left 5⁵⁰ am '07
7.07 border

2010
5:10 am

Along Interstate

14th Edition

75

2007 is the 400th Anniversary of the
arrival of the *Susan Conant*,
Godspeed and *Discovery* . . . three
English merchant ships bringing the
first permanent European
settlement to North America.

by Dave Hunter

"Local Knowledge" and *"Insider Information"*
for interstate travelers between
Detroit and the Florida Border

Along Interstate-75 is updated bi-annually and available from:

- **bookstores** in the USA, Canada and on the Internet

- **American Automobile Association (AAA)**
  offices in Ohio

- **Canadian Automobile Association
  (CAA)** in Ontario

- or by phoning **1-800-431-1579**
  (Visa, MasterCard & Discover accepted
   - all order shipped within 24 hours)

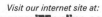

Visit our internet site at:
www.i75online.com
for **late breaking** Interstate-75
travel information
such as **detours, gas prices,
construction, road and traffic
information**, and much more.

i75online.com also includes a
complete **statewide
information section for Florida**,
with links to **Florida tourist
information, accommodation,
attractions, museums, golf,
parks, historical sites, etc.**

for further information, please contact:

Mile Oak Publishing Inc.
Suite 81, 20 Mineola Road East,
Mississauga, ON Canada L5G 4N9

e.mail: mile_oak@compuserve.com
phone: 905-274-4356
fax: 905-274-8656

To my wife and best friend of 44 years; without her, there would be no book.

—Kathy Hunter —

Sweetie, I know you don't want to be in the limelight but thanks so much for compiling all the exit information, editing the text, cross-checking page numbers ... and keeping me sane.
You are truly the Wind Beneath My Wings!

14th Edition of *"Along Interstate-75"* **by Dave Hunter, Mile Oak Publishing Inc.**

Editor and research assistance: Kathy Hunter

Cover: design by Margrie Wallace and Dave Hunter

Cover Background - An old Appalachian homestead in Tennessee.

Cataloging in Publication Data

Hunter, Dave, 1941 -

"Along Interstate-75, 14th edition. Local knowledge, Insider Information and Entertainment for those traveling between Detroit & the Florida Border."

ISBN-10: 1-896819-34-6   **ISBN-13: 978-1-896819-34-1**

1. Interstate-75 - Guidebooks.   2. United States - Guidebooks
3. Automobile Travel - United States - Guidebooks I. Title   II. Series

Graphic Credits:

Artwork courtesy of Softkey Clipmaster Pro and Corel Corporation's Gallery, Gallery 2, Mega Gallery and IMSI USA including: Image Club Graphics Inc., One Mile Up Inc., Techpool Studios Inc. and Totem Graphics Inc.

All **Photos** and **Photo Illustrations** taken or drawn by Dave Hunter, except as follows:

Booth Western Art Museum (125), FHA, DC (70), KY Travelers' Center (21 & 177), Macon (38), Marietta Diner (129, 164), NASA (74), Neil Armstrong Museum, Ohio (12, 186), Richmond, Kentucky (page 53), Road to Tara (132), Toyota, Ohio (88, 179), US Marine Corps (12, 186).

HELLO, I'M HERB . . .

YOU'LL SEE ME FROM TIME TO TIME THROUGHOUT THE BOOK, ADDING A BIT OF HUMOR TO THE PAGES. ON A SERIOUS NOTE THOUGH, I WANT TO THANK OUR LONG TIME PRINTER - GERRIE-YOUNG LITHOGRAPHY. THE G-Y FOLK TAKE A REAL PERSONAL INTEREST IN THIS BOOK . . . FROM THE PRESS OPERATORS TO THE BINDERY FOLK (AND EVEN BRIAN IN THE FRONT OFFICE), THEY'VE DONE AN INCREDIBLE JOB FOR ELEVEN EDITIONS. THANKS GUYS.

BY THE WAY, MANY PEOPLE THINK I'M DAVE - I'M NOT . . . AS THOSE WHO HAVE MET HIM WILL KNOW, HE'S MUCH BETTER LOOKING THAN ME!

Printed in Canada - *by Gerrie-Young Lithographic Inc,*
1008 Rangeview Rd, Mississauga ON Canada L5E 1H3

Contents at a Glance

Oops! _Did you notice I missed pages 143-144 in the chart above?_
I've included a couple of surprise maps on these pages, for you to enjoy.

Hello and Welcome to the
14th Edition of Along I-75

Don't you hate those company phone menu systems? The ones that tell you to *"press button 1"* to do this and *"press button 2"* to do that ... and so on. You usually end up at another menu and then perhaps, another. Well, it's not like that here at Mile Oak Publishing ... we don't have an automated system and never will. We want our readers to be able to reach us easily; in fact, Kathy or I often pick up the phone when it rings.

My favorite call is when somebody phones to pass on their thanks to the author. *"Oh do tell Mr. Hunter how much I love it,"* they will say. With a grin I answer, *"He's in the office now, would you like to tell him yourself?"* . . . and that's always the start of a fun conversation for both of us.

We've had some great calls this year ... and we've listened. For instance, thanks to ...

... the gentleman who wanted a quicker way of finding rest areas. We listened and added a special green symbol to the mile scale on the maps. Now he can quickly flip through the maps to easily see the next mark (rest area).

... the lady who said she was having a bit of difficulty reading the words in the brown (high ground) sections of the maps. We changed and emphasized the type face in these areas so it is much easy to read now.

And so it goes on as you and I, continue to improve *"Along Interstate-75"* together.

I've also had some interesting e.mails. In particular, a highway patrol officer was upset because of the radar trap locations revealed in the book. In an ongoing and friendly (he uses and enjoys the book) exchange, he felt it was unfair because I use the term "trap."

Now, I have no difficulty with a patrol car sitting in the open, beaming radar on oncoming traffic but, when it's hidden behind an overpass wall (see page 154) or in a wooded median, it's definitely an attempt to write tickets rather than slow down the traffic. After all, it's well known that purposely parking an empty patrol car on the soft shoulder, will slow traffic down to a safe legal speed ... but that doesn't write tickets.

In Britain, hundreds of speed cameras are installed (often in highly visible yellow road side boxes) often with a warning sign before you reach them. Although I disagree with the speed camera concept (in my opinion, it's against the principles of Common Law– the citation is mailed to the car owner, who may or may not be the perpetrator), they are effective and accident rates in areas where they exist, have decreased.

Finally, there are several things about radar traps which affect those of us obeying the speed limit. First, those 80 mph speed merchants careening down the fast lane create a hazardous situation when they suddenly see a radar trap and throw on their brakes. It dangerously disrupts the traffic flow behind them. And secondly, all I-75 states now require that you move over to clear the *"slow"* lane when an emergency vehicle is on the shoulder. We should all practice *"heads up"* driving but there is an extra margin of safety knowing that you may need to make a lane shift when traveling downstream from a radar trap ... you are better prepared to act.

Of course, it's the highest of compliments when a highway patrol officer complains about our radar trap notes. We always knew they were accurate (much of the information comes from police sources) but confirmation by a law officer is like winning an Oscar!

Safe travels,

Dave

"INTY"

Where Are We? ... a visual index to I-75

"A picture's worth a thousand words" – so I've replaced the *"Contents"* page with a visual index of the book's information. The next two pages relate the 25-mile maps (by map page #) to an aerial view of I-75. Mile-by-mile notes & Tips in the white Travelogue pages are similarly referenced.

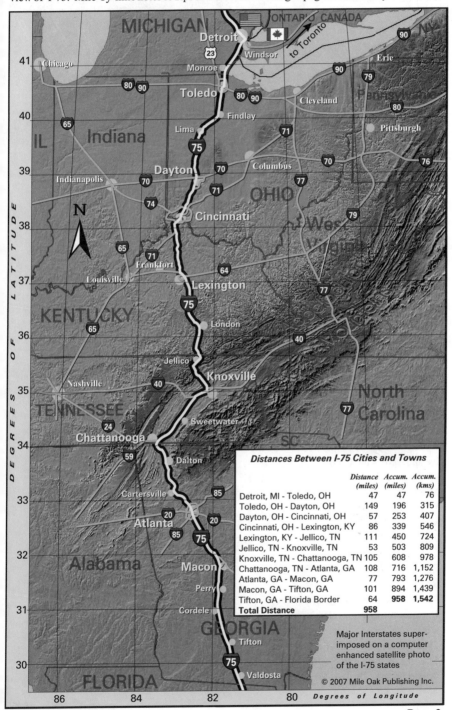

Distances Between I-75 Cities and Towns

	Distance (miles)	Accum. (miles)	Accum. (kms)
Detroit, MI - Toledo, OH	47	47	76
Toledo, OH - Dayton, OH	149	196	315
Dayton, OH - Cincinnati, OH	57	253	407
Cincinnati, OH - Lexington, KY	86	339	546
Lexington, KY - Jellico, TN	111	450	724
Jellico, TN - Knoxville, TN	53	503	809
Knoxville, TN - Chattanooga, TN	105	608	978
Chattanooga, TN - Atlanta, GA	108	716	1,152
Atlanta, GA - Macon, GA	77	793	1,276
Macon, GA - Tifton, GA	101	894	1,439
Tifton, GA - Florida Border	64	**958**	**1,542**
Total Distance	**958**		

Major Interstates superimposed on a computer enhanced satellite photo of the I-75 states

© 2007 Mile Oak Publishing Inc.

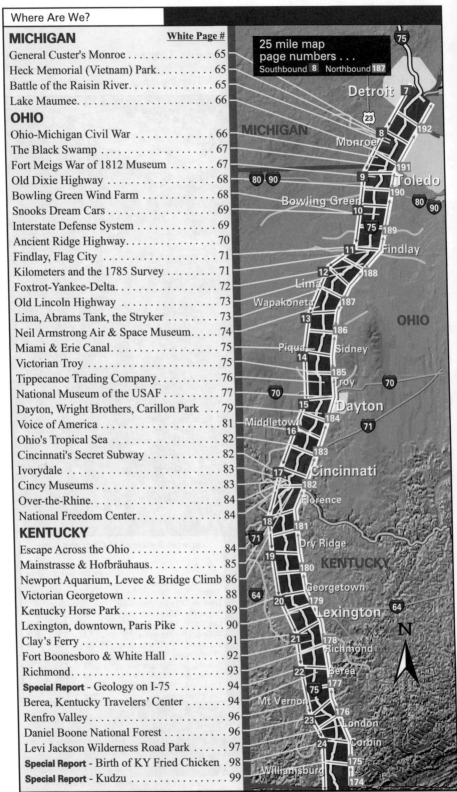

25 mile map
page numbers . . .
Southbound 8   Northbound 187

Jellico 25
174
26 75 173
Norris
27 172
40 28 75 Knoxville
40 171 Lenoir City
29 Sweetwater
170
30 Athens
31 169
Cleveland
168 Chattanooga
Ringgold
32 167 Dalton
Calhoun
33 166
75 Cartersville
34 165
85
Marietta N
35 164
20 Atlanta
36 163 20
Jonesboro
85 37 162
75
Forsyth 161
38 75 Macon
475 16
39 160
75
Perry
40 159
41 158
Cordele 75
42 157
Tifton
43 156
25 mile map
page numbers . . .
Southbound 43 Northbound 156
44 155
Valdosta
45 154
GEORGIA
FLORIDA

Southbound Route

First time readers: please read the *"Quick Start Hints"* on the inside of the front cover - this will quickly explain how the book is laid out in sections, to help you on your journey.   The Key to the **Road Speed** colors and **Map Symbols** is located on the front cover flap.

To get the maximum benefit from the 25 mile-per-page maps, remember . . .

- It takes approximately **½ hour to drive each page.** Add 20 minutes for every 8 maps (200 miles; 322 km), for gas and rest breaks..

- **Count Pages rather than miles.**
  In other words, if you are heading for a specific stop or destination, count the <u>number of pages</u> between your current position and the destination, and <u>divide by 2</u>.   This gives you your approximate driving time in hours.

- **Plan your day by the page.**
  I suggested a *"drive by the page"* strategy. Here it is (see top of next column) based on a 400 mile (16 page or 8 hour) day:

  Of course, the page strategy can be changed to meet your specific needs. "Morning" people may want to get an earlier start and drive for a few pages before stopping for breakfast;

Leave motel at 8:30am, and then drive . . .

four pages before 10:30am coffee break
   *15 minute coffee break
four pages before lunch at 12:45pm
   * 1 hour lunch
four pages before 3:45pm coffee break
   * 15 minute coffee break
four pages before the night stop at 6:00pm

families with young children may need to "time shift" to provide more frequent breaks.

- **Map information boxes:**
  This year, we have simplified the 25 mile-per-page maps by color-coding the information boxes (details on page 62).

  In particular, we have provided a quick reference to the nearest rest-room using a green arrow marker in the mile post scale (right side of each map). The marker also indicates the distance to the next facility (upper figure is in miles; the lower in kilometers).

Insider Tip for Southbound Travelers
Avoiding "Drive South" Sunburn

Did you know that you can get a sunburn and dangerous overload of cancer-causing ultraviolet (UV) light while driving south, especially if you are not used to being outdoors for long periods of time? Three days of driving into the sun - the average I-75 run from Michigan to Florida - can create a very high exposure to UV light on the face and arms, even on cloudy days.

The thick glass and plastic laminate of car windshields help filter UV light so that only about 15% of UVA* and virtually no UVB* reach the car's interior, but the extra long hours of constant exposure and UV light coming through the thinner, non-laminated side windows can mean that you are receiving much higher UV radiation than under normal circumstances.

To protect yourself from these harmful rays, wear long sleeves and use a sun screen with protection factor of at least SPF15 on your face - and of course, keep your side windows rolled up.

Note: UVA ages the skin and can cause skin cancer; UVB causes burning.

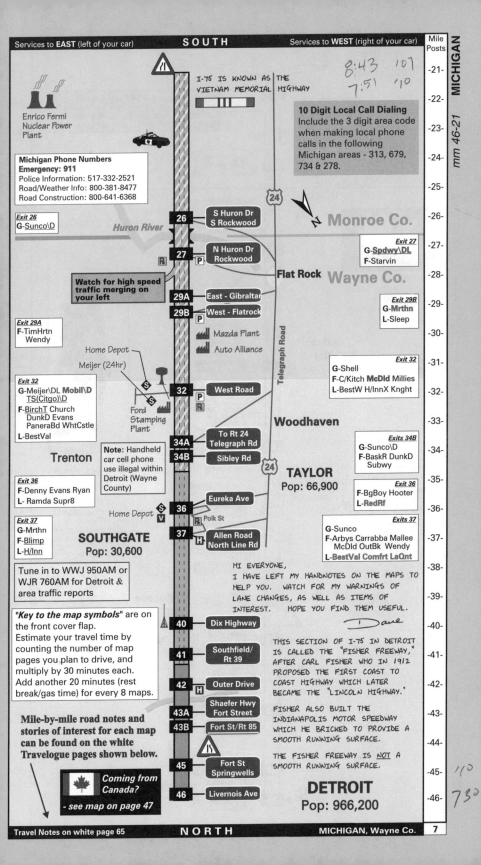

Enrico Fermi Nuclear Power Plant

I-75 IS KNOWN AS THE VIETNAM MEMORIAL HIGHWAY

8:43   107
7:51   '10

10 Digit Local Call Dialing
Include the 3 digit area code when making local phone calls in the following Michigan areas - 313, 679, 734 & 278.

Michigan Phone Numbers
Emergency: 911
Police Information: 517-332-2521
Road/Weather Info: 800-381-8477
Road Construction: 800-641-6368

mm 46-21

24

Exit 26
G-Sunco\D

Huron River

26   **S Huron Dr**
S Rockwood

N

Monroe Co.
-26-

27   **N Huron Dr**
Rockwood

Exit 27
G-**Spdwy**\DL
F-Starvin
-27-

Flat Rock   **Wayne Co.**
-28-

Watch for high speed traffic merging on your left

29A   **East - Gibraltar**

29B   **West - Flatrock**

Exit 29B
G-**Mrthn**
L-Sleep
-29-

Exit 29A
F-TimHrtn
Wendy

Mazda Plant

Auto Alliance

Telegraph Road
-30-

Home Depot

Meijer (24hr)

Exit 32
G-Meijer\DL **Mobil**\D
TS(Citgo)\D
F-**BirchT** Church
DunkD Evans
PaneraBd WhtCstle
L-BestVal

32   **West Road**

Exit 32
G-Shell
F-C/Kitch **McDld** Millies
L-BestW H/InnX Knght
-31-
-32-

Ford Stamping Plant

Woodhaven
-33-

Trenton

Note: Handheld car cell phone use illegal within Detroit (Wayne County)

34A   **To Rt 24**
Telegraph Rd

34B   **Sibley Rd**

24

TAYLOR
Pop: 66,900

Exits 34B
G-Sunco\D
F-BaskR DunkD
Subwy
-34-

Exit 36
F-Denny Evans Ryan
L- Ramda Supr8

36   **Eureka Ave**

Exit 36
F-BgBoy Hooter
L-RedRf
-35-

Home Depot

Polk St

Exit 37
G-Mrthn
F-**Blimp**
L-**H/Inn**

37   **Allen Road**
North Line Rd

Exits 37
G-Sunco
F-Arbys Carrabba Mallee
McDld OutBk Wendy
L-BestVal Comfrt LaQnt
-36-
-37-

SOUTHGATE
Pop: 30,600

HI EVERYONE,
I HAVE LEFT MY HANDNOTES ON THE MAPS TO HELP YOU. WATCH FOR MY WARNINGS OF LANE CHANGES, AS WELL AS ITEMS OF INTEREST. HOPE YOU FIND THEM USEFUL.

Dave
-38-
-39-

Tune in to WWJ 950AM or WJR 760AM for Detroit & area traffic reports

"Key to the map symbols" are on the front cover flap.
Estimate your travel time by counting the number of map pages you plan to drive, and multiply by 30 minutes each. Add another 20 minutes (rest break/gas time) for every 8 maps.

40   **Dix Highway**

41   **Southfield/**
Rt 39

42   **Outer Drive**

THIS SECTION OF I-75 IN DETROIT IS CALLED THE "FISHER FREEWAY," AFTER CARL FISHER WHO IN 1912 PROPOSED THE FIRST COAST TO COAST HIGHWAY WHICH LATER BECAME THE "LINCOLN HIGHWAY."

FISHER ALSO BUILT THE INDIANAPOLIS MOTOR SPEEDWAY WHICH HE BRICKED TO PROVIDE A SMOOTH RUNNING SURFACE.

THE FISHER FREEWAY IS NOT A SMOOTH RUNNING SURFACE.

-40-
-41-
-42-

Mile-by-mile road notes and stories of interest for each map can be found on the white Travelogue pages shown below.

43A   **Shaefer Hwy**
Fort Street

43B   **Fort St/Rt 85**

-43-
-44-

45   **Fort St**
Springwells

46   **Livernois Ave**

DETROIT
Pop: 966,200

-45-
-46-

110
730

Coming from Canada?
- see map on page 47

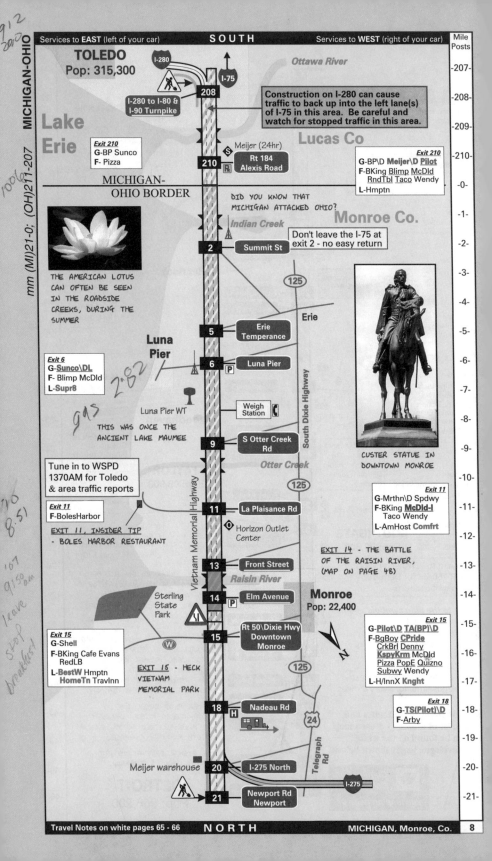

mm (MI)21-0; (OH)211-207

1006\208-207

912
2000

Services to **EAST** (left of your car)   **SOUTH**   Services to **WEST** (right of your car)   Mile Posts

TOLEDO
Pop: 315,300

I-280

I-75

-207-

Ottawa River

208

-208-

I-280 to I-80 &
I-90 Turnpike

Construction on I-280 can cause
traffic to back up into the left lane(s)
of I-75 in this area. Be careful and
watch for stopped traffic in this area.

-209-

**Lake
Erie**

Lucas Co

Exit 210
G-BP Sunco
F- Pizza

Meijer (24hr)
Rt 184
Alexis Road

210

S
R

Exit 210
G-BP\D **Meijer**\D **Pilot**
F-BKing Blimp McDld
  RndTbl Taco Wendy
L-Hmptn

-210-

-0-

**MICHIGAN-
OHIO BORDER**

DID YOU KNOW THAT
MICHIGAN ATTACKED OHIO?

-1-

Indian Creek

Monroe Co.

2

Summit St

Don't leave the I-75 at
exit 2 - no easy return

-2-

THE AMERICAN LOTUS
CAN OFTEN BE SEEN
IN THE ROADSIDE
CREEKS, DURING THE
SUMMER

125

-3-

-4-

Erie

5

Erie
Temperance

-5-

**Luna
Pier**

6
P

Luna Pier

2.82

-6-

gas

-7-

Exit 6
G-Sunco\DL
F- Blimp McDld
L-Supr8

Luna Pier WT

Weigh
Station
C

South Dixie Highway

-8-

THIS WAS ONCE THE
ANCIENT LAKE MAUMEE

9

S Otter Creek
Rd

-9-

Otter Creek

CUSTER STATUE IN
DOWNTOWN MONROE

Tune in to WSPD
1370AM for Toledo
& area traffic reports

125

-10-

Exit 11
F-BolesHarbor

710
8.51

11

La Plaisance Rd

Exit 11
G-Mrthn\D Spdwy
F-BKing **McDld-I**
  Taco Wendy
L-AmHost **Comfrt**

-11-

EXIT 11, INSIDER TIP
- BOLES HARBOR RESTAURANT

Horizon Outlet
Center

-12-

'07
9:50 am

leave

Vietnam Memorial Highway

13

Front Street

EXIT 14 - THE BATTLE
OF THE RAISIN RIVER,
(MAP ON PAGE 48)

-13-

Raisin River

stop

14
P

Elm Avenue

Monroe
Pop: 22,400

-14-

breakfast

Sterling
State
Park

Rt 50\Dixie Hwy
Downtown
Monroe

15

N

Exit 15
G-Pilot\D TA(BP)\D
F-BgBoy CPride
  CrkBrl Denny
  KspyKrm McDld
  Pizza PopE Quizno
  Subwy Wendy
L-H/InnX Knght

-15-

Exit 15
G-Shell
F-BKing Cafe Evans
  RedLB
L-BestW Hmptn
  HomeTn TravInn

W

-16-

EXIT 15 - HECK
VIETNAM
MEMORIAL PARK

125

-17-

18
H

Nadeau Rd

Exit 18
G-TS(Pilot)\D
F-Arby

-18-

24

-19-

Meijer warehouse

20

I-275 North

Telegraph Rd

I-275

-20-

21

Newport Rd
Newport

-21-

mm 207-182

-182-

25
DH

SIGN OF THE DIXIE HIGHWAY, THE "OLD ROUTE TO FLORIDA" (PAGES 68 AND 114)

County Airport

-183-

OHIO'S ROAD WEATHER INFORMATION SYSTEM (RWIS) MONITOR STATION IN THE MEDIAN

-184-

-185-

-186-

WAR OF 1812 - FORT MEIGS, PERRYSBURG

Pearl Harbor Memorial Highway

187 — Rt 582/Luckey Haskins

-187-

A favorite highway patrol aerial surveillance area - watch your speed carefully on this I-75 stretch

-188-

25
DH

-189-

N

Caution - watch for high speed traffic merging on your right

-190-

PERRYSBURG

Islamic Center of Greater Toledo

-191-

192 — I-475 & 23N Maumee Ann Arbor   **2** — I-475

Perrysburg Pop: 16,900

-192-

Exit 193
G-**BP\DL** Sunco
F-BKing BgBoy CrkBrl Evans McDld PaneraBd Ralph Subwy Taco
L-BestW Comfrt **Days** H/Inn H/InnX

193 — Rts 20 & 23S Fremont Perrysburg

Maumee River

Exit 193
G-Mrthn\D
L-LaQnt

-193-

K-Mart Kroger

S   G

Perrysburg Map, page 48

-194-

O.T.   I-80   I-90

Important - move to 2 left lanes

195 — I-80 I-90 Ohio Turnpike

O.T.   I-80   I-90

-195-

Exit 197
G-Shell\D
F-TimH Wendy
L-CrtYrd

EXIT 193 - FORT MEIGS (MAP PAGE 48)

197 — Buck Road

-196-

Exit 197
G-BP Sunco\D
F-Denny McDld
L-AmerInn

-197-

Exit 198
G-Shell\D
F-Subwy
L-AmHost Comfrt

198 — Wales/Oregon Rds/Northwood

Wood Co.

199A — Rt 65 North Miami Street

ENTERING THE "BLACK SWAMP"

-198-

-199-

Exit 199B
L-Days

199B — Rt 65 South/Rossford

Lucas Co.

-200-

Maumee River

Disalle Bridge

Stay in your lane - high speed traffic on your left creates a new L1

200 — South Ave

-201-

201A — Rt 25S/Maumee

OHIO Phone Numbers
Emergency: 911, *DUI (*384)
Road Help: 1-877-7-PATROL (728765)
Police Information: 614-466-2660
Road/Weather Info: 614-466-7031

202A — Washington St

Stay in 2 left lanes

202B — Collingwood Blvd

H

-202-

-203-

203B — Rt 24 Detroit Ave

TOLEDO

Move to 2 left lanes

204 — I-475W to Rt 23 Maumee Ann Arbor   I-475

-204-

Visitors Radio - tune 1610 AM

Willys Pkwy Jeep Pkwy

205A

-205-

206 — to Rt 24 Phillips Ave

10 Digit Local Call Dialing
Include the 3 digit area code when making local phone calls in the Toledo area - 419 & 567..

Follow overhead signs - "I-75 South to Dayton"

207 — Stickney Ave Lagrange St

-206-

-207-

EXIT 157 (NEXT PAGE), INSIDER TIP
"BISTRO ON MAIN" RESTAURANT

-157-

FINDLAY
Pop: 39,200

Blanchard River

-158-

Exit 159
G-BP\DL Spdwy\D Swfty
F-BKing DktaGrl KFC
LJSilvr McDld Mings
Pdrsa Pizza Ralph
StkShk Subwy Wendy
L-RedRf Rodwy Supr8
TravInn

Rts 224 & 15W
Findlay
Ottawa

159

Exit 159
G-Mrphy\D Shell\D
F-ChinaGdns CrkBrl
DennyDnr Evans
JacPizza OutBk Waffle
L-CtrylnnSte H/InnX
Hmptn QltyInn

-159-

(Roller) Skate City

-160-

Visitors Radio - tune
530 AM

CR 99   161

-161-

Jeffrey's Antique Mall

-162-

Weigh
Station

LEAVING THE "BLACK SWAMP"   Priebe Airport

-163-

Whirlpool

FINDLAY'S "DAVID
COPPERFIELD" HOUSE

Rt 613
Fostoria
McComb   164

Exit 164
G-PilotTS\D
F-Subwy Taco

-164-

Van Buren

Hancock Co.

-165-

Rocky Ford River

-166-

Wood Co.

Exit 167
G-Mobil\DL
PetroTS\D
F-IrnSklt McDld
Pizza

PetroShopping
Center

Rt 18
Fostoria
N Baltimore   167

ROUTE 18 IS A
"RIDGE" HIGHWAY

Exit 167
G-Sunco\D
L-Crown

-167-

North Baltimore

168

Eagleville Rd
Quarry Rd

Exit 168
G-FuelTS\DL

-168-

Needles Rd

Oil Center Rd

OHIO'S ROAD WEATHER
INFORMATION SYSTEM
(RWIS) MONITOR
STATION IN THE MEDIAN

-169-

CR603
Grant Rd

Insley
Road

-170-

Post Office

171

Rt 25
Cygnet

-171-

Cygnet

25

-172-

*Portage
River*

-173-

EXIT 161 OR 159
"DAVID COPPERFIELD"
HOUSE

-174-

DH

N

-175-

-176-

ROADSIDE WILDLIFE HABITAT AREA

-177-

Information 9:00-5:00 daily
Restrooms: 24 hours

25 m
40 k

EXIT 179 -
SNOOKS DREAM CARS

WOOD COUNTY
HISTORICAL
MUSEUM

Rest
Area

Rt 6/Fremont
Napoleon   179

WIND TURBINES

-179-

Co. Home Rd

BOWLING GREEN
Pop: 29,800

Gypsy Ln

-180-

Dunbridge

Bowling
Green WT

25

Napoleon

Exit 181
G-Meijer\DL
L-H/InnX

Rts 64 105
Pemberville
Bowling Green   181

Exit 181
G-BP\L Citgo\DL Spdwy\D
Sunco\D
F-BKing BgBoy Evans Frckers
Hunan McDld Subwy
Waffle Wendy Zarape
L-BestW BkEye Days Hmptn
QltyInn

-181-

Meijer (24hrs)

BGU Research Park

-182-

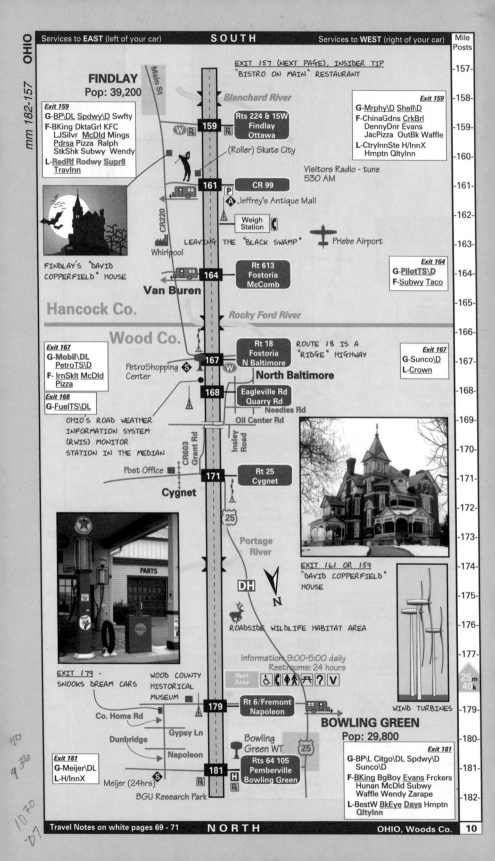

'07   10:23 '10

mm 157-132

-133-

-134-

Exit 135
G-Spdwy\DL

Exit 135
G-FlyJ\DL PilotTS\DL
F-Cookery McDld
Pepproni Subwy

-135-

U.S. 30

Napoleon

To Rt 30
Delphos
Beaverdam

135

Beaverdam

LINCOLN L HIGHWAY

San Francisco

-136-

Washington

Old Route 30
Lincoln Hwy

IKE'S CONVOY PASSED
BY HERE IN 1919

EXIT 135 - TO
THE "OLD LINCOLN
HIGHWAY"

Phillips Rd

-137-

-138-

Norfolk &
Western
Railway

-139-

Allen Co.

BRONZE BUST OF IKE HONORING
HIS ROLE IN CREATING THE
INTERSTATE SYSTEM OF HIGHWAYS,
LOCATED IN TIFTON, GEORGIA -
HOME OF THE FIRST I-75 MILES
BUILT (PAGE 140)

140

Bentley Road
Bluffton

H

-140-

Bluffton
Airport

Bluffton

-141-

Riley Creek

Exit 142
G-BP Sunco
L-Knght

142

W

Rt 103
Arlington
Bluffton

H

Exit 142
G-BP\D Mrthn
F-BKing KFC McDld-O
Subwy Taco
L-Comfrt

-142-

CR103

Hancock Co.

-143-

N

CR313

-144-

145

Rt 235/Ada
Mt Cory

-145-

IN 1784, IN THIS AREA
YOU WOULD BE LEAVING
CONNECTICUT AND
ENTERING VIRGINIA

-146-

-147-

I-75 WAS BUILT
ON TOP OF THE
DIXIE HIGHWAY,
BETWEEN FINDLAY
AND LIMA

DH

-148-

BLUFFTON'S NORTH MAIN STREET
IS A PRETTY DIVERSION FROM
THE INTERSTATE. WATCH FOR
THE TEDDY BEAR SHOP ON THE
CORNER

-149-

VORTAC FDY

THE FOXTROT DELTA YANKEE
MORSE SIGNAL OF THE
FINDLAY "VORTAC ON J47"

CR313

-150-

-151-

Dayton
100 MILES
161 KILOMETERS

-152-

No Information
Restrooms: 24 hours

Rest
Area

73 m
117 k

161 KILOMETERS TO
DAYTON (PAGE 71)

-153-

Findlay Municipal
Airport

♿ 🅿 🚶 ⛽ ❓ V

-154-

Lima Ave

Pioneer Sugar

-155-

FINDLAY

H

156

68 15 to 23
Kenton
Columbus

-156-

Exit 157
G-GasAm\D Mrthn\D
F-Blimp
L-BestVal

CR220 Main St

157

Rt 12
Findlay

V

FINDLAY IS KNOWN
AS THE "FLAG CITY"

Exit 157
G-TrvlCntr\D
F-Frckers
L-Econo

-157-

'10 10:01   10 5t '07

11:35 -07

Services to **EAST** (left of your car)   S O U T H   Services to **WEST** (right of your car)

Mile Posts

-107-
-108-
-109-

Cemetery Rd

25A

DH

RADAR

EXIT 111 - THE BEAUTIFUL NEIL
ARMSTRONG AIR & SPACE MUSEUM

110   St Marys
Belfontaine

P

-110-

Super Wal-Mart

111   Belfontaine
Street

P

Exit 111
G-TA(Mrthn)\DL
F-CFare
L-Days

EXIT 111 OR 110
RV HEAVEN (KOA)

Wapakoneta
Pop: 9,500

Exit 111
G-BP\DL Mrphy\D
Shell
F-Arby BKing CaptD
DQ Evans
GrndHog LkyStr
McDld Pizza Taco
Waffle Wendy
YangGdns
L-BestW H/InnX
HamltnInn Supr8
TravL

-111-
-112-

113   Rt 67
Unipolis
Wapakoneta

-113-
-114-

Truck
Area

LASER
GUN

DH

THIS LAND WAS ONCE COVERED
BY HUNDREDS OF FEET OF ICE
- OHIO'S ICE AGE

Auglaize Co.

-115-
-116-
-117-

*Caution - The Ohio State
Police run very active aerial
speed patrols from a small
airport a few miles west of
milepost 106. This stretch
of the I-75 is heavily
patroled from the air. On
clear days, watch for low
flying, high wing single
engine aircraft flying
parallel to the interstate.*

Dixie Hwy

118   Cridersville
W   **Cridersville**

Exit 118
G-FuelTS/D Spdwy\DL
F-Subwy

-118-
-119-

Allen Co.

120   Breese Rd
Fort Shawnee

Exit 122
G-Shell\D

-120-
-121-

McClain Rd

Exit 122
G-Spdwy\D

122   Rt 65
Lima
Uniopolis

-122-
-123-

HOME OF THE SECRET
"KRYPTONITE" ROOM

Exit 125
G-BP\D Mrphy\D Spdwy
F-Arbys BKing CaptD CrkBrl
Evans Hunan McDld Olive
Pdrsa Pizza Rally Ralph
RedLb Ryan SkylnStk Taco
TexStk Wendy
L-H/Inn Hmptn Knght Motel6

Super
Wal-Mart
K-Mart

124   Fourth Street

P

-124-

S

125   Rt 309 & 117

W   R

H

LIMA
Pop: 40,300

Exit 125B
G-Shell
F-IgnaGrl Kwpee
PJPizza
L-Economy Supr8

-125-
-126-

Ottawa River

STRIP   MINING
OPERATIONS

127   Rt 81 Ada
Lima

S

US Plastics Retail Outlet
(on Neubrecht Rd - ½ mile)

Exit 127
G-Mrthn\D
F-Waffle
L-Comfrt Days
Econo

-127-
-128-

N

Dixie Hwy

Norfolk &
Western Railway

-129-

Exit 130
G-Mrthn\D
L-BestVal

DH

130   Blue Lick Rd

-130-
-131-

Power Grid
Substation

-132-

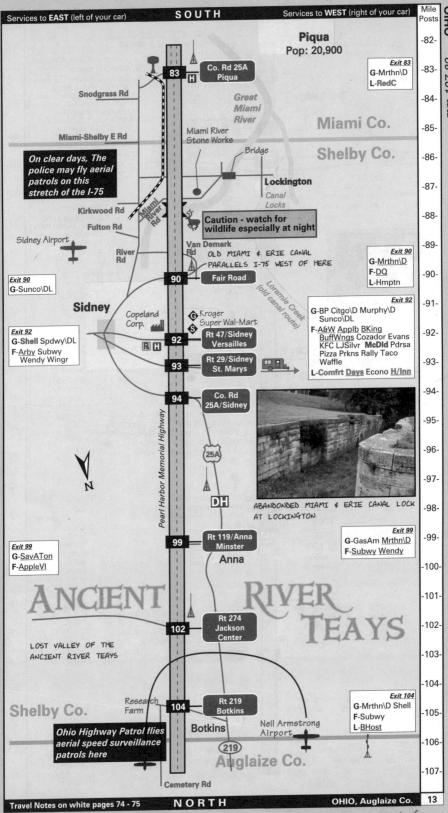

mm 107-82

Piqua
Pop: 20,900

-82-

83 Co. Rd 25A
Piqua   H

-83-

Snodgrass Rd

-84-

Great Miami River

-85-

Miami Co.

Miami-Shelby E Rd

Miami River Stone Works

Shelby Co.

-86-

Bridge

On clear days, The police may fly aerial patrols on this stretch of the I-75

Lockington
Canal Locks

-87-

Kirkwood Rd

-88-

Caution - watch for wildlife especially at night

Fulton Rd

Miami River Rd

Sidney Airport

River Rd

Van Demark Rd

-89-

OLD MIAMI & ERIE CANAL PARALLELS I-75 WEST OF HERE

Exit 90
G-Sunco\DL

90 Fair Road

-90-

Exit 90
G-Mrthn\D
F-DQ
L-Hmptn

Sidney

Loramie Creek (old canal route)

-91-

Copeland Corp.

Kroger
Super Wal-Mart

G
S

Exit 92
G-BP Citgo\D Murphy\D Sunco\DL
F-A&W Applb BKing BuffWngs Cozador Evans KFC LJSilvr McDld Pdrsa Pizza Prkns Rally Taco Waffle
L-Comfrt Days Econo H/Inn

Exit 92
G-Shell Spdwy\DL
F-Arby Subwy Wendy Wingr

R H

92 Rt 47/Sidney
Versailles

-92-

93 Rt 29/Sidney
St. Marys

-93-

94 Co. Rd 25A/Sidney

-94-

-95-

25A

-96-

-97-

DH

ABANDONDED MIAMI & ERIE CANAL LOCK AT LOCKINGTON

-98-

Pearl Harbor Memorial Highway

N

Exit 99
G-SavATon
F-AppleVl

99 Rt 119/Anna
Minster

-99-

Exit 99
G-GasAm Mrthn\D
F-Subwy Wendy

Anna

-100-

ANCIENT RIVER TEAYS

-101-

102 Rt 274
Jackson Center

-102-

LOST VALLEY OF THE ANCIENT RIVER TEAYS

-103-

-104-

Shelby Co.

Research Farm

104 Rt 219
Botkins

Exit 104
G-Mrthn\D Shell
F-Subwy
L-BHost

-105-

Botkins

Neil Armstrong Airport

Ohio Highway Patrol flies aerial speed surveillance patrols here

-106-

219

Auglaize Co.

-107-

Cemetery Rd

12:14 '01   11:27 '10

Exit 58
G-BP\DL Shell
F-BgBoy Hrdee
  McDld
L-BestW

EXIT 58 - NATIONAL
USAF AIRFORCE
MUSEUM - 6 MILES

DH

R
V
G Kroger

58 Needmore Rd

Post Office

Northridge

EXIT 59-58, INSIDER TIP
MILLER LANE LODGING

Exit 59-58; Miller Lane
G-Mrthn\D Spdwy\D
F-A&W Arby Chpotle CrabShck
  CrkBrl DonPedro Evans
  GldnC Hooter LJSilvr LoneS
  MaxEm Noodles O'Char
  Olive OutBk PaneraBd
  RedLb RubyT Ryan Sake
  SkyLnChili SmkyBnes
  StkShk Subwy TimHrtn
  Waffle Wendy Wnans
L-Comfrt CrtYrd CtrlnnSte
  Days Drury Fairfld Hmptn
  Knght Motel6 RedRf Rodwy
  Villager XStyAm

Exit 59
F-Subwy
L-HoJo

Visitors Radio -
tune 530 AM

59 Wyse Rd
Benchwood

I-70

R
V
P

61A I-70E
Columbus

61B I-70W
Indianapolis

I-70

Exit 63
G-Spdwy\D
F-BgBoy
L-CrossRd

EXIT 63 -
ROUTE 40 IS
THE HISTORICAL
NATIONAL ROAD

25A **Vandalia**

Exit 63
G-BP\D Shell Spdwy
F-Arby BKing-I KFC
  LJSilvr McDld Pizza
  SmHseDeli Subwy
  Taco Waffle Wendy
L-Supr8

Kroger G

63 Rt 40/Donnelsville
Vandalia

R
V

N

64 Northwoods
Blvd

Montgomery Co.

Miami Co.

Cox Dayton
International
Airport

DH

EXIT 68, INSIDER TIP
TIPPICANOE FRONTIER
TRADING CO

Tune in to WHIO 1290AM for
Dayton & area traffic reports

Tipp City R
Pop: W
9,200

North Dixie Rd

Exit 68
G-BP\DL Shell Spdwy
F-BKing Chinese FatDGrl
  McDld Pizza Subwy
  Taco

68 Rt 571/Tipp City
West Milton

V

Exit 68
G-Citgo\D Spdwy\D
F-Arby BgBoy Evans
  TipOTwn Wendy
L-H/InnX TravL

Exit 69
G-Citgo Mrthn
L-DairyM

69 Co. Rd 25A

V

25A

Gt Miami River

Exit 73
G-BP Shell
F-Waffle Wendy
L-BestW Econo
  Supr8

DH

PLANNING TO VISIT THE USAF
MUSEUM IN DAYTON? SAVE TIME
BY IGNORING THE "OFFICIAL"
BROWN SIGNS AND FOLLOWING
MY "LOCAL KNOWLEDGE" ROUTE
ON PAGE 49

Troy
Airfield

MT Picture Display

Kroger G

73 Rt 55/Troy/Ludlow Falls

Exit 74B
G-Meijer\DL
  Shell
  Spdwy\DL
F-Applb BKing
  BgBoy CJs
  Evans Fazoli
  Frndly HiMarks
  KFC LaPizza
  RubyT StlShk
L-BestVal Fairfld
  H/InnX Hmptn
  Radsn

Troy
Pop:
22,100
map on
page 76

H

74A Rt 41S/Troy
R

74B Rt 41N
Covington

R

Exit 74A
G-BP\DL
F- LJSilvr McDld
  Subwy TimHrtn

V R

Meijer/Super WalMart/Lowes
Troy Town
Center Mall

25A

Eldean Covered
Bridge

EXIT 74A - VISIT VICTORIAN
TROY - THERE ARE SOME
EXCELLENT RESTAURANTS AROUND
THE TOWN SQUARE (SEE MAP
                    PAGE 76).

Upper Valley
Medical Center H

78 Co. Rd 25A

Gt Miami River

PIQUA - HOME OF
THE MILLS BROTHERS

No Information - Restrooms: 24 hours

Rest
Area

Exit 82
G-Citgo Mrphy\D
F-A&W Arby
  ChinaGdns
  LJSilvr Pizza
  Subwy Taco
  Waffle Wendy

Home Depot S
K-Mart
Super Wal-Mart R H

Piqua Mall M P

Miami Valley Center Mall

M

82 Rt 36/Urbana
Piqua

R

Piqua
For local weather,
tune to 1610 AM

Exit 82
G-Spdwy
F-CrkBrl Evans
  McDld RedLb
L-Comfrt Knght
  LaQnt

54 m
87 k

-57-
-58-
-59-
-60-
-61-
-62-
-63-
-64-
-65-
-66-
-67-
-68-
-69-
-70-
-71-
-72-
-73-
-74-
-75-
-76-
-77-
-78-
-79-
-80-
-81-
-82-

133 '07   11:50 '10

mm 57-32

10 Digit Local Call Dialing
Include the 3 digit area code when making local phone calls in the following Ohio areas - 283 and 513.

On clear days, the police may fly aerial patrols on this stretch of I-75

DH

MIDDLETOWN
Pop: 51,900

Dixie Highway

4

Tune in to talk radio
WLW 700AM for
Cincinnati traffic reports

Great Miami River

Exit 36
G-**Exxon**\D **PilotTS**\D
  Shell\D
F-**McDld** Pizza Subwy
  Waffle Wendy
L-QltyInn

36

Rt 123
Franklin
Lebanon

Exit 36
G-Mrthn\D
  Sunco
F-WhtCstle

CRAFTER'S HEAVEN

Exit 38
F-Applb Arby Evans
  KFC LJSilvr McDld
  Taco TimHrtn
  TmKatz Wendy
L-H\InnX Hmptn

Kroger **G**

S

38

Rt 73
Franklin
Springboro

Franklin

Exit 38
F-BgBoy
L-Econo
  Knght

V

Chautauqua

■ Dayton Daily News
🏭 Franklin WT

Warren Co.

4

Springboro Pike

Dayton-Wright
Bros. Airport

Dixie Highway

Germantown

Montgomery Co.

I-675N exit 2
Many lodgings and
restaurants off this
exit including Fairfld,
Hampton, Sleep &
Quality.

2 675N

Dayton Mall

**Caution - High
speed merge
on right**

43

I-675 North
Columbus

M
Home Depot **H**
Lowes **S**

44

Rt 725
Centerville
Miamisburg

H
R
V

DH

Exit 44
G-BP\L Mrthn\D
  Shell
F-Evans Prkns
  Sushi TimHrtn
L-Knght RedRf
  Supr8

Exit 44
G-**BP****DL** Shell Spdwy
F-Applb BCRstr BKing BaskR
  BgBoy CaptD DunkD
  GrndSC KFC LoneS McDld
  Pizza SkylnChili Starbcks
  Subwy Taco Waffle Wendy
L-CrtYrd **H**/**Inn** Rsdnts
  Studio6+

Miamisburg
Pop: 19,500

Appleton Paper
Mills

Great Miami River

Left at i-15 pme

Kettering

GM Plant 🏭

47

Central Ave
W Carrollton

EXIT 51
CARILLON HISTORICAL
PARK, HOME OF THE
ORIGINAL WRIGHT
FLYER III, A NATIONAL
HISTORIC LANDMARK

Cooper Tire
& Rubber

*gas '07
$2.53/gal*

N

4

Moraine
V

50A

Dryden Rd
Moraine

Exit 50A
G-Sunco\D
L-**H**/**Inn** **Supr8**

50B

Rt 741S
Springboro Rd

Exit 51
L-CrtYd
  Marrtt

**NOTE - move into
2 left lanes - follow
*"I-75 to Cincinnati"***

51

Edwin C Moses
Blvd/Nicholas Rd

WRIGHT BROTHERS
CENTER

Exit 51
G-BP\D
F-McDld
  Wendy
L-Econo

Springboro Pike

52AB
H

Rt 35/Albany St
Stewart St

Dayton Map,
page 49

Rt 49/3rd St **53A**

Rt 49/1st St **53B**

EXIT 54B - DAYTON ART
INSTITUTE - LOVELY RED
ROOFED ITALIAN
RENAISSANCE BUILDING

**Caution -
ramps for exits
54A, 54C, 53B
and 53A - exit
on left side of
the freeway**

Grand Ave **54A**

54B Rt 48/Main St

Webster St **54C**

Dayton Map, page 49

55 Keowee St/Leo St

56A Stanley Ave E

56B Stanley Ave W

DAYTON
Pop: 167,100

EXIT 53B, INSIDER TIP
MENDELSON WAREHOUSE

Exit 57B
G-Sunco/L
L-**H**/**Inn**

57B
R

Neff Rd
Wagner Ford Rd
Siebenthaler Ave

-32-
-33-
-34-
-35-
-36-
-37-
-38-
-39-
-40-
-41-
-42-
-43-
-44-
-45-
-46-
-47-
-48-
-49-
-50-
-51-
-52-
-53-
-54-
-55-
-56-
-57-

1:54 '07   12:12 '10 lunch   1:25 '10 depart

CINCINNATI
Pop: 333,100

MOTORCYCLE POLICE WITH RADAR ARE NOW OPERATING ALONG I-75 IN CINCINNATI

THE LOCKLAND SPLIT - YOU ARE DRIVING IN AN OLD CANAL

Lockland

PSSST!!! CINCINNATI HAS A SECRET SUBWAY SYSTEM

ROUTE OF THE HISTORIC MIAMI-ERIE CANAL

Vine

9 — Rts 4 & 561 Paddock Rd Seymour Ave

10 — Galbraith Rd Ronald Reagan Hwy

A favorite location - hiding behind the concrete pillar of the exit 14 overpass, beaming radar on southbound traffic. See page 82.

Sharonville

GE Aircraft Engines

12 — Wyoming Ave Cooper Ave

13 — Shepherd Lane Lincoln Hts

RADAR

14 — Rt 126 Woodlawn

15 — Sharon Road

511 road information, see page 85

Exit 13
F-Taco Wendy

Exit 14
L-TravL

Exit 15
G-BP\L Sunco Thrntn\D
F-BgBoy Brbnk CrkBrl Evans JDandy RubyT RyIIndian SkyLnChili Waffle
L-CtryInnSte Drury H/Inn Hilton Hmptn LaQnt RedRf

Cincinnati Bypass I-275 East.

275E

16 — I-275 to I-71 I-74 Columbus Indianapolis

275W

Hamilton Co.

Cincinnati Bypass - stay in right lane & take exit 16 for I-275 East. Use map on page 194

Exit 19
F-Brova Champ Changs CldStnCream FishMkt PaneraBd PcakeHse RedRbn SmkyBnes StkShk

Streets of West Chester

Butler Co.

19 — Union Centre Rd

YOU ARE DRIVING OVER A TROPICAL SEA BED

Exit 19
G-BP\D Shell
F-Applb BKing Buffwngs Chpotle DonP Evans MaxEm Quizno RCityGrl Raffty RoadHs SkyLnChili Subwy UnoRest Wendy
L-Comfrt H/Inn Hmptn Marrtt Sleep

Exit 21
F-BgBoy
L-H/InnX

West Chester

Super Wal-Mart

21 — Cin-Day Rd

Voice of America SC Home Depot

Cincinnati Islamic Center

22 — Tylersville Rd

Exit 22
G-BP\L Sunco\L Thrntn
F-BKing BoneFsh Carino ChickF Chili CtyBBQ DtoPizza Evans IHOP KFC LJSilvr LongH McDld PaneraBd Prkns Quizno RubyT SOHO TGIF Taco Waffle Wendy
L-Econo

Cincinnati Enquirer

SITE OF THE VOICE OF AMERICA AND WLW

Meijer (24hr)

Butler Co. WT

Michael J Fox Highway

Exit 21
G-Mobil\D Mrphy\D Shell Spdwy
F-KspyKrm Waffle Wendy
L-Knght

Exit 22
G-Meijer\DL Spdwy\DL
L-Wingate

Dial Cellular 211 for free Cincinnati I-75 traffic information - (Mon to Fri only).

Butler-Warren Rd

24 — SR129W Hamilton

Butler Co.

N

Cincinnati Rd

Restrooms: 24 hours

Rest Area

29 — Rt 63/Monroe Hamilton

Traders World Flea Market

Turtle Creek Flea Market

Monroe

Exit 29
G-BP Mrthn\D Shell\D
F-BKing Chili TimHrtn Waffle Wendy WhtCstle
L-Days

Exit 29
G-BP\DL Spdwy\D Sunco\D
F-McDld Prkns SaraJ
L-Hmptn HoJo

Warren Co.

Union Rd

DH

Wal-Mart, Lowes
Kroger Meijer

Exit 32
G-BP\L
F-McDld Waffle
L-Comfrt Ramda Supr8 Value

32 — Rt 122 Middletown

Mall

Middletown

Exit 32
G-Murphy\D Spdwy
F-Applb BgBoy CrkBrl Evans Fazoli GldnC HmTnBft KFC LoneS O'Char Olive StkShk Wendy
L-BestW Fairfld H/InnX

44 m
71 k

-7-
-8-
-9-
-10-
-11-
-12-
-13-
-14-
-15-
-16-
-17-
-18-
-19-
-20-
-21-
-22-
-23-
-24-
-25-
-26-
-27-
-29-
-30-
-31-
-32-

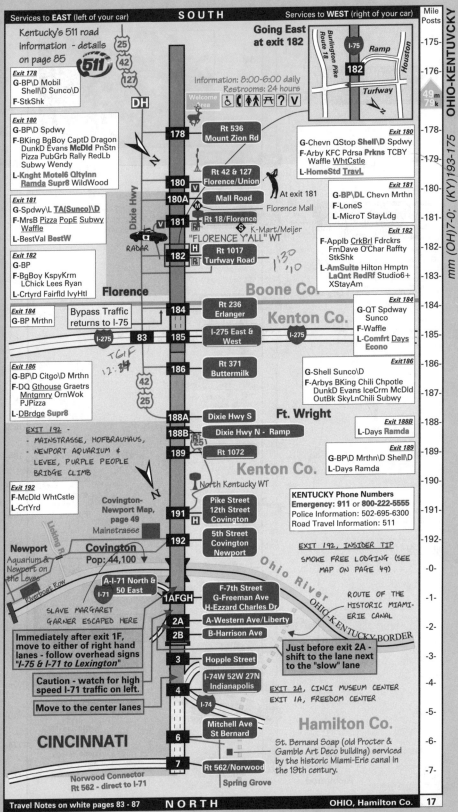

Kentucky's 511 road information - details on page 85

Going East at exit 182

Information: 8:00-6:00 daily
Restrooms: 24 hours
Welcome Area

Exit 178
G-BP\D Mobil Shell\D Sunco\D
F-StkShk

Exit 180
G-BP\D Spdwy
F-BKing BgBoy CaptD Dragon DunkD Evans **McDld** PnStn Pizza PubGrb Rally RedLb Subwy Wendy
L-Knght Motel6 Qltylnn **Ramda** Supr8 WildWood

Exit 181
G-Spdwy\L **TA(Sunco)\D**
F-MrsB Pizza PopE Subwy Waffle
L-BestVal BestW

Exit 182
G-BP
F-BgBoy KspyKrm LChick Lees Ryan
L-Crtyrd Fairfld IvyHtl

Florence

Exit 184
G-BP Mrthn

Bypass Traffic returns to I-75

Exit 186
G-BP\D Citgo\D Mrthn
F-DQ Gthouse Graetrs Mntgmry OrnWok PJPizza
L-DBrdge Supr8

EXIT 192 -
- MAINSTRASSE, HOFBRAUHAUS,
- NEWPORT AQUARIUM & LEVEE, PURPLE PEOPLE BRIDGE CLIMB

Exit 192
F-McDld WhtCstle
L-CrtYrd

Covington-Newport Map, page 49
Mainstrasse

Newport
Aquarium & Newport on the Levee

Covington
Pop: 44,100

SLAVE MARGARET GARNER ESCAPED HERE

Immediately after exit 1F, move to either of right hand lanes - follow overhead signs "I-75 & I-71 to Lexington"

Caution - watch for high speed I-71 traffic on left.

Move to the center lanes

CINCINNATI

Norwood Connector Rt 562 - direct to I-71

178 Rt 536 Mount Zion Rd

180 Rt 42 & 127 Florence/Union

180A Mall Road

181 Rt 18/Florence

At exit 181
Florence Mall
"FLORENCE Y'ALL" WT
K-Mart/Meijer

182 Rt 1017 Turfway Road

184 Rt 236 Erlanger

185 I-275 East & West

186 Rt 371 Buttermilk

188A Dixie Hwy S

188B Dixie Hwy N - Ramp

189 Rt 1072

North Kentucky WT

191 Pike Street 12th Street Covington

192 5th Street Covington Newport

A-I-71 North & 50 East

1AFGH F-7th Street G-Freeman Ave H-Ezzard Charles Dr

2A A-Western Ave/Liberty

2B B-Harrison Ave

3 Hopple Street

4 I-74W 52W 27N Indianapolis

6 Mitchell Ave St Bernard

7 Rt 562/Norwood

Spring Grove

Boone Co.

Kenton Co.

Ft. Wright

Kenton Co.

Hamilton Co.

Ohio River

OHIO-KENTUCKY BORDER

Going East at exit 182

Exit 180
G-Chevn QStop **Shell\D** Spdwy
F-Arby KFC Pdrsa **Prkns** TCBY Waffle **WhtCstle**
L-HomeStd TravL

Exit 181
G-BP\DL Chevn Mrthn
F-LoneS
L-MicroT StayLdg

Exit 182
F-Applb CrkBrl Fdrckrs FmDave O'Char Raffty StkShk
L-AmSuite Hilton Hmptn **LaQnt RedRf** Studio6+ XStayAm

Exit 184
G-QT Spdway Sunco
F-Waffle
L-**Comfrt** Days Econo

Exit186
G-Shell Sunco\D
F-Arbys BKing Chili Chpotle DunkD Evans IceCrm McDld OutBk SkyLnChili Subwy

Exit 188B
L-Days Ramda

Exit 189
G-BP\D Mrthn\D Shell\D
L-Days Ramda

KENTUCKY Phone Numbers
Emergency: 911 or 800-222-5555
Police Information: 502-695-6300
Road Travel Information: 511

EXIT 192, INSIDER TIP
SMOKE FREE LODGING (SEE MAP ON PAGE 49)

ROUTE OF THE HISTORIC MIAMI-ERIE CANAL

Just before exit 2A - shift to the lane next to the "slow" lane

EXIT 2A, CINCI MUSEUM CENTER
EXIT 1A, FREEDOM CENTER

St. Bernard Soap (old Procter & Gamble Art Deco building) serviced by the historic Miami-Erie canal in the 19th century.

238 -07   1:56 '10

KENTUCKY

mm 175-150

-150-
-151-

Miles 152 - southbound police cross median here to northbound lanes

-152-
-153-

A CIVIL WAR EXECUTION TOOK PLACE HERE

Williamstown WT

Williamstown

154 | Rt 36 Williamstown

H

Exit 154
G-Citgo\DL
Shell\D
F-EZStop

-154-

Exit 154
G-Mrthn\D
F-ClassicK
L-BestVal Days

-155-

Rock Cut

Miles 156-152 - Police very active with radar posted on the exit 156 overpass

156 | Barnes Road

PHOTO OPPORTUNITY JUST AHEAD AS YOU COME OVER THE BROW OF THE HILL AFTER MILEPOST 156

-156-

H

-157-

Exit 159
G-BP Mrthn
Shell\D
F-Arby BKing-I
DQ HpyDragn
KFC LJSilvr
McDld Pizza
Subwy Waffle
Wendy
L-MicroT Supr8

Super Wal-Mart
Dry Ridge WT

Dry Ridge

S

-158-

H

159 | Rt 22 Dry Ridge

R

P

Dry Ridge Outlet Mall

DH

Exit 159
G-Spdwy\D
Sunco\D
F-CrkBrl CntryGrill
Shony
L-H/InnX Hmptn

-159-

Arnold's River

-160-

-161-

EXIT 159, INSIDER TIP
THE COUNTRY GRILL

-162-

-163-

N

(25)

Grant Co. ✕

-164-

Crittenden

166 | Rt 491 Crittenden

P

-165-

Exit 166
G-Chevn
Shell\D
F-BKing
CntyPumkin
Subwy

-166-

Exit 166
G-BP Citgo\D
EZstop
Mrthn\D
F-McDld Taco

-167-

Weigh Station
ADVANTAGE-75?

Kenton Co.

ADVANTAGE 75

FOLLOW IN-CAB SIGNALS

-168-
-169-

Boone Co.

Walton

-170-

171 | Rts 14 16 Walton Verona

Exit 171
G-BP Citgo
F-DQ

Walton WT

-171-

Exit 171
G-FlyJ(Conco)\DL
F-Cookery Pepproni

-172-

(25)

I-71

173 | I-71 South to Louisville

Exit 175
G-PilotTS\D
TA(BP)\D
F-Arby BKing
CPride KspyKrm
Subwy Taco
WhtCstle
L-H/InnX

Exit 175
G-BP PilotTS\D
Shell\DL
F-Chili HngKng
McDld PapaDino
PennStn Raymnd
SkyLnChili Subwy
Waffle Wendy
L-Gatewy

-173-

-174-

175 | Rt 338 Richwood

Richwood

-175-

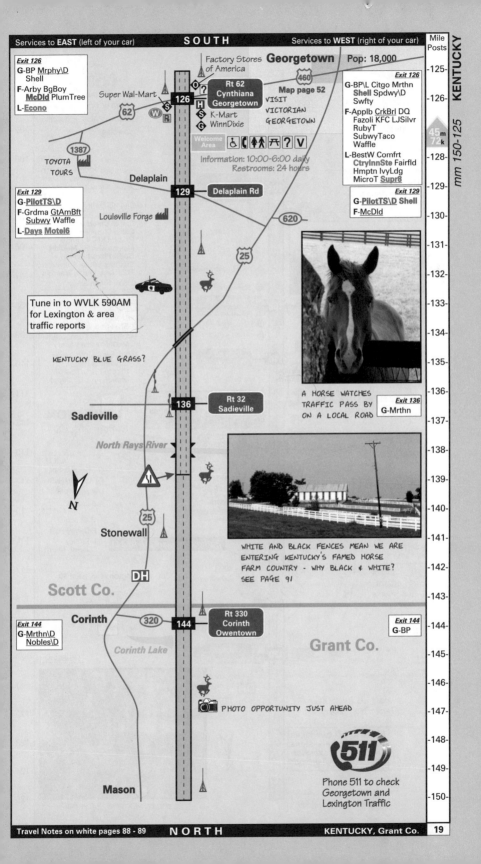

Exit 126
G-BP Mrphy\D
Shell
F-Arby BgBoy
McDld PlumTree
L-Econo

Factory Stores of America

Georgetown   Pop: 18,000

460

Rt 62 Cynthiana Georgetown

Map page 52

VISIT VICTORIAN GEORGETOWN

Exit 126
G-BP\L Citgo Mrthn
Shell Spdwy\D
Swfty
F-Applb CrkBrl DQ
Fazoli KFC LJSilvr
RubyT
SubwyTaco
Waffle
L-BestW Comfrt
CtryInnSte Fairfld
Hmptn IvyLdg
MicroT Supr8

Super Wal-Mart

62

126

K-Mart
WinnDixie

Welcome Area

Information: 10:00-6:00 daily
Restrooms: 24 hours

45 m
72 k

mm 150-125

1387

TOYOTA TOURS

Delaplain

129   **Delaplain Rd**

Exit 129
G-PilotTS\D Shell
F-McDld

Exit 129
G-PilotTS\D
F-Grdma GtAmBft
Subwy Waffle
L-Days Motel6

Louisville Forge

620

25

Tune in to WVLK 590AM
for Lexington & area
traffic reports

KENTUCKY BLUE GRASS?

A HORSE WATCHES
TRAFFIC PASS BY
ON A LOCAL ROAD

Exit 136
G-Mrthn

136   **Rt 32 Sadieville**

Sadieville

North Rays River

25

Stonewall

DH

WHITE AND BLACK FENCES MEAN WE ARE
ENTERING KENTUCKY'S FAMED HORSE
FARM COUNTRY - WHY BLACK & WHITE?
SEE PAGE 91

Scott Co.

Corinth   320   144   **Rt 330 Corinth Owentown**

Exit 144
G-Mrthn\D
Nobles\D

Exit 144
G-BP

Grant Co.

Corinth Lake

PHOTO OPPORTUNITY JUST AHEAD

511

Phone 511 to check
Georgetown and
Lexington Traffic

Mason

N

-125-
-126-
-128-
-129-
-130-
-131-
-132-
-133-
-134-
-135-
-136-
-137-
-138-
-139-
-140-
-141-
-142-
-143-
-144-
-145-
-146-
-147-
-148-
-149-
-150-

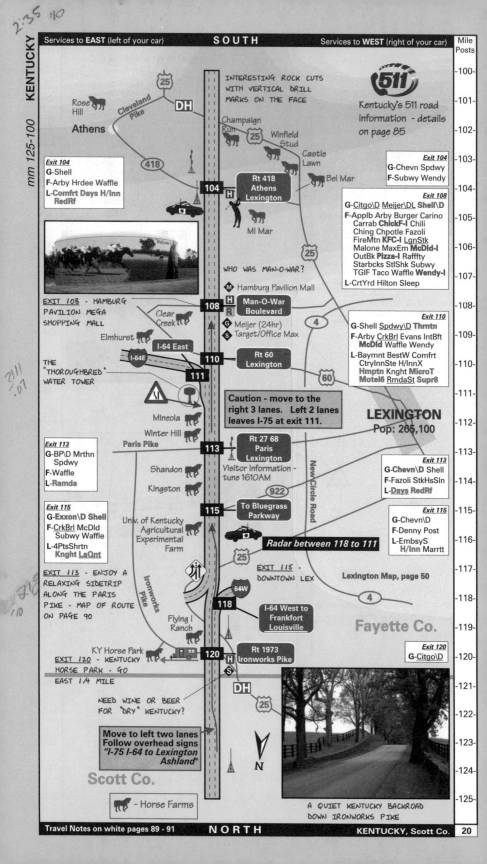

Services to **EAST** (left of your car)   **S O U T H**   Services to **WEST** (right of your car)   Mile Posts

2:35 110

-100-
-101-
-102-
-103-
-104-
-105-
-106-
-107-
-108-
-109-
-110-
-111-
-112-
-113-
-114-
-115-
-116-
-117-
-118-
-119-
-120-
-121-
-122-
-123-
-124-
-125-

INTERESTING ROCK CUTS WITH VERTICAL DRILL MARKS ON THE FACE

511 Kentucky's 511 road information - details on page 85

Rose Hill
Athens
Cleveland Pike
DH

Champaign Run
Winfield Stud
Castle Lawn
Bel Mar
Ml Mar

Exit 104
G-Shell
F-Arby Hrdee Waffle
L-Comfrt Days H/Inn RedRf

104 Rt 418 Athens Lexington **H**

Exit 104
G-Chevn Spdwy
F-Subwy Wendy

Exit 108
G-Citgo\D Meijer\DL Shell\D
F-Applb Arby Burger Carino Carrab **ChickF-I** Chili Ching Chpotle Fazoli FireMtn **KFC-I** LgnStk Malone MaxEm **McDld-I** OutBk **Pizza-I** Raffty Starbcks StlShk Subwy TGIF Taco Waffle **Wendy-I**
L-CrtYrd Hilton Sleep

WHO WAS MAN-O-WAR?

M Hamburg Pavilion Mall

EXIT 108 - HAMBURG PAVILION MEGA SHOPPING MALL

Clear Creek
Elmhurst

108 **H** **R** Man-O-War Boulevard
G Meijer (24hr)
S Target/Office Max

Exit 110
G-Shell Spdwy\D Thrntn
F-Arby CrkBrl Evans IntBft **McDld** Waffle Wendy
L-Baymnt BestW Comfrt CtrylnnSte H/InnX **Hmptn** Knght **MicroT** Motel6 RmdaSt Supr8

THE "THOROUGHBRED" WATER TOWER

I-64E I-64 East
110 Rt 60 Lexington
111

Mineola
Winter Hill
Paris Pike

Exit 113
G-BP\D Mrthn Spdwy
F-Waffle
L-Ramda

Caution - move to the right 3 lanes. Left 2 lanes leaves I-75 at exit 111.

LEXINGTON Pop: 265,100

113 Rt 27 68 Paris Lexington
Visitor Information - tune 1610AM

Shandon
Kingston

Exit 113
G-Chevn\D Shell
F-Fazoli StkHsSln
L-Days RedRf

New Circle Road

Exit 115
G-Exxon\D Shell
F-CrkBrl McDld Subwy Waffle
L-4PtsShrtn Knght LaQnt

115 To Bluegrass Parkway
922

Univ. of Kentucky Agricultural Experimental Farm

Exit 115
G-Chevn\D
F-Denny Post
L-EmbsyS H/Inn Marrtt

Radar between 118 to 111

EXIT 113 - ENJOY A RELAXING SIDETRIP ALONG THE PARIS PIKE - MAP OF ROUTE ON PAGE 90

Ironworks Pike

EXIT 115 - DOWNTOWN LEX

Lexington Map, page 50

64W
118 I-64 West to Frankfort Louisville

Fayette Co.

Flying I Ranch

KY Horse Park
EXIT 120 - KENTUCKY HORSE PARK - GO EAST 1/4 MILE

120 Rt 1973 Ironworks Pike **H** **S**

Exit 120
G-Citgo\D

DH

NEED WINE OR BEER FOR "DRY" KENTUCKY?

Move to left two lanes Follow overhead signs *"I-75 I-64 to Lexington Ashland"*

N

Scott Co.

🐴 - Horse Farms

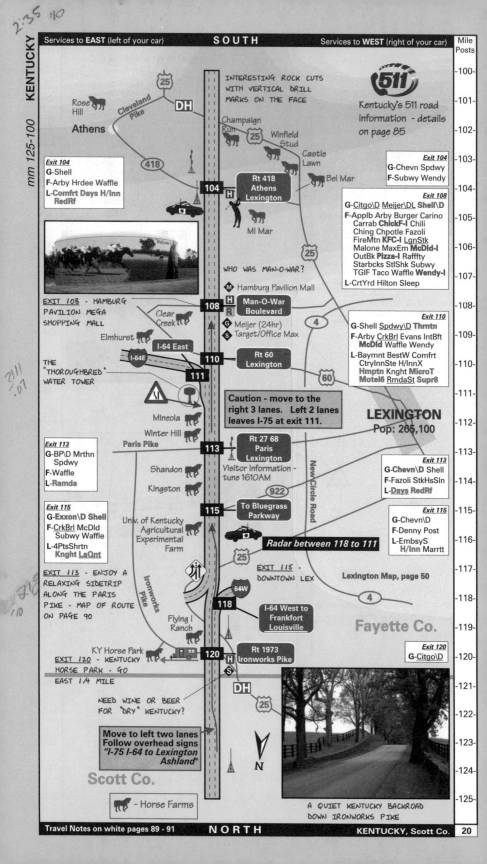
A QUIET KENTUCKY BACKROAD DOWN IRONWORKS PIKE

311 .07
311 .07

3:00,10   3:40 '07

Exit 76
G-BP Shell Spdwy\D
F-Arby BKing
Chinse CrkBrl KFC
LJSilvr Mario
McDld-I Pizza
Taco Waffle
Wendy
L-Hol/M Knght
Supr8

Super Wal-Mart

ANTIQUES

EXIT 76, INSIDER TIP
EL RIO GRANDE (MAP ON PAGE 52)

Exit 76
G-BP Chevn Mrthn\DL
F-Lees
L-Comfrt Econo Fairfld

-75-
-76-

mm 100-75

76 RT 21 Berea

Berea
Pop: 9,900

595

77 Rt 595 Berea

Exit 77
F-TravCenter

Berea Map, page 52

DH

EXIT 76 - BEREA, KENTUCKY'S ART & CRAFT CAPITAL - TOWN MAP ON PAGE 52

Exit 77
G-BP Shell
F-CasaReal
L-CdrVillage CtryInnSte Days H/InnX

-77-
-78-
-79-
-80-
-81-

421

25

Terrill

25

PHOTO OPPORTUNITY - FIRST VIEW OF THE MOUNTAINS

-82-

Rest Area ♿ ☕ 🚹🚺 🏕 V

83 m
134 k

No Information
Restrooms: 24 hours

-84-

Exit 87
G-BP\D Chevn Citgo\D Mrthn
Shell\D Spdwy
F-A&W Arby BKing Blimp
Fazoli HnyDipD Hooter
Krystal McDld Pizza Rally
Subwy Taco Waffle Wendy
L-BestW Econo QltyQtr

N

EXIT 77, INSIDER TIP
KENTUCKY TRAVELERS' CENTER

-85-

Richmond Mall

876

M

Rock Cut W

Rock Cut

87 Rt 876 Lancaster Richmond

P

Exit 87
G-BP\D Mrthn
F-Evans Ryan StkShk
L-Comfrt H/InnX Hmptn Jamsn

-86-
-87-

Richmond
Pop: 27,600

Richmond Map, page 53

Main

876

25

HV

EXIT 87 - "ACRES OF LAND" WINERY

-88-
-89-

Exit 90A
G-Shell
F-CrkBrl WSizz
L-Knght LaQnt RedRf

90A Rts 25S 421S Richmond

90B Rts 25N 421N

Exit 90B
G-BP\D Citgo Exxon\D
Mrthn Shell\D
F-Arby BgBoy DQ Hrdee
Pizza Subwy Waffle
Wendy
L-Days Supr8

-90-
-91-

EXIT 90A & 87
RICHMOND AND KIT CARSON
- TOWN MAP ON PAGE 53

DH

25

$36.73

GAS
$2.76

-92-
-93-
-94-

White Hall WT

Exit 95
G-BP\D Loves\D
F-Arby Blimp
McDld

95 Rt 627 Boonesborough Winchester

Exit 95
G-Shell\D

-95-

EXIT 95 - FORT BOONESBOROUGH AND
WHITE HALL - SPECIAL MAP PAGE 51

-96-

USA Flea Market

Exit 97
G-ExnTS\D
F-Hddle

closed

97 RTs 25S 421S

Kentucky River

Madison Co.

Fayette Co.

-97-

Clay's Ferry Map, page 92

Florida

99 Rts 25N 421 Clays Ferry

-98-
-99-

EXIT 99 - CLAY'S FERRY,
(MAP ON PAGE 92)

25

-100-

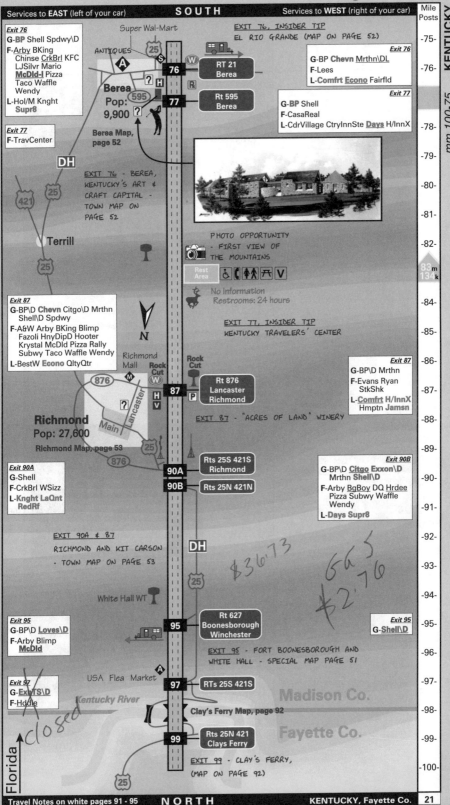

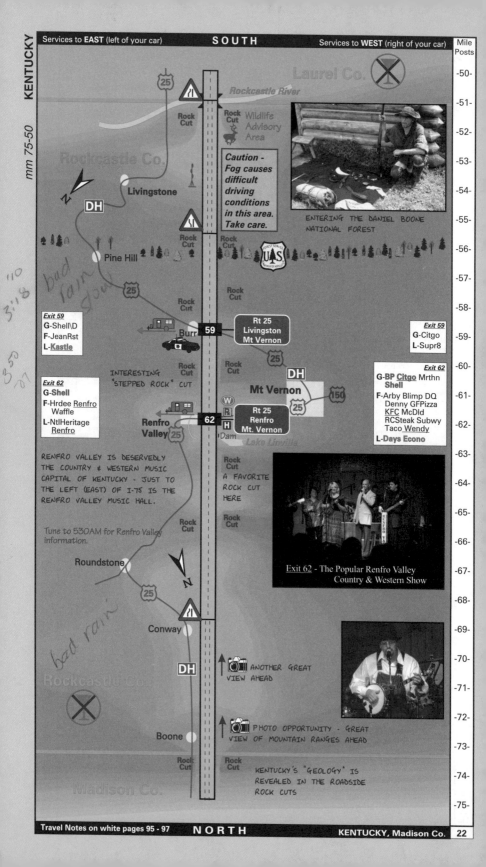

-50-
-51-
-52-
-53-
-54-
-55-
-56-
-57-
-58-
-59-
-60-
-61-
-62-
-63-
-64-
-65-
-66-
-67-
-68-
-69-
-70-
-71-
-72-
-73-
-74-
-75-

25

Rockcastle River

Laurel Co.

Rock Cut

Rock Cut Wildlife Advisory Area

Caution - Fog causes difficult driving conditions in this area. Take care.

Rockcastle Co.

Livingstone

DH

N

Rock Cut

ENTERING THE DANIEL BOONE NATIONAL FOREST

Pine Hill

Rock Cut

Rock Cut

U.S.

bad rain stou

'110
3.18

350
07

25

Rock Cut

Rock Cut

Exit 59
G-Shell\D
F-JeanRst
L-**Kastle**

Burr

59

Rt 25
Livingston
Mt Vernon

25

DH

Exit 59
G-Citgo
L-Supr8

INTERESTING "STEPPED ROCK" CUT

Rock Cut

Rock Cut

Mt Vernon

150

Exit 62
G-Shell
F-Hrdee Renfro Waffle
L-NtlHeritage Renfro

Renfro Valley

W R H

62

Rt 25
Renfro
Mt. Vernon

25

Exit 62
G-BP **Citgo** Mrthn Shell
F-Arby Blimp DQ Denny GFPizza **KFC** McDld RCSteak Subwy Taco **Wendy**
L-Days Econo

Dam Lake Linville

25

RENFRO VALLEY IS DESERVEDLY THE COUNTRY & WESTERN MUSIC CAPITAL OF KENTUCKY - JUST TO THE LEFT (EAST) OF I-75 IS THE RENFRO VALLEY MUSIC HALL.

Rock Cut A FAVORITE ROCK CUT HERE

Rock Cut

Tune to 530AM for Renfro Valley information.

Rock Cut

Rock Cut

Exit 62 - The Popular Renfro Valley Country & Western Show

Roundstone

25

N

bad rain

Conway

DH

ANOTHER GREAT VIEW AHEAD

PHOTO OPPORTUNITY - GREAT VIEW OF MOUNTAIN RANGES AHEAD

Rockcastle Co.

Boone

Rock Cut

Rock Cut

KENTUCKY'S "GEOLOGY" IS REVEALED IN THE ROADSIDE ROCK CUTS

Madison Co.

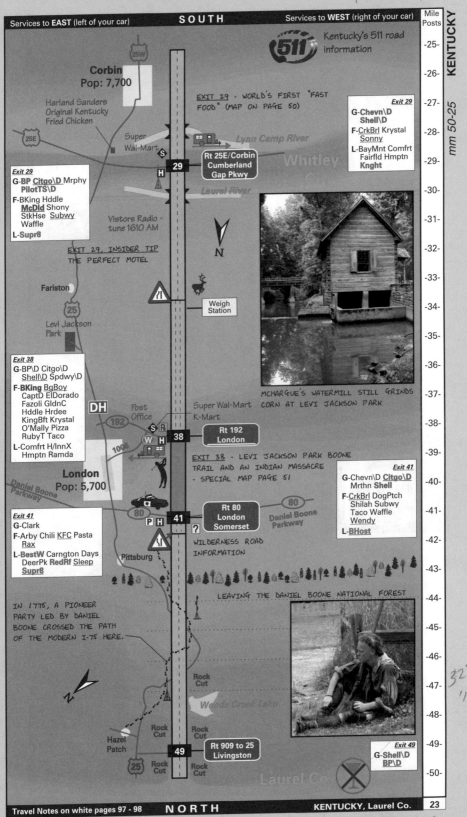

511 Kentucky's 511 road information

-25-
-26-
-27-

mm 50-25

Corbin
Pop: 7,700

Harland Sanders Original Kentucky Fried Chicken

EXIT 29 - WORLD'S FIRST "FAST FOOD" (MAP ON PAGE 50)

Super Wal-Mart

Lynn Camp River

Whitley Co.

Rt 25E/Corbin Cumberland Gap Pkwy

29

Laurel River

-28-
-29-
-30-

Exit 29
G-Chevn\D Shell\D
F-CrkBrl Krystal Sonny
L-BayMnt Comfrt Fairfld Hmptn Knght

Exit 29
G-BP **Citgo\D** Mrphy **PilotTS\D**
F-BKing Hddle **McDld** Shony StkHse **Subwy** Waffle
L-**Supr8**

Visitors Radio - tune 1610 AM

N

-31-
-32-
-33-
-34-
-35-
-36-
-37-

EXIT 29, INSIDER TIP THE PERFECT MOTEL

Fariston

25

Levi Jackson Park

Weigh Station

Exit 38
G-BP\D Citgo\D **Shell\D** Spdwy\D
F-**BKing** BgBoy CaptD ElDorado Fazoli GldnC Hddle Hrdee KingBft Krystal O'Mally Pizza RubyT Taco
L-Comfrt H/InnX Hmptn Ramda

DH

Post Office

192

1000

Super Wal-Mart
K-Mart

Rt 192 London

-38-
-39-

MCHARGUE'S WATERMILL STILL GRINDS CORN AT LEVI JACKSON PARK

London
Pop: 5,700

Daniel Boone Parkway

EXIT 38 - LEVI JACKSON PARK BOONE TRAIL AND AN INDIAN MASSACRE - SPECIAL MAP PAGE 51

Exit 41
G-Chevn\D **Citgo\D** Mrthn **Shell**
F-**CrkBrl** DogPtch Shilah Subwy Taco Waffle Wendy
L-**BHost**

-40-
-41-

Exit 41
G-Clark
F-Arby Chili **KFC** Pasta **Rax**
L-**BestW** Carngton Days DeerPk **RedRf** Sleep **Supr8**

80

Rt 80 London Somerset

80

Daniel Boone Parkway

WILDERNESS ROAD INFORMATION

?

-42-
-43-

Pittsburg

LEAVING THE DANIEL BOONE NATIONAL FOREST

IN 1775, A PIONEER PARTY LED BY DANIEL BOONE CROSSED THE PATH OF THE MODERN I-75 HERE.

N

Rock Cut

Woods Creek Lake

-44-
-45-
-46-
-47-
-48-

Hazel Patch

25

Rock Cut

Rock Cut

Rock Cut

49

Rt 909 to 25 Livingston

Laurel Co.

Exit 49
G-Shell\D BP\D

-49-
-50-

402 '07

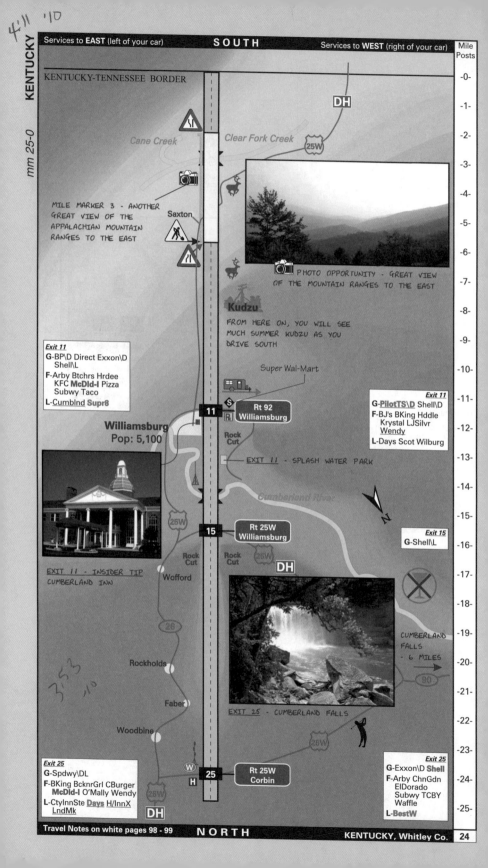

4.11 '10

Services to EAST (left of your car)   **S O U T H**   Services to **WEST** (right of your car)   Mile Posts

-0-
-1-

KENTUCKY-TENNESSEE BORDER

DH

-2-

Cane Creek   Clear Fork Creek   25W

-3-
-4-

MILE MARKER 3 - ANOTHER GREAT VIEW OF THE APPALACHIAN MOUNTAIN RANGES TO THE EAST

Saxton

-5-
-6-
-7-

PHOTO OPPORTUNITY - GREAT VIEW OF THE MOUNTAIN RANGES TO THE EAST

Kudzu

-8-

FROM HERE ON, YOU WILL SEE MUCH SUMMER KUDZU AS YOU DRIVE SOUTH

-9-

Super Wal-Mart

-10-

Exit 11
G- BP\D Direct Exxon\D Shell\L
F- Arby Btchrs Hrdee KFC **McDld-I** Pizza Subwy Taco
L- Cumblnd Supr8

Williamsburg
Pop: 5,100

11

Rt 92
Williamsburg

-11-

Exit 11
G- PilotTS\D Shell\D
F- BJ's BKing Hddle Krystal LJSilvr Wendy
L- Days Scot Wilburg

-12-

Rock Cut

EXIT 11 - SPLASH WATER PARK

-13-
-14-

Cumberland River

-15-

25W

15

Rt 25W
Williamsburg

Exit 15
G- Shell\L

-16-

EXIT 11 - INSIDER TIP
CUMBERLAND INN

Rock Cut

Rock Cut

25W

-17-

DH

Wofford

-18-

26

-19-

CUMBERLAND FALLS - 6 MILES

-20-

90

Rockholds

-21-

353 '10

Faber

-22-

EXIT 25 - CUMBERLAND FALLS

-23-

Woodbine

25W

Exit 25
G- Spdwy\DL
F- BKing BcknrGrl CBurger **McDld-I** O'Mally Wendy
L- CtyInnSte Days H/InnX LndMk

W
H

25

Rt 25W
Corbin

Exit 25
G- Exxon\D Shell
F- Arby ChnGdn ElDorado Subwy TCBY Waffle
L- BestW

-24-
-25-

25W

DH

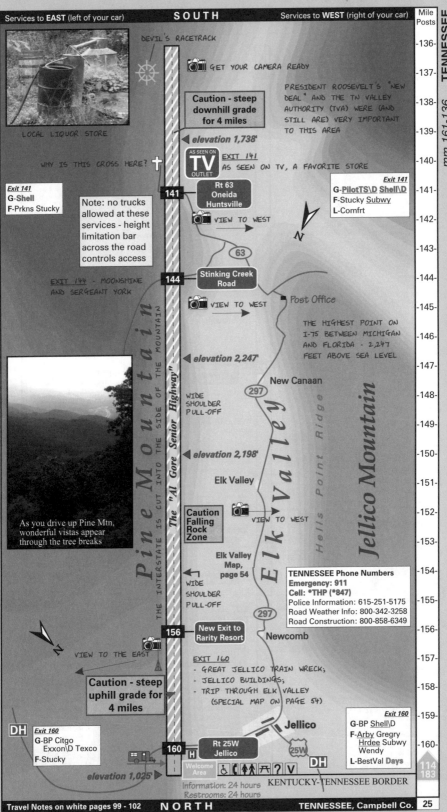

(handwritten top margin) '10 5:00pm

(handwritten left margin, vertical) 6 ie | '07 | left | 6 pm | dinner

TENNESSEE

mm 136-111

Exit 112
G-BP\D Chevn Pilot\D
F-Aubreys BudBBQ DQ
Deli Krystal McDld-I
RubyT StkShk TCBY
Taco Wendy
L-CtyInnSte H/InnX

Exit 112
G-Exxon
Shell\D
Weigel
F-Hrdee Shony
Waffle
L-Comfrt

Emory Rd

[R] [W]

112 | Rt 131
Emory Rd
Powell

Heiskell Rd

EXIT 112, INSIDER TIP
AUBREY'S RESTAURANT

Rock Cut

Knox Co.

Exit 117
G-BP
PilotTS\D

170

117 | Rt 170
Raccoon Valley

170

Anderson Co.

to I-75 via
Oak Ridge

Clinton A

EXIT 122 - JUST A FEW
MILE WEST OF I-75,
CLINTON HAS MANY
ANTIQUE SHOPS

Sevier Blvd

61

Clinton and Oak Ridge
Maps, page 56

25S

DH

Exit 122
G-Shell
F-Shony

Museum of the
Appalachia

61

441

122 | Rt 61/Norris
Clinton

?

Twin Gables
Antique Mall

A

Exit 122
G-BP Exxon\D GitnGo\D
Mrthn\D Phil66 Shell
F-Arby BKing BaskR
GitnGo GldnGirls
Hrdee Krystal McDld
Subwy Waffle Wendy
Zaxby
L-BestW Comfrt
CtryInnSte H/InnX
NorrisInn Supr8

Norris

Wildlife
Sanctuary

Norris Dam Map,
page 55

Clinch River

Lenoir
Museum

Grist Mill &
Threshing
Barn

EXIT 122, INSIDER TIPS
MUSEUM OF THE APPALACHIA

EXIT 122, INSIDER TIPS
GOLDEN GIRLS RESTAURANT

Bypass Knoxville? See
page 104; map on page 56

25S

Exit 128
G-BP Sunco

Lake City

128 | Rt 44
Lake City

Norris Dam

Norris
Park

129 | Rt S25W
Lake City

116

Exit 129
G-BP Citgo
Exxon\DL Shell
F-BKing Blimp CrkBrl
KFC McDld-I
Subwy
L-Days Lambs LkCty

Norris
Park

Anderson Co.
Campbell Co.

Kudzu

DH

Kudzu

(handwritten) Dragon on left

EXIT 128 - TAKE A SHORT BUT
FASCINATING SIDE TRIP OVER
NORRIS DAM (MAP ON PAGE 55)

Tune in to WNOX 100.3FM for
Knoxville & area traffic reports

N

EXIT 134, INSIDER TIP
HAMPTON ON THE HILL

H

134 | Rts N25W/E63
Caryville
Jacksboro
La Follette

Exit 134
G-BP
F-Scottys Shony
L-BHost

Exit 134
G-Exxon\D Shell
F-D/Bell Family
Waffle
L-Econo Family
Hmptn Supr8

Cove Lake
State Park

Caryville

[camera] VIEW - OFF TO THE WEST
◄ elevation 1,093'

Mile Posts:
-111-
-112-
-113-
-114-
-115-
-116-
-117-
-118-
-119-
-120-
-121-
-122-
-123-
-124-
-125-
-126-
-127-
-128-
-129-
-130-
-131-
-132-
-133-
-134-
-135-
-136-

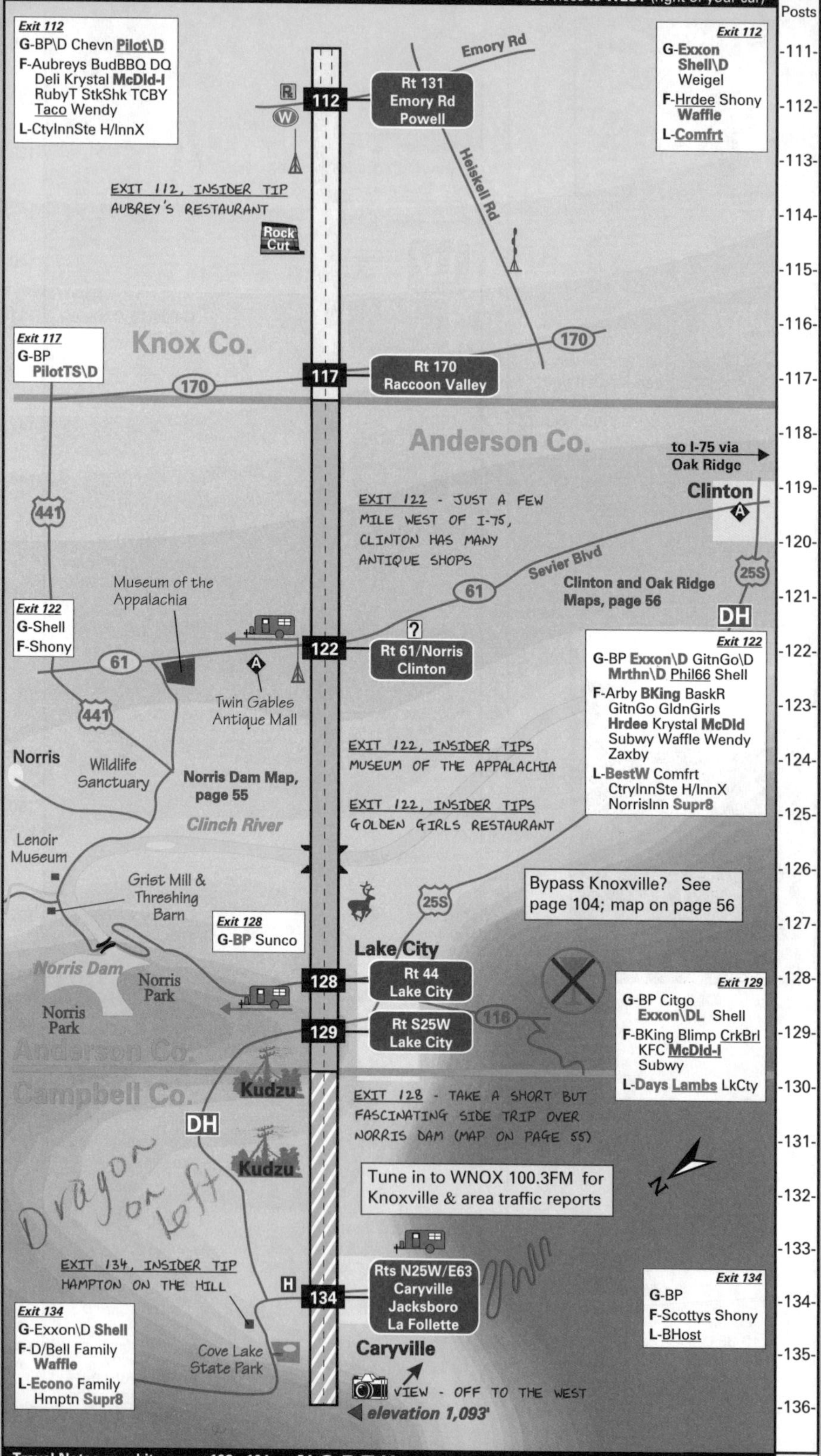

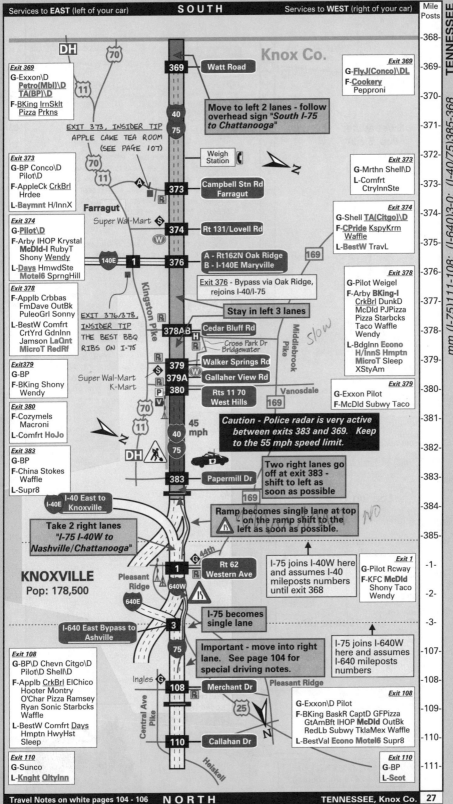

705 '07

TENNESSEE

mm (I-40/75)368; (I-75)83-59

-59-

Exit 60
G-Rcway
F-BKing **McDld**
L-BestVal Comfrt
Days Knght

EXIT 60 - THE "LOST SEA"

60

H

Rt 68
Sweetwater

A

Exit 60
G-BPTS\D Exxon\D
Phil66
F-CrkBrl J&JStk
L-BestW QltyInn

McMinn Co.

-60-

-61-

Exit 62
F-D/Bell

62

Rt 322
Sweetwater

-62-

Sweetwater
Pop: 5,600

DH

11

Monroe Co.

TENNESSEE'S WILDFLOWER PROGRAM,
PRODUCES MASSES OF BEAUTIFUL FLOWERS
ALONG I-75 IN SPRING AND SUMMERTIME.
RED CORN POPPIES, SHASTA DAISIES, YELLOW
COSMOS AND MANY OTHER WILDFLOWER
SPECIES PROVIDE CARPETS OF COLOR,
ESPECIALLY BETWEEN CHATTANOOGA AND
KNOXVILLE.
    "WITHOUT A DOUBT, THE TENNESSEE
    STRETCHES OF THE INTERSTATE ARE THE
    MOST BEAUTIFUL ON THE ENTIRE ROUTE."

-63-

-64-

-65-

-66-

Loudon Co.

-67-

Exit 68
G-BP\D

Philadelphia

68

Rt 323
Philadelphia

**Caution - Watch for Deer crossing
the road during the next 40 miles**

-68-

-69-

EXIT 68 - ENJOY A TENNESSEE
CHEESE AND FARM TOUR AT THE
SWEETWATER VALLEY FARM

ON ALMOST EVERY I-75 DRIVE, WE HAVE SEEN
DEER FEEDING IN THE ROADSIDE TREE FRINGE OR
IN THE WIDE MEDIAN AREAS - PLEASE BE CAREFUL
SINCE THEY SCARE VERY EASILY AND MAY BOLT
ACROSS THE ROAD IN FRONT OF YOU.

-70-

-71-

Exit 72
G-BP Shell\D
F-KspyKrm
McDld Wendy
L-Supr8

72 H

Rt 72
Loudon

Exit 72
G-Citgo
L-BestVal

-72-

11

N

Watts Bar
Lake

-73-

Mitchell W. Stout
Memorial Bridge

Tennessee
River

-74-

Loudon

WHO WAS MITCHELL STOUT?

-75-

Tennessee River

76

Rt 324
Sugar Limb Rd

-76-

EXIT 76 - TOUR TENNESSEE VALLEY WINERY
AND SAMPLE THEIR AWARD WINNING WINES

-77-

Exit 81
G-BP\D Exxon\D
Mobil Shell\D
Texco
F-BaskR BudBBQ
CrkBrl Shony
Subwy TokoyX
Waffle
L-**Days** H/InnX
Hmptn Kings

Kudzu

Kudzu

SUMMER NOTE - AN INCREDIBLE
STAND OF KUDZU HERE

-78-

Lenoir City

-79-

Dam
PARK

Super
Wal-Mart

S
R

81

Rt 321
Lenoir City
Oak Ridge

321

Exit 81
G-Citgo\D Shell
F-Krystal RubyT
L-Comfrt **Econo**
Ramda

-80-

-81-

Ft Loudon
Lake

75

**Watch for high
speed traffic
merging from left**

-82-

11

DH

70

368

I-40 West to
Nashville   40W

-83-

**Take Exit 368 (2 left lanes)
"South I-75 to Chattanooga"**

ROCK CITY?

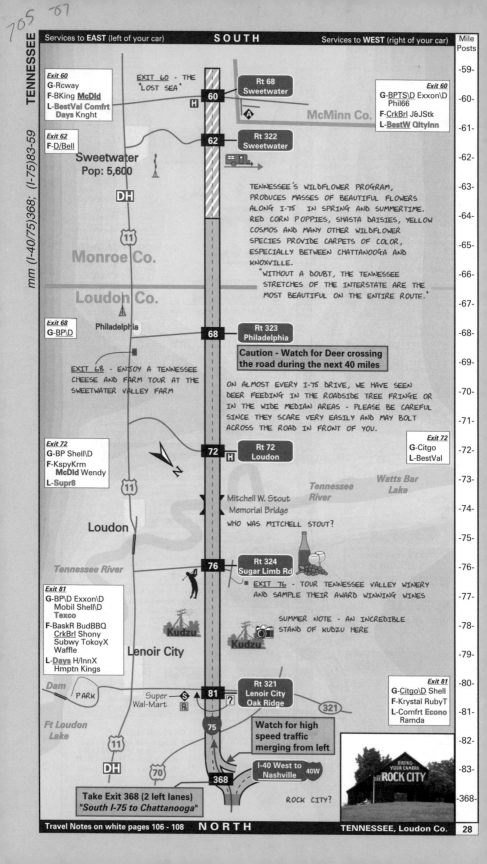

BRING YOUR CAMERA
SEE ROCK CITY

-368-

6:13 '10

TENNESSEE

mm 59-34

Bradley Co.

11

Hiwassee River

McMinn Co.

Bowater Paper

163   36   Rt 163 Calhoun

Calhoun

SPANISH EXPLORER HERNANDO DE SOTO AND HIS ARMY PASSED THROUGH HERE IN MAY, 1540

DH

The next 5 miles are extremely hazardous during fog - the electronic warning system will keep you advised. If conditions are foggy, please turn on your headlights (low beams) and exercise the utmost caution.

At mile 38.9 - watch for police radar hidden by trees in the wooded median strip

CAUTION FOG 15 SPEED LIMIT MPH

Riceville

42   Rt 39 Riceville Rd

Exit 42
G-Citgo
L-Relax

11

Electronic Fog Advisory System zone starts - please obey messages on overhead & roadside electronic signs - see page 109

Exit 49
G-BP\D Conco
  Kgroo Rcway
  Shell\D
F-Applb **BKing**
  Hrdee Krystal
  Montry RubyT
  Shony Subwy
  TCBY Waffle
L-**Days** Econo
  Hmptn Motel6
  Supr8

Rest Area   ♿ 🚻 🧍 🪑 V

49 m
79 k

No informatin - Restrooms: 24 hours

This police car radar trap is often on the rest area exit ramp facing back up towards I-75 southbound traffic as it comes around the curve

Exit 49
G-Shell\D

W   49   H   Rt 30 Athens Decatur

30

Athens
Pop: 13,200

N

Exit 52
G-Exxon GldnGln

Exit 52
G-Citgo
L-Motel

52   Mt Verd Rd Athens

11

EXIT 52 - TIME MAGAZINE'S "BEST ICE CREAM IN THE WORLD"

Welcome to Mayfield Home of The "World's Best Ice Cream"

Exit 56
G-BPTS\D
  CrzEd\D/
F-CrzEd

Niota

309   56   Rt 309 Niota

DH

EXIT 52 - A SPECIAL "MAYFIELD WELCOME" FROM MAGGIE, THE FAMOUS ICECREAM COW

McMinn Co.

Florida

Monroe Co.   McMinn Co.   ⊗

5:56 '10

-34-
-35-
-36-
-37-
-38-
-39-
-40-
-41-
-42-
-43-
-44-
-45-
-46-
-47-
-48-
-49-
-50-
-51-
-52-
-53-
-54-
-55-
-56-
-57-
-58-
-59-

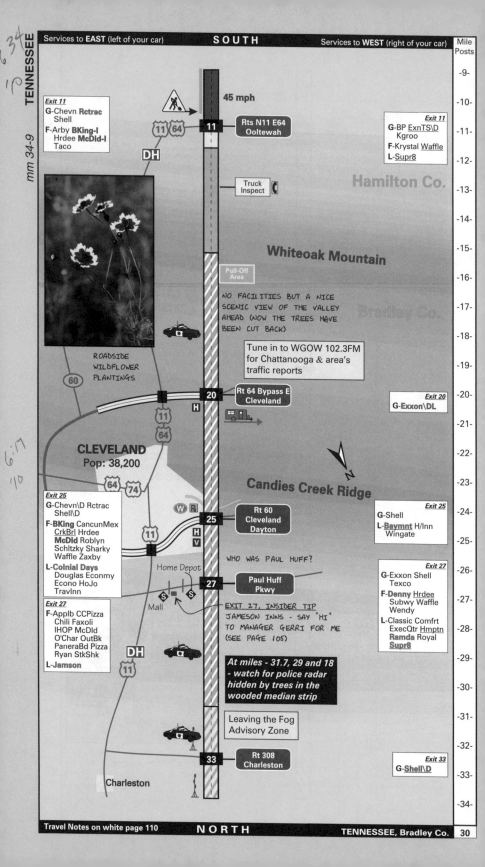

TENNESSEE

mm 34-9

634
1P

6:17
10

45 mph

Exit 11
G-Chevn **Rctrac**
Shell
F-Arby **BKing-I**
Hrdee **McDld-I**
Taco

DH

(11)(64) **11** Rts N11 E64
Ooltewah

Exit 11
G-BP ExnTS\D
Kgroo
F-Krystal Waffle
L-Supr8

Truck
Inspect

Hamilton Co.

Whiteoak Mountain

Pull-Off
Area

NO FACILITIES BUT A NICE
SCENIC VIEW OF THE VALLEY
AHEAD (NOW THE TREES HAVE
BEEN CUT BACK)

Bradley Co.

ROADSIDE
WILDFLOWER
PLANTINGS

(60)

Tune in to WGOW 102.3FM
for Chattanooga & area's
traffic reports

(11)
(64)

20 Rt 64 Bypass E
Cleveland

Exit 20
G-Exxon\DL

CLEVELAND
Pop: 38,200

(64) (74)

Exit 25
G-Chevn\D Rctrac
Shell\D
F-**BKing** CancunMex
CrkBrl Hrdee
McDld Roblyn
Schltzky Sharky
Waffle Zaxby
L-**Colnial Days**
Douglas Econmy
Econo HoJo
TravInn

W R

(11)

H
V

Candies Creek Ridge

N

25 Rt 60
Cleveland
Dayton

Exit 25
G-Shell
L-Baymnt H/Inn
Wingate

WHO WAS PAUL HUFF?

Home Depot

27 Paul Huff
Pkwy

S S

Mall

Exit 27
F-Applb CCPizza
Chili Faxoli
IHOP McDld
O'Char OutBk
PaneraBd Pizza
Ryan StkShk
L-Jamson

DH

(11)

EXIT 27, INSIDER TIP
JAMESON INNS - SAY "HI"
TO MANAGER GERRI FOR ME
(SEE PAGE 105)

Exit 27
G-Exxon Shell
Texco
F-**Denny** Hrdee
Subwy Waffle
Wendy
L-Classic Comfrt
ExecQtr Hmptn
Ramda Royal
Supr8

At miles - 31.7, 29 and 18
- watch for police radar
hidden by trees in the
wooded median strip

Leaving the Fog
Advisory Zone

33 Rt 308
Charleston

Exit 33
G-Shell\D

Charleston

TENNESSEE-GEORGIA

mm (TN)9-0; (GA)354-338

VIEW OF ROCKY FACE RIDGE CIVIL WAR BATTLEFIELD
JUST AHEAD - SEE FOOT
OF NEXT MAP

EXIT 341, INSIDER TIP
TUNNEL HILL HERITAGE
CENTER (PAGE 120, MAP
PAGE 59)

-338

EXIT 333 (NEXT PAGE)
INSIDER TIP
DALTON - BORN TO SHOP

Tunnel Hill

-339

33

DH

201

Rt 201
Tunnel Hill
Varnell

341
W

Tunnel Hill
Station

Chickamauga
River Bridge

Exit 341
G-Chevn Shell

-340

Whitfield Co.

Catoosa
Co.

-341

34

76

-342

GEORGIA Phone Numbers
Emergency: 911, 404-624-6077,
Cell: *GSP (*477)
Police Information: 404-657-9300
Road Construction
   and Conditions: 404-635-8000

Weigh
Station

41

Great Locomotive Chase Key
refers to story on page 117

1 = Andrew's Raiders (Union)

3 = Fuller (Confederate)

-343

-344

Exit 348
G-BP Conco
GldnGln\D_Shell\D
F-AuntEff CrkBrl
Hrdee KFC Krystal
LosReyes **McDld-I**
Pizza RubyT Subwy
Taco **Waffle**
L-BestW Days H/InnX
HomeTn Supr8

Exit 345
G-BP

345

Rts 41 76
Ringgold
Tunnel Hill

Civil War Battle
Ringgold Gap
Nov, 1863
(see page 116)

Exit 345
G-Chevn Kgroo
F-Waffle

-345

-346

Exit 348
G-Exxon Kgroo
F-KspyKrm Wendy
L-Comfrt

-347

Ringgold

Ringgold
Station
W
R

348

DH

Rt 151
Ringgold
LaFayette

-348

Exit 350
G-Exxon
Kgroo
F-KspyKrm

76
41

EXIT 348, INSIDER TIP
AUNT EFFIE'S

-349

H

350

Rt 2
Battlefield Pkwy
Ft Oglethorpe

Exit 350
G-Rctrac Shell
F-BBQCrl

-350

Georgia Welcome Center
Information: 8:30-5:30 daily
Restrooms: 7:00-11:00

GENERAL

35

EXIT 350
GEORGIA WINERY
AND SWEETWATER
FARM CHEESE

♿ ♟ 👫 🚻 ☕ ❓ Ⓥ

GA, Exit 353
G-BP Shell
F-Subwy

-351

Exit 353
G-BP Chevn
L-Knght

146

353
R

Rt 146/Rossville
Ft Oglethorpe

32 m
51 k

Chickamauga Creek

TN, Exit 1
G-BP Conco\DL Pilot Rcway Texco\D
F-A&W Arby **BKing** BaskR CatFsh
CrkBrl CtrlPark Hrdee Krystal
LJSilvr **McDld** Shony Subwy Taco
UncleBud Waffle Wallys
L-**Best** CreekL H/InnX **Supr8**

-353

TENNESSEE-GEORGIA BORDER

TN, Exit 1
G-Texco
L-BestVal Comfrt Crown
Econo HoJo **Ramda**

41

DH

1
R
A

Rt 41
East Ridge

-0-

-1-

Exit 3
G-BP
F-Subwy

2
M

West I-24
to I-59
Chattanooga

I-24

Missionary Ridge

CHATTANOOGA
Pop: 159,700

Chattanooga Map, page 56

-2-

Move to left 2
lanes - Follow
"I-75 Atlanta"

Eastgate Mall

-3-

EXIT 5, INSIDER TIP
STICKY FINGERS
FAMOUS DAVE'S

Hamilton
Place Mall

3

E Brainerd

EXIT 2, INSIDER TIP
A PRIVATE PARLOR
CAR FOR THE NIGHT

4
R

Chickamauga Dam

-4-

Famous Dave's
Sticky Fingers
M

11

dinner

-5-

63¢
eat

Exit 2 - Chattanooga's tourism
area is only 9 mins off I-75
(map on page 56)

S
R

5

Shallowford
Road

Exit 5
G-BP Citgo Exxon
F-Applb CrkBrl Fazoli GlenGene
McDld MexGrl O'Aces O'Char
RBravo Shony Subwy TexRdHse
Waffle Wendy
L-CtryInnSte Days Fairfld GuestHs
H/Inn H/InnX HltnGdn Hmptn
HomeWd Knght **LaQnt MicroT**
Ramda **RedRf** Sleep

-6-

7

Bonnie Oaks Dr
Lee Hwy
Rts 317 11S 64W

EXIT 4 -
TENNESSEE
VALLEY
RAILROAD

Gunbarrel

-7-

Exit 5
F-Acropolis Alexndr Arby
CntryPlace ElMeson
FmDave Krystal Olive
OutBk RedLb **StkSnk**
StkyFngr Taco
L-Comfrt CrtYrd Wingate

-8-

Exit 7
G-Texco
L-**Best** **BestW** Comfrt
Econo **Motel6** ParkInn

9
45 mph

Enterprise S
Industrial Pk

Hamilton Co.

-9-

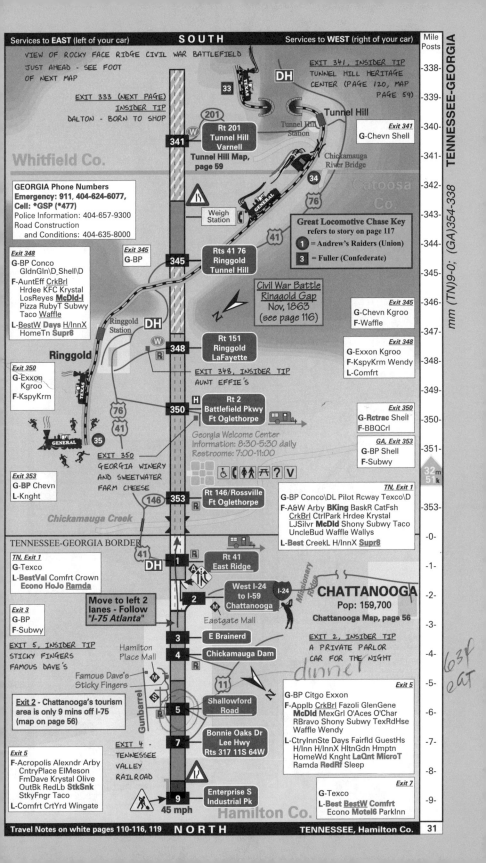

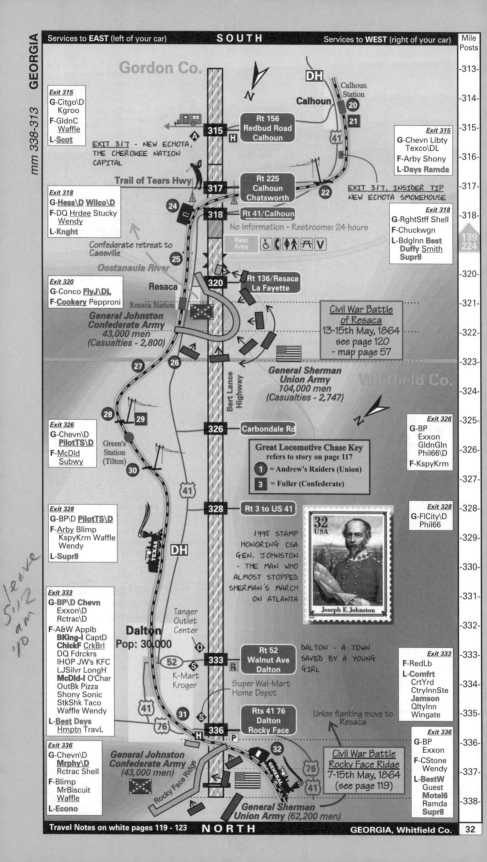

Gordon Co.

-313-

DH

Calhoun Station

Calhoun

-314-

20
21

Exit 315
G-Citgo\D Kgroo
F-GldnC Waffle
L-Scot

-315-

Rt 156
Redbud Road
Calhoun

41

Exit 315
G-Chevn Libty Texco\DL
F-Arby Shony
L-Days Ramda

-316-

EXIT 317 - NEW ECHOTA, THE CHEROKEE NATION CAPITAL

Trail of Tears Hwy

317

Rt 225
Calhoun
Chatsworth

22

-317-

EXIT 317, INSIDER TIP NEW ECHOTA SMOKEHOUSE

Exit 318
G-Hess\D Wilco\D
F-DQ Hrdee Stucky Wendy
L-Knght

24

318

Rt 41/Calhoun

No Information - Restrooms: 24 hours

-318-

139
224

Exit 318
G-RghtStff Shell
F-Chuckwgn
L-Bdglnn Best Duffy Smith Supr8

Confederate retreat to Caseville

25

Rest Area ♿ 🚻 🚶 🪑 V

Oostanaula River

Exit 320
G-Conco Fly.J\DL
F-Cookery Pepproni

Resaca

Resaca Station

320

Rt 136/Resaca
La Fayette

-320-

-321-

General Johnston Confederate Army
43,000 men
(Casualties - 2,800)

Civil War Battle of Resaca
13-15th May, 1864
see page 120
- map page 57

-322-

27

26

-323-

General Sherman Union Army
104,000 men
(Casualties - 2,747)

Whitfield Co.

-324-

28

29

Bert Lance Highway

Exit 326
G-Chevn\D PilotTS\D
F-McDld Subwy

326

Carbondale Rd

-325-

Exit 326
G-BP Exxon GldnGln Phil66\D
F-KspyKrm

-326-

Green's Station (Tilton)

30

Great Locomotive Chase Key
refers to story on page 117
1 = Andrew's Raiders (Union)
3 = Fuller (Confederate)

-327-

41

Exit 328
G-BP\D PilotTS\D
F-Arby Blimp KspyKrm Waffle Wendy
L-Supr8

328

Rt 3 to US 41

-328-

Exit 328
G-FlCity\D Phil66

32
USA

-329-

DH

1995 STAMP HONORING CSA GEN. JOHNSTON - THE MAN WHO ALMOST STOPPED SHERMAN'S MARCH ON ATLANTA

-330-

-331-

Joseph E. Johnston

Exit 333
G-BP\D Chevn Exxon\D Rctrac\D
F-A&W Applb BKing-I CaptD ChickF CrkBrl DQ Fdrckrs IHOP JW's KFC LJSilvr LongH McDld-I O'Char OutBk Pizza Shony Sonic StkShk Taco Waffle Wendy
L-Best Days Hmptn TravL

Tanger Outlet Center

Dalton
Pop: 30,000

52

K-Mart Kroger

333

Rt 52
Walnut Ave
Dalton

DALTON - A TOWN SAVED BY A YOUNG GIRL

-332-

-333-

Exit 333
F-RedLb
L-Comfrt CrtYrd CtryInnSte Jamson QltyInn Wingate

-334-

Super Wal-Mart Home Depot

41

76

31

336

Rts 41 76
Dalton
Rocky Face

Union flanking move to Resaca

32

76

41

-335-

Exit 336
G-Chevn\D Mrphy\D Rctrac Shell
F-Blimp MrBiscuit Waffle
L-Econo

General Johnston Confederate Army
(43,000 men)

Rocky Face Ridge

Civil War Battle
Rocky Face Ridge
7-15th May, 1864
(see page 119)

-336-

Exit 336
G-BP Exxon
F-CStone Wendy
L-BestW Guest Motel6 Ramda Supr8

-337-

General Sherman Union Army (62,200 men)

-338-

leave 5/12 am '10

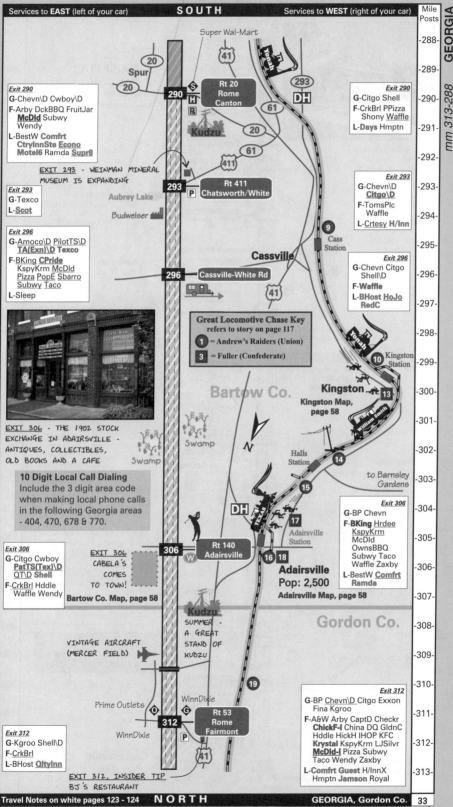

Services to **EAST** (left of your car)   **S O U T H**   Services to **WEST** (right of your car)

Mile Posts

GEORGIA

mm 313-288

-288-
-289-
-290-
-291-
-292-
-293-
-294-
-295-
-296-
-297-
-298-
-299-
-300-
-301-
-302-
-303-
-304-
-305-
-306-
-307-
-308-
-309-
-310-
-311-
-312-
-313-

Super Wal-Mart

41

Yonah

20

Spur

20

293

DH

290

Rt 20
Rome
Canton

61

Exit 290
G-Chevn\D Cwboy\D
F-Arby DckBBQ FruitJar
McDld Subwy
Wendy
L-BestW **Comfrt**
CtryInnSte Econo
Motel6 Ramda **Supr8**

Exit 290
G-Citgo Shell
F-CrkBrl PPizza
Shony **Waffle**
L-Days Hmptn

Kudzu

20

61

411

EXIT 293 - WEINMAN MINERAL
MUSEUM IS EXPANDING

293

Rt 411
Chatsworth/White

Exit 293
G-Texco
L-**Scot**

Aubrey Lake

Budweiser

Exit 293
G-Chevn\D
Citgo\D
F-TomsPlc
Waffle
L-**Crtesy H/Inn**

9
Cass
Station

Cassville

Exit 296
G-Amoco\D PilotTS\D
TA(Exn)\D Texco
F-BKing **CPride**
KspyKrm McDld
Pizza PopE Sbarro
Subwy Taco
L-Sleep

296

Cassville-White Rd

41

Exit 296
G-Chevn Citgo
Shell\D
F-**Waffle**
L-BHost **HoJo**
RedC

Great Locomotive Chase Key
refers to story on page 117
1 = Andrew's Raiders (Union)
3 = Fuller (Confederate)

Yonah

10 Kingston
Station

EXIT 306 - THE 1902 STOCK
EXCHANGE IN ADAIRSVILLE -
ANTIQUES, COLLECTIBLES,
OLD BOOKS AND A CAFE

Kingston
Kingston Map,
page 58

13
William Smith

10 Digit Local Call Dialing
Include the 3 digit area code
when making local phone calls
in the following Georgia areas
- 404, 470, 678 & 770.

Bartow Co.

Swamp

Swamp

N

Halls
Station

14

to Barnsley
Gardens

15

Exit 306
G-Citgo Cwboy
PatTS(Tex)\D
QT\D Shell
F-CrkBrl Hddle
Waffle Wendy

EXIT 306
CABELA'S
COMES
TO TOWN!
Bartow Co. Map, page 58

306
W

Rt 140
Adairsville

DH
TEXAS

17
Adairsville
Station

16 **18**

Exit 306
G-BP Chevn
F-**BKing** Hrdee
KspyKrm
McDld
OwnsBBQ
Subwy Taco
Waffle Zaxby
L-BestW **Comfrt**
Ramda

Adairsville
Pop: 2,500
Adairsville Map, page 58

Kudzu
SUMMER -
A GREAT
STAND OF
KUDZU

Gordon Co.

VINTAGE AIRCRAFT
(MERCER FIELD)

19

Exit 312
G-BP **Chevn\D** Citgo Exxon
Fina Kgroo
F-A&W Arby CaptD Checkr
ChickF-I China DQ GldnC
Hddle HickH IHOP KFC
Krystal KspyKrm LJSilvr
McDld-I Pizza Subwy
Taco Wendy Zaxby
L-Comfrt **Guest** H/InnX
Hmptn **Jamson** Royal

Prime Outlets

WinnDixie

Exit 312
G-Kgroo Shell\D
F-CrkBrl
L-BHost **QltyInn**

312

Rt 53
Rome
Fairmont

WinnDixie

41

EXIT 312, INSIDER TIP
BJ'S RESTAURANT

523 left

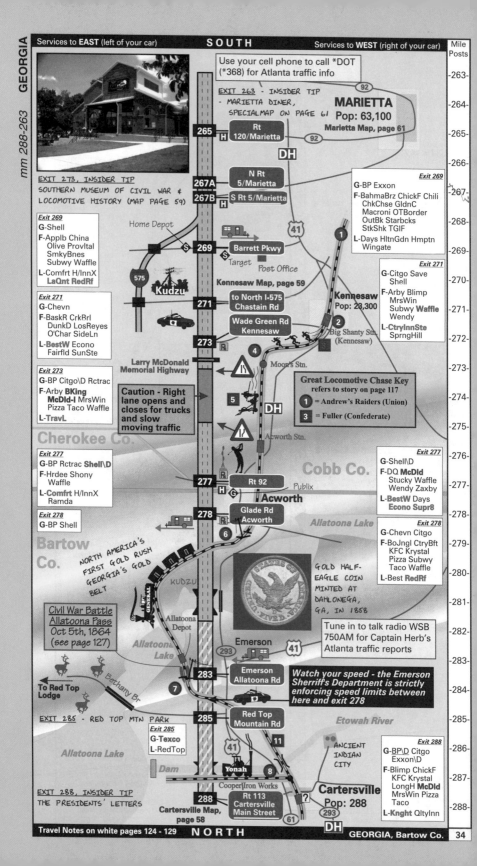

Use your cell phone to call *DOT (*368) for Atlanta traffic info

EXIT 263 - INSIDER TIP - MARIETTA DINER, SPECIAL MAP ON PAGE 61

MARIETTA
Pop: 63,100
Marietta Map, page 61

-263-
-264-
-265-
-266-
-267-
-268-
-269-
-270-
-271-
-272-
-273-
-274-
-275-
-276-
-277-
-278-
-279-
-280-
-281-
-282-
-283-
-284-
-285-
-286-
-287-
-288-

265 H Rt 120/Marietta

DH

267A N Rt 5/Marietta
267B H S Rt 5/Marietta

EXIT 273, INSIDER TIP
SOUTHERN MUSEUM OF CIVIL WAR & LOCOMOTIVE HISTORY (MAP PAGE 59)

Exit 269
G-Shell
F-Applb China Olive Provltal SmkyBnes Subwy Waffle
L-Comfrt H/InnX LaQnt RedRf

Home Depot

269 Barrett Pkwy

Target
Post Office
Kennesaw Map, page 59

Exit 269
G-BP Exxon
F-BahmaBrz ChickF Chili ChkChse GldnC Macroni OTBorder OutBk Starbcks StkShk TGIF
L-Days HltnGdn Hmptn Wingate

Exit 271
G-Chevn
F-BaskR CrkBrl DunkD LosReyes O'Char SideLn
L-BestW Econo Fairfld SunSte

575

Kudzu

271 to North I-575 Chastain Rd

273 Wade Green Rd Kennesaw

Kennesaw
Pop: 28,300

Exit 271
G-Citgo Save Shell
F-Arby Blimp MrsWin Subwy Waffle Wendy
L-CtryInnSte SprngHill

Big Shanty Stn. (Kennesaw)

Exit 273
G-BP Citgo\D Rctrac
F-Arby BKing McDld-I MrsWin Pizza Taco Waffle
L-TravL

Larry McDonald Memorial Highway

Caution - Right lane opens and closes for trucks and slow moving traffic

Moon's Stn.

Great Locomotive Chase Key
refers to story on page 117
① = Andrew's Raiders (Union)
③ = Fuller (Confederate)

DH

Acworth Stn.

Cherokee Co.

Cobb Co.

Exit 277
G-BP Rctrac Shell\D
F-Hrdee Shony Waffle
L-Comfrt H/InnX Ramda

277 H G Rt 92

Publix

Acworth

Exit 277
G-Shell\D
F-DQ McDld Stucky Waffle Wendy Zaxby
L-BestW Days Econo Supr8

Exit 278
G-BP Shell

278 Glade Rd Acworth

Allatoona Lake

Bartow Co.

NORTH AMERICA'S FIRST GOLD RUSH GEORGIA'S GOLD BELT

KUDZU

Exit 278
G-Chevn Citgo
F-BoJngl CtryBft KFC Krystal Pizza Subwy Taco Waffle
L-Best RedRf

GOLD HALF-EAGLE COIN MINTED AT DAHLONEGA, GA IN 1858

Civil War Battle
Allatoona Pass
Oct 5th, 1864
(see page 127)

Allatoona Depot

Allatoona Lake

Emerson

293

41

Tune in to talk radio WSB 750AM for Captain Herb's Atlanta traffic reports

283 Emerson Allatoona Rd

To Red Top Lodge

Bethany Br.

Watch your speed - the Emerson Sherriff's Department is strictly enforcing speed limits between here and exit 278

EXIT 285 - RED TOP MTN PARK

Exit 285
G-Texco
L-RedTop

285 Red Top Mountain Rd

Etowah River

Allatoona Lake

41

Yonah

Dam

ANCIENT INDIAN CITY

Exit 288
G-BP\D Citgo Exxon\D
F-Blimp ChickF KFC Krystal LongH McDld MrsWin Pizza Taco
L-Knght QltyInn

EXIT 288, INSIDER TIP
THE PRESIDENTS' LETTERS

Cooper Iron Works

288 Rt 113 Cartersville Main Street

Cartersville Map, page 58

Cartersville
Pop: 288

293
61
DH

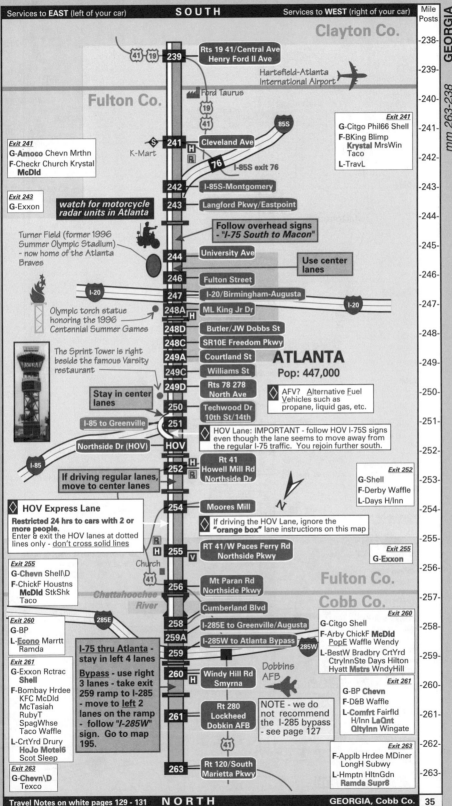

642 '10

Clayton Co.

mm 263-238

41 19 — **239** — Rts 19 41/Central Ave / Henry Ford II Ave — -238-

Hartsfield-Atlanta International Airport — -239-

Fulton Co.

Ford Taurus — -240-

19 / 41

85S

Exit 241
G-Citgo Phil66 Shell
F-BKing Blimp
Krystal MrsWin
Taco
L-TravL

Exit 241
G-**Amoco** Chevn Mrthn
F-Checkr Church Krystal
McDld

S — **241** — Cleveland Ave — -241-
K-Mart
H
R
76 — I-85S exit 76 — -242-

242 — I-85S-Montgomery — -243-

Exit 243
G-Exxon

243 — Langford Pkwy/Eastpoint

watch for motorcycle radar units in Atlanta — -244-

Follow overhead signs - "I-75 South to Macon"

Turner Field (former 1996 Summer Olympic Stadium) - now home of the Atlanta Braves — **244** — University Ave — -245-

Use center lanes

246 — Fulton Street — -246-

I-20 — **247** — I-20/Birmingham-Augusta — I-20 — -247-

Olympic torch statue honoring the 1996 Centennial Summer Games — **248A** H — ML King Jr Dr

248D — Butler/JW Dobbs St — -248-
248C — SR10E Freedom Pkwy

The Sprint Tower is right beside the famous Varsity restaurant — **249A** — Courtland St — **ATLANTA** Pop: 447,000 — -249-
249C — Williams St

Stay in center lanes — **249D** — Rts 78 278 North Ave — ◇ AFV? Alternative Fuel Vehicles such as propane, liquid gas, etc. — -250-

250 — Techwood Dr 10th St/14th

I-85 to Greenville — **251** — ◇ HOV Lane: IMPORTANT - follow HOV I-75S signs even though the lane seems to move away from the regular I-75 traffic. You rejoin further south. — -251-

Northside Dr (HOV) — **HOV** — -252-

I-85

Exit 252
G-Shell
F-Derby Waffle
L-Days H/Inn

If driving regular lanes, move to center lanes — H R — **252** — Rt 41 Howell Mill Rd Northside Dr — -253-

◇ **HOV Express Lane**
Restricted 24 hrs to cars with 2 or more people.
Enter & exit the HOV lanes at dotted lines only - don't cross solid lines

254 — Moores Mill — -254-

◇ If driving the HOV Lane, ignore the "orange box" lane instructions on this map.

R H — **255** V — RT 41/W Paces Ferry Rd Northside Pkwy — -255-

Exit 255
G-Exxon

Exit 255
G-Chevn Shell\D
F-ChickF Houstns
McDld StkShk
Taco

Church
41 — **256** — Mt Paran Rd Northside Pkwy — **Fulton Co.** — -256-

Chattahoochee River — Cumberland Blvd — **Cobb Co.** — -257-

285E — **258** — I-285E to Greenville/Augusta

Exit 260
G-BP
L-**Econo** Marrtt
Ramda

Exit 261
G-Exxon Rctrac
Shell
F-Bombay Hrdee
KFC McDld
McTasiah
RubyT
SpagWhse
Taco Waffle
L-CrtYrd Drury
HoJo Motel6
Scot Sleep

Exit 263
G-Chevn\D
Texco

259A — I-285W to Atlanta Bypass — -258-

259 285W — -259-

Exit 260
G-Citgo Shell
F-Arby ChickF **McDld**
PopE Waffle Wendy
L-BestW Bradbry CrtYrd
CtryInnSte Days Hilton
Hyatt **Mstrs** WndyHill

I-75 thru Atlanta - stay in left 4 lanes — **260** H — Windy Hill Rd Smyrna — Dobbins AFB — -260-

Bypass - use right 3 lanes - take exit 259 ramp to I-285 - move to left 2 lanes on the ramp - follow "I-285W" sign. Go to map 195.

261 — Rt 280 Lockheed Dobkin AFB — NOTE - we do not recommend the I-285 bypass - see page 127 — -261-

Exit 261
G-BP Chevn
F-D&B Waffle
L-Comfrt Fairfld
H/Inn **LaQnt**
QltyInn Wingate

41 — **263** — Rt 120/South Marietta Pkwy — -262-

Exit 263
F-Applb Hrdee MDiner
LongH Subwy
L-Hmptn HltnGdn
Ramda Supr8 — -263-

(handwritten top left: 7:04 '10)
(handwritten: mm 238-213)
(handwritten left margin: 645 break)

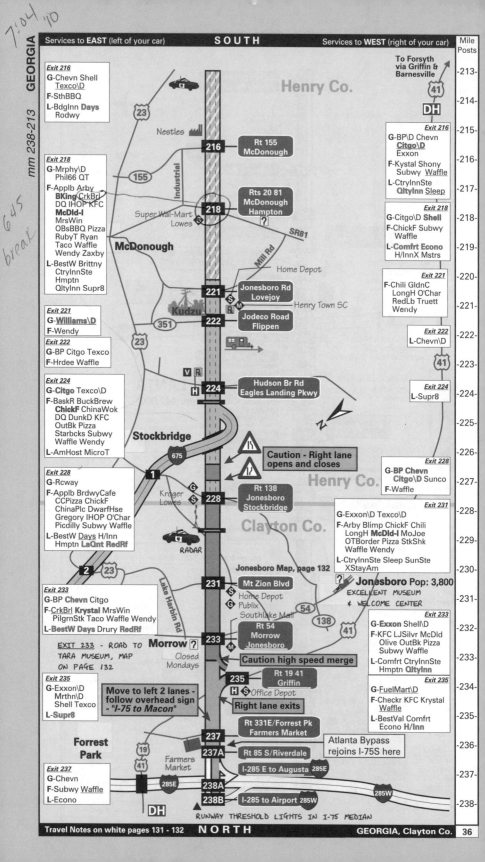

Exit 216
G-Chevn Shell
  Texco\D
F-SthBBQ
L-BdgInn **Days**
  Rodwy

Exit 218
G-Mrphy\D
  Phil66 QT
F-Applb Arby
  BKing CrkBrl
  DQ IHOP KFC
  McDld-I
  MrsWin
  OBsBBQ Pizza
  RubyT Ryan
  Taco Waffle
  Wendy Zaxby
L-BestW Brittny
  CtryInnSte
  Hmptn
  QltyInn Supr8

McDonough

Exit 221
G-**Williams\D**
F-Wendy

Exit 222
G-BP Citgo Texco
F-Hrdee Waffle

Exit 224
G-**Citgo** Texco\D
F-BaskR BuckBrew
  ChickF ChinaWok
  DQ DunkD KFC
  OutBk Pizza
  Starbcks Subwy
  Waffle Wendy
L-AmHost MicroT

Stockbridge

Exit 228
G-Rcway
F-Applb BrdwyCafe
  CCPizza ChickF
  ChinaPlc DwarfHse
  Gregory IHOP O'Char
  Picdilly Subwy Waffle
L-BestW **Days** H/Inn
  Hmptn **LaQnt RedRf**

Exit 233
G-BP **Chevn** Citgo
F-**CrkBrl Krystal** MrsWin
  PilgrnStk Taco Waffle Wendy
L-BestW Days Drury RedRf

EXIT 233 - ROAD TO
TARA MUSEUM, MAP
ON PAGE 132

Morrow [?]

Exit 235
G-Exxon\D
  Mrthn\D
  Shell Texco
L-Supr8

Move to left 2 lanes -
follow overhead sign
- "I-75 to Macon"

Right lane exits

Forrest Park

Exit 237
G-Chevn
F-Subwy Waffle
L-Econo

Henry Co.
23
Nestles
155
Industrial
Super Wal-Mart
Lowes
Mill Rd
SR81
Home Depot
Kudzu
351
23
V R
H
675
1
Kroger
Lowes
G
S
RADAR
2 23
Lake Harbin Rd
Jonesboro Map, page 132
S
Home Depot
Publix
Southlake Mall
54
138
41
M
Closed Mondays
H S Office Depot
Farmers Market
19 41
285E
DH

216 Rt 155 McDonough

218 Rts 20 81 McDonough Hampton [S] [?]

221 Jonesboro Rd Lovejoy [S] [M] R

Henry Town SC

222 Jodeco Road Flippen

224 Hudson Br Rd Eagles Landing Pkwy

Caution - Right lane opens and closes

Henry Co.

228 Rt 138 Jonesboro Stockbridge [S] G

231 Mt Zion Blvd [S]

233 Rt 54 Morrow Jonesboro [S] [M]

Caution high speed merge

235 Rt 19 41 Griffin

237 Rt 331E/Forrest Pk Farmers Market

237A Rt 85 S/Riverdale

238A I-285 E to Augusta 285E

238B I-285 to Airport 285W

RUNWAY THRESHOLD LIGHTS IN I-75 MEDIAN

To Forsyth
via Griffin &
Barnesville
41
DH

Exit 216
G-BP\D Chevn
  Citgo\D
  Exxon
F-Kystal Shony
  Subwy **Waffle**
L-CtryInnSte
  QltyInn Sleep

Exit 218
G-Citgo\D Shell
F-ChickF Subwy
  Waffle
L-**Comfrt Econo**
  H/InnX Mstrs

Exit 221
F-Chili GldnC
  LongH O'Char
  RedLb Truett
  Wendy

Exit 222
L-Chevn\D
41

Exit 224
L-Supr8

Exit 228
G-BP Chevn
  Citgo\D Sunco
F-Waffle

Exit 231
G-Exxon\D Texco\D
F-Arby Blimp ChickF Chili
  LongH **McDld-I** MoJoe
  OTBorder Pizza StkShk
  Waffle Wendy
L-CtryInnSte Sleep SunSte
  XStayAm

[?] **Jonesboro** Pop: 3,800
EXCELLENT MUSEUM
& WELCOME CENTER

Exit 233
G-Exxon Shell\D
F-KFC LJSilvr McDld
  Olive OutBk Pizza
  Subwy Waffle
L-Comfrt CtryInnSte
  Hmptn **QltyInn**

Exit 235
G-**FuelMart**\D
F-Checkr KFC Krystal
  Waffle
L-BestVal Comfrt
  Econo H/Inn

Atlanta Bypass
rejoins I-75S here

285W

-213-
-214-
-215-
-216-
-217-
-218-
-219-
-220-
-221-
-222-
-223-
-224-
-225-
-226-
-227-
-228-
-229-
-230-
-231-
-232-
-233-
-234-
-235-
-236-
-237-
-238-

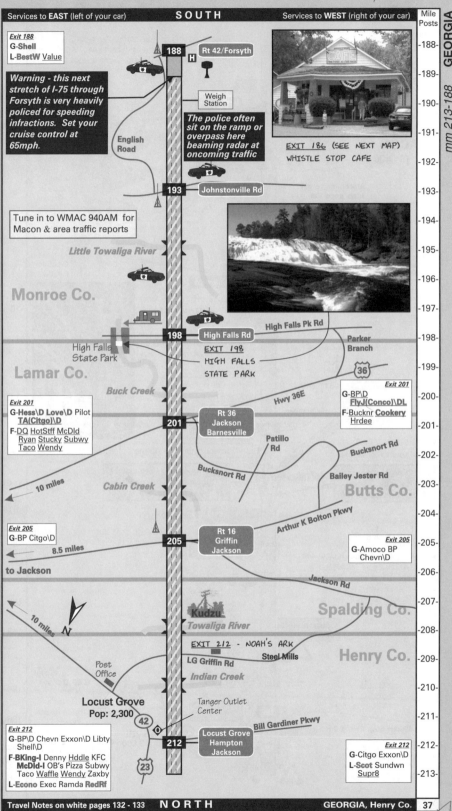

7,24 '10

GEORGIA

mm 213-188

Exit 188
G-Shell
L-BestW Value

Warning - this next stretch of I-75 through Forsyth is very heavily policed for speeding infractions. Set your cruise control at 65mph.

188   H   Rt 42/Forsyth

Weigh Station

The police often sit on the ramp or overpass here beaming radar at oncoming traffic

EXIT 186 (SEE NEXT MAP)
WHISTLE STOP CAFE

English Road

193   Johnstonville Rd

Tune in to WMAC 940AM for Macon & area traffic reports

Little Towaliga River

Monroe Co.

198   High Falls Rd   High Falls Pk Rd

High Falls State Park

EXIT 198
HIGH FALLS
STATE PARK

Parker Branch

Lamar Co.

Buck Creek

Hwy 36E

36

Exit 201
G-BP\D
FlyJ(Conco)\DL
F-Bucknr Cookery
Hrdee

Exit 201
G-Hess\D Love\D Pilot
TA(Citgo)\D
F-DQ HotStff McDld
Ryan Stucky Subwy
Taco Wendy

201   Rt 36 Jackson Barnesville

Patillo Rd

Bucksnort Rd

10 miles

Cabin Creek

Bucksnort Rd

Bailey Jester Rd

Butts Co.

Arthur K Bolton Pkwy

Exit 205
G-BP Citgo\D

8.5 miles

to Jackson

205   Rt 16 Griffin Jackson

Exit 205
G-Amoco BP
Chevn\D

Jackson Rd

Spalding Co.

10 miles

N

Kudzu
Towaliga River

EXIT 212 - NOAH'S ARK
Steel Mills

Henry Co.

LG Griffin Rd

Indian Creek

Post Office

Locust Grove
Pop: 2,300

42

Tanger Outlet Center

Bill Gardiner Pkwy

Exit 212
G-BP\D Chevn Exxon\D Libty
Shell\D
F-BKing-I Denny Hddle KFC
McDld-I OB's Pizza Subwy
Taco Waffle Wendy Zaxby
L-Econo Exec Ramda RedRf

212   Locust Grove Hampton Jackson

23

Exit 212
G-Citgo Exxon\D
L-Scot Sundwn
Supr8

-188-
-189-
-190-
-191-
-192-
-193-
-194-
-195-
-196-
-197-
-198-
-199-
-200-
-201-
-202-
-203-
-204-
-205-
-206-
-207-
-208-
-209-
-210-
-211-
-212-
-213-

34

8:4 '10

LAKE TOBESOFKEE RECREATIONAL AREA - THREE GREAT PARKS - RV CAMPING, FISHING, BOATING - OPEN YEAR ROUND. - PHONE: 912-474-8770

-1-

Exit 3
G-Mrphy\D Mrthn\D RcWay Spctrm
F-China CrkBrl J&L **McDld-I** Ryan Sonny Subwy Waffle Zaxby
L-BestW Comfrt Days Disc Econmy H/Inn Hmptn Motel6 QltyInn RedC Rodwy Supr8 TravL Villager

Super Wal-Mart

Exit 3
G-Conco\D Shell
F-BKing CaptD
L-Econo Knght Scot TravInn

-2-

Eisenhower Pkwy

80 **M** **S**

3 Rt 80/Macon Roberta

Eisenhower Pkwy

-3-

Macon Mall **M**

MACON
Pop: 104,400

Log Cabin Dr

Eisenhower Crossing SC

N Lizella Rd

-4-

74 **5** Rt 74/Macon Thomaston

Lake Tobesofkee Park Office

-5-

Exit 5
G-BP
F-Waffle

Macon (and area) Map, page 196

Exit 5
G-Shell
F-Church Subwy

-6-

Lower Thomason Rd

Thomaston Road

-7-

Exit 9
G-Citgo Mrphy\D Shell Spctrm
F-Buffalo ChenWok **ChickF-I** Fdrckrs Krystal **McDld-I** Mrgarita NuWyWnr PjPizza Pizza PopF Sonic Subwy Taco Waffle Wendy
L-Baymnt Fairfld LaQnt Sleep

Lamar Rd

Exit 9
G-LoBuck
F-Pollys

-8-

Larry Justice Highway

H **G** **9** Zebulon Rd **S**

Kroger Wal-Mart Lowes

-9-

475S

DURING THE CIVIL WAR, SHERMAN'S TROOPS BYPASSED MACON. AS A RESULT, MUCH OF ITS RICH ANTE-BELLUM ARCHITECTURE HAS SURVIVED.

-10-

Bibb Co.

-11-

DH

Monroe Co.

41 **N**

I-75

Bolingbroke **A**

For the next 15 miles you are on I-475 South, the Macon Bypass

-12-

-13-

To Macon

-14-

15 Rt 41 Bolingbroke

I-475, EXIT 15, RED TOMATO RESTAURANT

I-475 milepost numbers start here

-15-

177

If visiting Macon, stay in left 2 lanes - see Macon map page 196

Macon Bypass - take exit 177 (2 right lanes) - follow signs for *"I-475 to Valdosta"*

-178-

SAY "HI" TO BJ AND BERNICE FOR ME

Welcome Center ♿ 🚻 ♿ 🅿 ？ V

Information: 9:00-5:30 daily
Restrooms: 7:00-11:00

53 m
85 k

Exit 181
G-BP\D Shell\D

181 Rumble Rd Smarr

-180-

WHY NOT TAKE A FEW HOURS AND VISIT MACON. I'VE PROVIDED A DETAILED MAP (PAGE 196) SHOWING YOU AN EASY WAY TO REACH MACON'S FASCINATING MUSEUMS

Old Dixie Highway

-181-

-182-

Caution - left lane ends

41

Exit 185
G-BP Shell\D
F-Shony Waffle
L-Comfrt

-183-

-184-

EXIT 186, INSIDER TIPS THE GRITS CAFE

185 Rt 18/Gray **P**

42

83

Exit 186
G-BP\D Chevn Mrthn
F-DQ Waffle
L-H/Inn Hmptn Supr8

-185-

186 Tift College Dr Julliette Rd **?** **R** **H** Ingles

41 **DH**

83

Forsyth
Pop: 3,800

Whistle Stop Cafe (9.3 m)

-186-

Exit 187
L-Econo NFsyth Regncy

187 Rt 83/Forsyth Monticello **S** **R**

Wal-Mart

Exit 187
G-BP Citgo\D Exxon Mrthn Shell Texco
F-**BKing** Blimp CaptD Hrdee **McDld** Pizza Taco Waffle Wendy
L-Days Tradewnd

-187-

-188-

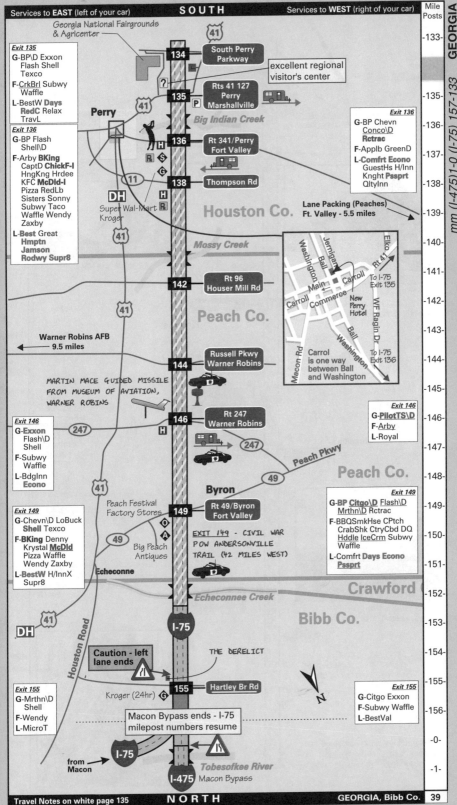

835

GEORGIA

mm (I-475)1-0 (I-75) 157-133

US 41

Georgia National Fairgrounds & Agricenter

134 — South Perry Parkway

? excellent regional visitor's center

Perry

135 — Rts 41 127 Perry Marshallville

Exit 135
G-BP\D Exxon Flash Shell Texco
F-CrkBrl Subwy Waffle
L-BestW Days RedC Relax TravL

Big Indian Creek

136 — Rt 341/Perry Fort Valley

Exit 136
G-BP Flash Shell\D
F-Arby BKing CaptD ChickF-I HngKng Hrdee KFC McDld-I Pizza RedLb Sisters Sonny Subwy Taco Waffle Wendy Zaxby
L-Best Great Hmptn Jamson Rodwy Supr8

Exit 136
G-BP Chevn Conco\D Rctrac
F-Applb GreenD
L-Comfrt Econo GuestHs H/Inn Knght Pssprt QltyInn

138 — Thompson Rd

DH

Super Wal-Mart Kroger

Houston Co.

Lane Packing (Peaches) Ft. Valley - 5.5 miles

Mossy Creek

142 — Rt 96 Houser Mill Rd

Peach Co.

Jernigan, Ball, Washington, Main, Carroll, Commerce, Carroll, New Perry Hotel, WF Regin Dr., Macon Rd, Elko, Rt 41
To I-75 Exit 135
To I-75 Exit 136
Carrol is one way between Ball and Washington

Warner Robins AFB 9.5 miles

144 — Russell Pkwy Warner Robins

MARTIN MACE GUIDED MISSILE FROM MUSEUM OF AVIATION, WARNER ROBINS

146 — Rt 247 Warner Robins

Exit 146
G-Exxon Flash\D Shell
F-Subwy Waffle
L-BdgInn Econo

Exit 146
G-PilotTS\D
F-Arby
L-Royal

Peach Pkwy

Byron

49

Peach Co.

Exit 149
G-Chevn\D LoBuck Shell Texco
F-BKing Denny Krystal McDld Pizza Waffle Wendy Zaxby
L-BestW H/InnX Supr8

Peach Festival Factory Stores

149 — Rt 49/Byron Fort Valley

Big Peach Antiques

EXIT 149 - CIVIL WAR POW ANDERSONVILLE TRAIL (42 MILES WEST)

Exit 149
G-BP Citgo\D Flash\D Mrthn\D Rctrac
F-BBQSmkHse CPtch CrabShk CtryCbd DQ Hddle IceCrm Subwy Waffle
L-Comfrt Days Econo Pssprt

Echeconne

Echeconnee Creek

Crawford C

Bibb Co.

I-75

Houston Road

DH

Caution - left lane ends

THE DERELICT

155 — Hartley Br Rd

Kroger (24hr)

N

Exit 155
G-Mrthn\D Shell
F-Wendy
L-MicroT

Exit 155
G-Citgo Exxon
F-Subwy Waffle
L-BestVal

Macon Bypass ends - I-75 milepost numbers resume

I-75

from Macon

I-475 Macon Bypass

Tobesofkee River

Mile Posts: -133- -135- -136- -137- -138- -139- -140- -141- -142- -143- -144- -145- -146- -147- -148- -149- -150- -151- -152- -153- -154- -155- -156- -0- -1-

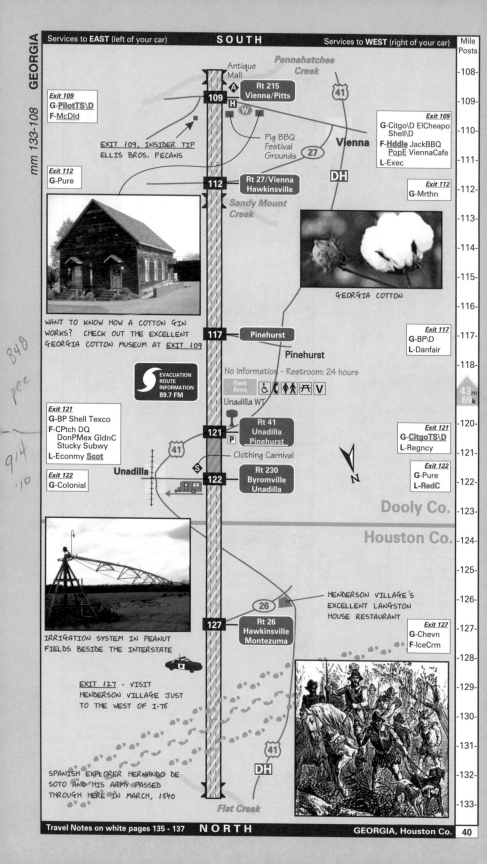

-108-

Pennahatchee Creek

Antique Mall

Ⓐ

109

Ⓗ

Ⓦ

Rt 215
Vienna/Pitts

🅤🅢 41

Exit 109
G-**PilotTS\D**
F-McDld

-109-

Exit 109
G-Citgo\D ElCheapo
Shell\D
F-**Hddle** JackBBQ
PopE ViennaCafe
L-Exec

-110-

EXIT 109, INSIDER TIP
ELLIS BROS. PECANS

Pig BBQ
Festival
Grounds

27

Vienna

DH

-111-

Exit 112
G-Pure

112

Rt 27/Vienna
Hawkinsville

Exit 112
G-Mrthn

-112-

Sandy Mount
Creek

-113-

-114-

-115-

GEORGIA COTTON

-116-

WANT TO KNOW HOW A COTTON GIN
WORKS? CHECK OUT THE EXCELLENT
GEORGIA COTTON MUSEUM AT EXIT 109

117

Pinehurst

Pinehurst

Exit 117
G-BP\D
L-Danfair

-117-

-118-

EVACUATION
ROUTE
INFORMATION
89.7 FM

No information - Restroom: 24 hours

Rest
Area ♿ 🚹🚺 🧺 V

43 m
69 k

Unadilla WT

-119-

Exit 121
G-BP Shell Texco
F-CPtch DQ
DonPMex GldnC
Stucky Subwy
L-Economy **Scot**

41

Ⓟ

121

Rt 41
Unadilla
Pinehurst

Exit 121
G-**CitgoTS\D**
L-Regncy

-120-

-121-

Clothing Carnival

Ⓢ

Exit 122
G-Colonial

Unadilla

122

Rt 230
Byromville
Unadilla

Exit 122
G-Pure
L-RedC

-122-

N

Dooly Co.

-123-

Houston Co.

-124-

-125-

IRRIGATION SYSTEM IN PEANUT
FIELDS BESIDE THE INTERSTATE

26

HENDERSON VILLAGE'S
EXCELLENT LANGSTON
HOUSE RESTAURANT

-126-

127

Rt 26
Hawkinsville
Montezuma

Exit 127
G-Chevn
F-IceCrm

-127-

-128-

EXIT 127 - VISIT
HENDERSON VILLAGE JUST
TO THE WEST OF I-75

-129-

-130-

41

-131-

SPANISH EXPLORER HERNANDO DE
SOTO AND HIS ARMY PASSED
THROUGH HERE IN MARCH, 1540

DH

-132-

Flat Creek

-133-

Mile Posts

GEORGIA

mm 108-83

9:46 '10

Exit 84
G-Citgo\D
F-DQ Oasis
  Subwy
L-Ashbrn

-83-

Exit 84
G-Shell\D

84

Rt 159
Ashburn
Amboy

-84-

-85-

W Fork Deep Creek

-86-

41

-87-

-88-

SOUTH GEORGIA IS FAMOUS
FOR ITS BEAUTIFUL DAYLILLIES

-89-

Turner Co.

Crisp Co.

COP on bridge

-90-

Plantation
House S

Exit 92
G-BP

92

Arabi

-91-

Exit 92
G-Chevn Pure
F-IceCrm
L-BdgInn

COP

Arabi

-92-

-93-

-94-

-95-

EXIT 101 - CLOSEUP OF THE
CORDELE TITAN ROCKET ENGINES

-96-

RV Park
Service

97

Rt 33
Wenona

Wenona

-97-

Exit 97
G-TA(BP)\D
F-CPride GtAmBft
  Pizza PopE

Exit 97
L-Royal

99

Rt 300
GA-FL Pkwy
Albany

41

-98-

-99-

EXIT 101 -
VIDALIA ONIONS;
& KING COTTON

COTTON

Super Wal-Mart
WinnDixie

280

-100-

Exit 101
G-Exxon\D
  PilotTS\D Shell
  Texco
F-**Arby** CSeaFood
  Denny GldnC
  Waffle
L-Days **Ramda**

280

101

Rts 280 90
Cordele

P S

R V

H

-101-

Exit 101
G-BP\D Chevn Libty
F-BKing CrkBrl
  CuttrsStk DQ
  GinaFD GldnC
  Hrdee KFC Krystal
  McDld-I Pizza
  Shony Subwy
  Taco Wendy
  Zaxby
L-Ashbrn Athens
  BestW Comfrt
  Deluxe Econo
  H/InnX Hmptn
  Premier **Supr8**

102

RT 257
Hawkinsville

257

Cordele
Pop: 11,600

-102-

Exit 102
G-Citgo

EXIT 101
- SLEEP IN AN
  ANTIQUE SHOP
- CHARLES SEAFOOD

PECAN
ORCHARDS

-103-

104

Bus I-75
Farmers Market
Rd/Cordele

-104-

257

Crisp Co.

-105-

Dooly Co.

9:25 '10

-106-

41

-107-

-108-

1002
1108
mm 83-58

DH

Exit 59
G-Love
F-Hrdee

Exit 60
G-Chevn
F-DrgnChina

41 **Tifton**

Exit 62
G-BP Citgo Exxon\D
F-Applb CSeaFood CrkBrl GldnC Sonic WSizz Waffle Zaxby
L-Comfrt CrtYrd Fairfld Hmptn MicroT Mstrs

7th W

Exit 63A
G-BP Chevn
F-Arby Asaki BKing Checkr CityBft Krystal McDld-I Pizza RedLb Shony SoCtryBft Taco Waffle
L-Econo Qltyinn Supr8

Main
2nd
E 12th

Lowes R
WinnDixie M
G
P
H
G

Tifton Mall
Food Lion

Exit 63B
G-Flash Texco
F-KFC Krystal LosCmpdres
L-Bdglnn

Exit 64
G-Chevn

EXIT 62 - ENJOY CHARLES SEAFOOD, ALSO SEE AUTO QUEST'S OLD CARS

EXIT 63B, INSIDER TIP PIT STOP BBQ

Exit 69
G-Phil66
L-RedC

Sue's Antiques A

Chula

Exit 71
G-BP\D

N

Tift Co.

Turner Co.

Hat Creek

EXIT 75 - BELL'S DAY LILLIES

Exit 75
G-Chevn

EXIT 78 - JEFFERSON DAVIS HISTORICAL CAPTURE SITE AND MUSEUM - 14.4 MILES EAST (19 MINS DRIVE TIME)

Exit 80
G-Exxon Shell
F-Subwy
L-Bdglnn

Swamp

Levelour

EXIT 82, INSIDER TIP ASHBURN'S FRENCH MARKET

Exit 59 -58-
Exit 60 -59-
G-PilotTS\D
F-StkShk Subwy

Exit 61 -59-
G-Citgo\D
F-Backyd Stucky WfflKing
L-Motel6

Exit 62 -60-
G-BP Chevn Rctrac Shell\D
F-BKing ChickF LongH RubyT Shony Sonny Starbcks Waffle Wendy
L-Days H/Inn Ramda Rodwy -61-

Tifton Map, page 53 -62-

After exit 63B, stay in left 3 lanes

Exit 63A -63-
G-Shell\D
L-Colony TravL

Exit 63B -64-
F-PitStopBBQ

EVACUATION ROUTE INFORMATION 91.1 FM -65-

BIRTHPLACE OF INTERSTATE-75, - MILE 63 TO 59, SEE SPECIAL REPORT ON PAGE 140 -66-

-67-
-68-

Chula-Brookfield Road -69-
-70-

Willis Stills Rd Sunsweet -71-

Sunsweet -72-

-73-

ALL ABOARD AT THE GEORGIA AGRIRAMA

Inaha -74-

Exit 75 -75-
G-BP
F-Stucky

No information - Restroom: 24 hours

Rest Area

29 m
47 k

Exit 82 - an "Insider" tip . . .
Visit the *Museum of Crime and Punishment*. Afterwards, have lunch at the *Last Meal Cafe*! -77-

Rt 32 Sycamore Ocilla -78-

41 -79-
DH

Bussey Rd Sycamore -80-

Sycamore

Exit 80 -80-
G-Chevn\D

-81-

Exit 82 -82-
G-BP Chevn
F-Hddle Hrdee KFC Krystal McDld Pizza Shony Waffle
L-BestW Days Ramda Supr8 -83-

Rt 112 Ashburn Fitzgerald

Ashburn

Interstate exits:
59 Southwell
60 S Central Ave
61 Omega Rd
62 Rts 82 319 Moultrie
63A 2nd Street
63B 8th Street
64 Rt 41 Business I-75 ABAC
66 Brighton Rd
69
71
75 Inaha Rd
78
80
82

Pit Stop BBQ
Agrirama
ABAC Abraham Baldwin Agricultural College

41

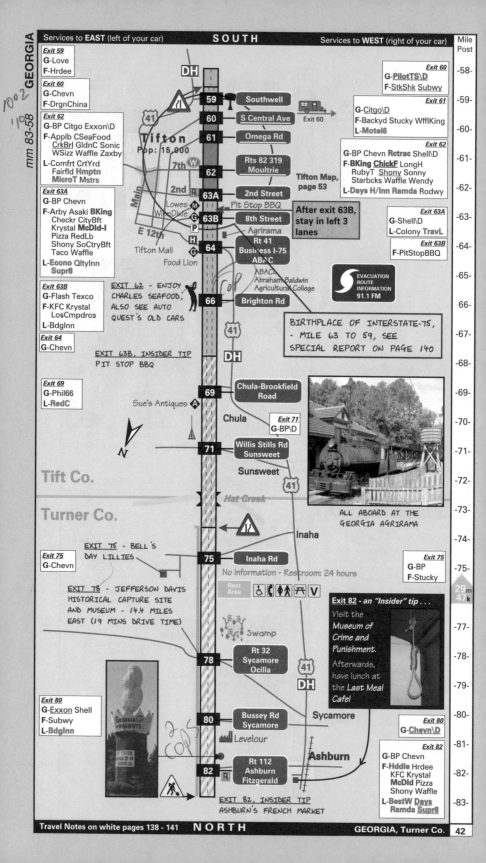

mm 58-33

South Georgia Motorsports Park

-33-

-34-

(41)

-35-

Georgia Forestry watch tower

-36-

Radar on ramp checking s/bound traffic

10:22 am '10 '07

-37-

37 Adel

-38-

Weyhauser Paper

King Frog Outlet Mall

Adel Ⓦ Ⓢ

-39-

39 Rt 37/Adel Moultrie

Ⓗ Ⓡ

Exit 39
G-BP CitgoTS\D
F-BKing CaptD Hddle IHOP KFrog MamaTbl PopE Stucky Taco WSizz
L-Days Hmptn

Exit 39
G-Shell\D Texco\D
F-Hrdee McDld-I Waffle
L-BdgLdg Scot Supr8

-40-

-41-

41 Roundtree Br Rd Sparks/Adel

Exit 41
G-Citgo

Sparks

(41)

BILL BOARD ROW

-42-

-43-

Tune your radio to 92.1 FM for shopping information at exit 39

-44-

Exit 45
L-RedC

Barneyville

45 Barneyville Rd

-45-

SLASH PINE - PINUS ELLIOTTII

-46-

Wagon Wheel

-47-

No Information - Restrooms: 24 hours

Rest Area ♿ 📞 🚹🚺 🎇 V

47 m 76 k

Lenox

49 Kinard Br Rd Lenox

-49-

Exit 49
G-Dixie\D
F-LenorDnr Pizza
L-Knght

Exit 49
G-BP\D Phil66\D

DH

FROM HERE TO THE FLORIDA BORDER, YOU WILL SEE SIGNS FOR VARIOUS FLORIDA WELCOME CENTERS (ALL IN GEORGIA!) - THERE IS ONLY ONE OFFICIAL FLORIDA WELCOME CENTER AND THAT'S IN FLORIDA, ONE MILE SOUTH OF THE FL/GA BORDER. MANY OF THESE UNOFFICIAL FLORIDA WELCOME CENTERS ARE "FRONTS" FOR CONDO SALES OPERATIONS.

N

-50-

-51-

-52-

🚫 **Cook Co.**

-53-

Tift Co. (41)

-54-

Exit 55
G-Citgo Pure\D

Magnolia Plantation Ⓢ
Eldorado

55 Eldorado Omega

-55-

Exit 55
G-Chevn

-56-

EVACUATION ROUTE INFORMATION 90.1 FM

-57-

-58-

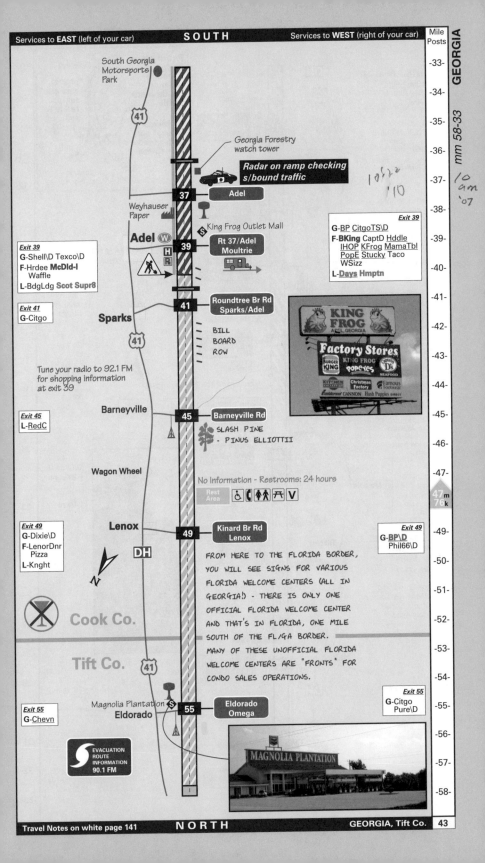

Services to **EAST** (left of your car)   **SOUTH**   Services to **WEST** (right of your car)   Mile Posts

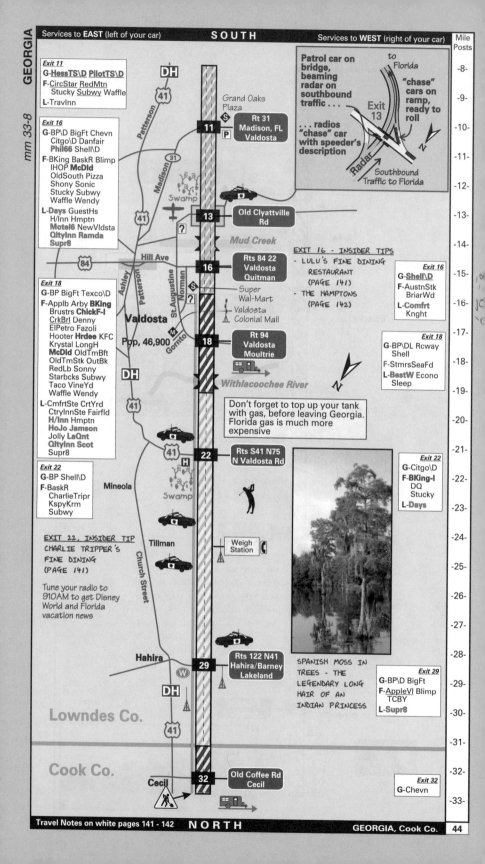

Exit 11
G-HessTS\D PilotTS\D
F-CircStar RedMtn
  Stucky Subwy Waffle
L-TravInn

Exit 16
G-BP\D BigFt Chevn
  Citgo\D Danfair
  Phil66 Shell\D
F-BKing BaskR Blimp
  IHOP McDld
  OldSouth Pizza
  Shony Sonic
  Stucky Subwy
  Waffle Wendy
L-Days GuestHs
  H/Inn Hmptn
  Motel6 NewVldsta
  QltyInn Ramda
  Supr8

Exit 18
G-BP BigFt Texco\D
F-Applbr Arby BKing
  Brustrs ChickF-I
  CrkBrl Denny
  ElPetro Fazoli
  Hooter Hrdee KFC
  Krystal LongH
  McDld OldTmBft
  OldTmStk OutBk
  RedLb Sonny
  Starbcks Subwy
  Taco VineYd
  Waffle Wendy
L-CmfrtSte CrtYrd
  CtrlnnSte Fairfld
  H/Inn Hmptn
  HoJo Jamson
  Jolly LaQnt
  QltyInn Scot
  Supr8

Exit 22
G-BP Shell\D
F-BaskR
  CharlieTripr
  KspyKrm
  Subwy

EXIT 22, INSIDER TIP
CHARLIE TRIPPER'S
FINE DINING
(PAGE 141)

Tune your radio to
910AM to get Disney
World and Florida
vacation news

DH
41
Patterson
31
Madison
41
Swamp
84
Hill Ave
Ashley
Patterson
St. Augustine
Norman
Valdosta
Pop, 46,900
Gornto
DH
41
Mineola
Swamp
Church Street
Tillman
Hahira
W
DH
41
Lowndes Co.
Cook Co.
Cecil

11   Grand Oaks Plaza   S   P   Rt 31 Madison, FL Valdosta

Patrol car on bridge, beaming radar on southbound traffic . . .   to Florida   "chase" cars on ramp, ready to roll   Exit 13   . . . radios "chase" car with speeder's description   Radar   Southbound Traffic to Florida   N

13   Old Clyattville Rd

Mud Creek

16   Rts 84 22 Valdosta Quitman
Super Wal-Mart
Valdosta Colonial Mall

EXIT 16 - INSIDER TIPS
- LULU'S FINE DINING
  RESTAURANT
  (PAGE 141)
- THE HAMPTONS
  (PAGE 142)

Exit 16
G-Shell\D
F-AustnStk BriarWd
L-Comfrt Knght

18   Rt 94 Valdosta Moultrie

Withlacoochee River

Don't forget to top up your tank with gas, before leaving Georgia. Florida gas is much more expensive

N

Exit 18
G-BP\DL Rcway Shell
F-StmrsSeaFd
L-BestW Econo Sleep

22   Rts S41 N75 N Valdosta Rd

Exit 22
G-Citgo\D
F-BKing-I DQ Stucky
L-Days

Weigh Station   C

29   Rts 122 N41 Hahira/Barney Lakeland

SPANISH MOSS IN TREES - THE LEGENDARY LONG HAIR OF AN INDIAN PRINCESS

Exit 29
G-BP\D BigFt
F-AppleVl Blimp TCBY
L-Supr8

32   Old Coffee Rd Cecil

Exit 32
G-Chevn

Travel Notes on white pages 141 - 142   **NORTH**   GEORGIA, Cook Co.   **44**

-8-
-9-
-10-
-11-
-12-
-13-
-14-
-15-
-16-
-17-
-18-
-19-
-20-
-21-
-22-
-23-
-24-
-25-
-26-
-27-
-28-
-29-
-30-
-31-
-32-
-33-

HAVE A SAFE TRIP TO YOUR FLORIDA
DESTINATION. DON'T FORGET TO STOP AT
THE WELCOME CENTER AND GET YOUR FREE
ORANGE OR GRAPEFRUIT JUICE DRINK!
ALSO, PICK UP YOUR DISCOUNT COUPON
BOOKS FROM THE BOXES NEAR THE VENDING
MACHINES. I'LL SEE YOU ON THE WAY BACK.

Dave

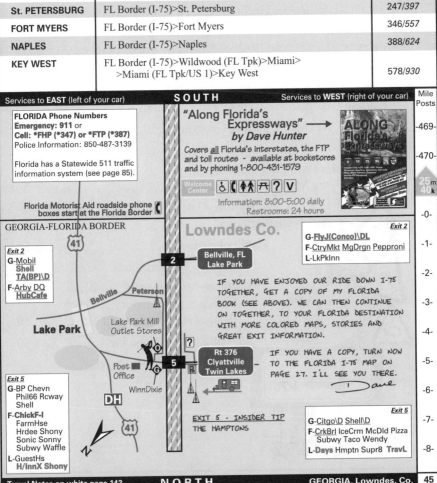

FLORIDA DESTINATIONS - Routes & Mileage

DESTINATION	ROUTE	MILES/Km
ORLANDO	FL Border (I-75)>Wildwood (FL Tpk)>Orlando	210/338
TITUSVILLE	FL Border (I-75)>Wildwood (FL Tpk)>Orlando (Rts528/427) Orlando (Rts528/427)>Titusville	250/402
JACKSONVILLE	Fl Border (I-75)>Lake City (I-10)>Jacksonville	113/182
DAYTONA BCH	FL Border (I-75)>I-10>I-295>I-95>Daytona	188/303
FT LAUDERDALE	FL Border (I-75)>Wildwood (FL Tpk)>Fort Lauderdale	407/655
MIAMI	FL Border (I-75)>Wildwood (FL Tpk)>Miami	422/679
TAMPA	FL Border (I-75)>Junction I-275> Tampa	226/364
St. PETERSBURG	FL Border (I-75)>St. Petersburg	247/397
FORT MYERS	FL Border (I-75)>Fort Myers	346/557
NAPLES	FL Border (I-75)>Naples	388/624
KEY WEST	FL Border (I-75)>Wildwood (FL Tpk)>Miami> >Miami (FL Tpk/US 1)>Key West	578/930

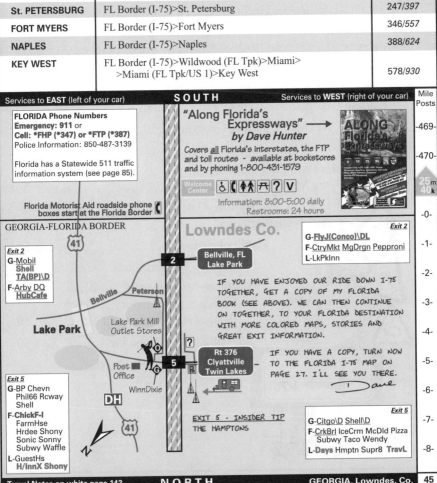

Services to **EAST** (left of your car)   **SOUTH**   Services to **WEST** (right of your car)

FLORIDA Phone Numbers
Emergency: **911** or
Cell: ***FHP (*347)** or **FTP (*387)**
Police Information: 850-487-3139

Florida has a Statewide 511 traffic
information system (see page 85).

Florida Motorist Aid roadside phone
boxes start at the Florida Border

"Along Florida's Expressways"
by *Dave Hunter*

Covers *all* Florida's interstates, the FTP
and toll routes - available at bookstores
and by phoning 1-800-431-1579

Welcome Center

Information: 8:00-5:00 daily
Restrooms: 24 hours

GEORGIA-FLORIDA BORDER

Lowndes Co.

Exit 2
G-Mobil
Shell
TA(BP)\D
F-Arby DQ
HubCafe

Bellville   Peterson

Exit 2
G-FlyJ(Conoco)\DL
F-CtryMkt MgDrgn Pepproni
L-LkPkInn

Bellville, FL
Lake Park

IF YOU HAVE ENJOYED OUR RIDE DOWN I-75
TOGETHER, GET A COPY OF MY FLORIDA
BOOK (SEE ABOVE). WE CAN THEN CONTINUE
ON TOGETHER, TO YOUR FLORIDA DESTINATION
WITH MORE COLORED MAPS, STORIES AND
GREAT EXIT INFORMATION.

Lake Park

Lake Park Mill
Outlet Stores

Post Office

WinnDixie

DH

Rt 376
Clyattville
Twin Lakes

IF YOU HAVE A COPY, TURN NOW
TO THE FLORIDA I-75 MAP ON
PAGE 27. I'LL SEE YOU THERE.

Dave

Exit 5
G-BP Chevn
Phil66 Rcway
Shell
F-ChickF-I
FarmHse
Hrdee Shony
Sonic Sonny
Subwy Waffle
L-GuestHs
H/InnX Shony

EXIT 5 - INSIDER TIP
THE HAMPTONS

Exit 5
G-Citgo\D Shell\D
F-CrkBrl IceCrm McDld Pizza
Subwy Taco Wendy
L-Days Hmptn Supr8 TravL

Mile Posts
-469-
-470-
25 m
40 k
-0-
-1-
-2-
-3-
-4-
-5-
-6-
-7-
-8-

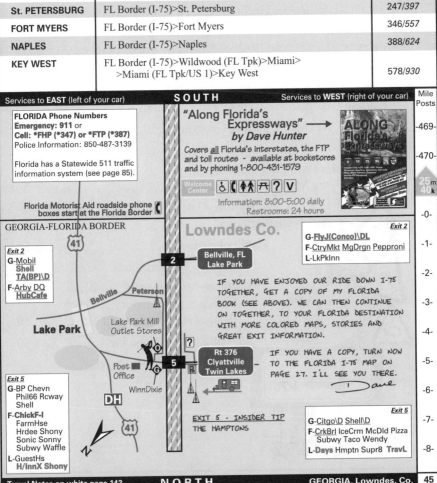

Off The Beaten Path

One of the most enjoyable aspects of a journey along Interstate-75 is the abundance of interesting places you can visit within just a few minutes of an exit ramp. Yet many travelers don't take advantage of this because of the fear of becoming lost in unfamiliar territory.

On the following pages we provide you with short side trips you can take - perhaps as a brief evening tour after checking into your motel or as a short excursion during your day's drive. Why not take an extra day on your journey, and enjoy the countryside around you?

Enjoy your drive . . . after all, getting there is half the fun!

Detroit's Ambassador Bridge to Canada - and Back

Finding the Ambassador Bridge to Canada from I-75 is easy - just take exit 47B, drive across the lights at Lafayette and you are at the bridge toll booths. Watch for trucks on your left as you enter the Toll Plaza - they have to cross to get to the right hand lane.

Getting back onto I-75 South is not so easy. This is nothing to do with Customs or Immigration, it is more to do with finding I-75 again (incidentally, this section of I-75 is called the *"Fisher Freeway"*). The signs are quite confusing and depending upon the season, covered by foliage in some cases. We have included this map to help you.

Finding the I-75 South

1. After clearing Customs, <u>drive across the lights</u> at Porter. <u>Do not go down the I-75 ramp to your left</u> - it goes north!

2. After passing Bristol (a small side street on your right, <u>move into left turn lane</u>.

3. <u>Turn left</u> at the Vernor intersection lights.

4. On Vernor, <u>move **immediately** into the left turn lane</u> as you cross the bridge over the I-75.

5. At the next lights, <u>turn left</u> onto Fisher Freeway W. Ignore sign at the corner that says *"Bridge to Canada."*

6. <u>Stay on</u> *"Fisher Freeway West"* - past Bagley, Lambie, Howard, 25th St, to the lights at Grand Boulevard.

7. Pass Vinewood, Hubbard and Scotten. Immediately after the lights at Clark, <u>move to the left lane and go down the ramp</u> onto the I-75 South.

8. If this ramp is closed for construction, continue on along the service road - there are at least 3 more I-75 Southbound ramps ahead.

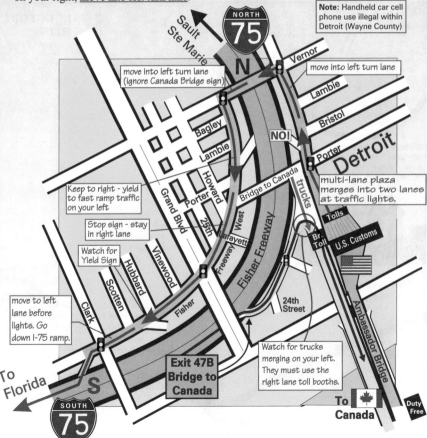

Note: Handheld car cell phone use illegal within Detroit (Wayne County)

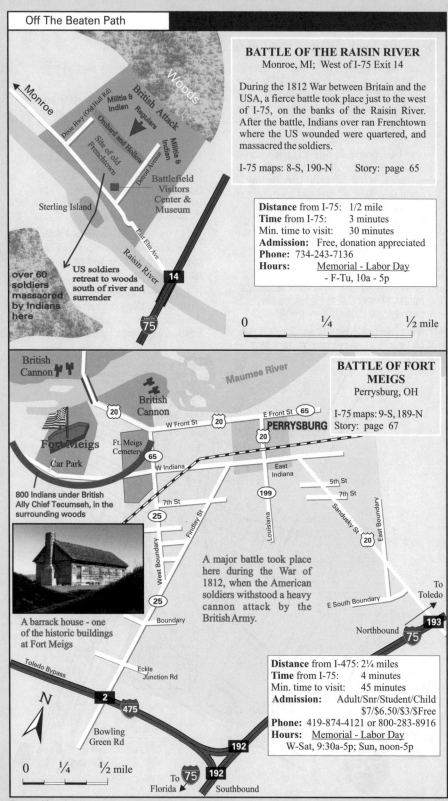

BATTLE OF THE RAISIN RIVER
Monroe, MI; West of I-75 Exit 14

During the 1812 War between Britain and the USA, a fierce battle took place just to the west of I-75, on the banks of the Raisin River. After the battle, Indians over ran Frenchtown where the US wounded were quartered, and massacred the soldiers.

I-75 maps: 8-S, 190-N   Story: page 65

Distance from I-75:   1/2 mile
Time from I-75:   3 minutes
Min. time to visit: 30 minutes
Admission: Free, donation appreciated
Phone: 734-243-7136
Hours: <u>Memorial - Labor Day</u>
             - F-Tu, 10a - 5p

Monroe

Woods

British Attack

Militia & Indian Regulars

Dixie Hwy (Old Hull Rd)

Orchard and Hollow

Militia & Indian

Detroit Avenue

Site of old Frenchtown

Battlefield Visitors Center & Museum

Sterling Island

East Elm Ave

Raisin River

14

over 60 soldiers massacred by Indians here

US soldiers retreat to woods south of river and surrender

SOUTH 75

0   1/4   1/2 mile

BATTLE OF FORT MEIGS
Perrysburg, OH

I-75 maps: 9-S, 189-N
Story: page 67

British Cannon

Maumee River

British Cannon

20

W Front St   **20**   E Front St **65**

PERRYSBURG

20

Fort Meigs

Ft. Meigs Cemetery

65

Car Park

W Indiana

East Indiana

5th St

7th St

199

7th St

Sandusky St

20

East Boundary

800 Indians under British Ally Chief Tecumseh, in the surrounding woods

25

West Boundary

Findlay St

Louisiana

A major battle took place here during the War of 1812, when the American soldiers withstood a heavy cannon attack by the British Army.

25

Boundary

A barrack house - one of the historic buildings at Fort Meigs

To Toledo

E South Boundary

Northbound

193

75

Toledo Bypass

Eckle Junction Rd

N

2 475

Bowling Green Rd

192

75 192

To Florida

Southbound

0   1/4   1/2 mile

Distance from I-475: 2 1/4 miles
Time from I-75:   4 minutes
Min. time to visit: 45 minutes
Admission: Adult/Snr/Student/Child
                $7/$6.50/$3/$Free
Phone: 419-874-4121 or 800-283-8916
Hours: <u>Memorial - Labor Day</u>
          W-Sat, 9:30a-5p; Sun, noon-5p

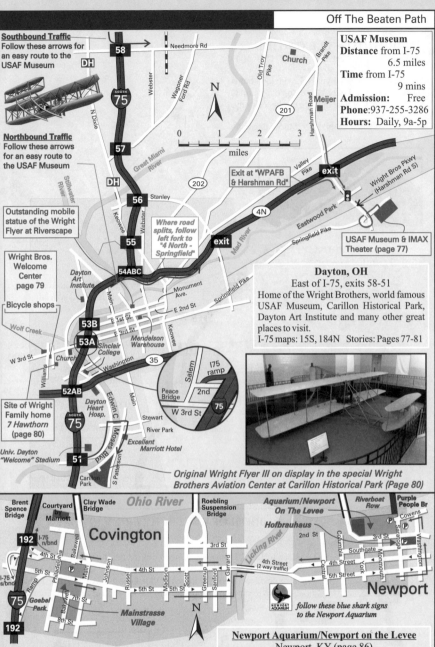

Southbound Traffic
Follow these arrows for an easy route to the USAF Museum

Northbound Traffic
Follow these arrows for an easy route to the USAF Museum

USAF Museum
Distance from I-75
6.5 miles
Time from I-75
9 mins
Admission: Free
Phone:937-255-3286
Hours: Daily, 9a-5p

Needmore Rd
Church
Brandt Pike
Old Troy Pike
Webster
Wagner Ford Rd
N Dixie
201
Meijer
Harshman Road
N

0 1 2 3
miles

Great Miami River
Stillwater River

Exit at "WPAFB & Harshman Rd"
Valley Pike
exit
Wright Bros Pkwy (Harshman Rd S)

Outstanding mobile statue of the Wright Flyer at Riverscape

Stanley
Eastwood Park
4N
Springfield Pike

Where road splits, follow left fork to "4 North - Springfield"
exit
Mad River

USAF Museum & IMAX Theater (page 77)

Wright Bros. Welcome Center page 79

Bicycle shops

Dayton Art Institute

Monument Ave.
E 2nd St
Springfield Pike

Dayton, OH
East of I-75, exits 58-51
Home of the Wright Brothers, world famous USAF Museum, Carillon Historical Park, Dayton Art Institute and many other great places to visit.
I-75 maps: 15S, 184N Stories: Pages 77-81

Wolf Creek
Main
Keowee
Webster
Keowee

E 1st St
E 3rd St
Mendelson Warehouse

W 3rd St
Williams
Church
Sinclair College
Washington

Salem
I75 ramp
Peace Bridge
2nd
W 3rd St
75

Site of Wright Family home
7 Hawthorn
(page 80)

Dayton Heart Hosp.
Edwin C. Moses Blvd
Patterson Blvd
Stewart
River Park
Excellent Marriott Hotel

Univ. Dayton "Welcome" Stadium

Carillon Park

Original Wright Flyer III on display in the special Wright Brothers Aviation Center at Carillon Historical Park (Page 80)

Brent Spence Bridge
Courtyard by Marriott
Clay Wade Bridge
Ohio River
Roebling Suspension Bridge
Aquarium/Newport On The Levee
Riverboat Row
Purple People Br
Cowens

192
I-75 n/bnd
Covington
Bakewell
Philadelphia
Johnson
3rd St
Hofbrauhaus
2nd St
Columbia
3rd St
Saratoga
Washington

4th St
5th St
Main
Russel
4th St
Madison
Scott
Greenup
Sanford
Garrard
Licking River
4th Street (2 way traffic)
Central
Southgate
York
Montmorth
4th Street
5th Street

I-75 s/bnd
Ramp
75
Goebel Park
Bakewell
7th St
5th St
5th St
Newport

192
8th St
Mainstrasse Village
N
follow these blue shark signs to the Newport Aquarium

Mainstrasse Village, Covington, KY *(page 85)*
Historic Mainstrasse is a restored 19th century German neighborhood of restaurants, art and craft shops, joined by cobblestone walkways.

Hofbräuhaus, Newport, KY *(page 85)*
Authentic Bavarian beer brewhouse and biergarten, modeled after the original 400 year old Hofbräuhaus in Munich, Germany.
Hours: From 11a daily until . . . whenever.
Lunch, 11a-3p, free lunch parking on site
Phone: 859-491-7200

Newport Aquarium/Newport on the Levee
Newport, KY (page 86)
I-75 maps: 17-S, 181-N
A superb and innovative aquarium experience. Enter glass tunnels and walk *through* the huge fish tanks. Don't miss the trip through the Ohio Valley Ice Age. Also enjoy the shops, boutiques and restaurants of *"Newport on the Levee"* beside the Aquarium.

Distance from I-75: 2¼ miles; **Time** from I-75: 5.5 mins
Hours: Summer, M-F & Su, 9a-7p; Sa, 9a-9p
Winter, 9a-6p
Admission: Adult/Snr/Child: $17.95/15.95/10.95
Phone: 859-261-7444 **Suggested time** to visit: 2hrs
Parking: $3, under "Newport On The Levee."

DOWNTOWN LEXINGTON
Lexington, KY; West of I-75 Exit 115 or 104

Most I-75 travelers bypass Lexington, but a short visit will add only ½ hour to your journey. Here's how to navigate through this historic city.

I-75 maps: 20-S, 178-N   Story: page 90

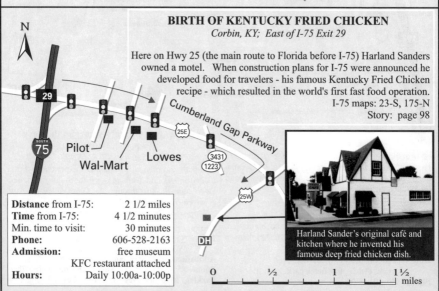

Rt 922 to I-75, Exit 115 →

60

Broadway

Main

S Mill

Vine St

Upper Limestone

Short

Elm

North Eastern

Midland to I-75 exit 110

Rose

Main

P

P

? Visitor Center

Statue of Horse Race

Paris Pike (exit 113)
- see map and special driving notes on page 90

Newtown Pike

115

68

DH 1.5 miles
25 1.2 miles

922

4

A●

113

27

LEXINGTON

111   64

Main St

60

Winchester   60   110

4   68

Limestone

Main St

DH

N

Man'o'War   108

25   421

Richmond Rd

4   New Circle Rd

25
DH

104

0   1   2   3   4 miles

Distance from I-75:   2 miles
Time from I-75:   5 minutes
Visitor Center, 301 E. Vine.
Phone: 800-845-3959
                  or 859-233-7299
Hrs: <u>Summer,</u>   M-F, 8:30a-5p
                      Sat, 10-5p
(summer only) Sun, noon-5p

A - Appleby's Park, home of the *"Lexington Legends"* ball team.

N

BIRTH OF KENTUCKY FRIED CHICKEN
Corbin, KY; East of I-75 Exit 29

Here on Hwy 25 (the main route to Florida before I-75) Harland Sanders owned a motel.   When construction plans for I-75 were announced he developed food for travelers - his famous Kentucky Fried Chicken recipe - which resulted in the world's first fast food operation.
I-75 maps: 23-S, 175-N
Story: page 98

29

SOUTH
75

Cumberland Gap Parkway

25E

3431
1223

Pilot

Wal-Mart   Lowes

25W

DH

Harland Sander's original café and kitchen where he invented his famous deep fried chicken dish.

Distance from I-75:   2 1/2 miles
Time from I-75:   4 1/2 minutes
Min. time to visit: 30 minutes
Phone: 606-528-2163
Admission: free museum
                      KFC restaurant attached
Hours: Daily 10:00a-10:00p

0   ½   1   1½ miles

WHITE HALL
Richmond, KY; West of I-75 Exit 95

Home of Abraham Lincoln's friend, and Kentucky's most colorful historical figure - Cassius Marcellus Clay. This magnificent Georgian style home dates from 1798 and is open to the public.

I-75 maps: 21-S, 178-N   Story: page 93

0   1   2   3 miles

N

River

Fort Boonesborough State Park

Coones Ferry Road

627E

Old Boonesborough Rd

McKinney Lane

627E

Rt 3377 Lost Fork Rd

White Hall

627W

75

95

FORT BOONESBOROUGH
Richmond, KY; East of I-75 Exit 95

Here in 1775 Daniel Boone established his frontier homesite on the bank of the Kentucky River. The reconstructed log fort is now a state park.

I-75 maps: 21-S, 178-N
Story: page 92

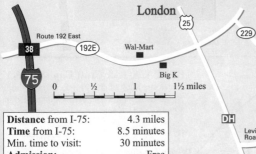

Catching up with daily chores at Fort Boonesboro

Distance from I-75:   1.9 miles
Time from I-75:   3 1/2 mins
Min. time to visit: 1 hour
Phone: 859-623-9178
Admission: Adult/Child $6/$3
Hrs: <u>Apr 1-Labor Day</u>, daily, 9-5:30
    <u>LabrDay-Oct 31</u>, W-Su, 9-5:30

Distance from I-75:   5.2 miles
Time from I-75:   6 minutes
Min. time to visit: 1 hour
Admission: Adult/Child $6/$4
Phone: 859-527-3131
Hours:
<u>Apr 1-Oct 31</u>   - Daily 9a-5p
<u>Winter</u> - phone, Fort may be closed

London

25

229

Route 192 East

38

192E

Wal-Mart

Big K

75

0   ½   1   1½ miles

N

Mountain Life Museum Village
Min. time to visit: 30 minutes
Admission:
    Adult/Child, $3/$2.25
Phone: 606-878-8000
Hours: Apr-Labor Day, daily 9a-5p
    From Labor Day, daily 9a-4p

DH

Levi Jackson Road

229

Mountain Life Museum

Cemetery

McHargue's Mill

Trail Rd

Site of Indian Massacre

Wilderness Road

Little Laurel River

25

Fariston Road

Levi Jackson Wilderness Road Park

Distance from I-75:   4.3 miles
Time from I-75:   8.5 minutes
Min. time to visit: 30 minutes
Admission: Free
Park Phone: 606-878-8000
Park Hours: daily, dawn - 11p
Mini-Golf: Adult/Child $4/$3
Pool: Adults/Child/under2 $5/$4/free
Camping all year
    - Apr 1-Oct 31 $21.00/Snr. $18.90
    - Nov 1-Mar 31 $12.00

LEVI JACKSON STATE PARK
London, KY; East of I-75 Exit 38

Levi Jackson Wilderness Road State Park is situated on a portion of Daniel Boone's pioneer trail which started at the Cumberland Gap.

I-75 maps: 23-S, 175-N   Story: page 97

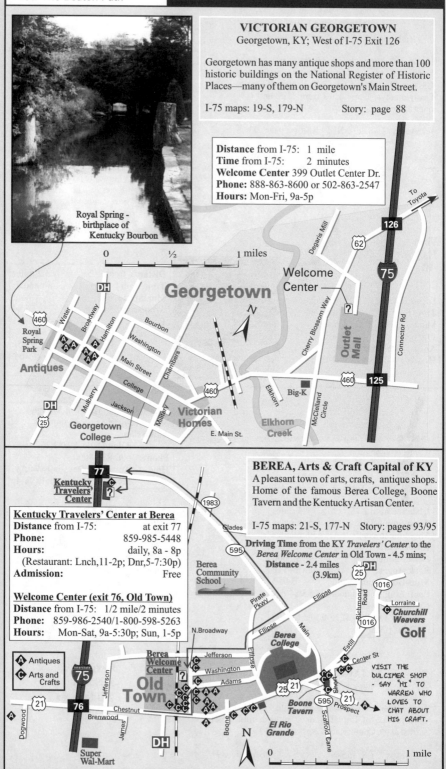

VICTORIAN GEORGETOWN
Georgetown, KY; West of I-75 Exit 126

Georgetown has many antique shops and more than 100 historic buildings on the National Register of Historic Places—many of them on Georgetown's Main Street.

I-75 maps: 19-S, 179-N   Story: page 88

Distance from I-75: 1 mile
Time from I-75:   2 minutes
Welcome Center 399 Outlet Center Dr.
Phone: 888-863-8600 or 502-863-2547
Hours: Mon-Fri, 9a-5p

To Toyota

Royal Spring -
birthplace of
Kentucky Bourbon

0   ½   1 miles

126
62
75

Welcome
Center

Georgetown

N

DH

460
Royal
Spring
Park

Water
Broadway
Hamilton

Bourbon

Washington

Antiques

Main Street
College

Mulberry
Jackson

DH
25

Georgetown
College

Chambers

Military

460

Victorian
Homes

E. Main St.

Cherry Blossom Way

Connector Rd

Outlet
Mall

125
460

Elkhorn

Big-K

McClelland
Circle

Elkhorn
Creek

Degaris Mill

BEREA, Arts & Craft Capital of KY
A pleasant town of arts, crafts, antique shops. Home of the famous Berea College, Boone Tavern and the Kentucky Artisan Center.

I-75 maps: 21-S, 177-N   Story: pages 93/95

77
Kentucky
Travelers'
Center
C
?

Kentucky Travelers' Center at Berea
Distance from I-75:   at exit 77
Phone: 859-985-5448
Hours: daily, 8a - 8p
  (Restaurant: Lnch,11-2p; Dnr,5-7:30p)
Admission: Free

Welcome Center (exit 76, Old Town)
Distance from I-75:   1/2 mile/2 minutes
Phone: 859-986-2540/1-800-598-5263
Hours: Mon-Sat, 9a-5:30p; Sun, 1-5p

1983

Slades

595

Berea
Community
School

Pirate
Pkwy

N.Broadway

Driving Time from the KY *Travelers' Center* to the
Berea Welcome Center in Old Town - 4.5 mins;
Distance - 2.4 miles
(3.9km)

DH
25
1016

Ellipse

Richmond
Road

1016

Lorraine
*Churchill
Weavers*

Golf

Ellipse
Ellipse

Berea
College

Main

Estill

Center St

A Antiques
C Arts and
   Crafts

75

Jefferson

21

76

Old
Town

Berea
Welcome
Center
?

C
C
Jefferson
Washington
Adams

C
C
C
C C
A A
A

Berea
College

25 21

Shopes

C C

21

595

Prospect

VISIT THE
DULCIMER SHOP
- SAY "HI" TO
WARREN WHO
LOVES TO
CHAT ABOUT
HIS CRAFT.

Dogwood

Chestnut
Brenwood

James

DH

Super
Wal-Mart

Boone

El Rio
Grande

N

Boone
Tavern

Scaffold Cane

0   1 mile

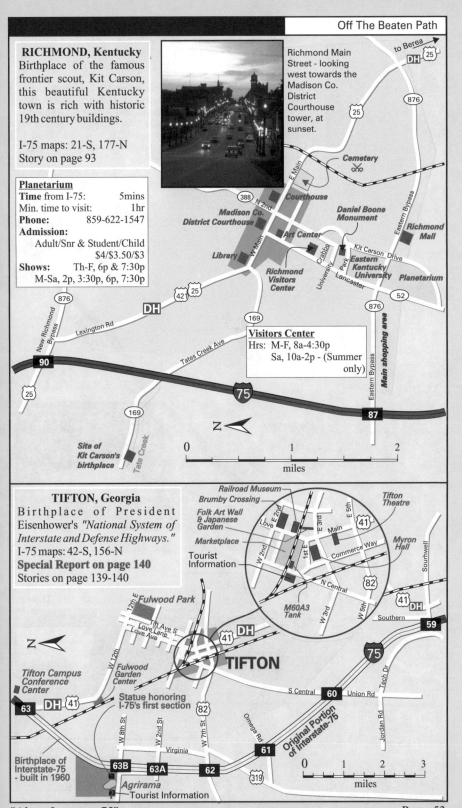

RICHMOND, Kentucky
Birthplace of the famous frontier scout, Kit Carson, this beautiful Kentucky town is rich with historic 19th century buildings.

I-75 maps: 21-S, 177-N
Story on page 93

Richmond Main Street - looking west towards the Madison Co. District Courthouse tower, at sunset.

Planetarium
Time from I-75:	5mins
Min. time to visit:	1hr
Phone:	859-622-1547
Admission:	
Adult/Snr & Student/Child	$4/$3.50/$3
Shows:	Th-F, 6p & 7:30p
	M-Sa, 2p, 3:30p, 6p, 7:30p

Visitors Center
Hrs: M-F, 8a-4:30p
     Sa, 10a-2p - (Summer only)

Site of Kit Carson's birthplace

0   1   2
miles

TIFTON, Georgia
Birthplace of President Eisenhower's *"National System of Interstate and Defense Highways."*
I-75 maps: 42-S, 156-N
Special Report on page 140
Stories on page 139-140

Railroad Museum
Brumby Crossing
Folk Art Wall & Japanese Garden
Marketplace
Tourist Information
Tifton Theatre
Myron Hall

Fulwood Park
Tift Ave S
Love Lane
Love Ave

Tifton Campus Conference Center

Statue honoring I-75's first section

Fulwood Garden Center

M60A3 Tank

TIFTON

Birthplace of Interstate-75 - built in 1960

Agrirama
Tourist Information

Original Portion of Interstate-75

0   1   2   3
miles

ELK VALLEY
Tennessee - S/Bound: exit 160,   N/Bound: exit 141

An alternative route to I-75.   An excellent paved, but winding road leading through tunnels of trees in the valley immediately to the west of I-75.   Caution - a great drive on a good day but do not use in bad weather or if you do not enjoy narrow twisting roads.   Not suitable for large Rvs. If northbound on I-75, take exit 141 and drive US63 west for 4.3 miles (6.9km); watch for the sharp right turn onto SR297 just past the Post Office.

I-75 maps: 25-S, 173-N   Stories: page 100/102

Jellico Mountain

5th Street

25W

Indian Mountain

JELLICO

160

Rt 25W Jellico

5th Street

Main St

297

Old Downtown Buildings

160

Newcomb

Railway

Florence

Sunset Trail

SOUTH 75

297

Gas

PINE MOUNTAIN

N

Zeb Mountain

Elk Valley

Stanfield Cemetery

SOUTH 75

"Tree Tunnel" on the Elk Valley road.

Potato Knob

New Canaan

Elk Valley

Elk Valley drive	24 miles (39 km)

Gobbler Knob

297

Hells Point Ridge

Highest Point 2,247 ft

Stinking Creek Rd

Time to drive between exits 141 & 160:
- via I-75   19 mins.
- via Elk Valley   40 mins.
Extra time needed for Elk Valley drive
- **difference   21 mins**

Post Office

144

Stinking Creek Road

4.3 miles 6.9 kms

63

63

Rt 63 Oneida Huntsville

To Huntsville

Turley Mountain

141

TV OUTLET

The winding drive down and northwards into Elk Valley. In the background, Pine Mountain carries Interstate-75 up more than 2,000 feet as it crosses the ridge on its journey south towards Knoxville.

US63 is also known as the *Howard Baker Highway*

AS SEEN ON TV - SEE PAGE 101

0   1   2   3 miles

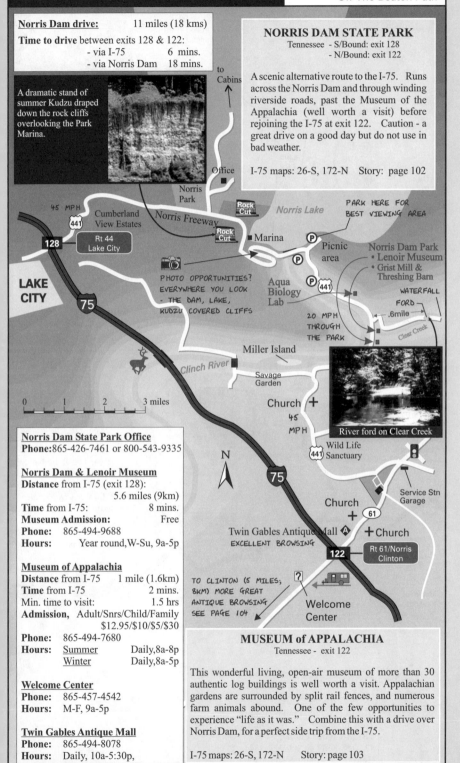

Norris Dam drive: 11 miles (18 kms)

Time to drive between exits 128 & 122:
- via I-75   6 mins.
- via Norris Dam   18 mins.

A dramatic stand of summer Kudzu draped down the rock cliffs overlooking the Park Marina.

NORRIS DAM STATE PARK
Tennessee - S/Bound: exit 128
- N/Bound: exit 122

A scenic alternative route to the I-75. Runs across the Norris Dam and through winding riverside roads, past the Museum of the Appalachia (well worth a visit) before rejoining the I-75 at exit 122. Caution - a great drive on a good day but do not use in bad weather.

I-75 maps: 26-S, 172-N   Story: page 102

to Cabins

Office

Norris Park

45 MPH

441

Cumberland View Estates

Norris Freeway

Rock Cut

Rock Cut

Norris Lake

PARK HERE FOR BEST VIEWING AREA

128

Rt 44 Lake City

■ Marina

Ⓟ

Picnic area

Ⓟ

Norris Dam Park
• Lenoir Museum
• Grist Mill & Threshing Barn

LAKE CITY

75

📷

PHOTO OPPORTUNITIES? EVERYWHERE YOU LOOK - THE DAM, LAKE, KUDZU COVERED CLIFFS

Aqua Biology Lab

Ⓟ

441

WATERFALL

FORD

.6mile

Clear Creek

20 MPH THROUGH THE PARK

Miller Island

Clinch River

Savage Garden

Church ✝

45 MPH

River ford on Clear Creek

0   1   2   3 miles

N

441 Wild Life Sanctuary

75

🚦

Service Stn Garage

Church ✝

61

Norris Dam State Park Office
Phone: 865-426-7461 or 800-543-9335

Norris Dam & Lenoir Museum
Distance from I-75 (exit 128):
     5.6 miles (9km)
Time from I-75:   8 mins.
Museum Admission: Free
Phone: 865-494-9688
Hours: Year round, W-Su, 9a-5p

Twin Gables Antique Mall ⬧ ✝ Church
EXCELLENT BROWSING

Rt 61/Norris Clinton

122

Museum of Appalachia
Distance from I-75   1 mile (1.6km)
Time from I-75:   2 mins.
Min. time to visit: 1.5 hrs
Admission, Adult/Snrs/Child/Family
     $12.95/$10/$5/$30
Phone: 865-494-7680
Hours: <u>Summer</u>   Daily, 8a-8p
     <u>Winter</u>   Daily, 8a-5p

TO CLINTON (5 MILES; 8KM) MORE GREAT ANTIQUE BROWSING SEE PAGE 104

❓

Welcome Center

Welcome Center
Phone: 865-457-4542
Hours: M-F, 9a-5p

Twin Gables Antique Mall
Phone: 865-494-8078
Hours: Daily, 10a-5:30p,

MUSEUM of APPALACHIA
Tennessee - exit 122

This wonderful living, open-air museum of more than 30 authentic log buildings is well worth a visit. Appalachian gardens are surrounded by split rail fences, and numerous farm animals abound. One of the few opportunities to experience "life as it was." Combine this with a drive over Norris Dam, for a perfect side trip from the I-75.

I-75 maps: 26-S, 172-N   Story: page 103

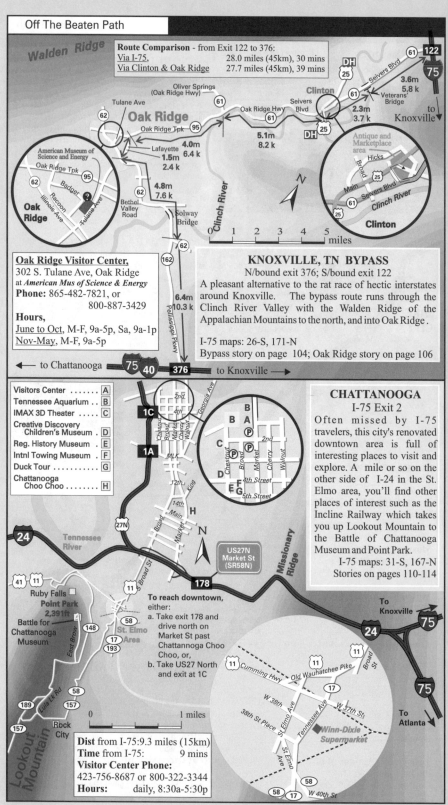

BATTLE OF RESACA & CONFEDERATE CEMETERY
Resaca, GA; Cemetery east of I-75 Exit 320

A bloody Civil War battle (5,547 men killed or injured) was fought here, between the 13th and 15th of May, 1864, as the Confederate Army was beaten back towards Atlanta.   To help you understand the scope of this large battlefield, the mile markers are shown on the I-75.   Directions and distances refer to the Confederate Cemetery which is well worth visiting.

Recent research has led to much greater knowledge of this battle; this revised map reflects that new knowledge.

I-75 maps: 32-S, 166-N   Story and Civil War Sidebar, page 120-121

Confederate Cemetery
Distance from I-75:
  2.5 miles (4km)
Time from I-75:
  4 minutes
Min. time to visit:
  20 minutes.

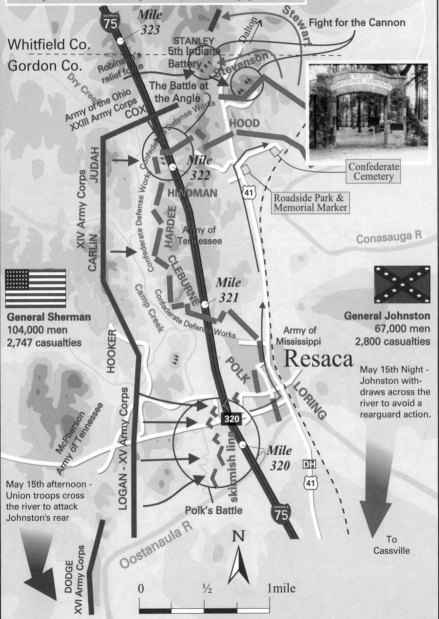

Mile 323

Whitfield Co.
Gordon Co.

Robinson's relief force

STANLEY 5th Indiana Battery

Dalton

Stewart

Stevenson

Fight for the Cannon

The Battle at the Angle

Army of the Ohio
XXIII Army Corps

COX

Defense Works

HOOD

Confederate Cemetery

Mile 322

JUDAH

Confederate Defense Works

HINDMAN

US 41

Roadside Park & Memorial Marker

XIV Army Corps

CARLIN

HARDEE

Army of Tennessee

CLEBURNE

Conasauga R

Camp Creek

Confederate Defense Works

Mile 321

General Sherman
104,000 men
2,747 casualties

Army of Mississippi

Resaca

General Johnston
67,000 men
2,800 casualties

HOOKER

McPherson
Army of Tennessee

LOGAN - XV Army Corps

POLK

LORING

May 15th Night - Johnston withdraws across the river to avoid a rearguard action.

320

skirmish line

Mile 320

DH

US 41

GEORGIA 75

May 15th afternoon - Union troops cross the river to attack Johnston's rear

Polk's Battle

Oostanaula R

DODGE
XVI Army Corps

To Cassville

N

0   ½   1mile

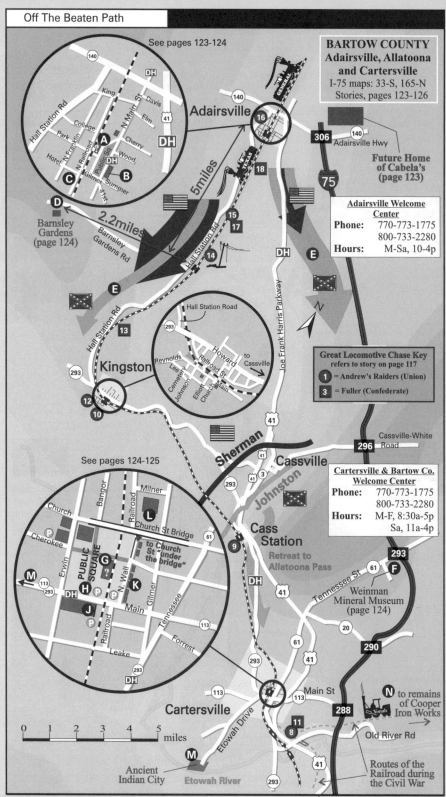

See pages 123-124

140

DH

King

Davis
St.
Elm

College

Hall Station Rd

Park
Franklin
N

N Railroad
A
Public Sq
Cherry

Hotel
N Franklin
DH
Wood
B

C
Gilmer
41st
Summer

D

Barnsley
Gardens
(page 124)

2.2miles

Barnsley
Gardens Rd

Hall Station Rd

E

Hall Station Rd

13

293

Kingston

293

12

10

140

Adairsville

16

18

Texas

15

17

14

5 miles

Hall Station Rd

Joe Frank Harris Parkway

Hall Station Road

293

Howard

Reynolds
Railroad St
to
Cassville

Lee
Cemetery
Johnson
Elliott
Church
Main

BARTOW COUNTY
Adairsville, Allatoona
and Cartersville
I-75 maps: 33-S, 165-N
Stories, pages 123-126

306

140
Adairsville Hwy

75

Future Home
of Cabela's
(page 123)

Adairsville Welcome
Center

Phone:	770-773-1775
	800-733-2280
Hours:	M-Sa, 10-4p

N

Great Locomotive Chase Key
refers to story on page 117

1 = Andrew's Raiders (Union)

3 = Fuller (Confederate)

41

Sherman

41

3

Cassville

293

Johnston

Cass
Station

Retreat to
Allatoona Pass

296
Cassville-White
Road

Cartersville & Bartow Co.
Welcome Center

Phone:	770-773-1775
	800-733-2280
Hours:	M-F, 8:30a-5p
	Sa, 11a-4p

See pages 124-125

Milner

Bangor
Railroad

Church

L

Church St Bridge

Church
Cherokee
P

61

Erwin

PUBLIC
SQUARE

G

to Church
St "under
the bridge"

M
113
293

DH
H
P
N Wall
P
K

J
P

Main
Gilmer

Railroad
Tennessee

Leake

Forrest

293

DH

113

9

DH

41

61

41

293

293

61

41

113

113
Main St

288

293

Cartersville

11
8

M

Ancient
Indian City

Etowah Drive

Etowah River

41

0 1 2 3 4 5
miles

F
61
293

Tennessee St

Weinman
Mineral Museum
(page 124)

20

290

N
Yonah
to remains
of Cooper
Iron Works

Old River Rd

Routes of the
Railroad during
the Civil War

Dave Hunter's

SOUTHERN MUSEUM of CIVIL WAR & LOCOMOTIVE HISTORY
Kennesaw, GA; I-75 Exit 273

Kennesaw was the starting point of the Great Locomotive Chase. Walk the grounds where the "General" was stolen and then cross the road and visit the newly renovated Museum, home of the famous locomotive.

This world class museum is associated with the Smithsonian Museum in Washington, DC, and has one of the finest collections of Civil War artefacts in North America.

I-75 maps: 34-S, 164-N;   Story page 128

Admission:	Adult/Snr/Child
	$7.50/$6.50/$5.50
Phone:	770-427-2117
Hours:	Mon-Sat, 9:30a-5p
	Sun, noon-5p

0   ½ mile

To Moon's Station

Park with historical markers

Museum home of the "General"

DH 293

Jiles

Cherokee Street

Shiloh

Cherokee Street

McCollum Pkwy

Maple

Poplar

Twelve Oaks

Timberlake

Ben King Road

Pine Hill

Cherokee St.

Main St

Parking

Big Shanty

N

Above: the famous railroad chase locomotive, "General"

Left: don't miss the fabulous reconstruction of a 19th century locomotive factory. Tour the Engineering office, Tool & Pattern shop, and Assembly ("Works") area.

TUNNEL HILL
Tunnel Hill, GA;
I-75 Exit 341

This 1849 tunnel became the scene of dramatic action during the Civil War's Great Locomotive Chase (see pages 117-119. The Tunnel Hill Heritage Center houses a Museum with much information about the tunnel, and its role in the epic railroad chase. Don't miss the blood stained bench!

I-75 maps: 31-S, 167-N
Stories: pages 116 and 119(32)

Lee Chapel Road

winding road

201

75

341

Spring Hill

Harper

201

Tanyard Creek

0   1/2 mile

N

Crawford

Fire Dept.

Church   Park

+

Heritage Center/Museum
Dist from I-75: 2.1mile (3.4km)
Time from I-75:   32.mins
Phone: 800-331-3258
Hours:
　　Summer: M-Sa, 10a-6p
　　Winter: M-Sa, 9a-5p
Admission:
　　Adult/Child $2.50/$1.50

C

41
DH

Church Rd

201

Mtn View

Varnell St

Post Office

Regal

Oak   Main

Parking

Tunnel Hill Heritage Center

covered br.

Clisby Ho.

Old Railroad Depot (inside ConAgra's trash dump)

Modern tunnel & track

fence

Old Civil War trackbed

Tunnel

Clisby Austin Rd

Railroad Car & push cart

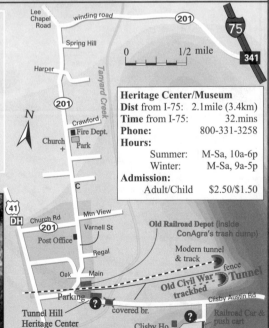

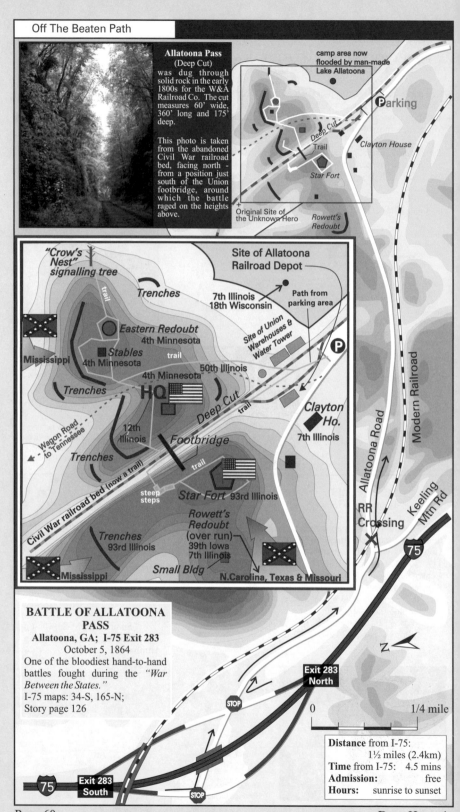

Allatoona Pass
(Deep Cut)
was dug through solid rock in the early 1800s for the W&A Railroad Co. The cut measures 60' wide, 360' long and 175' deep.

This photo is taken from the abandoned Civil War railroad bed, facing north - from a position just south of the Union footbridge, around which the battle raged on the heights above.

camp area now flooded by man-made Lake Allatoona

Parking

Deep Cut Trail

Clayton House

Star Fort

Original Site of the Unknown Hero

Rowett's Redoubt

"Crow's Nest" signalling tree

Site of Allatoona Railroad Depot

trail

Trenches

7th Illinois
18th Wisconsin

Path from parking area

Eastern Redoubt
4th Minnesota

Site of Union Warehouses & Water Tower

P

Mississippi

Stables
4th Minnesota

trail

50th Illinois

4th Minnesota

Trenches

HQ

Deep Cut

trail

Clayton Ho.

7th Illinois

Wagon Road to Tennessee

12th Illinois

Footbridge

Trenches

Civil War railroad bed (now a trail)

steep steps

trail

Star Fort   93rd Illinois

Rowett's Redoubt (over run)
39th Iowa
7th Illinois

Trenches
93rd Illinois

Small Bldg

Mississippi

N.Carolina, Texas & Missouri

Allatoona Road

Modern Railroad

Keeling Mtn Rd

RR Crossing

75

BATTLE OF ALLATOONA PASS
Allatoona, GA; I-75 Exit 283
October 5, 1864
One of the bloodiest hand-to-hand battles fought during the *"War Between the States."*
I-75 maps: 34-S, 165-N;
Story page 126

Exit 283
North

STOP

Exit 283
South

STOP

75

N

0   1/4 mile

Distance from I-75:	1½ miles (2.4km)
Time from I-75:	4.5 mins
Admission:	free
Hours:	sunrise to sunset

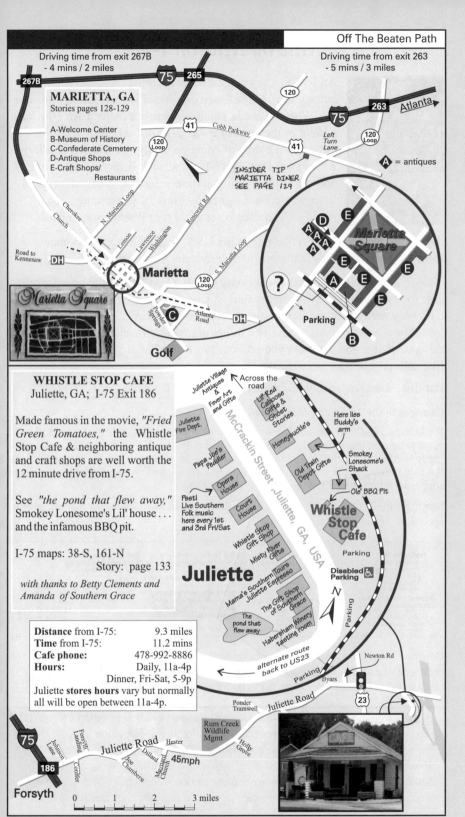

Driving time from exit 267B
- 4 mins / 2 miles

Driving time from exit 263
- 5 mins / 3 miles

75 265 267B

120

75 263 Atlanta

MARIETTA, GA
Stories pages 128-129

A-Welcome Center
B-Museum of History
C-Confederate Cemetery
D-Antique Shops
E-Craft Shops/
   Restaurants

41 Cobb Parkway

120 Loop

41 Left Turn Lane

120 Loop

Ⓐ = antiques

INSIDER TIP
MARIETTA DINER
SEE PAGE 129

Cherokee
Church

N. Marietta Loop

Lemon

Lawrence
Washington

Roswell Rd

S. Marietta Loop

Road to
Kennesaw DH

Marietta

120 Loop

Ⓓ Ⓔ
Ⓐ Ⓔ
Ⓐ Ⓐ
Ⓔ **Marietta Square**
Ⓐ Ⓔ Ⓔ
Ⓔ Ⓔ
Ⓐ
Ⓔ

?

Parking

Ⓑ

Marietta Square

Powder
Springs Ⓒ Atlanta
Road DH

Golf

WHISTLE STOP CAFE
Juliette, GA; I-75 Exit 186

Made famous in the movie, *"Fried Green Tomatoes,"* the Whistle Stop Cafe & neighboring antique and craft shops are well worth the 12 minute drive from I-75.

See *"the pond that flew away,"* Smokey Lonesome's Lil' house . . . and the infamous BBQ pit.

I-75 maps: 38-S, 161-N
       Story: page 133

with thanks to Betty Clements and Amanda of Southern Grace

Distance from I-75:	9.3 miles
Time from I-75:	11.2 mins
Cafe phone:	478-992-8886
Hours:	Daily, 11a-4p
	Dinner, Fri-Sat, 5-9p

Juliette **stores hours** vary but normally all will be open between 11a-4p.

Juliette Village Antiques & Fever Art and Gifts

Across the road

Lil' Red Caboose Gifts & Ghost Stories

Here lies Buddy's arm

Juliette Fire Dept.

McCrackin Street "Juliette, GA, USA

Honeysuckle's

Smokey Lonesome's Shack

Papa Joe's Peddler

Old Train Depot Gifts

Ole' BBQ Pit

Pssst! Live Southern Folk music here every 1st and 3rd Fri/Sat

Opera House

Court House

Whistle Stop Cafe

Whistle Stop Gift Shop

Misty River Gifts

Parking

Juliette

Disabled Parking

Mama's Southern Tour Juliette Espresso

N

The Gift Shop of Southern Grace

The pond that flew away

Habersham Winery tasting room

Parking

alternate route back to US23

Newton Rd

Parking

Byars

23

Ponder Tramwell Juliette Road

75 186

Johnson Lane

Forsyth Landing

Conifer

Juliette Road Hester

Joe Chambers

Dillard

Maynard Church

45mph

Rum Creek Wildlife Mgmt

Holly Grove

Forsyth

0   1   2   3 miles

Mile by Mile on I-75

Interstate-75 is dedicated to the Armed Forces that have defended the United States of America – it is officially known as the . . .

Blue Star Memorial Highway

An I-75 journey can either be a boring *"let's get there as quickly as possible"* race or a fun-filled adventure of discovery. Where else can you drive across a major **Civil War battlefield** or the **path of a 467 year old invading army** . . . or pass within a mile of America's <u>only</u> **"Presidents' Gallery,"** where each President has a specially dedicated area with portrait or photo, biographical information and an original letter written and signed by him . . . all presented in a world-class museum setting. From Washington to Bush, there is no other collection like this in the USA, and it's just a few minutes from the interstate. This is the magic of Interstate-75.

"Along Interstate-75" is written not only to assist you in locating your favorite gas, food and lodging exit services (on your side of the road), to help you negotiate busy sections of the freeway using our driving notes . . . but also to share local knowledge along the way. The following "white travelogue" pages provide this knowledge and entertain you on your journey. After all, there is nothing like entertainment to make the time go quickly!

But first, some notes about this edition of "Along I-75" . . .

Changes to the 25 mile Colored Maps

We listen carefully to you, our readers. Some of you wrote and said you would like the maps to be a bit less crowded, other said they had difficulty reading text on the dark brown "hilly" sections. Another reader had a great idea – he wanted to be able to quickly scan the pages ahead and see where all the restrooms are located. We took all your ideas and suggestions into consideration and made some changes.

Starting with this edition, we have organized the various notes on the 25 mile maps into specifically colored boxes as follows:

Restrooms? We have added a green marker in the "milepost margin" (on the right side of each map), locating each restroom facility and showing the distance in miles (m) and kilometers (k) to the next rest stop or Welcome Center.

In the following pages, you will find several features to help and entertain you during your I-75 trip. "Special Reports" provide detailed information about sights of particular interest along the way, "***Insider Tips***" will share local knowledge about interesting restaurants and other roadside "secrets." And our tried and true $aving Tip$ will save you money ... many of our readers have told us that these alone have saved them enough money to pay for this book, several times over!

I-75 Changes and Trends

Since writing the previous edition (13th) of this book two years ago, Kathy and I have driven I-75 many times and have been amazed at the significant differences we found in the available exit services and facilities along the way. A number have gone out of business (**331**), others have "come on line" as new businesses (**430**) ... for a total of **761** changes in exit services–in the 958 miles between Detroit and the Georgia/Florida border.

This represents a turnover rate of 22%, one of the largest we've seen in the 15 years we have been writing "*Along I-75.*"

In this edition (our 14th), we record **3,018** services within a mile of each exit, comprising **748** gas services, **1,531** fast food outlets & restaurants, and **739** lodging facilities.

We have seen some interesting trends during our travels; here is a summary of our findings:

♦ Again, the number of *hotels & motels accepting pets* has increased substantially over the past few years. The hospitality industry has come to realize that pets are part of the family and businesses were losing guests by restricting animals. The situation came to national attention when Oprah Winfrey encountered a problem while traveling with her dogs ... the hospitality industry could no longer ignore travelers with pets. As a compromise, many hotels–motels charge a small fee for accommodating pets. All the "pet friendly" lodgings are highlighted in blue on our colored "25-mile-per-page" maps.

Lane Talk - L1 to L4 . . . and more

I want to share the official lane numbering codes with you since I will sometimes use them in the driving (lane changing) directions, in these pages.

In police or DOT reports, the **lanes number from the center (median) strip, to the right** with the "**Fast**" lane (truckers "*hammer*" lane) as **L1**.

For instance in a three lane stretch, the "fast" lane is L1, the **middle** (also the truck overtaking lane) is **L2** and the "**slow**" or "**inside**" lane is **L3**.

Therefore, if I suggest you *move from L3 to L1/L2,* you know that I mean you should move from the *slow lane in a 3 lane stretch, to the center or fast lanes.*

♦ Several other increasing trends we have observed in the I-75 hospitality industry:

- a move towards completely *smoke-free* accommodations. For example, as of September, 2006, all Marriott properties (*Fairfield, Courtyard*, etc.), are now completely smoke-free.

- more lodgings offering *internet* (internet or wifi) connection in your room. Some charge for the service (you phone the front desk for a password) others provide it free.

- replacement of the traditional bathtub with walk-in *shower stalls.*

♦ There have also been some recent "brand" name changes:

- *LaQuinta* purchased all the *Baymont Inns*. The company operated ones are being converted to the *LaQuinta* flag; franchisee operated Baymont properties are continuing as *Baymont Inns*.

- *Amerihost* properties are all changing to *Baymont Inns*.

♦ The biggest of all the changes in the world of fast food is *McDonalds'* plan to change from traditional plastic interiors to a more relaxed, "club" style, a la Starbucks. More than half the 13,099 U.S. McDonalds will undergo this renovation by 2009.

Changes include using divider screens to split the interior into zones. The *"linger"* zone will have comfortable armchairs and sofas. The *"grab & go"* zone will be equipped with bar stools, high counters and plazma TV. The *"flexible"* zone will include fabric covered booths and other seating styles.

How will you be able to tell the difference between old and new McDonalds? As part of each renovation, the old familiar red/brown, double-sloped mansard roof line will change to an upscale flat metal one ... complete with newly designed shallow golden-arch curves–aka the *"swish eyebrow."*

♦ Salads are beginning to rule the day as fast food chain *menus change* to reduce fat content. One of our favorite lunch stops is *Chick-fil-A*, which has an excellent selection of salads and "cool-wraps."

♦ And bless their hearts, the marketing folk at one chain have not been asleep. In the face of growing criticism about huge meal portions, *Wendy's* has reclassified its

"Biggie" drinks and fries to *"Medium."* But it *is* a name change only. The "Medium" drink is still the same size as the former "Biggie" ... namely the equivalent of almost three 12 ounce cans of soda. Oh, and yes, the *"Great Biggie"* has been "downsized" to *"Large."*

♦ More *shopping opportunities*. As land becomes available alongside the interstate, the shopping mall developers move in. You will find more I-75 shopping opportunities on your next trip down the freeway. This also means that long established interstate businesses have a chance to relocate and upgrade their facilities. A case in point is **Bob Evans** at Findlay's exit 159 in Ohio; it is no longer on the east side. The popular restaurant has moved to premises in the new plaza on the west side of I-75.

▲ And of course, **Cracker Barrel** restaurants continue to open as the chain expands. We have all the latest locations on our maps.

▲ In service station circles, **Racetrac** is converting more of its company owned gas outlets to franchisee-owned, **Raceway**. It's all the same company though but you will see less Racetracs along I-75.

▲ Gas costs. Wow! Whoever would have thought a few years ago, we would be paying the pump prices demanded by today's markets.

In May, 2006, we completed an I-75 round trip between Detroit and the Florida Border, and used 107.6 gallons. An analysis of my gas bills (regular unleaded) shows that we paid $291.57, an average of $2.71/gallon. The national average price of regular unleaded gas for this period was $2.90, so I-75 prices were about 7% below national average, and this is a trend we have seen over the years.

So let me put this it into perspective, driving to Florida is still cheaper than other means of transportation. The cost per person with all our gear (and no need to rent a car on arrival) was $145.79/person, all taxes and surcharges included.

I haven't counted accommodation or meals because the drive was so relaxing and enjoyable, it was part of the vacation!

▲ In other news, the Federal Highways folk have decided that we drivers are getting older (demographically) and our eyesight is becomes less reliable. The answer? *"ClearviewHwy,"* a new highway sign lettering which apparently improves the readability of signs at night by as much as 16%. According to reports, this means that a car traveling at 45 mph will be able to identify that exit ramp 80 feet sooner! But who drives at 45 mph on I-75? The new typeface will be used on signs as regular maintenance replacement takes place.

Construction Delays: Don't be put off by stories of long construction zones on I-75. The problem is that state transportation agencies report construction by "project."

For instance, Georgia DOT reports a 10 mile construction project in Cook County. But most of it is dormant with only one work zone. There are no lane restrictions or merges so traffic flows through at a nominal 50 mph, with no backups, or other problems. It's an easy drive.

INSIDER TIPS

Throughout the following sections, you will find our famous "Insider Tips"– hints of special significance to help you save money and have a more enjoyable journey. In many instances, we recommend specific I-75 facilities (often first brought to our attention by our readers–see page 203) which, from our personal inspections have proven to offer exceptional value and service to interstate travelers.

No business has paid to be recommended in *"Along I-75."* There is no commercial content in this guide. In fact, none of our "recommendations" knew they were being inspected at the time of our visit.

You can trust our **"Insider Tips"**–here's where you get the **real local knowledge.**

WHAT'S IN A NAME?

Indian terms, historical characters, national heroes, town site descriptions–place names weave a colorful tapestry as we journey along Interstate-75. In some cases, early pioneers and settlers from east coast regions transferred the names of their original home towns to their new settlements (e.g.. Milford, Ohio), thereby perpetuating British and European names in the U.S. interior.

Throughout the following pages, we explain the meanings behind some of the more interesting place names encountered as we travel southbound to Florida:

INSIDER TIP - Java Fixes

Everybody (well almost everybody) loves a good cup of coffee in the morning and two things have happened along I-75 to help the day start well

Starbucks now has a number of new outlets on I-75, with the promise of more to come. You will find them at the following exits (State, exit #, east/west):

OH44E, **KY**108E, **TN**108E, **TN**(I-40/I-75)378W, **GA**269W, **GA**224E, **GA**62W, **GA**18E

OK baristas*, now translate a medium double, double for me. (*Starbucks counter person)

Tim Hortons is a Canadian national icon (there's even a Tim Hortons store in Kandahar, Afghanistan for Canadian forces on duty there). Since Wendy's purchased this outstanding coffee and doughnut company, expansion has been slow in the USA. But things are moving now as Canadian expatriates buy franchises. Here are their locations and the names of your hosts:

MI 29E - Corporate store

OH197E - Corporate store

OH Piqua - (planned - exit 82 or 83?)

OH74E - Ryan & Allison, London, ON
        (2 miles east of I-75)

OH59W - Bertha & Mark, unknown

OH44W - Julia & Richard, Niagara Falls,
        ON; open 24 hrs

OH38E - Julia & Richard, Niagara Falls, ON

OH29E - Corporate store

MICHIGAN: Detroit City (Wayne Co.): It is now illegal to use a handheld cell phone while driving within the City limits. This new law is being actively enforced.

Exit 15-Monroe: This exit leads to one of the oldest communities in Michigan, the historic town of Monroe settled by the French in 1780. *General George Custer* (of Civil War and Little Bighorn fame) lived here for many years before joining the army and making a name for himself in the cavalry.

Custer and his brother, Nevin, owned the Nevin Custer farm (now privately owned), just west of Monroe on the north bank of the Raisin River. The brothers purchased the farm in 1871, five years before George's death at Little Bighorn. George's favorite horse, Dandy is buried in the orchard near the barn. Visitors to the farm have included Buffalo Bill Cody and Annie Oakley.

Today, Monroe remembers Custer with a bronze statue of him astride his restless horse, Dandy, in downtown Monroe at the corners of Elm and Monroe Streets.

Just 1/2 mile to the west is a very interesting memorial to another Monroe hero–*Heck Park.* Named in memory of Capt. Norman (Rusty) Heck Jr., the first from Monroe Co. to be killed in Vietnam (December 8, 1964).

Two helicopters, a UH-1M "Huey" and a "Cobra" are on static display. A small but interesting museum is maintained by the local Vietnam Veterans of America Chapter.

Exit 14-Battle of the Raisin River: *(see map on page 48).* Just west of this exit on the north bank of the Raisin River, lies the site of an early settlement called Frenchtown. It was here that one of largest battles between the British and American Armies took place during the War of 1812.

On the evening of January 18, 1813, Frenchtown was occupied by an American force, mainly from Kentucky. The 700 men had faced a small British force earlier that day and after hours of tree to tree fighting, had driven them back north towards Detroit.

Several days later their leader, Gen. Winchester, arrived with the remainder of the troops, bringing the army to a strength of 934 men.

In the quiet pre-dawn of January 21st, a huge British force of 597 British soldiers supported by 800 Indians, crept towards Frenchtown to take their revenge. The attack lasted less than twenty minutes before the American right (closest to the I-75) was outflanked and the men retreated to the river. Of the 400 men who fled, over 200 were killed and 147 were captured–including General Winchester.

MICHIGAN - *an old Indian word of unknown origins. It could come from Mishi-mikin-nac or "swimming turtle," a descriptive term used to describe the shape of some of Michigan's land, or from Mitchisawgyegan (michi gama), an Indian term meaning "Great Lake."*

DETROIT - *from the French word "d'etroit" (of the strait). Founded on July 24th, 1701, by French explorer Antoine Cadillac, the early settlement lay on the stretch of land between Lake Erie and Lake St.Clair.*

The remaining 500 Kentuckians, fighting from behind Frenchtown's picket fences, were unaware of the collapse on their right, and drove off three fierce British attacks with their rifles. When they saw a British officer come towards them with a white flag, they thought that the British were going to surrender. They were surprised when the officer gave them orders from their own General, now a prisoner of the British, to surrender.

After the surrender, the British withdrew and the Americans gathered their dying and injured to the settlers' homes in Frenchtown. The following morning, the Indian forces attacked, burning and plundering the homes and scalping the American wounded. Over 60 were killed–the action became known as the *"Massacre of the Raisin River."*

The massacre shocked and enraged settlers throughout the Old Northwest Territory (today's Michigan). Ten months later, American troops chased the British army from Detroit to Ontario where a major battle took place on the banks of another river–the Thames. During this battle, the famous Indian chief and friend of the British, Tecumseh, was killed. The American battle cry at this engagement? *"Remember the Raisin!"* [Battlefield hours and other details on page 48].

Milepost 10 (N/bound)-Monroe Welcome Center: Welcome to the new Michigan Welcome Center and say "hi" to Manager Cathy and her counter folk, Lorean and Jo Ann. They will help you find the information you need in the Center's excellent stock of brochures for all areas of the State.

INSIDER TIP
Bolles Harbor Restaurant

Psst–this is why you bought this book ... for local knowledge! Hidden just half a mile to the east of exit 11 and overlooking the marina is the Bolles Harbor Café. It has won a number of awards including one from the AAA. Fresh perch and other lake fish are the specialties of the house.

Stop by and say *"hi"* from me to owner and chef, Silverio. I know you'll enjoy his tableside hospitality.

Hours, Tu-Sat, 6am-9pm; Sun, 6am-2pm, closed Mon. ☎ 734-457-2233

Exit 9-Lake Maumee: We cross through the plains south of Monroe giving little thought to the scene a million years ago when melting glaciers hundreds of feet thick formed an ancient lake which ran right across this section of Michigan and down as far as Exit 159 (Findlay) in Ohio. Geologists named it Lake Maumee and its water surface was about 230 feet above the present position of our car.

How can scientists tell? They found the beach ridges of the lake permanently etched into rock at an elevation of 800 feet above sea level (we are driving at 570 feet above sea level)–see page 70. The lake finally flooded the Grand River Valley in Michigan and as its water level fell, the current shoreline of Lake Erie appeared.

OHIO: Exit 210-Toledo and the Ohio-Michigan war: It is 1835 and this is where we find a forgotten war. The land between this exit and Ohio Exit 199 is disputed territory and both Ohio and Michigan have laid claim to it. That large crowd of men over there marching down the road with flintlock muskets slung over their shoulders is Michigan's Army led southward by Governor Mason (the stout, black hatted fellow on the roan horse). They are on their way to attack the small settlement of Toledo and settle this question once and for all. They don't know yet but before the week is out, they will capture one of Toledo's founding fathers and hold him as a prisoner of war. Congress will finally have to intervene. The war that has broken out will be resolved by awarding the territory to Ohio, and granting Michigan full statehood in 1837 along with all the copper and iron rights in the peninsula to their north.

The issue of "who owns Toledo" will not go away. In 1992, an editorial appeared in the *Toledo Blade*, questioning the ownership of Toledo by Ohio. It seems that some would still like to cede the city to Michigan!

Mile 205: Here's a southbound traffic tip, especially useful if driving an RV or towing a trailer. Immediately after the Willys/Jeep Parkway (exit 205 - caution, it exits on your left), *move in to L2*. You will not have to change lanes again until you leave Toledo.

OHIO - *early French explorers discovered the Ohio River, and used Iroquois words such as Oheo (beautiful) to describe it. The explored territory later acquired the name.*

TOLEDO - *because of its industrial heritage, named after the Spanish town of Toledo famous throughout history for "Toledo Steel."*

Miles 198 to 163-The Black Swamp: You wouldn't have wanted to be here 125 years ago, for this entire region (about the size of Connecticut) was the dreaded Black Swamp. A dense, dank, gloomy forest populated mainly by deer, panthers, rattlesnakes, wolves and bear.

The ground was an evil boggy quagmire of black muck which sucked pioneers to their knees and if the animals and insects did not get them, then malaria probably would. In 1850, farmers decided to try to drain the area, and by 1890 more than 22,000 miles of ditches had drained the land and revealed the rich fertile farmland beneath. In 40 years, the stinking swamp had been transformed into the productive farms of today's Ohio.

Exit 192-Fort Meigs: *(see map on page 48).* To set you in the mood, you enter the fort through the impressive orientation center. Take your time to go through the Museum first; it will greatly enhance your understanding of the War of 1812, and the actions which took place at this historic site.

After the massacre of the Kentucky troops at the Raisin River in January, 1813 *(see Michigan, Exit 14)*, fighting between the British and the Americans came to a temporary halt. U.S. Maj Gen. Harrison decided to build a new fort on the south banks of the Maumee River, named after Gov. Meigs of Ohio.

The fort quickly became central to the protection of Ohio; if it fell, Michigan & Ohio would become conquered British territory. At its peak it housed more than 2,000 American regulars from Ohio, Kentucky, Pennsylvania and Virginia. Let's go back in time for a visit.

Radar

When compared to national highway safety statistics, I-75 is a very safe freeway. State police mean to keep it that way by actively monitoring speed and issuing tickets for infractions as little as 5 mph over the limit.

Now, I *know* you have absolutely no intention of speeding but it is good to know where the regular I-75 radar traps are positioned. That way, you can be prepared for those speeders who sweep past you and throw on their brakes when they spot the patrol car in the bushes.

The "radar" symbols on our colored maps are very accurate–as many of our readers will attest.

It's late April, 1813; the fort is badly undermanned with twelve hundred troop of which only 850 are fit for duty. Will they be able to withstand the coming British attack? To protect his forces, Harrison orders long embankments of earth built across the fort parade grounds so his troops can burrow down into the muddy earth, behind them.

At 11 a.m. on May 1st, a British force of two thousand lays siege to Fort Meigs with 20-30 artillery pieces, pounding its earthworks and wooden blockhouses continuously for four days. Twenty-four pound cannon balls, red hot 12 pounders, mortar shells and fragmentation bombs rain down on the fort sending

---

Money Saving Tip

After entering a new state, stop at the Welcome or Traveler Information Center and get your free copies of the green covered *Traveler Discount Guide* and the red covered *Discount Lodging Guide* motel coupon books. They can usually be found lying in a pile on the counter or a rack inside the door. Ask the staff, if you don't see them.

These publications will save you many $$$$ on overnight accommodation. They are chock full of discount coupons for motels along the way. Typically, you will find discounts in the 20-45% range. Bargains we have seen recently were $65 rooms discounted to $36, and $42 rooms to $28. We use the books all the time on each trip and save literally hundreds of dollars.

Here's how they work. Every day, each motel listed in the coupon books sets aside a certain number of discount rate rooms based on their occupancy experience from the previous night. The discounts are provided on a first-come first-served basis to travelers with the discount book coupons. What are your chances of getting a discount room? We normally pull off the road around 5 p.m. and in all our years of traveling have only been turned down a couple of times at the motel of our choice. We quickly found another one nearby which accepted their coupon from the book.

---

deadly iron and wood splinter fragments in all directions.

Six days later, American reinforcements arrive and although the buildings and earthworks have been badly mauled, the American flag still flies. The garrison has held tight; the British lift the siege and withdraw northward into Ontario.

In a curious footnote to history, one and a half years later on September 14, 1814, a similar circumstance occurred at Fort McHenry in Baltimore Harbor, Maryland. After a heavy 24 hour pounding by British canon and mortar, the Fort survived and the American flag remained flying *"by the dawn's early light"* as immortalized by Francis Scott Key in *"The Star Spangled Banner."* But first honors for "survival under heavy British attack" should probably go to Fort Meigs!

Today, you can wander around this historic eight acre stockade overlooking the Maumee River, peer into the gloomy interiors of the log blockhouses and cast your mind back to the heroes who held this fort against a far superior force. Guides in period costume explain the actions which took place, and demonstrate some of the crafts of the time. [Hours and other details on page 48].

Escape Routes-The Old Road to Florida: By now, you will have noticed that our maps show roads that parallel I-75 (brown roads) and how they interconnect with I-75 exits. These are extremely useful should the interstate become affected by an accident. You will know how and where to get off I-75 to bypass such traffic problems - now that's the power of *"local knowledge."*

In using these "escape" routes, please note that they are not necessarily to scale on the east/west axis, across the map.

Most of these "escape" routes follow the tra-

ditional north-south route used by Florida snowbirds long before I-75 was constructed, the-*"Old Dixie Highway."* In some stretches, the interstate was built right on top of the old route but you can still follow the *"Old Dixie"* when US25 (in the North), and US411, US41 and US19(in the South) parallel the interstate.

Mile 186-RWIS: I bet you thought that the road surface beneath your wheels was just that–a road surface. Wrong! In this section of Ohio, and in sections north of Cincinnati and on Atlanta's I-75 in Georgia, the road surface acts as part of a giant input device which feeds information to traffic computers. Wire loops in the road record traffic information; cameras and other roadside devices send other types of data to a central computer.

This is all part of Ohio's multi-million dollar Traffic Information System (OTIS).

In fact, you are just about to pass one of the input devices at mile marker 186. The pole with the weather vane and wind cups (known as an anemometer) in the median strip and the coils of wire you've just passed over are gathering information and sending it electronically to the Road and Weather Information System (RWIS), all part of OTIS.

By the way, if you missed the sensor at this mile marker, you have a chance to see another one in the median strip just after exit 168.

Mile 183-Wind Farm: If the day is clear, look to the southwest between mile markers 183-182 and you might see the four huge towers and wind blades of the Bowling Green Wind Farm in the far distance. Each of these efficient three-bladed wind turbines produce 1.8 mega-watts of electricity when rolling. The towers are 256ft high and the blades are 134ft in length. Costing $2.4 million, each turbine can provide sufficient power for 900 homes.

INSIDER TIP - Cracker Barrel's Talking Books

Tired of the radio and need something different to pass the time as you drive? Then stop at the nearest Cracker Barrel Store *(see our maps for the closest "Cracker Barrel" exit to you)* and rent a tape or CD–yes ... Cracker Barrel now has some of the books on CDs–from their "Book on Audio" program. Pay for it–take it with you and after you've finished listening to it, drop it off at the next Cracker Barrel stop on your journey. Your total cost if you return it within a week? Three dollars & forty-nine cents!

Here's how the Cracker Barrel tape\CD-book program works. Go to the revolving stand in any Cracker Barrel store (usually just beside the counter) and choose the audio book you want. You pay Cracker Barrel the full price (marked on the tape\CD), and they give you a special receipt for this amount. After enjoying the book on your journey you stop at another Cracker Barrel, turn the audio-book in and receive your money back less $3.49 (per week) to cover the rental. A great way to catch-up with the "bestsellers."

To get a closer look (the Farm has become quite a tourist attraction), take exit 179 along Route 6. Although 6 miles west of I-75, you will see the huge wind towers long before you have reached the Farm.

Exit 181-BGSU: As we run southward, we pass the stadium and campus of Bowling Green State University. Founded in 1914, BGSU has developed into a major college campus of more than 100 buildings spread over 1,300 acres, and providing a diversity of programs to approximately 18,000 students.

Exit 179-Snook's Dream Cars: Believe it or not you will find a 1940s era Texaco gas sta-

tion less than a mile to the east of this exit. What started as a hobby for Bill Snook and his son, Jeff, has turned into a wonderful living museum of vintage automobiles and memorabilia, and a restored 1930s general store. See the colored maps for simple directions. If you love the 1940s and old cars, you'll love Snook's! [Daily, 11-4p; Adults/Snrs/Child, $5/$4/$3; ☎ 419-353-8338].

Milepost 178-Ohio Traveler Information Centers: I always make a point of pulling into the TIC at mile 178 and say "hello" to the knowledgeable counter staff of Blanca, Mindy and Quinn. Northbounders, say *"hi"* to Rose, Mary and Kate.

Incidentally, while here look for the marker designating Ohio's stretch of I-75 as the *"Pearl Harbor Memorial Highway,"* in memory of the many Americans who fought and died during the surprise attack.

Milepost 178-Interstate Defense System: As you pulled into the rest area, you may have noticed a historical marker which refers to the interstate as the *"National System of Interstate and Defense Highways."*

Here's the story behind this long title:

Just after World War I, the War Department in Washington wanted to "wave the flag" and thank the people of America who had generously supported the war effort in many ways. The Department decided that a "train" of America's military might—tanks, trucks, field guns—driven 3,251 miles across the continent from Washington to San Francisco would be

a suitable event. Named the Trans-Continental Motor Truck Trip, the convoy consisting of 79 vehicles & 282 men, would visit various towns on the way and give the public a closer view of the equipment which had help win the European war.

They turned to a young lieutenant colonel in the Tank Corps to lead this mission which he did with much enthusiasm. The convoy set off on July 7, 1919 and arrived on the Coast 62 days later.

From the first day, the expedition was a disaster. Heavy vehicles collapsed many wooden rural bridges and trucks were frequently mired to the axles in mud. Two months after the journey started, the convoy limped into Oakland, California–an average speed of 6 mph. Nine vehicles were so badly damaged they couldn't complete the trip.

The officer recorded in his memoirs,
"efforts should be made to get our people interested in producing better roads."

Others were also concerned about the state of the nation's roads and in the late 1930's during Roosevelt's administration, legend has it that during a meeting with the chief of the Bureau of Public Roads (the forerunner of the Federal Highway Administration), the President took a map of North America, drew equidistant three lines across the nation and three north-south lines ... and then handed the map over so roads could be built as indicated!

Finally, plans were being laid for a national grid of high speed freeways.

And then came World War II. The young Lt. Colonel who led the 1919 convoy had risen in rank and had become the Supreme Allied Commander with responsibility for coordinating the invasion of "Fortress Europe." He and his generals watched Hitler's ability to rapid-

A typical "road" from the cover of 1919 *Better Roads Magazine*

ly deploy his troops via the German superfreeway Autobahn system.

The commander of course, was Dwight Eisenhower who in 1953 became President of the United States. On June 29, 1956–the "official birth date" of the Interstate system–he signed legislation creating a *"National System of Interstate and Defense Highways"* – an extensive multi-lane limited-access freeway system designed not only to move people quickly from one place to another, but serve as a vital element of defense during a national emergency, so armies can swiftly move along its arteries.

Urban section of a 1950s interstate

Today however, the public at large is the beneficiary of what has become a miracle of modern engineering–the largest coordinated public works program in the entire history of mankind.

Defense isn't entirely forgotten though; sections of interstates have been designed to serve as tactical airstrips during times of crisis. During the 1960's, there was a concern that Soviet forces might attempt an invasion of the US mainland via Cuba. Sections of I-75 in lower Georgia would have been converted to airstrips to help meet this threat.

Incidentally, let me lay one myth about interstate highways to rest. There is absolutely no truth to the persistent rumor that one out of every five miles of freeway must be straight to accommodate the possibility of aircraft landings. It just isn't so. The rumor was born out of a study made in the 1950s to see if this was feasible. It wasn't and so the requirement was never designed into the freeway system.

Prior to the Interstate System, traveling long

EISENHOWER INTERSTATE SYSTEM

The familiar blue and white interstate logo, honoring President Eisenhower

distances could be painful; a trip from Detroit to Florida would take 5 to 6 days. Primary roads did not always go in straight lines–they often meandered around the countryside. Frequently they were single lane and at every community along the way,

traffic lights, stop signs and local cross traffic slowed the journey. Today, however, I-75 makes the drive to Florida a comfortable & pleasant experience.

Exits 167, 164 & 157-Ancient Ridge Highway: As the ancient Lake Maumee slowly receded to existing lake levels, it left beach ridges and sand dunes which can still be seen. Since these were on high ground, the Indians used the ridges for their trails through areas such as the Black Swamp. Pioneers cut their paths on top of Indian tracks, and these eventually evolved into the early roads and then the highways of today. I-75 crosses three highways which have been built on the backs of ancient Lake Maumee beach ridges–Route 18 at Exit 167, Route 613 at Exit 164, and Route 12 at Exit 157.

Exit 161-I75's Antique Roadshow: Those who watch this popular TV program will know that valuable treasures can still be found hiding among the bric-a-brac of antique malls and flea markets–and I-75 is particularly rich with such places.

To the right at this exit is Jeffrey's Antiques." Home to more than 250 dealers, the mall is over 700 feet long (2 football fields end to end) and occupies 40,000 square feet.

Without a doubt, Jeffrey's is the largest antique marketplace anywhere on I-75 and has an excellent cross-section of stock. Allow at least an 1½ hours to browse and visit all the rooms. [Hrs: 10-6p, daily; ☎ 419-423-7500].

Exit 159-Findlay: This is not exactly on I-75 but since so many people break their journey here, I thought I would mention something that has fascinated me for many years.

Many years ago, because of an accident I was routed off I-75 at this exit and had to drive north on Findlay's Main Street, which is also CR220. That's when I saw it! The most grotesque and yet beautiful Victorian house in the world–best viewed in the evening as the sun is slowly sinking behind it in the west. A perfect Halloween setting– go and judge for yourself.

The house was built in 1883 on part of a 300 acre farm owned by the Bigelow family and has only had a few owners since. It has seven magnificent fireplaces and many of the original gas jets, including one on the staircase newel post shaped like a dragon which breathes actual fire through its nostrils!

The beautiful main staircase of carved butternut wood, curves up to the second story in front of a magnificent stained glass window.

The *"House on the Hill"* is so impressive that master magician David Copperfield used it as a setting for his spectacular "burning house" illusion, in his 1995 TV special.

To find "my" house, take exit 159 east (Trenton Avenue) for 1 mile until you reach Main Street. Turn left at the lights and go north 1 mile until you reach the point just above the Bigelow Avenue traffic lights where Main Street changes from two lanes to one–the house is immediately to your left.

Catch it silhouetted in front of a sinking sun and you'll never forget it.

Some other notes of interest about Findlay. It was originally founded when natural gas was discovered in the area during the 1800's. This period was known as the great Ohio Natural Gas Boom.

Mile 157-The Flag Tank: Findlay also bills itself as *"Flag City, USA"*–a "tip o' the hat" to the patriotism of Findlay's citizens. A drive down Main Street in the summertime will attest to Findlay's claim since virtually every building is dressed with a flag or red, white and blue bunting.

And congratulations to Marathon Oil, whose magnificently painted tank beside I-75 leaves no doubt that Findlay really is *"Flag City."*

Mile 156: Just to the east is the Findlay Municipal Airport, the destination of *Tex Marshall's historic flight* in May, 1920, from Daytona, Florida, to Findlay. Marshall and his wife, Katherine, set off on their epic journey in a *Curtis JN-4D "Jenny"* with inaccurate maps and no set places to land and refuel. Weather became a major factor and they were very lucky to arrive at all.

Mile 153-Dayton's Survey: You might be surprised to see a highway sign announcing that we are 161 kilometers north of Dayton. There's a story here!

Shortly after the American Revolution, the Continental Congress was desperate to raise money since it was close to bankruptcy. How bad was it? Congress was $40 million in debt due to the War, and only had an annual income of $4.5 million. Ironically, with the cessation of hostilities, it had a fortune tied up in land. In fact, Congress was a classic case of *"asset rich and cash poor."*

The answer was to survey the land as quickly as possible so it could be sold and provide a cash flow to the Treasury.

Congress appointed an official Geographer, Thomas Hutchins, whose first task was to plot an east-west "baseline," known as the *"Geographer's Line of the Seven Ranges."*

From this, other lines would be plotted at right angles and the land divided into plots for quick sale.

But there was another problem. Virginian Congressman, Thomas Jefferson wanted to introduce a system of decimalized weights &

INSIDER TIP - Bistro on Main, Findlay

Don't miss this lovely restaurant with its distinctive green awning housed in an old Victorian building on Main Street in Findlay. From the moment you pass under the green awning and enter the warm interior with its mellow wooden booths, etched glass, old brickwork walls and tin ceiling, you know you are in for a treat. But it doesn't stop with the decor. The staff is friendly and welcoming–and the Northern Italian and American food is out of this world.

Owner Sam Fittante has a passion for people. His hospitality is exceptional and as his guests you will no doubt receive a friendly table visit from this affable restaurateur. The menu is extensive. This is fine dining at its best with entrees priced in the $18-$23 range and supported with an excellent wine list. As many know, I love desserts and Sam's Tiramasu, double Truffle cake or chocolate dipped strawberries are very much worth the short trip in from the interstate. Say "hi" to Sam for me.

Bistro on Main is easily reached from I-75 exit 157: travel east along W Main Cross St (Rt37) for 1.2 miles (1.9km) ; turn right onto S. Main St and drive south 1 block. Bistro on your left at number 407. [Hrs: Lunch, M-F, 11-2:30p; Dinner M-Th, 5-10p; F-Sa, 5-11p; closed Sunday ☎ 419-425-4900].

FINDLAY - *after James Findlay and a fort he built in this area during the 1812 War. Findlay later became the Mayor of Cincinnati for two terms and a Brigadier-General with the state militia.*

measures, and standardize them throughout the 13 states before the survey commenced.

But there was no time to waste-the need for money was urgent-and the survey had to be started in 1785, using the only measurement equipment available, the pre-Revolutionary, 100 iron-link Gunter's chain, of 66 feet. In use since 1624, ten chains equaled one furlong, 8 furlongs equaled one mile, and 6 miles equaled one Township.

To speed up the process, Hutchins hired several surveyors. One of these men, Israel Ludlow worked very fast but sacrificed accuracy for speed. Later, his work was described as having *"scarcely two sections of the same shape or of equal content."*

Sadly, Ludlow's survey became the basis for all the original land surveys in the Dayton area (the Miami Purchase) and violent disputes arose between settlers quarreling over the survey boundaries.

Even today, parcels of land in the Dayton area are disputed and it is said that there are more real estate lawyers employed in Miami County than anywhere else in North America.

Incidentally, Hutchins original survey was completed in June, 1787, and when the land went on sale a month later in New York, it only raised $117,108. Dayton land sold for $1/acre, but due to settlers redeeming paper warrants and war service credits, it only contributed about 12¢ an acre in real money.

I often wonder if the *"161 kilometers to Dayton"* sign we just passed was designed by somebody in ODOT, with a love of early settler history ... and a sense of humor.

Mile 150-Foxtrot Delta Yankee: Just to the east of I-75 at mile 150 is a round squat building with radio antennas on top. This is a signpost of sorts–an electronic signpost for aircraft called a VOR, or VHF Omnidirectional Range. It sits there transmitting its identification code, FDY in morse to anyone tuned into its navigation frequency.

Why does it do this? Just as interstates guide our car from city to city, aircraft are guided from place to place along invisible highways in the sky called, "airways." And just as interstates are given "I" numbers, airways are given "V" numbers, and their intersections are marked with VORs and other radio aids to

navigation, to keep the aircraft on course.

For instance, if we were traveling the airroute from Toledo to Cincinnati, which overflies just to the east of I-75 for most of the journey, our flight plan would be as follows:

Take off at Toledo and join the airway V47 at the Victor-Whiskey-Victor VOR–fly 30 miles to the Foxtrot-Delta-Yankee VOR (the one beside you at mile marker 150)–continue airway V47 for 42 miles to Romeo-Oscar-Delta VOR–and continue V47 for 82 miles to the Charlie-Victor-Golf VOR and Cincinnati's air traffic control zone.

As the journey proceeds, the pilot tunes in the frequency of the next VOR on the plane's navigational equipment, and displays indicate the distance away, the bearing towards, and whether the plane is on (or off) course for the next VOR–"highways in the sky."

And now let's step back several hundred years in terms of navigation . . .

Mile 142-Yesterday's Virginia: What a difference a few hundred years make. If it had been possible to travel the I-75 route southward in 1784, you would now be leaving Connecticut and entering Virginia–and after leaving Virginia 300 miles south of here, you would enter the Carolinas before arriving in the Spanish territory of Florida.

According to a map drawn in 1784 by Abel Buell, the four Atlantic states of Connecticut, Virginia, North and South Carolina stretched westward from the sea to the Mississippi River. Territorial disputes led to much of this land being designated as *"Northwest Territory"* (present day Michigan, Indiana, Ohio, Kentucky and Tennessee) in 1787.

Thomas Jefferson, proposed that the land be sliced into fourteen new states, with names such as *Cherronesus, Assenesipia, Illinoia, Michigania* and *Polypotamia.* Congress rejected this proposal however and granted statehood to Kentucky and Tennessee in 1792 and 1796, respectively. In 1803, the eastern part of the remaining Territory gained statehood – with the Iroquois Indian name for beauty–*"Ohio."*

Mile 141-Wildflowers: If you are driving through here in summertime, you cannot help noticing the masses of wildflowers along the banks and median of I-75. Blues, mauves, pinks and whites. Like many other states, Ohio's Department of Transportation has an active wildflower planting program which provides motorists with a rainbow of colors at more than 200 sites throughout the State.

Begun in 1984, the Ohio program now annually plants more than 2,000 pounds of wildflower seed along the roadside. In addition to providing carpets of red, blue and yellow flowers, the program helps preserve native vegetation and reduces costs along the way.

Between mile markers 137 and 138, you'll notice an ODOT sign announcing the Tree Source program, which is a similar initiative–planting trees for Ohio.

Mile 140-Bluffton: I know you are heading south, but as a small break from freeway driving, I'm going to suggest that you head off at exit 140 and drive the short distance west to County Road 313 (S Main St), turn right and drive north through the very pleasant town of Bluffton. There are only a couple of traffic lights so it's a very pleasant drive of about 2.3 miles (3.7km). At the intersection of Jefferson, turn right onto Route 103 to rejoin I-75.

If you have children in the car, don't miss *Grove's Bears*, the teddy bear store on the corner of Main and Jefferson. Just around the corner is also an interesting wall painting.

Mile 133-Old Lincoln Highway: On an overpass above us is US Highway 30–the Granddaddy of all of our super-roads–the old *"Lincoln Highway."*

It's the route which taught young 29 year old Dwight Eisenhower that America's roads were inadequate for heavy transportation *(see "The Interstate Defense System"–page 70).* The first of the trans-continental roads, it was originally a Dutch settler's trail called the *"Old Plank Road"* starting near Philadelphia and linking with Indian paths through Ohio and the midwest. It connected with the Oregon Trail in the Platte Valley and then ran through the mountains and past Salt Lake for the Overland Stage Route into California.

In 1912, Carl Fisher, a visionary from Indianapolis, tried to raise funds to develop this route into the first proper road across the nation–but little progress was made. Eventually, Fisher's dream came true as the Federal Government began its freeway building program, and the Old Lincoln Highway became the US 30 and I-80, a continuous modern route from Philadelphia to San Francisco.

Exit 127-US Plastics Corp: As you approach exit 127, you cannot miss the huge US Plastics Corporation plant on the right-hand side of the interstate. We decided to go in and have a closer look, and found ourselves in an incredible world of plastic. The US Plastics retail outlet covers 18,000 square feet and according to one of their sales staff, has the largest assortment of plastic goods in the world. If you have a plastic product need–no matter how unusual–you will probably find it here.

To reach US Plastics, go west at exit 127 and turn right on to Neubrecht Road. Run north parallel to I-75 for ½ mile and US Plastics is on your right. It's well signposted. [Hrs, M-F, 8:30-5p; ☎ 800-537-9724 or 419-228-2242].

Mile 124 -Lima's Kryptonite Room: A mile or so to the west of I-75 is a manufacturing factory of General Dynamics Land Systems Division, the Lima Army Tank Plant (LATP). Here they build, arguably the best army tank in the world–the famed M1 Abrams Main Battle Tank.

In his excellent book, *"Armored Cav,"* Tom Clancy takes us for a tour of the plant and gives insight into the manufacturing processes. Based on a British innovation called Chobham armor, the M1's outer shell uses interleaved layers of high quality steel alloys and ceramic. But that's not all, using a secret "black art" process in the Kryptonite room, a layer of depleted uranium is somehow bound to the armor shell, more than doubling its effectiveness. Superman would be proud!

LATP also builds the hull portion of what is another awesome machine –the 8 wheeled Stryker Combat Vehicle. With the upper deck built in London, Ontario, and the final assembly in Anniston, Alabama, this 19 ton assault vehicle greatly enhances the safety and speed

---

LIMA - *pronounced "lime-uh"...although named after Lima, Peru (pronounced "lee-mer")*

WAPAKONETA - *possibly named for the distinguished daughter of a Shawnee Chief.*

PIQUA - *the French explorer derivation of the name of a local Shawnee Indian tribe, from which the famous Indian Chief Tecumseh rose to fame.*

at which the US military is able to deploy on the battlefield.

Exit 118-Historic Cabin: In Cridersville, just 2/10ths of a mile west of here is the love-

Bowsher 1836 Cabin

ly 1836 log cabin built by Daniel Bowsher, one of the earliest settlers in this area. Furnished in the pioneer lifestyle of the 1830s, it is open from May-October, first & third Sundays, between 1-5p.

Miles 116 to 91-Ohio's Ice Age: During a winter drive, a glance out of the window at the snow laden landscape gives a sense of what it must have been like during the Pleistocene Ice Age. At that time, huge glaciers rumbled southward from Canada dragging boulders, rocks and other debris which slowly ground the Ohio countryside down under their massive weight. As the earth warmed and the glaciers melted and receded, the rubble was left in large ridges known as "end moraines"–gigantic piles of debris which were slowly assimilated into the surrounding landscape. The interstate between Lima and Piqua is rich with such moraines–a good view of a typical glacial moraine can be seen by looking behind your car and to the right (northward) at Mile 114.

Mile 114-Portable Potty Heaven: The facilities at this rest area have been closed and the area designated as *"truck parking,"* although we have seen RVs and cars pull in there for a rest stop. Portable toilet units have been installed for the desperate. The next *real* toilet facility is another 33 miles south (53km) although I note there is a McDonalds in three miles at Wapakoneta exit 111.

Exit 111-Neil Armstrong Air & Space Museum: If you are in your 30s, I am sure you remember the hazy TV pictures on July 20, 1969, of Neil Armstrong climbing down the ladder of the Lunar Exploration Module, "Eagle," and saying–*"That's one small step for a man; one giant leap for mankind."* Neil Armstrong was the first human to set foot on the moon.

Neil was born and raised at 601 West Benton St. (now a private residence), Wapakoneta, just to the west of I-75. Here as a boy, he built model aircraft and worked part-time delivering for the local pharmacy.

Today, there is a magnificent museum just to the west of I-75, to honor his achievements and showcase exhibits from America's space program. Built by the state of Ohio, the museum is housed in the low gray concrete building that looks like it has a white golf ball on top. Inside, there are seven galleries devoted to the history of space exploration. Exhibits include moon rock and meteorite samples, rocket engines, space suits, actual space rockets and spacecraft.

A special display records the early days of space exploration, including many personal items and Russian space artifacts.

Aspiring astronauts can try their hand at the new space shuttle landing simulator. This unit uses computer programs designed to help train the shuttle crew. After a short training session, you take over the controls and have command of the shuttle on its final approach.

The Neil Armstrong Air and Space Museum is very easy to find. Simply take exit 111 west; turn right at the first road and you are in the museum parking area. [Hrs: Tu-Sa, 9:30-5p; Sun & Holidays, noon-5p; Closed Monday.; Adults/Snrs/ Child-$7/$6.50/$3; ☎ 800-860-0142 or 419-738-8811]

Exit 110-A Great RV Park: It's been a few years since I headed off on an RV trip but I remember enough to recognize an above average campsite when I see one. John and Debbie Schuettler, the owners of the *Wapakoneta KOA*, run an excellent campsite; I heartily recommend it. Non-RVers, they have 6 cabins available–a great change to a night at a motel.

Miles 104 to 99-Lost River Teays: Ohio is rich in ancient geological history. Between these mile markers, you are crossing the lost River Teays–a major North American river of pre-glacial times with a valley as deep as 400 feet deep below the present position of the I-75. But the glaciers spelled its death. The rubble they dragged along blocked the course of the Teays, burying the valley and erasing it from the landscape forever.

Mile 88-The M&E: A few pages ago, I mentioned the invisible "highways in the sky" – the "airways" used to guide commercial aircraft. For several miles now, I-75 has been paralleling a much older transportation system and just before crossing the Great Miami River Bridge, we traversed the abandoned and dried course of the Miami & Erie feeder canal from Sidney. This branch used to join the Miami and Erie canal just above Piqua.

The Marguerite II - a typical narrow canal barge

Opened in 1841, the M&E canal system provided valuable barge transportation between Lake Erie at Toledo and the Ohio River at Cincinnati–a distance of 250 miles–but the growth of much faster railroad transportation (horse drawn barges averaged 3 mph) spurred on by the needs of the Civil War, quickly made canals obsolete.

Capacity and speed of delivery have always been the main keys driving the constant improvement in transport systems, whether carrying goods or people. Consider the much greater capacity of a horse drawn canal barge over a horse drawn cart, it's little wonder that canal routes were built as rapidly as possible when the only alternative was the horse and buggy.

And then along came the steam locomotive with its network of railroads, and of course far greater capacity and delivery speed than the canal barge. The canal era was over.

Mile 87-Lockington: To the west lies the small village of Lockington. Here you will find impressive remains of the five Lockington Locks which in the mid-19th century lowered canal barges 67 feet within 1/2 mile. Today, the stone walls remain in almost original condition.

Unfortunately, although so close to the interstate (about a mile away), there is no easy access from I-75 other than through various

county roads running west from exits 90 or 82. I've added these roads to the colored maps (brown lines) so if you feel adventurous, leave the interstate at either of these exits and head over to Lockington.

Exit 82-The Mills Brothers: John Jr., Herbert, Harry F.and Donald F. Mills were born in Piqua. Their famous "sound" started when, during a talent contest at the Piqua Mays Opera House, Harry discovered that he had lost his kazoo and, cupping his hands around his mouth, imitated a trumpet. *"Paper Doll"* and *"Glow Worm"* are among their international hits.

Exit 78-The Eldean Covered Bridge: If you would like a diversion from the interstate, let's go and visit another of Ohio's covered bridges. It's only a mile or so out of our way.

Eldean Covered Bridge was built in 1860 to cross the Great Miami River; its 224 foot span makes it the second longest covered bridge still in use in Ohio (the longest is in Brown Co.) To reach the bridge, go east of I-75 on CR25A South (past the Medical Center and towards Troy). In 1.6 miles (2.6km, just past concrete silos on the right), turn left on to CR33 (Eldean Road)–the bridge is ahead.

After, you can either backtrack the 1.8 miles to I-75 or continue down CR25A to return to I-75 via Victorian Troy (see map on next page). If this is your choice then continue south on CR25A.

Exit 74-Troy: What a perfect place to stop for lunch. Take this exit and drive east for 1.7 miles (2.7km). Here you will find Troy town square with many historical buildings listed on the National Register of Historical Places, such as the lovely red brick Dye building, fronted with the fountain and flower beds. Where Market Street meets the Square are some excellent restaurants and antique & collectible shops. Ample parking can be found along the roads or in the open parking areas at the corners of the Square. Go and visit *Leo & Michael* at the upscale *La Piazza Pasta & Grill*, share a joke with *Karen ("Cookie")* at the *O'Brian Pub*, enjoy *Margaret's* fresh

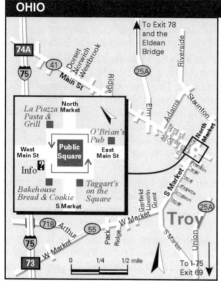

drive along the pleasant Main Street of Tipp City (Old Tippecanoe), with its many antique & craft shops, cafes and 89 historical buildings. If you have a chance, pick up a copy of the *"Visitors Walking Tour"* map from the Information Kiosk at 12 East Main.

Tipp City is another 1840s M&E Canal town and when you reach the river just past First St, you'll see a canal "narrow" boat, the *Marguerite II*, on the left, in a small grassy park where you can turn around.

This short drive is a very pleasant diversion from I-75, and will take less than 5 minutes if you don't stop and shop.

Mile 67-Dayton Traffic: Turn on your car radio to 1290AM and get a Dayton traffic report if you can. Check to see if traffic is slow around the I-70/I-75 Interchange.

bread sandwiches at the *Bakehouse Bread & Cookie Co.* (there is none better!), and savor the gourmet dishes of *Chef Joyce* at *Taggart's On The Square*. Say *"hi"* to them for me (and don't believe one word of what Karen says!).

The Miami County Visitors Bureau is located at 405 SW Public Square, Suite 272 [☎ 800-348-8993] pick up their map of the downtown area–and stroll around for a while.

Once back in your car, leave the Square via Market Street (Route 55), and drive in a southwest direction towards I-75 exit 73.

Exit 68-Tipp City: A mile is all it takes to

If traffic is busy, get off the interstate at exit 64 or 63, and drive south through the small town of Vandalia on the old Dixie Highway *(see map page 14)*. It's an easy drive. After 4.5 miles (7.2km), watch for Needmore Rd. Cross Needmore and Wagoner roads, watch for easy to see I-75 signs. Follow I-75 South and rejoin the interstate at exit 56 (Stanley).

Exit 63-Ohio's Historical National Road: We are just passing US Route 40 which has been designated a Historical National Road.

George Washington and Thomas Jefferson believed that a trans-Appalachian road was essential for expanding the young nation and

---

INSIDER TIP - Tippecanoe Frontier Trading Company

When you walk through the door of the Tippecanoe Frontier Trading Company at Tipp City, you will quickly realize you have traveled back in time. Old lanterns hang from the ceiling, wall racks hold swords and flintlock guns and a sign in the window announces that black powder cartridges are available. In a corner is a tub of lye soap beside a rack of men and women's 1700 style clothing. From old Indian arrows to hunting knives, gun flints and musket balls, this store

has everything for the frontier country.

No, it's not a museum; it's a real frontier trading company and everything is for sale. Owner Mara, says that she specializes in the 1700-1840 and 1870 to 1898 eras, mainly for re-enactors, but anybody can shop there. I was surprised how reasonably priced many of the reproduction items were. For instance, men's American Revolutionary shirts and breeches are about $45; women's long dresses of the same era are about $60.

For anybody with a love of American frontier history, a stop at this store is a must.

At I-75 exit 68 (Tipp City), go east for about 8/10ths mile (1.3km); the store is on your right at 114 E Main. [Hrs: Tu-F, 10-6p; Sat, 10-5p; close Sun-Mon; ☎ 937-667-1816].

in 1806, their dreams were realized when a road was constructed (the first road to be federally funded) running from Maryland to the Ohio River. US 40 is the later extension of this route and now runs to the border of Illinois. Today, the route has been designated as one of significant historic value.

USAF museum visitors: ignore the brown roadside signs instructing you to take exit 61. There is a much better "local" route to the museum; it's shorter and avoids heavy traffic. Just follow my map and details on page 49.

Exit 61 I-70/I-75 Interchange: Built in the late 1960s, $145 million is being spent on a three phase construction project to transform this exit into one of the safest and most modern interchanges in the Nation. Phase II has been completed and the final phase to rebuild the exit and entrance ramps is underway.

South of the interchange, note the interesting Wright Brother bas-relief on the retaining walls beside the northbound lanes.

Exit 60-It's gone!: Welcome to Exit 59. As part of the Interchange redesign described above, it was necessary to change a few of the exits in this area. One historical name which has disappeared with these changes is *"Stop 8"* road. Familiar to many old-timer "snowbirds," this was the eighth stoplight on the old Dixie Highway, on the way south to Florida. Stoplights 1 to 7 disappeared many years ago.

Exit 59: Known locally as the *Miller Lane* exit, has picked up much of the business which used to be reached by exit 60. Miller Lane is actually a sideroad running parallel to I-75, from exit 59 (Benchwood Rd) to exit 58 (Needmore Rd). It has arguably, the largest cluster of restaurants and lodging services to be found on I-75. Many of these properties are new, meaning that there are some excellent overnight bargains here as the businesses build their guest lists. And of course, dining at your choice of just about any major restaurant is just a minute or so away.

Dayton and the Wright Brothers: In 2003, we celebrated the 100th Anniversary of the Brothers famous first powered flight–120 feet in length and 12 seconds in duration–at Kitty Hawk, in North Carolina.

But it is really a Dayton, Ohio story since this is where the brothers went to school, grew up and as young men discovered the principles behind "heavier than air" flight. This is where they ran their printing and bicycle businesses, and where they built their famous Wright

Flyer which was then taken to pieces and transported to Kitty Hawk for its 1903 flight.

Why was Kitty Hawk chosen? According to a report written by Orville Wright in 1920, the Brothers decided upon Kitty Hawk for their experiments after consultation with the US Weather Bureau, looking for the *"windiest place in the country."*

It was here at Dayton where the Wright Brothers developed by experimentation the principles of flight, built practical airplanes capable of sustained and steerable flight, the first airport, the first permanent flying school and the first airplane factory.

Exit 58 (N/bound-54C)-National Museum of the USAF: *(see Dayton map with Museum information on page 49).* You must visit this awesome museum if you have any interest in flight. Nearly 350 military aircraft and missiles fill its four huge halls, and range from very early wooden biplanes to the most modern non-secret and experimental aircraft–and admission is absolutely free!

When you arrive, make sure that you go to the Information Desk in the main hall and ask about reservations to visit the *Presidential Gallery.* This fabulous collection includes many of the aircraft used by the nation's first executives, including *Air Force One* which flew JFK back from his fateful Dallas trip. You can actually go aboard many of these famous aircraft. The Gallery however, is located on the airbase and because of security restrictions, you are taken there by bus. If you want to see this outstanding collection of historic aircraft, you must make a reservation as soon as you arrive at the Museum. Seating is limited.

Another gallery requiring reservations since it is also located on airbase, is the *Research & Development/Flight Test Hangar.* It includes the world's only *XB-70 "Valkerie"* bomber on public display.

The Museum continues to expanded its facilities. The extra space gives you a much better appreciation of each aircraft and has allowed

---

INSIDER TIP
Favorite Miller Lane Lodgings

In the past last year, Kathy and I have really enjoyed the following Miller Lane (exits 59-58) lodgings ... ❋ *Hampton Inn & Suites*, GM Larry, ☎ 937-387-0598, and ❋ *Country Inns & Suites*, GM Sital, ☎ 937-937-890-1221. We highly recommend them both.

the staff to add dioramas and other small displays of particular interest to specific aircraft. The latest display area is the Missile and Space Gallery. Here you can get "up-close" to a number of famous InterContinental Ballistic Missiles (ICBMs).

Let's have a quick look at the other museum galleries and display areas:

The _Early Years Gallery_ features many aircraft from the "pioneer of flight" days, through WWI and on through the 1930s into WWII–from the Wright 1909 Military Flyer, Bleriot monoplane to a superb British WWII Hawker Hurricane. A huge barrage balloon brought memories of a wartime childhood on the southeast coast of England, flooding back to me. A recent addition to this gallery is a WWI Spad XIII fighter, in mint condition.

The _Air Power Gallery_ tells the World War II story, from the European and Pacific theaters, to China-Burma-India and of course, the home front.

Next is the _Modern Flight Gallery_ with aircraft from the Korean Conflict and War in Vietnam eras, to the present. Here you will find classics such as the _F86 Sabrejet_ and the latest modern aircraft such as the _YF-22,_ prototype of the F/A-22 Raptor.

As you enter the last hangar, the _Cold War Gallery_, you cannot help but be impressed by its 200,000 sq.ft. The space is dominated by the massive _B-36J,_ the largest bomber ever built–but it is the spaceship appearance of the _B2 stealth bomber_ just inside the door which will probably capture your attention.

Walk through the gallery past the _thermonuclear bomb_ sitting insidiously on its cradle, and view an _F-117 stealth fighter_, _B-1B "Lancer"_ bomber, the awesome _SR-71 "Blackbird"_ and a _U-2 spy plane._

Thermo-Nuclear Bombs – Cold War Gallery

Throughout the museum complex, you will find other special exhibits such as the tribute to _Bob Hope_. Here you can sit and watch him entertaining the troops overseas.

Everyone should visit the _Holocaust Exhibit_. Chillingly, you enter it under the stark wrought iron sign–_"Arbeit Macht Frei"_ meaning _"Work Brings Freedom."_ Nazi Rudolph Hess required that these words be installed over the entrance gates of Auschwitz, and other concentration camps. Beyond is a very rare concentration camp uniform, which was worn by prisoner 114600 Moritz Bomstein.

In another section, a _VE Day_ diorama shows bomb ruins in Berlin. Amidst the rubble lies a golden eagle with its outspread wings–the icon of the Nazi party. This eagle was one of two which stood either side of the entrance to Hitler's office in the Reich Chancellery. Several feet away, is a battered bust of Hitler, with bullet holes through the head.

WWII Luftwaffe Junker 52 Transport

Veterans from the European theater of WWII, shouldn't miss the _Nissen Hut_ and _Control Tower_ exhibits just outside the main museum building. As you enter the hut, you walk into a briefing for a bomb run over Germany–a very authentic visual and sound presentation.

Finally, it's time to rest your feet and enjoy the awesome experience of the _IMAX Theater_. With its high six-story, wide screen, you feel as if you are actually strapped into the cockpit and it is here that you can come the closest to experiencing flight as you fly a helicopter on a mercy mission in Europe or fly as a passenger with the Blue Angels. [Museum, see page 49 for details].

Huffman Prairie Flying Field: Two miles (3.2km) to the east of the Museum is the National Park Service _Huffman Prairie Flying Field Interpretive Center_ and the _Wright Brothers Memorial._

Huffman Prairie was the field where the Wright Brothers conducted most of their post-Kitty Hawk flights. They made hundreds of flights from here and also ran a flying school training the first military flyers for the US Army Signal Corps.

While there, make sure you chat with Ranger Bob; he's very knowledgeable about the early days of flight and loves to share his Wright Brother stories with visitors to the shop.

From the national USAF museum, turn right onto Springfield Pike. Go to 2nd traffic light and turn right on to Kauffman Road, and then immediately right into the first driveway;the park entrance is on your right. [Open all year, daily, 8:30-5p; ☎ 937-425-0008].

Mile 56: For an easy drive through Dayton, just follow the white lane markings on the road–*"I-75 through City."* The bad news is that their white paint does not show up on a snowy winter surface.

Mile 55-Dayton Inventors: Dayton must be the #1 city in the World for inventors; if society needed it–it was probably invented here. The downtown RiverScape Park, located where Dayton's five rivers meet (Twin Creek, Wolf Creek, Great Miami, Mad and Stillwater), honors many of these inventors with gold stars set into the park's paths.

So what did these Dayton inventors invent? Of course, you already know about the Wright Brothers inventing powered flight, but how about Dayton's other inventors and these everyday items: parking meters (ugh!), office building mail chutes, parachute, cash register, pull tab & pop top soda cans, microfiche, stepladder, cellophane tape, movie projector, ice cube tray, gas mask, auto starter motor,

The original 1905 Wright Flyer III, now housed at Dayton's Carillon Park

price tag machine ... and the list goes on.

Exit 54B-Dayton Art Institute & Jonathan Winters: *(see map on page 49)* While driving through here I must mention the Dayton Art Institute–the beautiful red tile-roofed, warm stone Romanesque building you see to your right just north of this exit. It's well worth a visit–free parking, free admission and world-class special exhibitions. I particularly enjoy the incredible beauty of the modern glass sculptures in the *Eileen Dicke Gallery of Glass*-each piece is dramatically displayed with hidden lights. My favorite? *"Bold Endeavor"* by Jon Kuhn.

Incidentally, *comedian Jonathan Winters* (remember Ma Fricker) lived in an apartment just behind the Institute. He studied art and met his wife, Eileen, here. Later, Winters entered a local talent contest and as a result, started working as an early morning disc jockey at local radio station, WING.

[Hrs, Daily 10-4, Th-F, open to 8p; Admission-free; ☎ 937-223-5277].

Exit 53-Wright Welcome Center: *(see map on page 49)*. A visit to the Wright Welcome Center is a must for those following the footsteps of the famous brothers. Located at 22 Williams Street, the center is housed in one of the original buildings used by the Wrights for their printing business, and includes a 1900s grocery shop on the street level and the Wright's print shop on the second. The information desk on the ground floor is an excellent place to start your visit to the Wrights' Dayton. Say "hi" to Ranger Judi for me... and don't forget the gift shop.

Next door is the building used by the Wrights as one of their bicycle shops. It's hard to imagine that this small red-brick 19th century building with its original wood plank flooring, located on a quiet Dayton side street was the birthplace of aviation. And yet this is where, from 1895 to 1897, Orville and Wilbur

22 Williams Street

ran their printing and bicycle repair business in the day–and by evening's oil-lamp light developed the concepts of powered flight.

The second of four locations for the brothers' bicycle business, it was here they read about experiments in Germany, analyzed and rejected the concepts involved, designed and built a wooden wind tunnel with which they developed a set of radically new pressure tables and started drafting what would eventually be the first flying machine, the Wright Flyer 1.

The Wright Welcome Center is administered by the National Park Service as part of the Dayton Aviation Heritage National Historical Park. [Hrs: daily 8:30a-5p, ☎ 937-225-7705].

1127 West Third St–the Wright Brothers moved here from 22 Williams, in 1897 and occupied the premises until 1916. While continuing their bicycle business, they continued research into flight and on these premises built their kites, gliders and the first flying machine–the Wright Flyer 1–which was successfully flown at Kitty Hawk, NC, on December 17, 1903.

In 1936, the building was acquired by Henry Ford, who moved it to the Henry Ford Museum & Greenfield Village, in Dearborn, MI, where it is open to public display.

7 Hawthorn Street–the Wright family home from 1869-1878 and 1885-1914. Bishop Milton Wright and his wife, Susan, purchased this new home in 1869, and raised their family of 4 boys and a girl. It was here that Bishop Wright brought home a small flying top toy which motivated Wilbur and Orville's interest in flight.

This building was also acquired by Henry Ford, and can now be visited at the Greenfield Village, in Dearborn, MI.

Incidentally, all these Wright Brother sites are all within a couple of blocks of each other, and only a few minutes from I-75.

Designed by Orville Wright, The *John W*

Berry Sr. Wright Bros Aviation Center is located in Carillon Park *(see below)*. After walking through a faithful replica of the 1127 W Third St Bicycle Shop, and enjoying a multimedia movie about flight, you enter a hall housing the actual 1905 Wright Flyer III–the world's first practical airplane which was flown at Huffman Prairie.

The Brothers felt that this was their most definitive craft since it could not only sustain heavier-than-air flight for a long time but it was completely maneuverable. This is the only airplane which has been recognized as a National Historic Landmark.

As with the other local Wright Brother sites, the Carillon Park Aviation Center is administered by the Dayton Aviation Heritage National Historical Park.

Exit 51-Carillon Historical Park: *(see map on page 49)* Carillon Historical Park is a "feast" of historic Ohio buildings and transportation exhibits, arranged in a bygone street scene. Twenty-five buildings include the 1796 Newcom Tavern, gristmill, covered bridge, 1924 gas station, canal office & locks, 1894 railroad station and vintage vehicles dating back to 1835. Culp's Cafe, a 1930s era restaurant serving soup & sandwiches.

All the buildings are open to the public and suitably equipped and furnished. Each is staffed by knowledgeable guides who enjoy demonstrating some of the machines and relating to life at that time.

The exhibits are diverse–from early transportation such as locomotives and luxury passenger cars, canals, bicycles, automobiles, to many of the major inventions created by area entrepreneurs, such as the famous Barn Gang who, with Charles Kettering, invented the electric starter for automobiles.

[The park is now open year round; Hrs, M-Sa, 9:30-5p; Su & Holidays, noon-5p; Adult/ Seniors/Children-$8/$7/$5; ☎ 937-293-2841].

Model of the 1903 Wright Flyer 1, built and owned by the author

Exit 50-Shawnee War Parties: Two hundred years ago you would be in the heart of Indian country, for the main Shawnee camp of Old Chillicothe lay on the banks of the Little Miami River, just thirteen miles (21km) to the east. The Shawnee were the most fierce of the Ohio tribes. Their war parties ranged the countryside down to the mountains in South Kentucky (Cherokee lands), often attacking the white settlers who were invading their lands from the east.

In 1778, the famous frontiersman Daniel Boone was captured by the Shawnee Chief Black Fish, and for four months lived as a member of the Shawnee tribe at Little Chillicothe. Learning of an Indian plan to attack his home at Boonesborough (just east of exit 95 in Kentucky) he escaped and made his way through the country alongside today's I-75 route, to warn the Boonesborough settlers.

Mile 41.3: If you look to the east (your left if southbound), you will see the hangar where the 1909 Wright Flyer "B"–built for the US Army Signal Corp–is kept. Several years ago, I was fortunate to take the controls of this early flying machine while in the air, an awesome experience.

Exit 38-Crafter's Heaven: (parking not suitable for large RVs) It would probably be easier to list all handcraft supplies that are not carried–leathercraft and woodworking, for instance–but supplies for virtually everything else can be found in this huge warehouse retail outlet just west of the interstate.

Pick up a free catalog just inside the door–and if you are reading it in your motel room that evening and find something else you need–they have a mail order service.

Factory Direct Craft Supply is at 315 Conover Drive. From the exit, turn west on to State Route 73 then left on to Conover Drive. The craft supply outlet is halfway down on the right. [Hrs, M-Sa 9-6p; Su 11-5p; ☎ 937-743-5855].

Mile 30.1-Holy Head: It's impossible to miss. The 62 foot high "sculpture" was commissioned by the evangelical Solid Rock Church and stands in a pond on the organization's roadside 100 acre campus. Made of Styrofoam and fiberglass over a steel frame, the image weighs 16,000 lbs & cost $250,000 to build and install.

The statue known by the Church as *"King of Kings,"* has gained international fame. Irreverently, it has been given other names, such as

"Touchdown Jesus" or *"Help, I'm Sinking."* Incidentally, in a recent poll, 75% of the local residents said they did not like it.

Exit 29-Flea Market Paradise: If you enjoy flea markets, then the northeast and northwest sides of exit 29 must be pure paradise. Trader's World (to the east) and Turtle Creek (to the west) markets are open on weekends from 9-5pm, all year round.

Mile 28-Travelers Information Center (N/bound): Jerome, Sheila and Todd await you at the northbound TIC, ready to help with free Ohio travel information. To find them, go past the restrooms to the center of the building where you will find them "hidden" in a corner. This Center also has a Family restroom–one of only two on I-75.

Mile 24-Voice of America (VOA) & WLW: On your left once stood the tall towers and curtain antenna arrays of the former *VOA Bethany Relay Station.* For more than 50 years, this facility transmitted its signals to the World.

Early photo of VOA Bethany's powerful transmission towers

During WWII, the station played a major part beaming messages of freedom into the heart of Nazi Europe. As you drive by now, it's strange to think that this tiny parcel of land east of I-75 once incensed Hitler so much that he screamed during a Reichstag speech, *"the lying propagandists in Cincinnati."*

Exit 22-Voice of America Center: The new huge *Voice of America* (shopping) *Center* now occupies the lands previously dedicated to the antenna arrays of the Bethany Station. For those who enjoy shopping, all the big-box names are here.

Exit 22-WLW: While on the subject of radio transmitters, I must mention what was once the most powerful radio station in North America–Cincinnati's WLW. Between 1934-39, WLW's transmission tower at Mason, OH (on the ridge about 3 miles (3.2km) east of exit 22) radiated 500,000 watts! This is much more powerful than the 50,000 watt "clear" AM radio stations currently allowed by the FCC, which can easily reach 10-16 states at nighttime. In the 1930s, local residents complained that they could receive WLW on their "water taps" and "fence posts"!

The huge glass valve transmitters generated so much heat that they had to be water cooled and ponds for the cooling outflow were built on the transmitter's premises.

The original 1933 antenna is still in use. Weighing about 135 tons of steel, this massive antenna reaches 747 feet into the sky and is 35 square feet wide at its midpoint.

Mile 25-Cincinnati's Traffic System: The Greater Cincinnati area has implemented the *511 traffic information system* now in use in Kentucky (see page 70). So you can now obtain Cincy traffic information at any time by dialing 511 from any phone (including your cell phone). The service is available on a 24/7 basis, the information is completely up-to-date ... and it's free!

Miles 20 to 14-Ohio's Tropical Sea: You are now traveling across the ancient bed of a warm, shallow tropical sea *(see Geology chart on page 94; Paleozoic Era–Ordovician Period–400 million years ago)*. The shale and limestone outcrops along I-75 are rich in fossils, particularly around Miles 20.5 to 19.5 and 14.8 to 14.3. As the teeming sea life of small animals (examples, trilobites, primitive fish) and other life forms died, they settled to the bottom and slowly over millions of years, became the familiar layered (geologists call it sedimentary) rock that you see in exposed roadside rock cuts on your journey down the I-75. Often, the ancient animals' hard shells and skeletons remained intact in the rock, creating the fossils of today.

One of the best places to find extensive fossil beds is at the Hueston Woods State Park (near Oxford, OH), but this is 22 miles (35km) west

Fossil found in the Cincinnati area while building the interstate

of here. Phone the park office at 513-523-6347 for further information.

Exit 19-Streets of West Chester: Welcome to another new I-75 shopping experience -the *Streets of West Chester*. Here you will find upscale restaurants, boutiques and a Barnes & Noble bookstore.

Mile 16-(Cincinnati Bypass map–page 194).

Exit 14-Hidden Radar: As you approach the concrete pillars of the overpass by exit 14, watch your speed *very* carefully. The pillar near the slow lane soft shoulder is a favorite hiding place for a radar equipped patrol car, beaming its radar gun at oncoming southbound traffic as it leaves the 65 mph zone and enters the 55 mph speed reduction.

Incidentally, Cincinnati monitors its city interstate routes using motorcycle police equipped with radar guns. Motorcycles are much more effective than police cars in urban areas since the officer can sit in the concrete median area beaming back over their shoulder ... and then easily chase through heavy traffic to flag down the offender.

Mile 14-Driving the Old M-E Canal: Few will remember that from mile 14 southward, I-75 actually runs on the bed of the old Miami-Erie Canal (drained in 1910). South of mile 13 where the southbound lanes veer away from the northbound and become separated by high concrete walls (known locally as the *"Lockland Split"*) you are driving in a very old part of the freeway system which has not changed that much over the years. In this area stood the series of canal locks (hence, *"Lockland"*) which once took the barges down to the level of the Ohio River!

The first freeway built here was not I-75, but the *"Wright-Lockland Highway,"* a 1941 WWII project to help Cincinnati workers reach the Wright Aeronautical Plant (now GE Engine Plant) where they built engines for

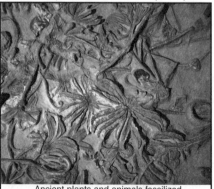
Ancient plants and animals fossilized in an Ohio tropical seabed

RAF fighters and the American B29 bomber.

As I drive through here, I'm often reminded of what it was like to drive I-75 when it was first constructed –as you came around the blind curve of the *"Split"* surrounded by the high walls, you had to be very careful you didn't hit slow traffic pulling into your path from the several gas stations which were still open on the righthand side of the road. A drive through the "Lockland Split" is still very much a "time warp" experience.

Mile 7.3-Ivorydale: One of Cincy's earliest manufactories was the Proctor & Gamble soap making complex to the west. P&G started making white *"Ivory"* soap in 1878, shipping it aboard barges of the Miami-Erie Canal, which docked right behind the factory buildings. The area became known as *"Ivory-dale,"* and in 1900, employed 600 workers.

Off to the west you can see the finely detailed Art Deco building of the St. Bernard Soap Factory. One of the original P&G factory buildings.

To view these buildings close up, take exit 6 and turn right on to Mitchell Ave; turn right on to Spring Grove. The building is at 5177 Spring Grove, about 1 mile from exit 6.

Exit 3-Cincinnati Subway System: If you ask most Cincy folk where you can find the closest subway station, they will probably look at you as if you are crazy. Cincinnati doesn't have a subway ... or does it?

Well actually, it does, but it has been silent

Subway tunnel entrances just before I-75, exit 3

and abandoned since it ran out of money in 1927, before it could be put into operation. In fact, it was so badly in debt that it took until 1966 for the City to make its final payment on the original 1916 $6 million bond issue.

In 1916, the scheme sounded like a good idea. The old M&E canal running down to the Ohio River had been drained and there was a perceived need to build a transportation system to move people out from the downtown area of the Queen City. What would be more logical than to build a railroad on the old canal bed, and burying it!

Eleven miles of the 16 mile subway project–including two miles of downtown tunnels and three stations with platforms–were completed and ready for the track laying crews, before the money ran out.

Some of the finished sections between the River and mile marker 3 were used during Interstate-75's construction, but most of the other sections were abandoned.

Northbound drivers can see the sealed tunnel entrances where the proposed subway right-of-way was to curve off the path of today's freeway and disappear underground, just to their right as they approach Interstate-75's Hopple St, exit 3.

So today, under the streets of Cincinnati lie subway tunnels and stations, and nobody knows what to do with them.

Mile 2-*"Pardon me boy, is this the Cincinnati Choo Choo"*: "*Cincinnati Choo Choo*, Dave ... surely that should be *Chattanooga Choo Choo*?"

Well, actually, no ... but you'll have to wait until we arrive at Chattanooga for me to explain.

Exit 2A (S/bound), 1G (N/bound)-Cincinnati Museum Center: I rarely recommend leaving the interstate in large cities because it is so easy to become lost, but the *Cincinnati Museum Center*, housed in the beautiful 1933 Art Deco Railroad Terminal is not to be missed.

It's really three museums in one–Cincinnati History, hands-on Children's Museum and the Museum of Natural History & Science. The Center includes an OMNIMAX Theater showing the latest in giant screen movies.

I find the *Cincinnati History* galleries the most fascinating of the three. As you step through its doors, you enter *Cincinnati in Motion*–a huge moving and highly detailed model of the city in 1910 with every building in superb detail. For example, I took a photo of the "Ivorydale" St. Bernard Soap building described above and you can actually see the barges being loaded in its rear (see photo below). The detail is really incredible. Streetcars glide down urban streets, locomotives haul freight and passengers along the many railroad tracks and traffic is moving everywhere. There's even an airplane flying overhead. You actually walk through the model so you are surrounded by this city throbbing with miniature life.

Continuing down a tunnel we come out into the dark, starlit ancient hills of prehistoric Ohio and then slowly work our way through time until we step out into a Cincy street of the 1850s. Ahead is a paddle-wheeler being loaded ready for its run down river.

This wonderful museum is well worth the short trip from I-75. To reach the museum: S/bound traffic take exit 2A (Western Ave). N/bound traffic take exit 1G (US50W-River/Linn Sts), take Gest St exit on left, go north to Freeman, then north to Ezzard Charles Dr, turn left museum is at end of road. [Museum Hrs, M-Sa, 10-5p, Su, 11-6p; Adult/Snr/Student/Child-$7.25/$6.25/ $5.25/$4.25; ☎ 513-287-7000; OMNIMAX - ☎ 513-287-7001 for show times and prices].

Mile 1.5-Over-the-Rhine: To the east of the interstate is an important district in Cincinnati. Many German immigrants were attracted to this area in the late 19th Century and called it *"Over-the-Rhine."* It was so popular that by 1900, there were 30 German language newspapers, 48 German churches and a number of traditional beer gardens and singing societies. The annual consumption of German beer among the local populace was 50 gallon per person! *Das ist gut, Ja?*

Exit 1A-National Freedom Center: This

$110 million Museum is located on the north banks of the Ohio River, on the very location where in the 1800s, many fugitives escaped from slavery and set foot on free soil. The Center covers the many discriminatory acts which haunt our history–from the Cherokee *"Trail of Tears,"* to the terrible days of Slavery and later, Segregation. In particular, it helps us understand the secret *Underground Railroad*, the human network which enabled slaves to escape their southern shackles, to the free north states and Canada.

The entire subject is beautifully presented with many interesting and informative displays. It's a very "up beat" experience.

Whatever your color, whatever your ethnic background and whatever your age, this is a "must see" museum for us all.

One word of caution. Normally parking in the Center's vicinity is $4. When a sporting event is scheduled in either of the adjacent stadiums, it increases to a whopping $12. Try and visit on a non sports event day if possible. To find the Center, from I-75 take exit 1A (Downtown-2nd St) & follow signs ⁿ the *Freedom Center*. [Hrs: Tu-Su,   -5p; Adult/Snr/Student/ Child, $12/$10/$10/ 8; ☎ 513-333-7500]

Cincinnati Museum - working model of Ivorydale

THE PROCTER & GAMBLE CO. FACTORIES

CINCINNATI - *settled in 1788 and called Losantiville, the Governor of the then Northwest Territories renamed the village after a Revolutionary War officers' association called the Society of Cincinnati, which in turn was named after Lucius Quinctius Cincinnatus (519 B.C.), a Roman dictator and soldier who was also a keen farmer.*

Mile 0-Escape Across the Ohio: As you cross the busy Brent Spence Bridge, it's hard to imagine how desolate and lonely the river to your left would have been on a wintery night in late January, 1856. It was ... and an historical marker on the south bank of the Ohio records a very tragic event which took place below you, that evening:

"On a snowy night in January, 1856, seventy slaves fled at the foot of Main Street (in Covington, Kentucky) across the frozen Ohio River. A Margaret Garner was in the group. When arrested in Ohio, she killed her little daughter rather than see her returned to slavery. This much publicized slave capture became the focus of national attention because it involved the issues of Federal and State authority"

Here is the story behind the escape.

On that snowy January night, 22 year old freed-slavewoman Margaret Garner, gathered her children and met with twelve other slaves at a nearby church. Here they boarded a horse drawn sled and galloped through the darkness north to Covington, where they crossed the frozen Ohio on foot.

The Garners sought the "safe" house cabin of a friend, but this was their undoing since their "owners" were in hot pursuit and quickly discovered the Garners' whereabouts.

Surrounding the cabin, a battle commenced during which one of the deputies was shot. The door was broken down and seeing no escape, Margaret took a knife and killed her youngest daughter, Mary, so she would no longer have to suffer the horrors of slavery.

The trial that followed raised many legal and moral questions about slave ownership since one of the key arguments was that Margaret and her children were not slaves, but free due to earlier circumstances. Sadly however, the Court's decision was to return her to slavery in Kentucky. She died in 1858, still a slave.

KENTUCKY: Statewide 511: Increasingly, the 511 phone number mandated by the Federal Government for road conditions and travel information is spreading through the I-75 states. Todate, the system is fully implemented statewide in Kentucky (including Cincinnati, OH) and statewide in Florida.

The service is free and can be dialed from any phone within the area for information about local travel. It uses voice-recognition technology but has a live operator over-ride in case you experience difficulty.

It really works. We were able to get traffic conditions on I-75 ahead of us (using a cell phone in the car) while southbound above Lexington and lower in the State near Corbin.

Exits 192-MainStrasse, Hofbräuhaus Newport and the Newport Aquarium: *(Town map on page 49).* This exit opens the door to some very interesting attractions just east of the Interstate.

Mainstrasse Village: this picturesque five block area of restored 19th century German buildings will make you think you have landed in Europe. Antique, art and craft shops abound, and of course, restaurants serve the finest Bavarian food such as sauerbraten, schnitzel and wurst, washed down with German lager.

Mainstrasse people are proud of their heritage and offer old world service. Summer or winter, it's fun to wander the cobbled walkways and visit establishments such as the *Linden Noll Gift Haus* or *MainStrasse Arts.* Or sit under the trees near the Goose Girl fountain watching others go by while listening to the glockenspiel tower playing its 43 bell carillon in the nearby park.

Hofbräuhaus Newport: After visiting Mainstrasse, we drove a few minutes further east along 5th Street and across the Licking River, to the only authentic HofbräuHaus in the USA. Modeled after (and licensed by) the famous 400 year old HofbräuHaus in Munich, this traditional Bavarian bräuhaus

The double-decked Brent Spence Bridge crosses the Ohio River, separating Kentucky & Ohio

brews its own München beers–from creamy

and dark Hofbräu Dunkel & Weizen to lighter Kunzel Lager, and seasonal favorites such as Maibock, Doppel Bock and Weizenbock.

Can't make up your mind which beer to try? Do as I do and get a "paddle" of "tasters" at $1 per 4oz glass.

Traditional bräuhaus lunches and dinners are also served while the Om-pa-pa band plays traditional drinking songs & polkas. This comes, of course, with

much *Gemütlichkeit* (fun & good times) which is part of the Bavarian beer hall experience. When the chicken dance starts, climb on the table and start wiggling your tail–*Ein Prosit*.

The parent, Munich Hofbräuhaus has done everything to ensure the authenticity of this Newport location. Most of the fittings come from Munich; even the chairs (dating from the 1930s) were shipped from the original Bavarian beer hall.

Every day is Oktoberfest in the Hofbräuhaus Newport–Wunderbar!

Newport Aquarium & Newport on the Levee: Just a block away is one of the finest aquariums in North America. If driving, park your car in the indoor parking area beneath *"Newport on the Levee"* and take the elevator up to the Levee and Aquarium level.

If you are traveling with "children" this is a "must see" attraction. Not only do you walk around the seventeen dramatic themed galleries–*Dangerous and Deadly, Bizarre & Beautiful, Jellyfish, Shore, River Bank and Penguins*–to name a few, but you also can wander through

"Inside" a tank tunnel

the huge tanks by means of 200 feet of acrylic tunnels. One 85 foot tunnel takes you to the middle of a shark feeding ground, and if the fish don't provide enough excitement, the scuba divers you will see in most tank, probably will!

In particular, don't

Look up! A hungry shark swims overhead

miss *Shark Central*– the new, permanent exhibit about sharks; it will give kids a fun and interactive way to learn about these unique animals. [Hrs: Daily, 10-6p, with longer hours in the summer; Adult/Snr/Child, $17.95/15.95/10.95; ☎ 859-261-7444].

While parked for the aquarium why not also enjoy *Newport on the Levee* and nearby *Riverboat Row*. The *Levee* has some interesting shops, a cafe and a great seafood restaurant, *Mitchell's Fish Market*. We particularly enjoy the burritos at *Moe's Southwest Grill*.

Purple People Bridge Climb: Sidney, Australia has one and now so does Newport, Kentucky, although this latest attraction is not for the faint-of-heart. After being outfitted with

KENTUCKY - *a Wyandot Indian name "Kentahteh" meaning "land of tomorrow," or as early settlers used to call it - Caintuck.*

your climbing gear and going through a orientation session (including a climb simulation) at the Base Camp, your climb leader takes you up into the girder spans for a two hour adventure of your life, 140 feet over the Ohio River.

It looks scary but is quite safe. Safety lines tether you to the bridge for the duration of your climb which can be easily handled by youngsters 12 years (must be 48" in height) and older. [Further info, ☎ 859-261-6837].

To find all of the Covington/Newport attractions described in the last few pages, use the map on page 49. You will also find hours and phone numbers on the map.

Mile 182-*"Florence Y'all"*: Do you see the warm welcome on the side of the water tower to our right? Now–y'all know you are in the "South;" on the sunny side of the famous Mason-Dixon line (if extended this far west).

But there is an interesting story behind the greeting, *"Florence Y'all."* It was never intended as a sign of welcome to Northerners. Originally, a local company used the publicly owned water tower to advertise their nearby business, the Florence Mall. Other area retailers were upset that public property was being used for this purpose and convinced the authorities that the tower should be repainted removing the offensive advertising. But although it agreed, the City lacked the budget to pay for the work.

Then an enterprising city employee suggested removing the *"M"* from *"Mall"* & replacing it with *"Y'"*–that's how it remains to this day.

Exit 181-Graeter's Ice Cream: Psst! There's an excellent local ice cream place just about ½ mile east of this exit–Graeter's. Founded in 1870, this family business has never compromised its traditional method of hand-making ice cream–the French Pot process–2 gallons at a time. With flavors ranging from Tangerine Cream and Black Cherry, to traditionals such as Chocolate and Vanilla, I know you will not want to miss this local delicacy [☎ 859-341-3005].

Exit 180-Wildwood Inn: Kathy and I spent an interesting evening in an African Safari hut here last summer. We could have slept in a cave or by a waterfall but opted for a kraal in our own African village. If you are traveling with children, you will certainly find a night in one of the Wildwood Inn theme rooms

something they will remember for a long time to come. ☎ 859-371-6300 or 800-758-2335.

Mile 177-Welcome Center: Need Kentucky information or discount coupons? Then this is the place to get them. Say "hi" to Manager Jeff, Brad and Judy. They all know Kentucky well and would love to help you.

Mile 169-Advantage-75: Are you curious about the *"Advantage-75"* signs you see at truck weigh stations? This is an electronic scanning system which uses computers to automatically identify the equipment rolling through the weigh scales. Introduced in 1994 at a cost of $150,000 per weigh station, it is now speeding trucks through the documentation process at many of I-75's weigh stations.

This is the beginning of the elimination of interstate weigh stations. Eventually, all trucks will carry mini-transmitters (transponders) similar to those used by aircraft for traffic control purposes. A truck will roll down I-75 without slowing down, pass a road side scanner which reads the truck's load and destination data, drive over an electronic plate in the right lane road surface to record the load's weight, and get a green signal in their cab which indicates that they may continue–or a red signal to pull over for an inspection. Electronic sensors will monitor the other lanes to ensure that no trucks bypass this invisible

INSIDER TIP - The Country Grill

Every year we stop at exit 159 and eat at the Country Grill family restaurant.

It's easy to spot the Country Grill as you come off the interstate it sits on the side of a small hill to the west, on the left side of the road. Parking is available in front of the restaurant and in an unpaved area just behind the building.

All meals are prepared from fresh ingredients by Chef Edward Smain; "front of house" operations are run by owners Edward and Greg Melcher–Greg will probably seat you at your table.   [Hrs: Su-Th, 8-9p; F-Sa, 8-10p; ☎ 859-824-6000].

data collection system.

Mile 156-153-Radar: We passed the police patrol car parked on the overpass at exit 156 beaming radar in our direction, not in itself an unusual occurrence on I-75. Then, spotting flashing lights on the soft shoulder ahead, we moved over from L3 into the center lane (it's the law now in all I-75 states). And then we saw another patrol car stopped beside the interstate writing a citation–and another–and another–and another. In fact in the next few miles, we counted 5 patrol cars looking after "clients" by the side of I-75. But soon the excitement was over. At mile 153, we saw a sixth vehicle using the median emergency "U" turn, to head back north and begin the process all over again. I guess this gives a whole new meaning to *"cash flow."*

Exit 154-A Civil War Execution: Just a quarter of a mile east of this exit is an historical marker commemorating a sad Civil War event which took place in 1864. Three Confederate soldiers were brought here from the Union prison in Lexington. At this spot, the three were hanged as a reprisal for the guerrilla murder of two Union sympathizers.

Mile 132-Blue Grass: Sixty miles back we passed over the mighty Ohio River and into Kentucky. The scenery is very pleasant as we drive through the gently rolling Kentucky countryside, but try as we might, we cannot see any famous bluegrass–and yet it is supposed to be all around us–but the grass is distinctly green!

So what is Kentucky Bluegrass? It is a type of grass which grows lushly in the State's rich limestone soil. It is not really blue–it's green, but in the spring, Bluegrass develops bluish-purple buds which, when coated with early morning dew and viewed from a distance,

---

INSIDER TIP - Picnic

Tired of the fast food "factories" and their consistently predictable food? Recently we've been trying another way of handling lunch while on the road. Most rest areas have picnic areas away from their main buildings, so we look on our 25 mile strip maps for such a facility ahead of us (look for the picnic table symbol) which we will reach about lunch time, and then a Subway (or similar fresh food outlet) at an exit before it. Stopping at the Subway, we get our sandwiches and drinks–and then head of for our picnic. No crowds, no fuss–just us, food and pleasant surroundings.

---

appear as a rich, blue blanket cast across a meadow. Early pioneers found it growing in abundance when they crossed the Appalachian Mountains in their wagons. They shipped it back east and soon traders began asking for the *"blue grass seeds from Kentucky"*–and the name stuck.

Exit 129 or 126-Toyota: Toyota Motor Manufacturing in Georgetown is huge. Its 1,300 acres property includes a test track, 7.5 m i l l i o n square foot plant and administration offices. Two vehicle production lines produce  the popular Camry, Avalon and Solara vehicles, as well as engine and axle components.

The Visitor Center Lobby, is open M-Fr, 9am-4pm (to 7pm on Thurs). Here you can book a free tour of the plant where you'll have a chance to see some of the 500,000 cars and engines which are built here, annually. After an introductory video, you are taken on a guided tram ride through the stamping, body welding and assembly shops. Here is your chance to watch robots at work!

Drive east on Cherry Blossom Way, from exit 129 or 126. Travel towards the plant chimneys–you can't miss them–you are looking for the Visitor's Center at Gate 2.

Plant's tours depart the Center M-Fr, at 10am, noon and 2pm. On Thursday there is also a 6pm tour. The plant is closed holidays & the third week in July. There is a maximum of 64 people/tour so reservations are required. Children must be at least 8 years old. No shorts. ☎ 502-868-3027 or 800-866-4485.

Mile 128-Welcome Center: If stopping for Georgetown or Lexington information, say hello to Manager Jean and Becky, Gaynell and Pat at counter.

Exit 126-Georgetown: *(Town map on page 52).* Just west of I-75 at this exit is the pleasant community of Georgetown–the *"Antiques Capital of Kentucky."* If you have a few minutes to spare, take a drive down and back up Main Street–I-75 is easy to rejoin.

Main Street between Hamilton and Water Streets is an antique and specialty shopper's heaven. Brick sidewalks, old-fashioned lamp posts and more than 100 buildings listed on the National Register of Historic Places make this short sidetrip a visit to a bygone era.

An excellent County Museum is located 229 East Main. Located in the former Post Office building, its exhibits cover prehistoric occupation 12,000 years ago, to recent times. [Hrs: M-F, 9-4p, Sa, 10-4p; donations appreciated; ☎ 502-863-6201].

Finally, an historical marker at the west end of Main Street tells us that the first Bourbon whiskey was distilled here using the fine limestone water from nearby Royal Spring.

Named after the county name *"Bourbon"* when this land was part of Virginia, in 1789 Georgetown founder Rev. Elijah Craig, set up a still at the spring and brewed the first batch of this potent potion.

Exit 120-Time to Top Up: With wine and beer, that is. Soon you will be in Kentucky "dry county" country, and just to the west of this exit is the perfect place to pickup "supplies." Not only does *Post Time Liquors* have an excellent selection of wines but next door's convenience store has a whole refrigeration section of ice cold beer. *Post Time Liquors* even has a drive through window! Incidentally, this exit is an "easy off–easy on" (i.e., little traffic; just a stop sign on the exit ramp). [Hrs: M-Th, 10-10p; F-Sa, 10-midnight; ☎ 859-255-7277].

Exit 120-Kentucky Horse Park: Kentucky is famous for its horses and horse breeding, and Lexington is at the heart of horse country. If you enjoy anything to do with horses (and even if you don't) then you owe it to yourself to stop at the Kentucky Horse Park (exit 120, Iron Works Pike–go east for ¼ mile).

Here you will be welcomed by a statue of that most famous horse of all–Man O'War *(see story at Kentucky, exit 108)*, who is buried at the park. The Visitor Center has a spectacular

film presentation, *"Thou Shalt Fly Without Wings."* Journey through time and trace the history of horses from prehistoric to modern times, along the spiral ramp of the International Museum of the Horse.

Afterwards, take the park shuttle, horse-drawn carriage or horseback (in snowy winter, horse-drawn sleigh) and enjoy the beautiful Kentucky park with its many horse related activities. The park houses an educational department where students are trained in skills to enter careers in the horse industry, so there is always something going on.

[Hrs, Winter: W-Su, 9-5p; Summer: Daily, 9-5p; Admission, includes the American Saddlebred Museum: Adult/Snr/Child (winter)-$9/$8/$6, (summer)-$15/$14/$8; Parking, $3

summer, winter is free); ☎ 859-233-4303].

And now for some BIG Lexington news. From Sept. 20 to Oct. 3, 2010, Lexington has been chosen to host the *Fédération Equestre Internationale (FEI) Games*, and the *Kentucky Horse Park* will serve as the focal point for the events.

How big is this? The FEI Games are the "Olympics" of the equestrian world. Held every 4 years, the events (there are eight disciplines–dressage, vaulting, endurance, reining, driving, jumping and eventing) will attract 400,000 people including international royalty to the area, and more than 1,000 horses will participate. The Games will be televised in over 50 countries.

I'm sure we will hear more about this over the next few years.

Mile 120-Lex on Central Time: If you were driving through the Lexington area before 1961, you would have your watch back by an hour since you would now been in a *Central Time* zone. That year, it was changed to the *Eastern Time* zone because of the problems

LEXINGTON - *named in 1775 after Lexington, Massachusetts, by a group of colonial hunters who camped close by after the first skirmish with British troops during the War of Independence.*

the hour's difference cause local businesses.

Exit 120-Ironworks Pike: This road got its name from the early 1800's transport route which ran from the Slate Creek Ironworks about 40 miles (64km) east of Lexington, to Frankfort on the Kentucky River. War materials from the Ironworks were carried along this road for shipment by river down the Mississippi to Andrew Jackson in New Orleans during the War of 1812.

Exit 115-Lexington Downtown area: *(City map page 50)*. One and a quarter miles (2km)– south on Newtown Pike (Rt 922) will bring you to the Lexington downtown area. Lexington was a settlers' campsite in 1775 and yet had become a bustling commercial center within twenty-five years. Turn onto West Main Street, bear right onto Vine (one way), cross Broadway, S Mill, Upper, Limestone and stop at the Visitor Center at Vine and Rose [Hrs–see map on page 50; 301 E. Vine St; ☎ 800-845-3959 or 859-233-7299].

While there, pick up a map and a guide book for there is lots to see and do in Lexington. Also, ask for a free copy of *"Lexington Walk & Bluegrass Country Driving Tour."* One side of this folded map details a walking tour of the downtown area with descriptions of the history and architecture; the other side provides driving plans for short but spectacular car trips around Lexington's nearby horse

Lexington's superb horse race statue

country. The accompanying maps are beautifully drawn in colored pastel–the brochure is in itself, a work of art.

While at the Visitors Center, take a few minutes to walk over to *Thoroughbred Park* and see what I consider to be one of the most fascinating statues in the world! If you are in your car, you can park in the area just behind the statue *(see map on page 50)*.

This bronze statue by Gwen Reardon is of a "frozen" horse race, and you can easily spend a half-hour wandering around between the horses just looking at the expressions on the riders' faces. Colored in subtle earth tones, you can see the supreme effort on the faces of the leading jockeys as they attempt to eke out just one more inch of horse flesh on the finish line. And don't miss the look of desperation on the face of the tail end jockey who already knows that he has lost. Take your camera–the close-ups you take will be memorable.

Exit 113-Paris Pike: (not suitable for large RVs) If you have time on your hands and would like to see some of the lush Kentucky horse farm land close up, you might enjoy a country drive east of this exit, along Paris Pike–routes 27 & 68. But first a caution. This route is used heavily in the "rush hours" by commuters traveling between Paris and Lexington so best not to do this drive in peak travel periods.

This section of the Pike was widened several years ago and this caused a very unusual problem since the new right-of-way cut through heritage lands which have dry-laid stone walls, some dated back to the late 1800s. These walls were carefully moved by hand and rebuilt stone-by-stone as the road

Key to Horse Farms

1-Castleton-Lyons	10-Dixiana	19-Fairway
2-Due Process	11-Spendthrift	20-Manderly
3-Whileaway	12-Clovelly Farm	21-Tree Haven
4-Kingston	13-Whitaker	22-Thoroughbred Center
5-Pillar Stud	14-Walmac	23-CV Whitney
6-Fairfield	15-Elmendorf	24-Gainesway
7-Pharamon	16-Normandy	25-Greentree Stud
8-Shandon	17-Hagyard	26-Payson Stud
9-Domino Stud	18-Winter Hill	27-Duntreath

construction proceeded eastward. Well, back to the drive.

Designated a "Scenic Route" you will travel past the old stone walls and white fenced meadows of horse farms such as *Walmac International, Bittersweet, Clovelly, C.V. Whitney, Elmendorf, Normandy, Spendthrift and Domino Stud.* Many of these farms have bred thoroughbred champions running in major events around the world, most notably in the USA and France. *Man o' War's* sire, *Fair Play* and dam, *Mahubah*, are buried on *Normandy Farm. CV Whitney's Farm* is often host to film stars, international business and political figures.

A few moments ago, I mentioned white fences ... but you might have noticed that there is now a trend towards black. Sadly (because the white fences look much nicer), this is a sign of the times.

White fence paint is a bit more expensive than other colors and such fences needed painting every year. Until recently, black could not be used because of its lead content which would have been very bad for the horses cribbing on the wood while watching traffic go by. Lead-free black paint is now readily available and the fences only need to be painted 6 to 8 years.

The *Castelton-Lyons* farm (No. 1 on the Paris Pike map) has recently switched to tan paint, and my local expert tells me it is very pleasing to the eye. Perhaps this is the horse farm, fence paint, color of the future.

The drive takes you 3 miles (4.8km) to the junction of Rt1973 (Ironworks Pike), in a further 2 miles (3.2km) turn left on to Hughes Lane. Turn left again in 1 1/3 miles (2.8km) onto Kenny Lane and drive to the junction of Ironworks Rd in 2 miles (3.2km).

Here you can either turn left to rejoin the Paris Pike in 1 mile (1.5km) where you turn right to drive the 3 miles (4.8km) back to I-75, or, turn right to head north on historic Ironworks Pike. After 1.2 miles (1.9km) you will reach the junction of Russell Cave Rd (route 353). Cross the intersection and continue on Ironworks Pike for 2.4 miles (3.9km) until you reach the Newtown Pike (route 922). Turn left and drive 2.3 miles (3.7km) until you rejoin I-75 at exit 115.

Total mileage? Thirteen miles (21km) if you took the shorter route or 15 miles (24.1km) for the longer route–both of wonderful Kentucky countryside–20 mins of pure pleasure.

If short of time, just drive the 3 miles (4.8km) to the junction of Rt 1973, carefully turn around and drive back to the interstate.

Exit 111-Blue Water Tower: Speaking of monuments, if you have any doubts that Lexington is the center of the horse world, check the blue water tower on the east side of I-75 just north of exit 111. This project was a joint effort on the part of nine organizations.

Exit 108-Man O'War: Man O'War Boulevard is of course, named after the famous Kentucky thoroughbred-foaled in 1917–who put many new records into the book. *Man O'War* (WWI was in progress at the time) was said to have had a 25 foot stride and was once clocked at 43 MPH during a workout. He was only beaten once in his racing career, ironically by a horse named, *"Upset."*

In retirement, *Man O'War* and his groom, *Will Harbot*, became inseparable friends for 17 years. Will died in 1947; Man O'War died one month later–many said of a broken heart.

Lexington is thoroughbred horse country. The lush grass meadows growing on limestone soil make ideal horse grazing conditions. As you travel the I-75, the neat horse farms to the east with their trim plank fences–Kingston, Shandon, Winter Hill and Meadowcrest–are a delight to the eye. Check our I-75 maps–we have named them for you.

To the west of this exit hidden from the freeway lies the huge shopping mall, *Hamburg Pavilion*. With its Meijer 24 hour superstore, Target, Barnes & Noble super bookstore, Office Max, Radio Shack, Old Navy, Garden Ridge, etc., it's a great place to stop if you need a bit of time away from the interstate.

Exit 99-Clay's Ferry: (not suitable for large RVs). If you're getting a bit tired of the freeway, I've got a small diversion for you. It will only take a few extra minutes–the entire distance is 2.9 miles (4.7km). Let's go down and visit the Kentucky River and see the site of historical Clay's Ferry.

Actually, there's very little to see now but the scenery is pretty and the drive interesting (don't try this if icy!). After leaving I-75 at

Lexington's Blue Water Tower

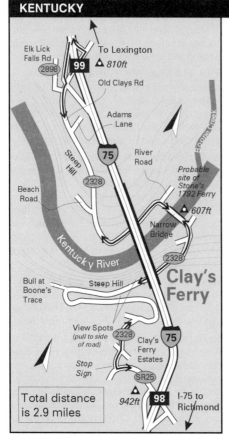

Elk Lick
Falls Rd
(2898)
99 △ 810ft
To Lexington
Old Clays Rd
Adams
Lane
Boone Creek
75
River
Road
2328
Probable
site of
Stone's
1792 Ferry
Beach
Road
△ 607ft
Narrow
Bridge
2328
**Clay's
Ferry**
Kentucky River
Bull at
Boone's
Trace
Steep Hill
View Spots
(pull to side
of road)
2328
Clay's
Ferry
Estates
75
Stop
Sign
SR25
Total distance
is 2.9 miles
△
942ft
98
I-75 to
Richmond

exit 99, follow the winding road down 200 ft into the river valley. Here you'll find a narrow single-lane road bridge-drive across this carefully after yielding to any oncoming traffic.

As you drive across the bridge, glance to your left (east) for it was here that Valentine Stone operated his ferry in 1792. Stone sold the ferry to Gen. Clay in 1798 and it stayed in the Clay family ferrying people and carts back and forth until 1865.

As you drive up the hill away from the river there are several impressive views of the valley below. If you park by the side of the road, pull well off even though there's not a lot of

I-75 crosses the Kentucky River

traffic here. Do you hear that rumbling overhead? Its I-75 on the bridge high above you.

Finally, drive around the hairpin bend at Boone's Trace and follow the winding road to the stop sign at SR25. A left turn will bring you back to I-75.

Mile 98-The Kentucky Knobs: Now we have crossed the Kentucky River, the road becomes hillier for we are in the region known as the Kentucky Knobs. Geologists refer to this area as the Jessamine Dome, an area of sedimentary rock which was uplifted millions of years ago.

Exit 95-Fort Boonesborough: *(see map on page 51 for details).* Just five miles (8km) east (about an eight minute drive) along route 627 lies Fort Boonesborough–a reconstruction of the wooden fortified settlement built by Daniel Boone in 1775. As you wander around inside the wooden stockade you may visit the settlers in their period costumes and watch them make soap, spin wool, & practice many other frontier arts and crafts. This is a "hands-on" experience so if there is something you would like to try, just ask.

In 1778, Boone escaped from an Indian village in Ohio (Little Chillicothe–Ohio exit 52) and returned here to warn the settlers of an impending Indian attack. With the help of the British Army, the Indians lay siege to this fort for ten days. Heavy rains and the strong defense by Boone and his men broke the siege. On the tenth day the Indians gave up, disappearing into the trees around the fort.

As you peer through the half opened gateway into the dappled sunlight of the still green forest beyond, it's easy to imagine that the cawing sound you just heard was not a bird but one of a Shawnee war party signaling the band to move closer to the stockade walls.

Exit 95-Driving Tip: Don't forget to use the brown "escape routes" shown on the colored maps. They can save you lots of time and stress. While driving in this area several years ago, we heard on the radio that the interstate traffic had backed up several miles at mile 92, due to an accident. So, I checked the map and found that we could cut off of I-75 at exit 95 and come back on at exit 90B. It was a great drive. We came back to an almost empty road and avoided all the stressful bumper-to-bumper traffic.

Exit 95-White Hall: *(see map on page 51 for details).* In the opposite direction just 1.9 miles (3km–3½ minutes) to the west lies the famous White Hall. This magnificent Georgian and Italianate building was the home of Cassius Marcellus Clay, Clay is one of Kentucky's most colorful and historical figures–a noted abolitionist, publisher, ambassador to Russia and friend of Abraham Lincoln.

White Hall is really two houses in one. The original Georgian building–Clermont–was built in 1798, by Clay's father. In the 1860s while Clay was on service in Russia, his wife, Mary Jane supervised the construction of the second house over the original. The transformed building designed by prominent architects Lewinski and McMurtry became known as *"White Hall."*

Exit 90A-Richmond: *(Town map page 53)* Home of East Kentucky University, Richmond is an attractive town which has done an excellent job of protecting its 19th century heritage with more than 100 buildings on the National Register of Historic Places. Many of these fine homes and public buildings can be seen in the "downtown" area on East and West Main, Lancaster, Water & Irvine streets.

South of East Main Street just past Baker Court lies the old Cemetery. This was the scene of Civil War action, during the Battle of Richmond in August, 1862.

Having been beaten in two skirmishes between Berea and Richmond on the previous days, the Union forces retreated to the Richmond Cemetery. Their commander, Maj. General Nelson, a huge man of 300 pounds, rode up and down in front of them, brandishing his sword and berating them as cowards for retreating.

"Boys," he said, *"if they can't hit something as big as I am, they can't hit anything."*

Suddenly, a gun was heard and Nelson fell, shot in the thigh. He was carried off the field.

The Confederates overran the Cemetery resulting in a significant Confederate victory which opened the way for the CSA's advance to the North. The Union suffered 80% losses.

Route 169 (Tates Creek Road) runs west out of Richmond where in about 12 miles (19.3km) it reaches the Kentucky River and the famous Valley View Car Ferry, Kentucky's oldest continuous business.

It's along this road that the famous pioneer and explorer, <u>*Christopher "Kit" Carson*</u> was born in a small log cabin beside Tates Creek, on Christmas Eve, 1809. Kit Carson, went on to become a living legend as a frontiersman.

His skill as a hunter and rifleman was thought by many to be second to none. The publication of his adventures during his 1842-1844 exploration of the West was widely read in the eastern cities and spurred many on to life on the new frontier.

Exit 87 Acres of Land Winery: Several readers have reported that there is a winery six miles west of this exit, with an excellent restaurant. The winery itself took a number of impressive silver and bronze medals at the 2005 Florida State Fair International Wine competition, so a trip to its Tasting Room might be worth the drive.

The restaurant also has interesting lunch ($7-$11) and dinner ($8-$20) menus, with lots of variety. [Restaurant hours are Tu-Th, 11-9p, F-Sa, 11-11p, closed Sun and Mon; ☎ 859-328-3000].

Mile 86-Sedimentary Rock: We pass through an interesting cut of stratified limestone–successive layers of sedimentation from an ancient tropical sea which have been heaved up by the Earth's colossal, mountain folding forces. In summer, this cut is particularly pretty–topped with stands of young lush trees and carpets of wildflowers.

Exit 77-Kentucky Travelers' Center: Over the next year or so, Kentucky will be beautifying the median area of this exit, to complement the Kentucky Travelers' Center *(see Sidebar next page and map on page 52).*

Exit 76-Berea: *(Town map page 52).* Literally seconds to the east of I-75, the town of Berea is a hidden jewel that many drive by in their haste to reach Florida. If you enjoy crafts and antiques, make sure you plan an overnight stop here for Berea is exciting and vibrant. In 1988, it was designated the *"Folk Arts and Craft Capital of Kentucky"* by the State Legislature. More recently, Southern Living magazine recognized it as a *"favorite small town"* in America.

RICHMOND - *named by early settlers after the capital of Virginia, which in turn was named after Richmond, Surrey, England.*

Geology and Dinosaurs along I-75.

The I-75 winds its way across an ancient land with many rock cuts revealing the geology of very early times. To help you understand the age of the land around you and the life forms which were present at that time, here is a simplified chart of the Geological Time Scale.

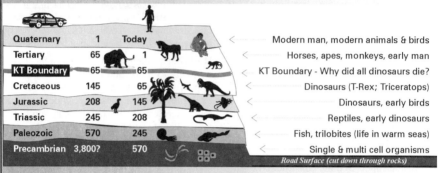

Quaternary	1	Today	<	Modern man, modern animals & birds
Tertiary	65	1	<	Horses, apes, monkeys, early man
KT Boundary	65	65	<	KT Boundary - Why did all dinosaurs die?
Cretaceous	145	65	<	Dinosaurs (T-Rex; Triceratops)
Jurassic	208	145	<	Dinosaurs, early birds
Triassic	245	208	<	Reptiles, early dinosaurs
Paleozoic	570	245	<	Fish, trilobites (life in warm seas)
Precambrian	3,800?	570	<	Single & multi cell organisms

Road Surface (cut down through rocks)

Think of the Time Scale as an eight layer cake; each layer representing a period of time (numbers are in millions of years). The oldest layer is at the bottom and the newest (today) is at the top:

Incidentally did you notice that according to the chart, Tyrannosaurus Rex, the huge flesh eating monster in the "Jurassic Park" movies, was not around in the Jurassic period? It did not appear until the Cretaceous Period, 63 million years later–the movie should have been called, "Cretaceous Park."

continued top or next page

INSIDER TIP - KY Travelers' Center

To the east of I-75 at exit 77 is Kentucky's spectacular Travelers' Center (see map on page 52). Built in a French Chateau style from limestone quarried near Harrodsburg, KY, this 20,000 sq feet building showcases the finest of Kentucky arts and crafts, as static displays and hands-on demonstrations by crafts folk from all over the State. A huge gift shop with well lit display cases sells much of this local artwork. Whether it's music, pottery, weaving or one of the other many Kentucky craft forms, you will almost certainly find it here.

The magnificent building with its high pine-beam ceiling also has a tourist counter with well-stocked information racks and a "not to be missed" cafe serving Kentucky food for breakfast, lunch and dinner. Oh yes, and the restrooms are super clean!

The Center is open from 8a to 8p daily; admission is free. There is loads of parking space (including RVs and buses) so why not stop and say hello to manager Victoria, and the friendly counter folk–BJ, Bonnie, Cindy, Connie, Cori, Debra, Glenna, Hannah, Ima Dale, Kathi, Kim, Lucian, Marilyn Opal, Rick, Roy & Traci–they would love to share stories about their beautiful state with you.

The largest concentration of working studios and craft galleries can be found in *"Old Town Berea,"* located near the Berea Welcome Center on North Broadway. During my last visit, I counted 32 such places.

Head to the Welcome Center (just follow the railroad tracks) housed in the town's original *1917 L&N Railroad Depot* building and get a copy of the excellent Berea guide and foldout map–it's a great help in navigating around the town. When leaving, don't forget to say

INSIDER TIP - El Rio Grande

It's hard to ignore a letter when a reader writes to say that they have discovered one of the best Mexican restaurants north of the Border. In fact, equal to the restaurants in Puerto Vallarto where they normally vacation. And it's in Berea!

Now I must admit, I'm not keen on Mexican food so I have to take this recommendation on faith. The manager speaks a bit of English and the waiters *"no comprende Inglés"* If you decide to try it, let me know.

El Rio Grande is at 305 Chesnut Street (the road connected to exit 76). Drive east from I-75 for 1.2 miles (1.9km).

And if you *"habla Español,"* the phone number is 859-985-0314.

Special Report–continued from top of previous page

Dinosaurs disappeared 65 million years ago, possibly as the result of a major natural catastrophe. Geologists have identified a dark narrow band of material called the KT Boundary, which appears in rock strata of that time. This layer contains iridium, an element rare on earth but common in asteroids. It also contains tectites, small beads of glass fused under tremendous pressure and heat (most powerful nuclear bomb times 500,000). One theory is that a 6 mile wide asteroid collided with the earth (the Chicxulub Crater) in the ocean off the Yucatan Peninsula, Mexico, causing a massive, earth circling cloud of sulphur fog and debris. This blocked the sun plunging the world into a dark cold ice age, killing all land animals in the process. The KT Boundary may consist of debris from this cloud which settled back onto the earth's surface and was gradually covered by later geological layers.

As we drive along I-75 we travel over an ancient section of landscape, for time has seen many of the more recent geological layers eroded away. Today, the surface geology is often the rocks of the seventh Paleozoic period–a time when warm tropical salt seas covered the land. During that period, sediment suspended in the sea water continually dropped to the bottom accompanied by dead fish, shell invertebrates and vegetation debris. Over time, the ocean bed hardened layer by layer into sedimentary rock such as limestone and shale; the trapped fish and shell remains became the fossils which can be found today in the sedimentary (many-layered) rocks of the cuts along the I-75. All the way from Ohio, through Kentucky and Tennessee and down into Georgia, the surface geology is of this Paleozoic period.

But what about the Dinosaurs? Did they ever stalk the lands through which the I-75 now runs? Not according to the surface geology for this is too old. But marine dinosaur bones of the late Cretaceous period have been found in southwest Georgia.

"goodbye" to Tux the black and white Depot Cat. Tux and her kittens owe their lives to Berea's cat rescue unit. Ask Director Belle or staff members Lynda and Martha, to tell you the story.

Outside the Welcome Center is an interesting log cabin which is open to view from 9-5:30. Although a modern structure, the interior portrays settler life in early years. As a keen gardener, I really enjoy the pioneer herb garden, during the summer months.

If you are a "rock hound" you should spend a few minutes visiting *Hosfeld's Jewelry and Repair* across the road from the Center. Not only does Mr. Hosfeld specialize in Kentucky Agate, but apparently, he can fix any piece of jewelry needing repair while you are wandering around Old Town Berea. {Hrs: Tu-Fri, 10-6p; ☎ 859-985-5353].

Don't miss the historic *Boone Tavern* located in the heart of *College Square* along with numerous galleries and shops.

Berea, where the bluegrass meadows meet the rugged mountains, is truly a living celebration of the Appalachian culture. Stop for a night and enjoy it.

Mile 73-Rock Springlets: We are approaching the Cumberland Mountain region of Kentucky, an area rich with timbered ridge scenery, dense stands of forest, and interesting rock cuts. A favorite of mine is on the west side of the interstate at Mile 63. The face of the cliff is covered with vines and the rock often weeps from hidden springlets of ground water. In the warm sunlight of a spring day, it is magical.

Hawks: Two or three hawks glide above us, riding the air currents of the ridges, their sharp eyes focused on the ground looking for the tiny, almost imperceptible movement of a delectable field mouse or baby rabbit. Suddenly, one of them swoops down–sharp talons extended earthward– dropping like a stone. You look away knowing that once again a small animal has given its life to ensure that in death, life goes on. Such is Nature's food chain.

Exit 62-Renfro Valley: Renfro Valley Entertainment Center is one of Kentucky's best loved places and is less than a minute east of I-75 at this exit. Known as *"Kentucky's Country Music Capital,"* the Renfro Valley

BEREA - *for the Biblical city in ancient Syria.*

complex has everything you need for an enjoyable stay– restaurant, gift shops and its most recent addition, the world class *"Kentucky Music Hall of Fame & Museum."*

But it's the stage shows in the entertainment Barn Theater which brings most people to Renfro Valley. Fiddling, banjo picking, singing, clogging, bluegrass, and vaudeville comedy make up the best country music and entertainment show this side of Nashville. Over the years, many stars have graced the Renfro Valley stages . . from Red Foley to the Osborne Brothers, or Loretta Lynn to Patty Loveless. Enjoy the Renfro Valley Barn Dance, Jamboree, Mountain Gospel Jubilee and traditional Festivals.

Funny man, Bun Wilson harasses show host, Jim Gaskin during the Renfro Valley Music show

The newly opened Music Hall of Fame & Museum is outstanding. Among the 12 first inductees are Merle Travis, The Osborne Bros., Loretta Lynn, Rosemary Clooney and Clyde Julian "Red" Foley. Here you will find special exhibits honoring these folk–their costumes and dresses, instruments, etc.

The Valley's musical venues run from March to December. From May to October, the entertainment of various forms, runs from Wednesday to Sunday. The programs and stars vary, so it's best to call ahead at 1-800-765-7464 for your reservations. At the very least, there is a *Barn Dance* and *Jamboree* every Saturday night and a *Sunday Gatherin'* every Sunday morning at 8:30 am.

Mile 61-Interstate Engineering: As we drive through more rock cuts, we cannot help wondering about the massive engineering and construction task presented to I-75 road

builders. The roadbed was built through anything which stood in its path. At times, I-75 cuts deep into the side of a hill and at others, it traverses a short valley on top of an embankment.

At this mile marker, you notice how the rock face on both sides of the road has been blasted and cut back in steps. If you look carefully, you will often see evidence of drill holes running vertically down the rock face. These holes were drilled down through the rock a few feet apart; dynamite charges dropped down each hole were set off at the same time slicing the earth away from the face where it could be gathered and trucked away at the road bed.

The building of America's Interstate system is often quoted as the largest public works project of all human times–larger than the building of the Egyptian Pyramids; broader in scope than the digging of the Suez Canal.

As we whiz by on our way to Florida, we take our hat off to you, the builders of I-75. Thanks for your Herculean work.

Mile 56-Daniel Boone National Forest: We are about to cross into the Daniel Boone National Forest. From I-75, it doesn't look very big; most of it lies to the east and west of us covering 21 counties and over 670,000 acres of rugged terrain–steep slopes, narrow valleys, picturesque lakes, rocks and cliffs. The Forest is a primary recreation area with many miles of hiking trails and opportunities for outdoor activities such as picnicking, camping, fishing and water sports.

As we cruise down the freeway on automatic control at 65 MPH, I often think about the hard life of the early pioneers as they pushed their way inland from the settlements of the Atlantic shore. The Appalachian (pronounced locally as, "App-er-latch-urns") Mountains blocked their path and until the Cumberland and Pine Mountain gaps were discovered in 1750 by Dr. Thomas Walker, the journey by oxen-drawn wagon laden with all their household possessions was next to impossible. Measuring their forward progress in days–not minutes–they overcame obstacle after obstacle to finally emerge into that wonderful land just beyond the next misty horizon–*Caintuck.*

The difficult terrain of the settlers' journey was not the only hazard. As the War of Independence raged up and down the Atlantic Coast the British Army incited the warlike Indians tribes of Ohio and Kentucky to attack the pioneers and turn them eastward again. Soon small warbands of Cherokee, Shawnee, Miami and Wynadot braves were treading the paths in the forests beside which we travel, to ambush and tomahawk the settlers.

In 1775, a man called Henderson formed the Transylvania Company and purchased the lands we now know as Kentucky from the Cherokee Indians–his wish was to sell land grants to white settlers from the east, and he hired Daniel Boone to help with this mission.

The country we are now passing through is named in honor of Boone, for it was he who blazed the original trail across the mountain passes and into Kentucky, in 1775. Later, with 30 axe-men, he broadened the trail cutting trees down below wagon axle height, so that settlers could follow his path, known as the *Wilderness Trace*. He and his men opened the entire trail in less than three weeks!

In the next few miles, I-75 crosses the original path of Boone's pioneer trail *(see map pages 23-S and 175/176-N)*. The modern terrain matches the 200 year old frontier trail well. It is still easy to imagine those deerskin clad woodsmen with their wide brimmed beaverskin hats and flintlock muskets crooked over their arms, near the rocks beside the freeway. We can still hear the rumbling of the wagon wheels and snorting of the pack horses as the first settlers move northward on their journey to Boonesborough, Kentucky.

Exit 41-Wilderness Rd: This is the "official" intersection of I-75 and the Wilderness Road although research has shown that the actual path was a few miles to the north of here.

Exit 38-Levi Jackson Wilderness Road State Park: *(see map on page 51 for details).* Nine minutes to the east of this exit lies the Levi Jackson Wilderness Road State Park, honoring both the first judge in Laurel County and the famous pioneer trail which runs through the property.

The park is home to McHargue's Mill (closed for renovations) with its picturesque mill pond and ducks.

Nearby is the Mountain Life Museum, a living collection of old log buildings representing the different aspects of pioneer life in *Caintuck*. The 19th century folk (actors) bake bread, make candles and carry on with their life as usual while enjoy a chat with their "visitors from the future." Be careful if you go there and you're a man though. On the day I visited, the mother tried to marry her daughter off to me. I thought I was in serious trouble until Kathy rescued me!

"Unmarried" daughter with Levi Jackson Mother

On a sadder note, within the park lies the site of Kentucky's worst Indian massacre, Defeated Camp. During the night of October 3, 1786, under a hunter's moon, the McNitt party became the victims of a bloody Indian massacre in which at least 24 of the travelers were killed.

The group of approximately 60 pioneers, representing 24 families, had been traveling for over a month and had stopped for the night on the Boone Trace near the Little Laurel River.

Unknown to them, Indians–Shawnee and Chickamauga–were in the area to observe religious ceremonies. A war band may have

---

INSIDER TIP - We find the Perfect Motel

I've been recommending this Inn–the Baymont west at exit 29, since Kathy and I first visited it many years ago while escaping from a terrible I-75 snow storm. Since then, owner Bob Adkins has won many awards; the Inn is always clean and the staff, friendly.

The well decorated, high ceiling rooms have a full reclining armchair, large 25" screen TV, and coffee maker with full supplies. Heavy noise-killing drapes ensure a quiet stay even though next to the interstate. The separate vanity-bathroom (very important for traveling couples and fast morning getaways) has a modular shower with an excellent shower head and a GREAT steam extractor fan–the perfect room in a perfect motel.

But there is more. On the ground floor is an indoor/outdoor swimming pool which is maintained at a tepid 97°F (36°C); an even warmer bubble spa is right alongside.

We often eat at the Cracker Barrel within walking distance next door. The following morning, we enjoyed a free breakfast and paper in the Baymont "breakfast room," enabling us to make an early start. I continue to highly recommend this motel. ☎ 606-523-9040.

Birth of the World's Fast Food Business

Hidden in the valley just to the east of the Interstate in south Kentucky is a gem of a discovery–the birth place of America's (and the world's) fast food industry. For this is where Harland Sanders ran his Sanders Court Motel and Restaurant for many years (long famous with travelers for its clean rooms, country hams and pecan pie), right alongside the main route to Florida–Highway 25 *(see map on page 50)*.

Imagine Mr. Sanders' consternation in 1956 when he learned about the Government's plan to build a super highway (the I-75) to Florida just two miles to the west of his property. Sixty-six year old Sanders decided that his reputation for good wholesome food could continue to attract customers so he set about developing a new type of food for the traveler which they could take along on the road with them–deep fried chicken.

The Colonel's original kitchen - note the tub of secret herbs and spices in the corner.

The rest, of course, is history. His 11 secret herbs and spices combined with pressure frying techniques, developed into his famous Kentucky Fried Chicken, the first fast food business in the world. Later, the Commonwealth of Kentucky honored him by granting him the title of Colonel, and the name "Colonel Sanders Kentucky Fried Chicken" was born.

Today, you may visit the free museum which includes a typical Sanders Court motel room, the Colonel's office and the kitchen where he developed his special recipe. You sit in the original restaurant which was restored and re-opened in September 1990, and eat where it all began! Order the Colonel's original recipe from the adjoining modern KFC store.

How much money did Harland Sanders' Motel and Restaurant make? Here are his financial results for 1945:

RESTAURANT	- Food Sales	$1,847	
	- Cost of Sales	1,081	
	- Net Food Sales	$766	
	- Expenses	777	
	- **LOSS**	$10	$11
MOTEL	- Revenue	$906	
	- Expenses	542	
	- **PROFIT**	**$364**	364
TOTAL PROFIT FOR 1945			**$353**

become disturbed when it observed the settlers singing and playing cards at their overnight camp–also a sacred Indian place beside the river.

The scalped bodies were found later by local settlers, who buried the remains by the camp. During the raid, up to ten pioneers were taken prisoner, including 8 year old Polly Ford who spent nearly 15 years living with the Indians before being rescued.

Exit 29 & 25-Corbin: In May, 2003, Corbin held a "liquor" referendum and to the surprise

of virtually all residents, the town voted "wet" after more than 60 years of temperance. However, the new law will only allow sale of alcohol by the glass and only in restaurants which have more than 100 seats. As of press time for this edition, no restaurant has risen to this challenge although I have heard a rumor that one of the locally owned restaurants at exit 25 is considering selling to a large chain which serves liquor.

Exit 29-KFC: *(see Special Report.. Also see the map on page 50)*.

Exit 25-Inn on top of the Hill: When we started driving I-75 in the 1960s, the inn at the top of the hill on the southwest corner of this exit, was a particular favorite of our. Sadly, over the years it has gone "down hill" (pun intended) as it has changed hands from one brand to another. It is now closed and the gates chained ... another loss from the past.

Exit 11-Splash Water Park: Kentucky's largest family attraction is just 1/2 mile west of exit 11. Twenty-five acres of fun–Wave Pool, 900ft long Castaway (driftin') River, Tad Pole Island, three water slides of varying intensity, 300 gallon dump bucket–ensure all will enjoy themselves.

And if this is not enough, try the go-kart track, batting cages or 18 hole championship miniature golf.

I should also tell you from my own personal experience that if you are a chocolate lover, you must try *Mrs. Whitey's locally made chocolate chip brownies!* You can get them from the concession stand beside the ticket counter. [Hours vary seasonally. ☎ 606-549-6065 for information].

Mile 8 & 3-Mountains: Soon we will be crossing the Kentucky–Tennessee border and climbing from Jellico up into the sky. At Kentucky Miles 8 and 3, the freeway ahead gives us a glimpse of what is to come–a panoramic view of the mountain ridges to the south. Taylor, Patterson, Vanderpool, Chestnut Oak, Walnut and Brushy Mountains march across the horizon and recede into the bluish hazy distance.

Mile 6 Asphalt Rehabilitation: It's long overdue but, the Kentucky Transportation Cabinet is finally doing something about the washboard road surface through here. The project should be complete by early 2007, but should traffic become heavy, use the parallel US25W route (see brown route on colored maps). It's easy to reach from all I-75 exits in lower Kentucky, and comes back to the interstate through Jellico's exit 160, in Tennessee.

Mile 1 (N/bound)-Welcome Center: Say "hello" to counter folk Dallas, Debbie, Steve and Janelle.

TENNESSEE: Mile 161 (N/bound)-Graveyard: Notice the tiny graveyard beside I-75 just before this mile marker? Here is stark evidence of the way the interstate planners slashed the new freeway across landscape, dividing businesses, farms, homesteads, and

Kudzu

If it is summer and you look at the hillside ahead at Kentucky mile 8, you will see an incredible stand of Kudzu (pronounced *cut-zoo*, with the stress on the first syllable). This prolific vine (Pueraria) grows rapidly, covering everything in its path. You often see it in South Tennessee or Georgia covering telephone poles, fences and surrounding trees. Brought to America from Japan in 1876, it was first grown in the Japanese Pavilion at the Philadelphia Centennial Exposition and then became popular as a house plant.

Until 1955, it was used to stop soil erosion in the South, but it escaped and rapidly became a menace to the point where it has been described as a "national disaster." Growing as much as a foot a day in hot weather, the vine develops roots wherever its leaves touch the ground. In one season, it can easily grow 100 feet away from its original stem, enveloping everything in its path. The good news, however, is that cattle like to eat it. It has been used for its herbal and medicinal properties; recently, it has been found to be very useful in alcohol addiction therapy.

Money Saving Tip

Pickup your free copies of the green covered *Traveler Discount Guide* and the red covered *Discount Lodging Guide* motel coupon books at the Tennessee or Kentucky Welcome Centers (mile TN 161 or KY 1). Coupons in these books can save you <u>as much as 45%</u> off regular motel rates.

in this case–separating the local folk from their departed loved ones. The graveyard is lovingly maintained by the Gibson, Hyslope, Corbin and Parrott families; the cemetery is always well groomed and the flowers fresh.

Tennessee-the State that almost wasn't: Did you know that Tennessee would have been called *Franklin* if a Rhode Island delegate to an 18th century Congress had not been too late to vote? Here's what happened:

In 1769, settlers from Virginia illegally crossed the mountains and moved into the protected lands of the Cherokee, homesteading along the banks of the Watauga river.

Neighboring North Carolina refused the settlers appeals for help against the Cherokees who attacked the settlers so, four years before the American Revolution, they formed the Watauga Association, wrote the first American constitution (the Watauga Compact) and later in 1784, created the State of Franklin (after Ben of the same name).

In 1788, the state approached the Philadelphian Congress requesting entry into the Union as the 14th state, but the motion was lost by a single vote (remember that tardy delegate from RI?) and the State of Franklin disappeared forever–except in the hearts of Tennesseans. For being a descendant of a Watauga Association settler is as revered in Tennessee as a proven genealogy back to the *Mayflower* is in Massachusetts.

Over the next few years, Congress annexed Franklin to North Carolina, then designated it as part of the "SW Territory." The settlers finally achieved statehood in 1796, when Tennessee was admitted as the 16th state. The first Governor was John Sevier, one of the leaders of the original efforts for statehood.

Mile 161-Welcome Center: It's always a joy to stop at this older but well maintained Welcome Center. Say hello to Rick, Debbie, Joyce or Suzette, who are usually at the counter helping travelers with their journeys through Tennessee.

Exit 160-Jellico: *(Town map on page 54).* The small town of Jellico guards the northern gateway to the southernmost range of the massive Appalachian Mountains chain which sweeps across the northeast U.S.A., from New Brunswick, Canada to the Carolinas and Tennessee. Jellico, possibly named after the mountain Angelica plant which was used by settlers to brew an intoxicating drink called "Jelca," was settled in 1795 and incorporated in 1883. Some say the town was incorporated to provide a legal means of selling Tennessee whiskey.

It is remembered for a terrible train crash which occurred here during WWII. A speeding train hauling 15 cars loaded with over 600 soldiers on their way to army camp, derailed and crashed into the deep gorge of the Clear Fork River, about 1½ miles (2.4km) to the east. More than 35 men were killed.

Elk Valley: *(map page 54–although paved all the way, the route is not suitable for large RVs).* If you have time–this will only take you an extra 21 minutes–and the weather is reasonable, I suggest you turn off I-75 at exit 160, drive through Jellico and take the Elk Valley road which parallels the interstate. It rejoins I-75 at exit 141. For those who ply the freeway year after year, this might be a refreshing break. As you drive through the Jellico main street, note the old storefronts on either side. This is an unusual opportunity to see some really old buildings in their original state. Although they are designated as historical landmarks, they have not been renovated.

Route 297 continues on past the buildings and becomes a very pleasant country byway through leafy tunnels formed by overhanging trees, winding corners and occasional vistas to the east of I-75 as it climbs Pine Mountain.

Mile 159-Pine Mountain: The road seems to climb forever as it starts its four mile (6.4km) ascent toward the highest point on our southward journey. We are climbing the Pine Mountain Ridge of the Appalachian chain with Elk Fork Valley and Jellico Mountain to

TENNESSEE - *after the major Cherokee Indian town of Tanasi, located on the river which is now known as the Little Tennessee, in the eastern part of the State.*

our right; the Cumberland Mountain range to our left. The interstate tops at Mile 147 *(see next paragraph)*, and then, as it descends to Caryville, we come across one of the most famous exit signs on our journey–the one that everybody remembers– Stinking Creek.

Exit 156-Road to Rarity: I'm always intrigued when I see a new exit being built. Although we don't know the official signage wording yet, this one will link up with *Rarity Mountain*, a mountain top gated retreat offering magnificent views over East Tennessee.

Mile 147-the highest point on your journey: You are now at the highest point on your journey to Florida–2,247 feet above sea level–from now on it's all downhill!

Exit 144-"Stinking Creek Road": With all the names available to county planners, how did *"Stinking Creek"* ever get its name? As usual, the answer is rooted in history.

Years ago, there was a very harsh winter in the Tennessee mountains and wildlife were unable to forage and find food. They gathered at the local creek where water and sustenance had always been plentiful but the creek was frozen; eventually the animals died of starvation and thirst. In the Spring, all the carcasses thawed out and soon a horrible stench pervaded the area. So with great imagination, the creek was named, *"Stinking Creek."*

Moonshiners: (note–don't try this without a local map or GPS system in your car). On past trips I've wandered around the backwood tracks leading off of Stinking Creek Road – among the hills, valleys and hollows with their sweetwater creeks and room for a small corn patch. It's not difficult to imagine the smell and sounds of a different time–wood smoke, sour mash and the hiss of a copper still. The clink as another wide-mouthed Mason jar is set aside after receiving its potent fill of "white lightning," which trickles from the still's copper pipe.

Here is a photo of an abandoned still we found traveling on back mountain roads

(somewhere in Tennessee!) several years ago.

One evening, I was having dinner with some of the local folk when the conversation turned to moonshine. My neighbor asked if I'd ever tasted it. I told him I hadn't

and thought little more about it as we continued our meal. Just as dessert was being served, I felt something heavy drop in my lap–it was a Mason Jar of clear liquid. I don't know where it came from–I think I had my eyes closed at the time. Well, of course, later that evening I had to try it to make sure it wasn't just water ... and let me tell you ... we will never have another fuel crisis ... that stuff is *very, very* potent.

Many say that stock car racing owes its roots to these early moonshine activities since the moonshiners were often outracing the Revenue men, in their constant battle of outwitting each other. Soon, bragging rights for the fastest car were established by racing each other–is this how NASCAR was born?

Sergeant York: A famous World War I hero lived and hunted in the mountains just beyond Elk Valley to our west–Sergeant Alvin York. He grew up with guns and as a boy, was a crack shot and had the reputation of making every single bullet he fired, count.

Drafted into the Army in 1917, he struggled with the moral issue of shooting humans, but all this changed in Europe's Argonne Forest, on a cool day in October, 1918.

While attempting to move forward, York's platoon was trapped and surrounded by a large German force of machine gunners. In the next few minutes, York single-handedly took out 35 machine gun nests and captured 132 enemy soldiers–all in one action and with only 18 rifle shots and 6 shots from his .45 Colt pistol.

At one point, he was charged by a German Major and six men with fixed bayonets. York coolly picked them off one by one with his pistol, starting at the rear so the men in front weren't aware of their fallen comrades. He then captured the lone survivor, the Major!

Sergeant York was awarded the Medal of Honor for his heroic stand. Every single shot from his rifle and pistol had counted–a legacy from his hunting days in these mountains beside I-75.

Exit 141-As Seen on TV: How can you not stop when you see the enticing red and white *"As Seen on TV"* sign? Sheer curiosity took me off I-75 recently. Do they really have TV specials? Is the selection current or are they just leftovers? Well, the

The "New Deal" and Tennessee Valley Authority (TVA)

As you travel through Tennessee, you will encounter the massive works (Norris Dam & Chickamauga Dam, for example) of the Tennessee Valley Authority, the TVA ... what's it all about?

In the 1930's, the country was hurting from the effects of the Great Depression, and no where was this more evident than in the state of Tennessee. Newly elected President Franklin Roosevelt decided that the answer was to put the country back to work, and in 1933 proposed a "New Deal" which created many public works agencies and projects thus producing employment, and jump starting the economy.

Tennessee needed electrical power so work projects were implemented to build dams and generating plants on the Tennessee River. Senator George Norris of Nebraska led a fight to create an agency to keep such projects out of private hands, and the Tennessee Valley Authority (TVA) was born.

During the Second World War, the TVA's ability to produce massive amounts of electrical energy was crucial to the development of the atomic bomb (see Oak Ridge story on page 106). Today, the TVA is a powerful agency controlling all water issues such as power generation, flood control and navigation on the state's river system.

answer to all the above is a resounding, "yes."

The store is jammed with just about every "special" I've seen advertised on TV over the last 10 years; the diversity of the store's stock is huge. And yes, they have the most recent merchandise as well as items from *"As Seen on TV"* history.

You pay the same price advertised in the TV offer, but with no waiting or shipping & handling charges. Be aware that there is local sales tax added though.

I left proudly carrying a wire thing which I am assured, slices and dices faster and more efficiently than anything else on the Planet! [Hrs: Daily, 8-10p; ☎ 423-562-7777].

Mile 142-The Cross: What's that huge cross on the east side of the road? There are no churches nearby, just a building which very visibly advertises that it sells "adult" products. And that's exactly what it's all about.

According to local people, a wealthy Tennessean travels the state trying to stamp out such shops. Whenever one opens, he buys a small plot of land close by and erects one of his crosses.

I spoke to the owner of the RV park at the top of the lane which starts near the foot of the cross. He isn't very happy with the "Adult" shop either. Although he has no ties with the "Cross" man, he says it does provide a convenient landmark to guide RVs in to his site.

Mile 137-Devil's Racetrack: About 1/4 mile to the east of the interstate is a cone-shaped hill with vertical runs of sandstone rock up its sides. This is the "Devil's Racetrack," a formation of Pennsylvanian rock (late Paleozoic Age–see the geological strata diagram on page 94), about 340 million years old. People come from miles to explore this unique geological feature, rich with fossils.

Exit 128-Norris Dam: *(see map on page 55).* Here is an opportunity to take a short scenic trip off the I-75, for very little extra

NORRIS - named after George William Norris, Senator and a great champion of public electric power. Norris was instrumental in promoting the Tennessee Valley Authority (TVA) as the agency to harnessing the power of water. Norris was built to house the builders of the Dam.

investment in time. This side trip across the picturesque Norris Dam will only add an extra 12 minutes to your journey, and bring you back to I-75 at exit 122.

For a really interesting time, you might wish to visit the Lenoir Museum at the Norris Dam State Park or the Museum of Appalachia (see Insider Tip), both are excellent.

Several years ago, Kathy and I stopped at the Grist Mill, just below the Museum on the east side of the dam, and chatted with a Park Ranger. She told us that the road below the Grist Mill led to a ford and waterfall–so off we went. We discovered a narrow leafy road which ran alongside Clear Creek. After driving slowly through the shallow ford, we found the waterfall. Below it, the creek meandered across a bed of small rocks and pebbles, in a small valley speckled with yellow winged butterflies–a beautiful sight on a warm, sunny day. The whole adventure only took fifteen minutes; if you would like to repeat our adventure, just follow our "waterfall" road on the Norris Dam map on page 55.

Just to the west of Norris Dam lies the Norris Dam State Park where you can rent a cabin. Ten of them are labeled deluxe or "AAA," 19 are rustic or "AA." If interested, give the Park office a call at 865-426-7461.

Mile 126.5 and 125 (Northbound): As we

start to leave the relative flat lands of the Clinch River Valley, ahead you will see the Pine and Walden Mountain Ridges with the Vowell Mountain peak at 2,603 ft, and far to the left is the Flag Pole at 3,500 ft.

We will leave these peaks on our left as we continue to climb northbound towards the Cumberland Mountain Ridge at mile 136.

Exit 122-Museum of Appalachia: (see Insider Tip, map on page 55).

Exit 122-Welcome Center: Next door to the Golden Girls, is the Anderson County log cabin Welcome Center. Stop by and say

INSIDER TIP - A Mountain Man's Gift to the Future

When you arrive at the **Museum of Appalachia** and enter the main building, you know this is a special place. The smell of warm, freshly baked bread wafts by as you purchase your tickets. You follow the signs to this huge outdoor museum, passing the brick fireplace where flaming logs pop and snap on ancient andirons. These are all good omens.

As you move out into the bright mountain sunlight, you have stepped back into time. Nestled close to rounded hay stacks are a few sheep while a small herd of Scottish Longhorn cattle drink from a pond. The faint sounds of fiddle and banjo waft across the meadow on the still morning air as a group on the verandah of an old mountain house, enjoy a few moments away from field chores.

This is a living mountain village–the Museum of Appalachia. A wonderful experience of 38 original mountain buildings, displayed in such a way that you would believe the inhabitants have just stepped out back for a few moments.

Barns contain museum displays of Appalachian mountain living. Of particular interest are the many different types of musical instruments, including a long horn which was used by Grandma for warning everybody within miles, that "revenue men" were in the valley.

To John Rice Irwin, founder of this wonderful museum, it has been a lifetime labor of love and this dedication shows in the detail around you. John Rice has created a true gift for future generations–we heartily recommend it. See the map on page 55 for phone number, hours and admission details.

"hello" to Stephanie, Becky and Ethel. If you decide to take the Knoxville bypass via Clinton and Oak Ridge, they will be able to help you. [Hrs, M-F, 9-5p; ☎ 865-457-4542].

Exit 122-Bypass Knoxville via Oak Ridge: *(Route map on page 56)* Sometimes it would be great to get off I-75 for a little while–and exit 122 provides such an opportunity while still moving you ahead in your journey. Rather than continue running south and through the sometimes heavy traffic of Knoxville's I-40, you could "cut the corner" and taking the *"Oak Ridge"* route.

The bypass leaves west from exit 122 on SR61-Seivers Blvd, crosses the Clinch River and cuts through the "antique shop" town of Clinton *(see next topic)*.

INSIDER TIP - Aubrey's

If it's time to stop for a meal then I know you will enjoy Aubrey's Restaurant at exit 112. As soon as you enter the door, you know this is going to be a wonderful dining experience–the greeting could not be friendlier. Aubrey's meets all our criteria for a *"Dave Hunter* **Insider Tip."** Service is excellent, a wide choice of entrees are reasonable priced ($9-$22) and the food, tasty. Try the Potato Soup topped with cheese, with crispy sweet rolls to start–yummy!

Take time to check out the unusual artwork hanging from the ceiling. Artist Bobbie Crews has decorated 4'x8' blackboards with pictures from bygone times, in colored chalk. They are quite a feature.

Go east at exit 112 and turn left up the hill towards the Holiday Inn Express; the restaurant is across the road. [Hrs: 11-10p daily; F-Sa, 11-11p; ☎ 865-938-2724].

After crossing US25, SR61 (now called the *Oakridge Hwy*) the road follows the northern bank of the Clinch with the Walden Ridge of the Appalachian Mountain chain to the north–and becomes the *"Oak Ridge Turnpike."*

Just east of Oak Ridge, the *Turnpike* becomes SR95 and you enters the secret WWII town of Oak Ridge *(see Tennessee exit 376A for the story of Oak Ridge and the Atomic Bomb)*.

Turn left on to Lafayette Dr, travel its length and turn left to join SR62-Illinois Road which

leads to SR162-the *Pellissippi Parkway*. The *Parkway* joins I-75 west of Knoxville at I-40/I-75, Exit 376.

The total distance from exit 122 to exit 376 is 27.7 miles (45km) and takes about 39 minutes to drive. Alternatively, staying on I-75 will take about 30 minutes (depending upon construction activity and traffic), but the Oak Ridge route is much more interesting and will only cost you an extra 9 minutes.

Exit 122-Clinton: this old Tennessee town, 5 miles (8km) west of I-75 is an antique hunters heaven. Clustered around Main & Market Sts are 11 antique shops and a large mall. Enjoy!

Here you will also find the marketplace where in 1895-1936, freshwater pearl producers traded their wares harvested from the Clinch River. Clinton pearls were so well known that dealers came from New York to buy; pearls from this area have even been featured at the International Exposition, in Paris.

Mile 107-Southbound Driving Notes: If continuing on I-75 past exit 122, you will need the following notes.

As Interstate-75 swings south and around Knoxville to the west, it briefly joins and assumes the mile post numbers of two other freeways (I-640 and I-40). It can be a little tricky driving through here without local knowledge, so let me "talk" you through it. You'll find all the lane change instructions clearly marked on the colored map page 27 (pp171-172 for northbounders).

First, we want the westbound branch of I-640 (Knoxville's northern "ring road")–here's how we join it. Several miles after exit 108, you will see an *"Exit 3 I-640 East"* sign.

As you approach it, make sure you stay well over to the right. At exit 3, the left 2 lanes bear off to the east and continues on to down-  town Knoxville–don't follow it! Instead, stay over in the right lane (the *I-75 South* lane) which becomes a single lane ramp until you merge with the traffic of I-640 West. The mile posts now change to Interstate-640's numbering system.

KNOXVILLE - *originally called White's Fort, in 1791 it was renamed after General Henry Knox (1750-1806), a soldier during the American Revolution. General Knox was the army Commander in Chief (1783-84) and the Nation's first Secretary of War under President Washington (1785-95). The main depository of the Nation's gold bullion, Fort Knox, is also named after him.*

INSIDER TIP - Best BBQ Ribs on I-75 - Calhoun's or Rafferty's?

Over the years, I have eaten in just about every BBQ rib place beside I-75, and for many years, considered Calhoun's to be tops. But now some readers are challenging me since they consider Rafferty's, two miles east of Calhoun's to be better ... so I want YOU to be the judge.

Calhoun's: locals flock to Calhoun's which claims to be the *"Home of America's Best Ribs."* As soon as you step through the front door, you know that manager Jonathan Rosner is ready for our challenge. Food is fresh, service is warm and friendly. [Hours: opens daily at 11 am. ☎ 865-673-3444, *10020 Kingston Pike–take exit 376B (I-140E-Pellissippi Pkwy), take exit 1A (US11E/US70-Kingston Pike east). Calhoun's is on your right past the lights*].

Rafferty's: seems that locals flock to Rafferty's as well. Again, great hickory smoked ribs, loaded baked potato, real "homemade" french fries and a side salad for a comparable price. Manager John Steed is looking forward to impressing you. [Hours: opens daily at 11 am. ☎ 865-539-1323, *8906 Kingston Pike –take exit 378 (Cedar Bluff Rd) south, cross Peter St and turn left to US11E/US70-Kingston Pike. Rafferty's is on your right*].

When you arrive at either restaurant, make sure you take your copy of *"Along I-75"* in with you and let them know that this is a *challenge* situation. We want to know **which really is the best**–results will be announced in the book's 15th edition.

I've marked both locations on map 27 and 171 for you; each is just a few minutes off I-40/I-75.

After three miles (4.8km), the left lanes continue ahead to *I-40 East-Knoxville*. Move into the right two lanes and follow the *I-40West/I-75 South - Nashville/Chattanooga* sign.

On the ramp, the two lanes quickly become one, so move left as soon as possible–and move left again once you are on I-40 since the ramp lane disappears.

The mile posts numbers change once again–this time to I-40's "380" series.

Watch for police along this stretch since it is actively patrolled for out of state speeders (the "locals" seem to whiz by at excessive speeds with complete immunity).

Well, how did we do? You should now be driving westward along I-75/I-40. If you see exit 383-Papermill Dr ahead of you, you know you are going the right way.

Mile 383-The Body Farm: Now, if you are squeamish (or just about to stop for a meal), please skip the following paragraphs. If you continue to read, I make no apology for the subject matter . . .

About 2 miles (3.2km) southeast of where you are right now is the 3 acre Bass Anthropological Research Facility. Also known by its initials BARF (I kid you not!), or the *"Body Farm."* Made famous in crime writer Patricia Cornwell's novel of the same name,

INSIDER TIP - Jameson Inns, Clean and Friendly

Consistency in the quality of accommodation is very important to me as a traveler. I much prefer staying at a regional inn chain, than the large franchise-operated "Nationals." "Regionals" are often operated by the inn company's own trained and managed staff–thereby ensuring a consistent lodging experience. When traveling in the Southeast, my choice is Jameson Inns (based in Atlanta) and in a few miles at exit 378, we'll have a chance to enjoy one.

In my experience, Jameson Inns offers safe, quality accommodations at a very reasonable price. Rooms include a luxurious 13" mattress bed and recliner chair, executive desk with data ports, TV with free HBO, microwave/fridge, coffee/tea maker, iron and board ... in fact, everything to make your overnight stay as comfortable as possible. Oh, and local phone calls (including 1-800 access) are free.

The front desk is staffed around the clock and I've always found the Jameson people to be friendly and helpful, no matter the hour.

In the morning, you'll find that a breakfast of fresh fruit, Belgian waffles, baked pastries, cereal, juices, coffee, etc., is included with your overnight stay, as is a free *"USA Today."* When comparing motel rates, don't overlook these extras. For instance, if you buy a morning paper, making a couple of phone calls and have breakfast "on the road," you are probably spending another $14 per couple–a stay at a Jameson saves you these additional costs.

I heartily recommend Jameson Inns–you'll not be disappointed. ☎ 1-800-526-3766

the Body Farm is a highly secured area where corpses are placed in various situations (in the open, buried under leaves, in water, etc.) and in different environments (burnt out cars, old trunks,)–and in the interests of forensic science, left to deteriorate.

Operated by the University of Tennessee, the facility is famous in the world of crime detection. Organizations such as Interpol, the FBI and regional police authorities use the Farm's findings to determine how long a corpse might have been dead (given climate and environment of the discovery site).

How is this done? Well, out of a sense of propriety I'm not going to tell you unless you ask me in person–or better still, read Patricia Cornwell's best selling book. You'll find the answers in lurid detail.

Oh! by the way, you cannot visit the Body Farm–it's not an "attraction" and is surrounded by razor wire fences. However, since this book claims to be a complete guide to I-75–I just wanted you to know it was there.

Exit 376-Exit Letters: Some travelers have found this exit confusing. I-75, exit 376 services a short multi lane "service road" which then splits into exits 376A-to Oak Ridge, and 376B-Maryville. So if you are looking for the "lettered" exits, you must take exit 376 first.

Exit 376A-Oak Ridge: *(see map on page 56 for details).* 12.3 miles (19.8km) to the north of the I-40/I-75 lies a city built in 1942, for the workers of Clinton Engineering Works. A city so "secret" that it was on no map and anybody asking casual questions about it would be arrested as a possible spy.

One hundred years ago, Albert and Mileva Einstein published their Special Theory of Relativity and revealed the famous equation $E=MC^2$. In essence, this formula states that there is an incredible amount of energy locked up in matter.

But how to unlock it? In 1939, the US Government realized that the Nazis in Germany understood the possibilities of unlocking this energy and creating an atomic bomb. Their scientists had recently succeeded in splitting atoms of uranium at Berlin's Kaiser Wilhelm Institute. An atomic bomb in the hands of the Nazis would have guaranteed their world domination so it was vital that the USA protect itself by beating the Germans by developing the bomb first. President Roosevelt authorized a full-scale atomic bomb program,

code named the *Manhattan Project*; work started in 1942.

Three top secret sites were chosen to perform different phases of the project. Plutonium production was located at site W (Hanford, WA); Uranium (U235) extraction at site X in Tennessee, and site Y, a lonely mesa in New Mexico called *Los Alamos* where the various components from "W" and "X" would be assembled under the direction of Robert Oppenheimer, and the finished bomb tested.

Site X was to become the secret city of *Oak Ridge*. Named after *Black Oak Ridge*, one of a series of three valleys northwest of Knoxville, it was chosen because of the availability of huge amounts of hydro-electricity generated by the TVA dams; the valleys offered shelter to adjacent operations should one of the atomic plants explode, and finally, it was very sparsely populated by farmers who could be easily relocated. Its remoteness also ensured security from Nazi spies.

So the secret city of Oak Ridge was born and scientists & workers moved in. Very few residents were allowed to leave and until 1949 it could only be visited by special permit.

Three plants with code names K25–uranium extraction and enrichment, X10–atomic pile and Y12–uranium atom separation were built in parallel valleys under a secret organization, the Clinton Engineering Works. The entire area, including the town of Oak Ridge with housing and amenities for all the workers, was enclosed by barbed-wire with access controlled by seven gates. Life in the area was very basic and made difficult by the ever present mud.

Today things are much different, an excellent visitors' center and several attractions –the *American Museum of Science and Energy*, *New Bethel Church* (where the Project scientists used to meet), the *Graphite Reactor* and the K-25 visitor overlook–are well worth a visit for those interested in the birth of the Nuclear Age. Since 9/11, security has been tightened at some of the sites so if planning to visit them, I suggest you phone or visit the *Visitors Center* first *(See map and other details on page 56).*

Exit 373-Apple Cake Tea Room: *(see* **Insider Tip***).*

Exit 368-Driving Notes: Here I-75 leaves the I-40, and continues south towards Chattanooga. I-75 mile marker numbers resume.

INSIDER TIP - Apple Cake Tea Room

I cannot rave enough about the Apple Cake Tea Room, just south of the interstate at exit 373. Housed in a cozy log cabin, the minute you enter the door you know this is going to be a special occasion. Tasty home cooking aromas greet your senses and prepare you for the meal to follow. Take a look around the interior. The Henry family has lived here for many generations and owner Mary Henry furnished the interior with many of her treasured family heirlooms.

Now to the lunch menu. First, a very presentable chicken soup and then on to the main course. There are a number of sandwich choices; I enjoyed the grilled chicken sandwich on a fresh croissant. Side orders of honey butter, cheese toast and banana nut bread help round out the course. Don't miss trying the Cornucopia for dessert–a wonderful blending of vanilla ice cream, sauteed bananas and homemade chocolate or butterscotch sauce nested in a crunchy basket. Scrumptious!

To find this wonderful restaurant, take exit 373 south towards Farragut. The Apple Cake is in Appalachian Log Square plaza on the left side of Campbell Station Road, almost immediately opposite the Pilot gas station. Hrs: M-Sa, 11-2:30 ☎ 865-966-7848

Exit 81-Wild Flowers: I happened to drive through this stretch of I-75 last May which is an unusual time of year for me, and was awed by the profusion of flowers. Carpets of red corn poppies, white and yellow shasta daisies and yellow cosmos blanketed the ramp slopes and median strips along the interstate.

In fact, the Tennessee Department of Transport plants more than 700 acres of wildflowers along interstate routes, under the State's Bicentennial Beautification Act. As somebody recently remarked,

"Without a doubt, Tennessee stretches of the interstate were the most beautiful of the entire journey."

Exit 81: Lenoir City: 1/5th mile east of I-75, is the pleasant Lenoir City (pronounced, "Len-ore") Visitor Center, with its waterfall and koi pond. Say "hi" to Director Mary, and counter staff Alice and Becky, who have all sorts of area information to share with you.

Mile 81-Rock City: Those who drove to Florida in the pre-I-75 days will remember the classics of roadside advertising–*Burma Shave* and *Rock City*. Most of these were dis-

continued when federal legislation required the removal of all private roadside signs along the interstates, but several have survived.

"Rock City" signs were very prolific and adorned the roofs of barns, outhouses, and farm buildings throughout the South (Rock City is an attraction in Chattanooga), announcing the number of miles you had to travel to *"See Rock City."* If you look very carefully to the left at mile marker 81, you will see a barn with an original *"Rock City"* sign painted on its roof.

Exit 76-TN Valley Winery: A quarter of a mile to the west of exit 76 (Sugar Limb Road) lies the entrance to the *Tennessee Valley Winery.* For 21 years the Reed family–Tom, Jerry, John and Christine–have practiced the Tennessee wine making tradition, producing more than 26,000 gallons of table wines each year from their 22 acres of plantings at the Wildwood Vineyards, located 15 miles (24.1km) south in Roane County. Winemaker, Tom, is proud of the fact that the family's estate has won medals and awards from all over the United States. Since 1984, the wines have earned more than 800 medals

Tom and Christine sample one of their gold medal wines

in national and international competition.

Tastings and picnic facilities are all available here; the Reeds invites you to stay a while and enjoy a picnic lunch on the sun-deck where you can relax and take in the magnificent view across the Loudon Valley. [Hrs: M-Sa, 10-6p, Su, 1-5p; ☎ 865-986-5147].

Mile 74-Mitchell W. Stout Bridge: You are just about to pass over the wide Tennessee River, on a bridge named after a Korean War hero, Sergeant Stout. Here's what happened:

While his unit's bunker came under heavy attack while guarding the Khe Gio Bridge, a grenade was thrown into their midst. Stout, knowing that it might explode at any

moment and kill them all, grabbed it and hugging it close to his body like a football to shield them all, ran for the door. It exploded killing him–but his action saved his fellow soldiers.

Mitchell Stout was awarded the Medal of Honor, posthumously. He died at age 20.

Exit 68-Tennessee Cheddar: As a youth, I spent several months living on an English dairy farm which owned a huge herd of black & white cows, or *"Friesans"* as we called them. Kathy, my Canadian wife, calls the same breed, *"Holsteins."* Who is right?

This question arose again recently when we drove in to Sweetwater Valley Farm to meet owners John and Celia Harrison and to sample the famous Tennessee cheese we had been hearing so much about.

Let me say, the question of b&w cows (I still call them *Friesans!*) quickly disappeared as I sank my teeth into nibblets of Sweetwater's award winning *1999 Tennessee Aged, Mountain White, Hickory Smoked* and *Burch's Champion Reserve.* These cheeses are so good the Harrisons actually mail them to customers in Wisconsin! By the way, while you are tasting the cheese, you can watch it being made through the large glass windows of the cheese "Make" room.

We then took a Farm tour and saw baby calves in their "nursery" pens. Next, we visited the milking facility where machines milk the herd of 700 *"Friesans"* three times daily. Dairy farming has become so sophisticated that computers now track how far each cow has walked during the day, and her milk yield.

If you are traveling with children–who have never seen a cow and believe that all milk comes in bottles–this farm visit and tour is an absolute must!

The farm is only a 4 minute drive from I-75. Take exit 68 and drive east for 2 miles (3.2km) on Pond Creek Rd (SR323), turn left on to US 11 and drive 1/5th mile to the farm entrance (white pillars) which is on your left. [Store Hrs, M-Sa, 8:30-5p, Su, 1-5p (summer only); Farm tours: (weather permitting), M-

Sa, 10-4p, tour leaves store on the hour; ☎ toll free 877-862-4332, 865-458-9192].

If you don't have time to visit the cheese shop here, you have a second chance when you reach Georgia. Sweetwater Valley Farm have opened a cheese outlet just 250yds west of I-75, at Georgia exit 350.

Exit 60-Lost Sea: Seven miles (11.3km) to the east of I-75 (91/2 minutes along Route 68) lies North America's largest underground lake–the *"Lost Sea"*–4.5 acres of water deep within the Craighead Caverns.

As you glide across the mirror lake in the dimly lit cavern, unusual rock formations, limestone deposits and strange cave flowers heighten the mystery; through the glass bottomed boat, speckled trout can be seen in the crystal clear water below.

During the Civil War, the caves were a source of saltpeter for gunpowder. Close your eyes and imagine smoky lanterns casting their flickering shadows on the cavern walls as Confederate soldiers swing their pickaxes. Listen to the ring of metal against stone. These are spooky surroundings.

If you decide to tour the caves, dress warmly because below ground, the air is a constant 58 degrees summer or winter. Also wear solid shoes–the tour includes a walk of about 3/4 mile. [Daily Hrs: Nov-Feb, 9-5p, Sep-Oct/Mar-Apr, 9-6p; May-June/Aug, 9-7p, July, 9-8p; Adult/Child- $13.95/$6.95; ☎ 423-337-6616].

Exit 52-*"The World's Best Ice Cream"*: It's that time again ... the time when Kathy and I must sit down at a table covered with cups of different ice creams, to sample them and ensure that Mayfield Dairy Farms is still churning out (pun intended) the *"World's Best Ice Cream"* (Time Magazine).

So once again, we leave I-75 at Tennessee's exit 52 (Mt. Verd Road) and follow route 305

Colorful "farmyard" painting on the wall outside the Mayfield Dairy building

eastwards for 4.3 miles (6.9 km) through pleasant countryside towards Athens, TN.

Mayfield Dairy is well marked on the left side of the road, you can't miss the big round brown and yellow billboard at Mayfield Lane stating:

"Mayfield Dairy Farms–Home of
the World's Best Ice Cream."

As we draw close to the building, we see the colorful wall mural of farmyard scenes. As usual, we head directly to the Ice Cream Parlor and put ourselves in the hands of Chad, Donna and the Mayfield counter staff, to start sampling the wares.

Somebody has to do it!

As always, I ask about the most popular flavors for adult. It seems that *Vanilla*, *Moosetracks* (vanilla ice cream & peanut butter cups swirled with fudge) and *Turtle Tracks* (vanilla ice cream with chocolate caramel Turtles, chocolate covered pecans and a caramel swirl) are the big ones.

For the youngsters, its *Super Cow* (vanilla ice cream with pink, blue and yellow swirls), *Birthday Cake* (sugar cookie flavored ice cream with a blue icing swirl and colored buttercream freckles) and *Play Dough* (yellow vanilla ice cream with red & blue cookie dough).

We dutifully sampled all of these and agreed that the Mayfield's ice cream is still the *"World's Best!"*

Just as we are about to leave, Donna said that we haven't tried the others yet.

What others? She told me that they have four new flavors which are part of the Mayfield *"Flavor Decision '06"* campaign and only one of them will be retained as a permanent flavor; we must record our votes before we leave.

So, it's back to the table and tasting cups for *Extreme Moose Tracks* (rich chocolate ice cream with fudge-filled cups and fudge lumps), *Blueberry Cream Pie* (cream cheese ice cream with blueberry swirl and sugar pie pieces), *Peanut Butter Cookie Dough* (cookie dough-flavored ice cream with peanut butter swirl and cookie dough pieces), and *Triple Brownie* (brownie batter-flavored ice cream with brownies and a swirl of brownie batter). Phew!!! Next year, I want danger pay.

Finally, for dessert, we decided to try a flavor a reader recommended, *Lemon Meringue Pie* (lemon chiffon ice cream with meringue nougat and graham pieces). It was awesome but my palate may have become a bit jaded by now.

After thanking the staff, we staggered back to our car, feeling grateful that we were at least half-an-hour from our next food review for the book, a popular BBQ Rib restaurant.

You too can have a Mayfield Dairy tasting experience. The ice cream parlor is open year round: M-F, 9-5, Sa, 9-2p, closed Su & major holidays. Ice cream prices are very reasonable, starting at $1 for a single scoop & $2 for a double.

Plant tours are held Monday to Saturdays, every half-hour. The last tour is 1 hour before closing time. Admission is free; comfortable slip-resistant shoes are recommended for the plant tour. Further information?
☎ 423-745-2151 or 1-800-629-3435.

Mile 44-Electronic Fog Detection & Warning System: You are about to enter a "high-tech" portion of the freeway. Born out of tragedy–the Hiwassee River Valley electronic Fog Detection and Warning system.

Man-made fog is a frequent problem on this five mile section, caused primarily by industry east of here–and it can be deadly.

Since the opening of this stretch of highway in 1973, there have been 18 fatalities and 130 injuries in more than 200 fog related crashes. In December, 1990, a terrible traffic accident of massive proportions was caused by fog rapidly enveloping I-75. On the southbound downgrade towards the River, 83 cars and trucks piled into one another. The end result? Thirteen killed and 50 injured.

This tragedy provided the impetus needed to deal with this deadly section, and the fog advisory system was born. The Fog Detection and Warning system uses eight fog sensors and 44 speed detectors to constantly monitor visibility and traffic flow. In the same manner

HIWASSEE RIVER - *Cherokee Indian word meaning "meadow."*
CHATTANOOGA - *a Cree Indian word meaning "rock rising to a point" (Lookout Mountain).*

as an optical smoke detector, the fog sensors measure the clarity of the air between its detection cells–if you look closely you will see the two arms of the sensors on some of the roadside poles.

Data from the monitors are relayed to a central computer at the Highway Patrol office where it is analyzed and translated into messages displayed on the overhead electronic signs. If it senses heavy fog, the system can even activate barriers at six I-75 entry ramps, closing off the fog shrouded freeway to traffic.

Since installation in late 1993, there have been no fog related accidents or fatalities in this area.

Mile 42-Spanish Explorers: And now for a change of pace. In May, 1539, the Governor of Cuba, Don Hernando de Soto landed in Tampa and started an extensive exploration of North America with an army of 600 men.

For more than four years, he traveled over 4,000 miles while searching for gold and silver–and a north passage to China. Ranging up the US mainland through Georgia, he led his army into the Carolinas, Tennessee–and as far away as modern Chicago, until he turned southward through Missouri and into Arkansas where he died in 1542.

Extensive journals were kept documenting his exploration. Since most of the Indian sites mentioned are known today and many modern roads are built over early Indian trails, the track taken by his expedition is well known. The path of I-75 crosses the path of de Soto's army in two places–Athens, TN & Perry, GA.

From his journals for May, 1540, we know that while in Tennessee he spent a night at Madisonville. The next day an Indian chief visited him and led him to Athens. Here he was joined by a scouting party he had sent up the Tennessee Valley towards Knoxville, where they discovered Indian mines.

He and his army then traveled to, and camped on, Hiwassee Island, at the confluence of the Hiwassee & Tennessee Rivers. Examination of the terrain indicates that he would have crossed the modern path of I-75 in the vicinity of this mile marker.

Mile 18-Radar Alert: Be careful here in case

the traffic ahead of you suddenly brakes! The interstate runs downhill and gently curves to the left with trees lining the median area.

At the bottom of the hill an emergency vehicle path cuts through the trees between the south and northbound I-75 lanes, and the police love to hide here with radar beamed up the hill. Cars cannot see them until they are right on top of the trap and speeders violently brake to avoid getting caught. Watch the traffic ahead of you as you descend this hill. We don't want you rear-ending a speeder.

Exit 27-Paul Huff Pkwy: Tennessee sure has its fair share of Medal of Honor winners.

Infantryman and Cleveland resident Cpl. Paul Huff was awarded the Medal for intrepid leadership and daring combat skills during the US attack on Carano, Italy, in 1944.

Exit 9-Enterprise Boulevard: $23 million has been spent on this new exit built to service a new industrial park venture. Originally, the lands to the southwest of mile 9 were occupied by the *Volunteer Ordnance Works*, a factory established in 1942 to manufacture TNT explosives for WWII. Later renamed, Volunteer Army Ammunition Plant (VAAP), it provided explosives for the Korean and Vietnam Wars. Production ceased in 1977 and the property was converted to various other purposes such as the manufacture of nitric and sulphuric acids, and ammonium nitrate, the latter for fertilizer production.

After a huge environmental clean-up, the lands have been redeveloped into a major industrial campus facility called, *"Enterprise South Industrial Park."* I'm sure we will hear more about this complex in the years to come.

Exit 5-Shallowford Road: Every so often on I-75, you find exits with huge selections of lodging, restaurants and shopping. This is such a place. To the west is a choice of 15 lodging properties. On the east side of I-75 are many restaurants and the Hamilton Place Shopping Mall (see map inset on page 168; northbound traffic can take exit 4A for direct access to the Mall).

Exit 4-Tennessee Valley Railroad: As a kid, I loved the smell and noise of steam locomotives as they chugged their way through the countryside. Now you can experience it (again ... if you are over 40 years old!) with a ride on the Tennessee Valley Railroad.

You board your coach *(see* **Insider Tip***)* at the *Grand Junction Station* where your locomo-

Old Number 349

tive–*Southern Railway #4501*, old *Central Georgia #349* or perhaps engines *#610* or *#630*–waits to follow the Civil War track of the *Tennessee & Georgia Railroad*; once a vital supply link, first for the Confederacy and then for the Union as the tides of war shifted.

You can sense the Civil War atmosphere as the train winds through the Chattanooga country and plunges into the darkness of the *1858 Missionary Ridge Tunnel*, on its way to the *East Chattanooga Terminus* where the locomo-

From the cab as we head into the tunnel

tive is turned around on the turn table ready for the trip back.

Afterwards, enjoy the audio-visual show and railroad exhibits, visit the repair shop or browse the gift store.

Grand Junction Station is 3.8 miles (6.1km) from I-75, take exit 4 (Chickamauga Dam) and follow Rt153N to the fourth (Jersey Pike) exit. Turn left and follow the *"TVRM"* signs to Cromwell Rd. [Hrs, M-Sa, 10-5p; Su, 11:30-5p; Adult/Child, $12.50/$6.50; ☎ 423-894-8028].

Exit 2-Chattanooga: *(City map on page 56).* Many people bypass downtown Chattanooga because it seems such a long trek to the west of I-75, but I-75, exit 2, and along I-24 to exit 178, will get you there *in 9 minutes*.

And believe me, it is well worth it. Not only is the short trip a scenic and interesting drive as the excellent freeway winds down the face of historic Missionary Ridge, but downtown

INSIDER TIP - Ride in the Cab

Psst! If you are planning to ride the TN Valley Railroad, few know you can ride up front in the cab with the engineer. It costs $10 extra but is well worth it. Phone ahead to makes sure cab space is available–there are only two spaces per trip.

Chattanooga has become a mecca for visitors.

The Interstate physically separates Chattanooga's two tourist areas. As you approach Chattanooga, the **Lookout Mountain/St. Elmo area** is on your left, and **Downtown Tourist area** is to your right. Let take a quick look at the St. Elmo area before heading downtown.

I-24 exit 178-Lookout Mtn/St. Elmo: follow the sign for *Lookout Mountain*–turn left on to Broad St–pass back under I-24–follow the enlarged section on my map on page 56.

Lookout Mountain Attractions: On the mountain–*Rock City*, *Ruby Falls*, *Battle for Chattanooga Museum* and *Point Park*. You need to drive to the first two; I suggest you take a ride up the *Incline Railway* from its St. Elmo station and at the top, walk the 2 blocks along to the museum and park–the view over Chat-

INSIDER TIP
Sticky Fingers and Famous Dave's

Sticky Fingers - A long time downtown favorite of mine, *Sticky Fingers* also has a location on the Hamilton Place perimeter road. Arguably, the best authentic Memphis-style ribs and barbecue in the South. Our hickory-smoked ribs, wings, barbecue pork and five signature Sticky Fingers barbecue sauces (yes, we tried them all) were to die for. Joe, our hospitable server just kept them coming, and coming, and coming.

If you enjoy ribs, you'll understand its name although they serve many other entrees as well. Enjoy!

The restaurant is located beside I-75 on the western edge of Hamilton Place - see inset map on page 168. [Hrs, Su-Th, 11-10p; Fr-Sa, 11-11p; ☎ 423-899-7427].

Famous Dave's - With a name like this, you would think they'd let me go to the front of the line ... but they didn't.
(Tip: phone ahead to get your name put on the "wait" list before you arrive).

We arrived around 7pm, and enjoyed sitting outside chatting with some local folk until our pager started flashing.

The wait was definitely worth it. The pit cooked BBQ food (ribs, steaks, etc) was well prepared and very tender. Our server, Dave, was excellent. Famous Dave's is located at 2122 Gunbarrel Road, just east of Hamilton Place - see inset map on page 168. [Hrs, M-Th, Su, 11-10p; Fr-Sa, 11-11p; ☎ 423-954-3227]

tanooga with the river winding around, is spectacular.

<u>Raccoon Mountain Power Plant</u>: Farther west lies *Raccoon Mountain* with its intriguing power generation plant. It works rather like a large storage battery. At times of low electricity consumption (night, for instance), river water is slowly pumped up 990 feet through a concrete tunnel drilled through the mountain, to a huge reservoir at mountain top.

When electricity is needed, the water is released down the same tunnel, powering the same pumps which now serve as generators. The system can run for 22 hours driven by the mountain top water, generating 1,530 megawatts of electricity. People thought this generation system was crazy when proposed

in 1970 ... but it works! [A Visitor Center is open daily from 9-5; ☎ 423-751-0011 for further information].

I-24 exit 178-Downtown: Downtown Chattanooga is based on a square grid pattern so it's very easy to navigate–just watch for one-way signs. Use the distinctive Aquarium building (brown angular building with glass triangles on top) as your area landmark.

To reach it, take I-24, exit 178 and take the first ramp on your right following signs for *Downtown/Market St*. Drive along *Market Street*, past the *Chattanooga Choo Choo* Holiday Inn *(see* **Insider Tip***)* until you see the

---

INSIDER TIP - a Private Parlor Car for the Night

How would you like to spend a night in your own private railroad Parlor car? All this is possible at the *1909 Chattanooga Railroad Terminus*, operated by Holiday Inn. On the rails beside several Victorian platforms stand personal Parlor Sleeping cars awaiting lucky guests. Each is well appointed with a large bedroom (including TV & phone), and a separate toilet/shower compartment (and before you ask ... yes, it's OK to flush while the train is standing in the station. The cars are permanently attached to the hotel's plumbing system). After spending a night in Car 764, I can appreciate what a magnificent lifestyle the railroad barons of the 19th century lived! Call ahead to the hotel to ensure a car is available for you–they are very popular.

Our personal luxury Parlor Car

As darkness settled, I sat under a flickering gas lamp on the old platform reflecting upon a wonderful evening dining in the station's restaurant. I'm sure I sensed the rustle of petticoats as ghostly passengers swished by–and then I heard what I'd been waiting for, *"Pardon me boy, is this the Cincinnati Choo Choo?"* Was it the wine? I knew it was time to climb the steps up into my mahogany furnished sleeping car–and go to bed.

The *Holiday Inn Chattanooga Choo Choo* is just north of I-24 (exit 178), at 1400 Market St *(see map page 56)*. A free shuttle operates between the hotel and downtown; you can be at the Aquarium and other Chattanooga attractions in less than 5 minutes. If you are traveling with

... and so to bed

children the "Choo Choo" is an experience they will never forget. ☎ 423-266-5000 or 1-800-872-2529.

People often stop and ask us what's inside the Parlor Car. So here's a peek inside ...

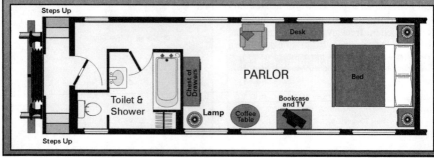

Tennessee Aquarium with the *Visitors Center* in the building to its right. There is lots of parking ahead or to your left. Stop at the Visitors Center for one of their excellent maps.

Every time I return to visit the downtown area, I'm amazed at the new attractions and restaurants which have opened since we were here last. Everywhere you look, there are tourists enjoying the sights and attractions; downtown Chattanooga has become a veritable theme park, with little similarity to the commercial downtown areas of other cities.

The newest additions since our last visit are the magnificent $120 million *21st Century Waterfront* parks on the Tennessee River, new $30 million *Ocean Journey* aquarium annex building and *Trail of Tears Memorial* waterfall, and $20 million revitalized *Hunter Museum of American Art* and *Bluff View Art District*. New restaurants such as, *Blue Plate, Easy Seafood Co.* and *Hennen's,* can be found beside the grassy areas around the Waterfront and main Aquarium building.

And of course, the other downtown attractions we have visited and written about over the last few years are still there to be enjoyed –*Tennessee Aquarium River Journey, Imax 3D Theater* (incredible!!!), *Regional History Museum, Creative Discovery Museum, Tow & Recovery Hall of Fame, "Southern Belle" Riverboat, African-American Museum, Houston Museum,* and ... *Candyland.*

To me, the whole of the downtown area is now an attraction–with easy parking, great restaurants and shops, and excellent sidewalks for walking–downtown Chattanooga has experienced a renaissance and grown into a wonderfully interesting place for visitors. Now let me share a few specifics with you:

Tennessee Aquariums: The main Aquarium, *"River Journey"* has been joined by a new one, *"Ocean Journey,"* just a few steps away behind the Chattanooga Visitors' Center.

As you know from previous *"Along I-75"* editions, *River Journey* in the main Aquarium is a self-guided tour. Starting at the top of the building, you follow the flow of the Tennessee River–from its beginnings as a drop of water in an Appalachian Mountain Cove Forest with dripping rocks, ferns and moss cov-

ered trees–through mountain stream and otter pools–down into the great Mississippi Delta and onward towards the salt waters of the Gulf of Mexico. Fabulous vistas of birds, animal and marine life accompany your journey as you descend through the aquarium building.

The new *Ocean Journey* aquarium tells the story of a tropical reef, modeled after the *Flower Garden Banks National Marine Sanctuary*, off of Galveston, Texas.

An easy walking ramp takes you from the ocean's surface, down 4 stores, to the caves at the foot of the reef. Along the way you encounter all sorts of colorful and unusual marine life. The "adventure" is very much a "hands on" experience so, yes, you actually get to touch a shark (see above) or sting ray, if you wish. At the cave level, you can get very close to marine life by popping up in a seabed "bubble." This young lady is just a few inches away from these giant crab!

The new Ocean Journey aquarium is certainly a great attraction, for young or old.

"Cincy Choo Choo"

Remember when we were driving in Ohio and I was singing, *"Pardon me boy, is this the Cincinnati Choo Choo?* Well, here's the story I promised.

The famous train actually ran between the termini in Chattanooga and the Queen City–so there's no point in being at

the Pennsylvania Station at a quarter to four. It won't be there! According to an historical marker at the Chattanooga Railroad Terminal,

"On March 5, 1880, the first passenger train leaving for Cincinnati was called the "Chattanooga Choo Choo. This historical occasion opened the first major link in public transportation from the North to the South. "Choo Choo" was operated by the Cincinnati Southern Railroad."

Don't you just love historical markers?

Tickets for your Aquarium visit are purchased from the Visitor Center building, just to the east of the River Journey (main) building, and include admission to both aquarium adventures.

[Hrs, 10-6p. daily; Adult/Child-$17.95/$9.50 –children under 3yrs are free; The Aquarium also operates an IMAX 3D theater showing nature oriented films with images that leap off the screen. Imax tickets $7.95/$5.50. Combination aquarium and theater are also available at $22.95/$13.50; ☎ 800-262-0695 or 423-265-0695].

Running across the forecourt of the aquariums is a slow meandering course of shallow water. With stepping stones, small pools and low bridges, it's a natural place for the kids to cool off on a hot day. In its final turn, the water flows down steps to the Tennessee River, creating a lovely Memorial to the *Cherokee Trail of Tears* (see page 122 for more about this tragic episode in our history).

It was a hot day while we were there so we decided to take an *amphibious "Chattanooga Duck" tour* of downtown and the River. The Chattanooga Duck's are unique ex-military amphibious vehicles made for the US Army to land troops on beaches during wartime. They are equally at home on land as well as water.

We started our journey (by land) at the duck depot at the corner of Broad & 5th Streets (see map on page 56). What a surprise–the depot contains an excellent Command Post Museum with lots of memorabilia from past wars. Once aboard the Duck, it's off to explore historic downtown Chattanooga and then down a long ramp and into the river. Our Duck Captain gave a running commentary on all the sights (and some sounds) which was downright fun. We really enjoyed this fascinating one hour journey and will make sure that when we return, we will "Duck" it, again. [Hrs: 10-dusk; Adult/Snr/Child-$22/13/8; ☎ 423-756-3825]

Chattanooga and the Old Dixie Highway:
While visiting the excellent Regional History

Museum (4th & Chestnut Sts), I was fascinated to discover that the famous Dixie Highway–the route all snowbirds used before I-75 was built, was actually started as an initiative of the Chattanooga Auto Club (now part of the AAA). In 1915, the Club organized a meeting of the governors of seven states to discuss the possibility of creating a north–south route, and the Dixie Highway was born.

Each section was financed by local communities along the way and this led to some problems–but by 1927, most of the route from Detroit to Miami had been opened. Red & white "DH" signs nailed to telephone and telegraph poles along the way, marked the route since in those early days, there were no route numbers.

DH

[Hrs: M-F, 10-4:30p, Sa-Su, 11-4:30p; Adult/ Snr/Child-$4/3.50/3; ☎ 423-265-3247].

Chattanooga and Coca Cola: As we head towards the Georgia border, I have to remind Kathy that we will soon be entering "Coca-Cola Country." She is such a Pepsi fan, she's liable to ask for diet Pepsi in the *"World of Coca Cola"* museum in Atlanta! But Coca Cola is so strongly identified with Georgia that in days gone, the State's welcome centers handed out free Coca Colas to greet tourists.

However, if it hadn't been for two Chattanooga business men, you might never have heard of this drink! For it was here that changes were made to the marketing of the beverage which helped Coca Cola change from being a local soda fountain drink, to the huge international success it is today.

In 1899, Benjamin Thomas and Joseph Whitehead sat in the Atlanta office of Coca Cola owner, Asa Chandler, explaining how they would like to take the drink and sell the brown liquid in little green straight-sided bottles. Chandler laughed and said it would never work. He was convinced that Coca Cola's future lay in drug store soda fountain sales–he sold the two men the rights to bottle and distribute Coca Cola within the USA, for $1!

Thomas and Whitehead set up the first bottling plant in Chattanooga on the ground floor of a pool hall (the building is still there, on the corner of Broad and 2nd, across the road from the Aquarium), and the rest is history.

Bottling a soda to increase sales may sound like basic common sense today, but in the late 1800's it was a novel approach for a soda fountain drink. Soon, the Chattanooga group sold bottling franchises to other businessmen across the Nation, became rich beyond their wildest dream–and Coca Cola was on its way to become a national and then international, success. The original bottling plant is currently under renovation to become a museum, with boutiques and restaurants.

RC Cola and Moonpie: a final Chattanooga thought I cannot resist before we leave.

Moonpies, a combination of rich, sugary chocolate covered marshmallow on a round graham cookie were created by the Chattanooga Bakery in 1917 and have been a strong Chattanooga favorite ever since.

Royal Crown Cola, cool & sweet, more affectionately known as RC Cola or just RC, has also been around the South for many years.

Both came together as a combo strongly identified with the southern middle-class lifestyle through song and word in the 1950s. As one old-timer said, *"RC and moonpie are as southern as grits and chicken-fried steak."*

St. Elmo and Lookout Mountain: *(see map on page 56)*. On the other side of I-24 rises Lookout Mountain, peaking at 2,391 feet. On the mountain you'll find other Chattanooga attractions–Battle of Chattanooga Museum, Incline Railway, Ruby Falls and Rock City. The drive up the mountain *(see map)* to the Point Park at the top is well worth the effort.

Exit 1-East Town Antiques: Just to the west of this exit (behind the Cracker Barrel) is an interesting plaza of six antique shops and an Antique mall.

Mile 1- (N/bound)-Welcome Center: After a year of closure due to draining problems, the newly renovated northbound Welcome Center is open once again for business.

GEORGIA- Mile 352-Welcome Center: One of my very favorite stops is to pull in here and chat with my friends–and find out what's new in Georgia. Teresa and Janice have been sharing their knowledge with me

since I started to write *"Along I-75"* in 1992–we actually met in Tampa but that's another story. Barbara, Betty, Jane, Linda and "T" have also become special I-75 friends over the years. Betty always bakes cookies for me if she knows we are coming. Please say *"hi"* to them for me.

Exit 350-Georgia Wine and Cheese: Go west for 250 yds and turn right at the first road-KOA Campsite Rd.

The *Georgia Wines Tasting Center* has expanded and now has a great selection of local wine and other delectables. A huge parking area (suitable for RV parking) is surrounded by the company's vineyards. Stop and say "hi" to Patty, who would love to share some of her favorite reds, whites and fruit wines with you. [Hrs, M-Sa, 10-6p, Closed Sun; ☎ 706-937-2177].

The *Sweetwater Valley Cheese Shop* is next door in the flat red-roofed building. This is the Georgia outlet for the cheese shop I recommended when we visited their farm at Tennessee exit 68. At this location, manager Stephanie carries over 20 of the farm's famous cheeses including, Sweetwater Colby, Fiery Fiesta and Hickory Smoke, and invites you to sample them.
[Hrs. M-Sa, 10-6p; ☎ 706-935-5159]

Exit 350-Firing Pits: In 1898, America went to war with Spain and one of the conflict's theaters was Cuba, with its protecting Spanish army of almost 200,000 men. At the time, US army strength was 26,000 but a Mobilization Act called for a further 125,000 volunteers who of course, needed training.

Many volunteers came from the Southeast, and to the west of I-75, down the hill just behind the Racetrac gas station are the target

---

GEORGIA - *in honor of King George II of England, by early explorer James Oglethorpe who received a Royal Charter in 1733, to settle the area.*

RINGGOLD - *in memory of Samuel Ringgold, professional soldier and Indian fighter who died of wounds received in action during the Mexican War, 1846.*

War Between the States - the Ringgold Gap

Special Report

There is much history just to the east of I-75 in Ringgold, so let's leave the freeway for a while and drive the 5.2 miles (8.4km) through the town and the Gap where the Battle of Ringgold took place, until we rejoin the freeway at exit 345. Because of a narrow bridge with an 11' 7" height restriction, this sidetrip is not suitable for large RVs.

Exit 348 - at the bottom of the s/bound ramp, turn left to cross the interstate bridge heading east. On the bridge, look south at the Ringgold Gap. It was on the sides of these hills in November, 1863, that Gen. Cleyburne's 4,100 men stopped the 12,000 Union soldiers of "Fighting Joe" Hooker long enough to allow the Confederate forces under General Bragg to reorganize at Dalton. Although this battle only lasted six hours, hostilities did not recommence until 6 May, 1864, when south of Ringgold Gen. Sherman gave his famous orders to *"Advance on Atlanta."*

For the next .6 mile (10km) we are driving east along the old Alabama Road used by Andrew Jackson as a supply route in his war against the Creek Indians. Pass "Aunt Effie's" *(see **Insider Tip***) on your right and turn right at the next set of traffic lights, on to Nashville St, or US41S.

Drive south on US41 towards Ringgold for .7 miles (1.1km), you will cross Maple Street and enter the main street area of Ringgold. Imagine the street scene on the night of Nov 27, 1863 the town was occupied with the thousands of Union troops who had not been able to get through the Gap during the day's battle.

Two tenths of a mile (.3 km) further on is the Train Depot where Generals Grant, Sherman and Hooker rested their maps on barrels on the porch and planned their next moves. After the battle they attempted to blow it up but were only successful in destroying the roof.

Just beyond the Depot is the narrow railway bridge. Drive through it following US41. Half a mile (.8km) is a small park on your right, commemorating the battle.

Continue driving for 1.8 miles (2.9km) until you reach the Stone Church at the junction of US41 and GA Route 2. Built in 1850, the Confederates used it as a hospital during the battle. You can still see blood stains on the floor and teeth marks on the benches, which date from its founding.

After leaving the Church, continue along US41 for a mile (1.6km). where you will rejoin I-75 at exit 345.

---

pits used for live ammunition training exercises.

Exit 348-Ringgold & the Great Locomotive Chase: *(see Special Report on next page, side trip maps on page 59, Bartow Co. map on page 58, and detailed 25 mile maps between exit 348 and exit 273).* One of the best known adventures of the Civil War–made even more famous by a Walt Disney movie, *"The Great Locomotive Chase,"* starring Fess Parker, and Buster Keaton's classic of the Silent era, The General–was exactly that–an epic chase where a steam locomotive stolen by Union soldiers, was chased through the Georgia countryside by its Southern crew, who used their feet, a push car, and three other locomotives before they successfully recaptured their errant ward.

But best of all, the route of this chase from Kennesaw in the south, to Ringgold in the north, criss-crossed the path of the modern I-75 as it winds its way from the Tennessee-

Georgia border towards Atlanta. We have mapped this chase alongside the modern interstate for you on southbound map ages 31 to 34 & northbound map pages 164 167.

Exit 341-Tunnel Hill: *(map with details on page 59).* The famous 1850 railroad tunnel at Tunnel Hill played a very significant role in the Civil War's Great Locomotive Chase *(see page 122)* and in General Sherman's 1864 Atlanta Campaign.

Across the field, the Clisby-Austin House is also a special Civil War site. It was used as a

continued on page 119

INSIDER TIP - Aunt Effie's

Just a few blocks east of exit 348 is Aunt Effie's Restaurant, a very popular favorite with the locals. Serving Southern and American meals, it can be noisy and crowded at times but definitely a good place to meet the folk from Ringgold. [Hrs, M-F, 11-8p, Su, 11-3p, closed Sat; ☎ 706-935-6525].

War Between the States - The Great Locomotive Chase

During the Civil War, the Western & Atlantic railway line between Chattanooga and Atlanta was of great importance to the Confederacy, moving freight and soldiers between these two important railway centers. This vital link was a single track railway with passing tracks at various stations along the route. Kentuckian James Andrews, a Federal spy, devised a plan to steal a train near Atlanta and destroy the track and bridges along this line as he traveled northward. Andrew's tiny band of Union soldiers became known as Andrew's Raiders, and the subsequent actions of Saturday, April 12, 1862–the "Great Locomotive Chase."

Note: This Special Report tells the story of the chase from the theft of the "General" at Big Shanty (Kennesaw–exit 273) to its conclusion at Ringgold (exit 348). The chase therefore ran from south to north. If southbound on I-75, I suggest you read this report first so you understand the significance of the various locations as you run south towards Kennesaw. The entire adventure is shown on the I-75 map pages covering the exits mentioned above, supported by special sidetrip maps on pages 58 and 59. Numbers in the report refer to the locations marked on the maps–numbers in circles represent Andrew's Raiders (Union) actions; numbers in squares represent Fuller's (Confederate) actions.

Kennesaw   **Ringgold**

1. 5:30 a.m.–on a wet, rainy day, James Andrews and 23 Union soldiers from Ohio ride from Marietta to Big Shanty (Kennesaw) as passengers on a northbound train pulled by the locomotive, *General*. William Fuller is the train's conductor

2. 6:00 a.m.–while the train stops for breakfast at Big Shanty, Andrews' Raiders capture the *General* and with three boxcars, head north towards Chattanooga. Andrews and two men ride the locomotive while the rest of the armed band are hidden inside the boxcars.

3. 6:10 a.m.–Fuller, disturbed at breakfast and believing that Confederate conscripts had stolen his train to get clear of Big Shanty's army camp and would shortly abandon it, decides to give chase on foot. The General's engineer, Jeff Cain and a railroad engineering foreman, Anthony Murphy run with him.

4. The *General* runs out of steam a few miles up the track from Big Shanty. Andrews did not realize that the boiler dampers had been closed while the crew were at breakfast. The dampers were quickly opened and fires re-stoked with oil-soaked wood while the Raiders cut trackside telegraph wires to prevent "intercept" messages going north.

   After a quick run north, the *General* arrives at Moon's Station, and the Raiders "borrow" an iron bar from a track repair crew. The Raiders intend to remove rail sections behind them to halt pursuit, but later find the bar is inadequate for the task.

5. A breathless Fuller and companions arrive at Moon's Station, and take a *pole-car*. The three continue their pursuit by poling the car northward at 7-8 mph.

6. After passing through Acworth Station, the Raiders stop and cut more telegraph wires and damage a rail section.

7. The *General* halts just below Allatoona to cut telegraph wires.

8. Andrews sees the *Yonah*, a work locomotive belonging to the Cooper Iron Works on the north banks of the Etowah River, with steam up. He is concerned since he knows that if a pursuit message gets this far north, there is now an operational locomotive and armed crew, to give chase. He does not stop since destroying the Etowah Bridge would not fill a purpose now.

9. The *General* pulls up at Cass Station (near Cartersville). Andrews convinces a suspicious railway worker that he is carrying much needed gunpowder north to the Confederate Army. The patriotic worker gives Andrews his only railway schedule so that Andrews can plan his northbound run to meet and pass southbound trains at appropriate stations.

10. The Raiders pull into Kingston Station, a major passing point on the railroad. Here they wait for a southbound train but when it finally arrives, they find that there are two unscheduled southbounds on the same track section. The Raiders are forced to wait until the next section of track is clear.

In the meantime, the station personnel are getting very suspicious of the northbound "gunpowder" train.

11. Fuller cannot stop the pole-car in time and it runs off the track at the broken rail section, dumping the crew and car down an embankment. Uninjured, they carry the car back up and resume the chase. After an epic pole-car journey of 20 miles, Fuller and crew arrive at the Etowah River and commandeer the *Yonah*.

12. After a wait of more than an hour, the *General* pulls out of Kingston to continue its northbound journey, just eight minutes before the arrival of Fuller aboard the *Yonah*. Andrews is now aware that pursuit is close since he has heard the frantic whistle of the *Yonah* as it approaches Kingston.

Yonah

13. Fuller cannot get past the southbound trains so once again, he and his companions take to foot, running across the Kingston railroad yards to commandeer another locomotive, the *William R. Smith*. They give chase northwards alongside Hall Station Road towards Adairsville Station. To warn of obstructions, Fuller hangs onto the locomotive's cowcatcher while scanning the track ahead.

14. Aware that a chase is now on hand, the Raiders stop to cut wires and pile railroad ties across the track as a delaying tactic.

15. Several miles further, the Raiders stop to remove a rail section but find that their crowbar is too small to easily pull the spikes. By brute strength, the men manage to bend and snap a rail and throw it in the bushes.

16. Feeling safe once more, the Raiders pull into Adairsville Station where they find a long southbound train pulled by the locomotive, *Texas*. The suspicious engineer refuses to pull his train forward to clear the north switch of the passing track. After another delay, Andrews manages to convince the driver, and tries to send him southbound to either collide with their pursuers or derail on the broken section.

17. The *William R. Smith* is stopped in time to avoid being derailed by the missing section of rail. Fuller and company take off on foot for the third time, running up the track where they manage to flag down the southbound train pulled by the *Texas*.

18. They hear the engineer's story and commandeer the *Texas* for their chase–running in reverse. As they pass through Adairsville, Fuller, without stopping the

train, uncouples the cars, runs ahead, turns the switch to a side track diverting the cars into it, returns the switch for the mainline movement, jumps back on board the *Texas* and the pursuit continues unencumbered by the weight of the cars.

19. The Raiders hear the whistle of the *Texas* to the south. They create as high a head of steam as possible by burning wood soaked in oil. The *General* careens up the railroad, leaning out and almost toppling on the curves.

20. The *General* and the last train southbound from Chattanooga pass at Calhoun Station without incident.

21. As the *Texas* steams through Calhoun a few minutes behind the General, Fuller spots a 13 year old telegraph boy, and grabs him onto the moving train. He writes a telegram to the Confederate commander in Chattanooga.

22. Desperately, the Raiders stop and attempt to remove a rail section but are only able to bend it slightly out of shape. They also cut the telegraph wire. They quickly scramble back on board when they see their pursuer for the first time–the reversed *Texas* with a full head of steam charging in their direction.

23. The *Texas* miraculously rides right over the damaged rail section.

24. Around a curve and out of sight, the Raiders uncouple a box car and let it run down a grade onto Fuller, who reverses his direction of travel to "catch" the boxcar. He couples it to the *Texas'* tender and resumes the chase with the box car leading.

25. The Raiders do not have time to burn and destroy the covered Oostanaula River Bridge (a major target) so drop the second boxcar in its center span hoping to slow down the pursuers. As before, the Fuller "catches" the boxcar, couples it and later drops them both at a siding near Resaca Station.

26. A mile north of Resaca Station, Andrews cuts the Calhoun-Dalton telegraph wire and piles ties across the track.

27. The tactic of dropping railroad ties onto the track works to delay the *Texas*. Each time, the engineer must throw the locomotive into full reverse, skid to a halt while Fuller and his men jump down, clear the track and start on their way again. Seeing this, Andrews decided to punch a hole through the rear wall of the remaining boxcar, and drop a succession of ties on the track behind him.

28. Aware their pursuers are close again, the Raiders stop to cut wires and pile railroad ties across the track as a delaying tactic. Just south of Green's Station (Tilton), the Raiders stop again and attempt to remove a rail. They can only pry it out of shape, however. Andrews puts another rail underneath the bent rail, to try and derail the fast approaching *Texas*.

29. Thinking the damaged rail will have stopped the pursuit, a mile north of Tilton, Andrews' Raiders stop to take on much needed wood and water, but have to cut this short when they hear the whistle from the fast approaching *Texas* again. For the second time that day, the *Texas* has managed to run over damaged railway track without derailing.

30. After two more miles, the *General* stops again. Telegraph wires are cut and the track obstructed.

31. The Raiders decide to speed through Dalton, a major Confederate camp. A mile north of Dalton, they stop to cut the telegraph wire to stop messages getting through but they are unaware that minutes behind them, Fuller has dropped off the boy telegraph operator, who manages to get a portion of the message through to Chattanooga.

32. A few miles ahead is the Tunnel Hill railroad tunnel, and the Raiders discuss whether to ambush the *Texas* or perhaps travel through the tunnel and then reverse the *General* locomotive back towards the

pursuing *Texas* for a collision. They decide to speed on northwards.

33. The *Texas* approaches the smoke filled tunnel. They cannot see ahead and are aware of what the Raiders might plan. Fuller decides to plunge into the tunnel's darkness at full speed, regardless of safety.

34. To their horror, Andrews looks back and sees the *Texas* emerge from the tunnel hard on their heels. They are approaching a covered wooden bridge across the Chickamauga River so he orders the last box car set on fire and then uncoupled in the middle of the bridge. Wet wood and the driving rain of the hour prevents this last attempt to escape, from working.

35. After a frantic dash through Ringgold, the Raiders are out of wood and oil and the *General* is slowing down. Andrews orders his men to jump from the train and find their own ways back to Union lines.

The mission failed because of the dogged pursuit by the General's conductor, William Fuller. Of the Raiders, sixteen were captured and eight were able to escape back to the safety of the Union. Of the captured men, eight were taken to Atlanta (including James Andrew) where they were hanged. Six were exchanged and two "enlisted" in the Confederate Army. After the war, most of the surviving Raiders were awarded the first Medals of Honor.

continued from page 116

hospital during the war and later, as General Sherman's HQ during his campaign against Atlanta. After General John Hood lost his leg at the battle of Chickamauga, he and the limb were transferred to the House; the leg was buried in a nearby cemetery.

Mile 339-Battle of Rocky Face Ridge: Ahead of you looms the craggy heights of Rocky Face Ridge, shielding the strategic town of Dalton behind. Here, for eight days starting on May 7th, 1864, Confederate General Joseph Johnston held off General Sherman's Army of the Ohio, under the command of Major General Schofield. The Rebs were well entrenched along the ridge (known locally as "Buzzards Roost") and as you can see, the terrain was very difficult for the attacking forces. In places, the men could only advance along its precipitous paths in

single file; General Sherman described this gap as "the door of death."

While General Schofield pursued his attack, Sherman decided to outflank the Confederates and sever the railroad further south. On May 9th, he sent his Army of the Tennessee to the west through Snake Creek Gap and down towards the sleepy town of Resaca (mile marker 320). On May 11th, realizing the assault on the Ridge was impossible,

The War Between the States - Resaca

As you drive through north Georgia, you will pass a number of nearby Civil War battlefields–Chickamauga and Chattanooga's Lookout Mountain. Interstate-75 follows the route of Sherman's march toward Atlanta with its resulting destruction by flame–and you will actually drive through two of the battlefields *(see Resaca map on page 57)*.

Imagine the scene–it is May 13,1864. Strung out across the path of the southbound I-75 a few yards south of mile marker 323 is a thin line of young men crouched in hurriedly constructed trenches cut deep into the red Georgian earth. Banks of rubble have been thrown forward to give added protection from the whining Minie balls which zip overhead like angry hornets waiting to administer the sting of death. A fountain of red soil suddenly shoots skyward in front of them, followed by the vibration of the ground shock wave and deep crumping sound of a distant explosion. A Confederate field gun is ranging in on their position.

Sweltering under the hot Georgian sun in their heavy flannel uniforms of dark blue, they wait their officer's command to rise up and charge over the rough ground toward the wooded rise where they can see the gray hunched shapes of the Confederates behind log spiked palisades. Behind the wooden barriers, the distinctive saltire cross of the red and blue Battle Flag floats lazily overhead.

On closer look, the mud and sweat streaked faces are of very young men–frightened, quietly exchanging comments of bravado in nervous, throat-tightened voices. Many, only in their sixteenth or seventeenth year, will not see nightfall.

Continued top of next page

Sherman left a token attacking force and followed his main army down towards Resaca. Johnston found out about this flanking movement from prisoners a day later, and rapidly pulled his troops from the *"Door of Death"* and retreated to defend the railroad at Resaca.

Exit 336-CornerStone Grill: Just west and on the south side of Rt41, is a new restaurant recommended by several readers and obviously popular with local folk–the *Cornerstone Grill*. Dinner entrees $14-$29. It's been getting excellent reviews so you might wish to try it. [Hrs: Lnch, M-Fr, 11-2p, Dnr, M-Sa 5-9p; ☎ 706-529-2500].

Exit 336 Driving Note: If taking this exit to go east, be carefully of the very sharp curve.

Exit 333-Carpet Capital of North America: Dalton is the *"Carpet Capital of North America,"* and it all started in the early 1900s with a young farm girl, Catherine Whitener, who supported her family by making tufted bedspreads & scatter rugs at home. Other women joined her and soon Dalton had a booming cottage industry, saving the area from the pangs of the Depression.

In these early days, one of the most popular

INSIDER TIP- Tunnel Hill Heritage Center & Museum

The Whitefield County (Dalton) tourism folk have moved into the new Heritage Center right by the Civil War Tunnel at Tunnel Hill, and have included a magnificent museum in the same building. You will find counter staff Vivian & Ralph very friendly and knowledgeable about not only the local Civil War history, but Dalton & the surrounding area.

Of particular interest is a blood-stained pine church bench. Modern forensic experts have been able to determine that 3 badly wounded soldier slumped here awaiting treatment, and the nature of their gruesome wounds (including bayonet stabbings).

See page 59 for details and phone number. Incidentally, the large adjacent lot has pull-through spaces for RV parking. Now that's convenience!

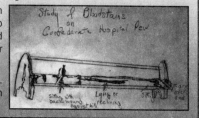

Dave Hunter's

They are showing the strain of the Atlanta campaign–many escaped death only a few days earlier facing the same enemy in the battle of Rocky Face Ridge, 14 miles north of here. They were lucky, for they survived and flanked General Johnston's Gray forces who have now retreated southward to make yet another stand here–at Resaca–as the Rebels fall back toward Atlanta's main defense line in a losing war.

These are the men and boys of the General Sherman's 35th Indiana, under the command of Brigadier General Stanley. Little do they know that the Confederates have already spotted a weakness to the left of their line and at 4 o'clock that afternoon, six divisions of General Hood's best Rebs will charge down the slope and drive them from their position. The situation will be saved by the 5th Indiana gunners firing double-shotted canister into the Grays, and the timely arrival of General William's Union Army of the Cumberland, currently positioned a mile to their right.

Before the end of this battle three days later, 5,547 men and boys will have been killed or injured, and the Confederates will have pulled back across the Oostanaula River to make yet another retreating stand at Cassville (just west of I-75 at exit 296, opening the door to Sherman's Union victories at New Hope Church, Kennesaw Mountain–and ultimately, Atlanta.

All this action took place across the modern I-75 as you approach Exit 320 *(see page 57)*.

Path of modern I-75 laid on an 1864 engraving of the Resaca battlefield — **East** — Confederate General Johnston — Union General Sherman — **West**

designs incorporated two colorful peacocks facing each other. Since the women used to hang the newly made carpets and rugs on lines strung near the old US 41route to Florida, the Dalton section of the *"Dixie Highway"* became known as *"Peacock Alley."*

By the 1950s advances in machinery and dyeing opened the door to the modern carpet industry. The entrepreneurial spirit of the local residents turned the cottage bedspread industry into multi-billion dollar carpet manufacturing. Today, more than 65% of the world's carpets are made in Dalton!

Miles 323 to 319.8-Battle of Resaca: *(see battle map on page 57).* I-75 is just about to cross the actual Resaca battlefield, which involved over 171,000 men and boys for 3

days, in May, 1864. During the construction of this stretch of I-75, in Oct., 1960, many artifacts were uncov-

ered but unfortunately much of the field's earthworks and trenches which lay in the path of the interstate, were destroyed. Archaeologists were given eleven weeks prior to construction, to excavate the three mile long site–an impossible task.

So let's sit back in the car, and I'll give you a mile-by-mile account of the battle action:

Mile 322.8-*"Fight for Cannon"* - just to the left on top of the hill, 6 Union cannon batteries held the northern boundary of the field.

DALTON - *in honor of Tristram Dalton (politician & Senator from Maine), whose grandson was the engineer who laid out the town and donated land.*

The position was attacked by Confederate (CSA) forces using bayonets; the attack was turned by a relief Union force, which rode from the west across I-75's path at this point.

Mile 322.2-*"Battle at the Angle"* - a bloody attack by the Union forces took place right here on the path of I-75, as they attempted to breach the CSA defenses.

Mile 322-*Confederate Territory* - although the interstate is running through cuts in the hills, we are now driving across what would have been the CSA encampment.

Mile 321-*Southern edge of the CSA Defense line* - here we leave the CSA encampment and run down towards "no-man's land" in the valley of Camp Creek. Polk's Confederate Army is to our left and Logan's Union XV Army Corp is to our right.

Exit 320-*Resaca Confederate Cemetery* - nowhere can the atmosphere of that day in 1864 be better felt than at the Confederate Cemetery just a few minutes east of the I-75. The map on page 57 will help you find it.

The first time I visited this site it was dusk and I was by myself. It was lonely yet somehow peaceful–just row upon row of old but tidy graves–in the soft fading light filtered through the leafy boughs of the trees above.

The United Daughters of the Confederacy had recently put tiny flags by many of the tombstones; even 130 years later, the men are still cared for. Imagine the anguish of wives and daughters, of families left behind who didn't know where their men had gone. But we know where they went–their journey ended here.

Mile 320-*Polk/Logan Skirmish Line* - the open muddy land north of the Oostanaula River with small hill fortifications left a very vulnerable section in the CSA defenses. The Union capitalized on this. After a pounding bombardment by General Logan's artillery (fired from the west and in the direction of the modern I-75), nine Union regiments charged the small hills held by Polk's mainly untried recruit troops.

Logan won the positions; Polk counter- attacked several times with

little success and the hills were still in Federal hands by nightfall. These hills now posed a major threat to the CSA's southern flank but Sherman did not grasp this tactical situation and spent the following day repairing the hill defenses. Wisely, General Johnston decided to fall back across the river that night before the Union forces realized the situation. Thus began the Confederate retreat to Cassville.

Exit 320-*The Skeleton at the SW Exit Ramp* - Several years ago, new research about the battlefield came to light and was published in a book I highly recommend, *"The Battle of Resaca,"* by Philip Secrist (Kennesaw State University). Prof. Secrist recounts the discovery of a grave by a Resaca historian, working ahead of the interstate road builders.

The grave contained a brass lined tobacco pipe, a few unfired minie ball cartridges–and a skeleton with an amputated foot. Just above the knee around the femur lay an iron tourniquet buckle. The skeleton was reburied in the Confederate Cemetery.

Exit 317-New Echota and the Cherokee Nation: Route 225 crosses I-75 here and for very good reasons, the route is known as the *"Trail of Tears"* highway. During the early 1800's, north Georgia was the heart of the sovereign Cherokee Indian Nation. By this time, the Cherokee was one of the most progressive Indian tribe in North America.

In 1821, they became the first American Indians with a written language, invented by *Sequoyah*. *New Echota* (pronounced "airchot-er"), the Cherokee national capital, was located just 1/2 mile from here (take exit 317–and follow Rt 225 east for 1 minute). There, a constitutional government with executive, legislative and judicial branches ruled the nation. Once the largest town in this area, New Echota consisted of houses, stores, taverns, a Council house, Supreme Courthouse, and a printing office which published a bilingual newspaper, the *Cherokee Phoenix.*

In 1838, under the presidency of Andrew Jackson, the Cherokee were rounded up at gun point and imprisoned by state and federal armies. Later that year, these peaceful people

Chief Sequoyah

RESACA- *originally called Dublin by Irish railroad workers, renamed after the Mexican town of Resaca de la Palma, by returning Mexican War veterans.*

OOSTANAULA RIVER - *Cherokee name, "place of the rocks across the stream," for a shallow place to ford.*

were forced to what is now Oklahoma. Four thousand Cherokee died on the terrible march west known as the *"Trail of Tears."*

Today, you can visit New Echota where the State of Georgia maintains an excellent museum and seven of the original houses. [Hrs. Tu-Sa, 9-5; Su 2-5:30; Adults/Senior/Child–$4/$3.50/$2.50; ☎ 706-624-1321].

Mile 310-Mercer Air Field: Sadly, Mercer air field and its deteriorating but historic aircraft (across the freeway beside the northbound lanes–best seen in the winter when the trees are bare) is rapidly becoming a junk yard. I wonder whether our news about exit 306 (see below) will revitalize it, or mean that the collection will be sold. Only time will tell.

Miles 307-277-Bartow County: This next stretch of I-75 has so many things to see that I've drawn a special map for you on page 58. Various attractions are identified by "A," "B." etc. on the map and in the following text.

Exit 306-BIG NEWS!!!: *Cabela's,* the huge *"World's Foremost Outfitter"* of hunting, fishing and outdoor gear, is going to be building one of its famous 165,000 sq.ft. (about 3½ football fields) retail mega-stores, on the northeast side of this exit, just behind the QT gas station ... and you heard it here first, in *"Along I-75."*

Now if you are not familiar with *Cabela's,* it is almost like an outdoorsman's theme park with lots of great things to buy.

Bringing its own mountain, waterfalls, rivers, fish ponds and attractions such as an archery range and signature gun library–all indoors.

It's a tourist destination. The typical Cabela's store attracts visitors from hundreds of miles away. And this Northwest Georgia store will be no exception since the closest neighboring Cabela's is at Wheeling, WV!

Which means of course, there will be many changes to this exit in terms of new hotels, restaurants and other visitor facilities, since *Cabela's* customers tend to make an overnight stay of their shopping experience.

The store will occupy 40 acres stretching northward beside I-75 and is expected to open as early as Fall, 2007.

Exit 306-Adairsville: *(Town map page 58).* Just 1.3 miles (2.1km) west of I-75 is Adairsville. This historic town lies on the strategic Atlanta-Chattanooga railroad line which during the Civil War, became a bustling supply depot. This ended abruptly when Sherman marched through on his way to Cassville. Today though, it's enjoying a renaissance and has become a great place to stop and relax for a while. The entire town with its many heritage buildings, is listed on the National Register of Historic Places.

I suggest you park in the public square just outside the historic **Train Depot** *(A).* This original Western & Atlantic Depot pre-dates the Civil War and played a part in the Great Locomotive Chase *(see page 118, item 16),* for it was here that the Conductor Fuller commandeered the southbound Texas and started chasing the stolen General backwards, towards the north.

Across the square the **1902 Stock Exchange** *(B)* (124 Public Sq.) is a fine example of an historical restoration. Inside, you'll find antiques, gifts, crafts, used hardcover quality books, a cafe-style gourmet tea room and an Antebellum dinner theater. Owner Rita Pritchard loves chatting with visitors and showing them her architectural treasure. She invites you in to use her clean restroom and also enjoy free coffee. [Hrs, Tu-Sa, 10-5p; Tea room, 11-2:30p; ☎ 770-773-1902].

Turn around, look across the railroad track and you will see a white frame house with a silver roof. This is the **childhood home of Charles Arthur Floyd** *(C),* who became bet-

INSIDER TIP - the Most Romantic Place in Georgia

Let's visit one the most romantic place in Georgia–the haunting ruins and beautiful Antebellum roses of **Barnsley Gardens (D)**. Add a Civil War action, *"Gone With The Wind"* connections, a ghost, acres of flowers and a water garden–and I think you will have to agree that this is a place you will never want to leave.

And if that is your wish and you're in a mood to "splurge," Barnsley is also a five star resort with a village of "cottages" styled in 19th century architecture and a first class restaurant beside a championship golf course. But let me tell you Barnsley's story:

In 1824, penniless Godfrey Barnsley, arrived in North America, where he rose to become a prominent and rich cotton planter. Needing an estate, he purchased this property and named it *Woodlands*. During his business travels abroad, Barnsley collected rare and exotic plants,

brought them back and planted the famous Woodlands gardens–perhaps best known for their countless varieties of roses.

The untimely death of his wife, Julia and the Civil War bought an end to his fortunes, and sadly, Godfrey died as penniless as the day he arrived on these shores. Disaster struck again in 1906 when a tornado ruined the main house and nearby gardens. In later years, Margaret Mitchell was a visitor and some believe that Godfrey Barnsley's Woodlands provided inspiration and background to Tara in *"Gone With The Wind."*

Today, we can enjoy Barnsley's roses, ferns, fruit trees, rockeries and woodland gardens–over 30 acres of cultivated delight surrounding the ruins of Godfrey's Italianate villa.

Don't miss the excellent museum to the right of the ruins. Here you will find Barnsley's knowledgeable historian, my friend Clent Coker. I'll leave it to Clent to explain the stain from a large pool of blood on the floor of the old building–and the hauntings!

Admission to the gardens, ruins & museum-Adults/Snrs/Student: $10/$8/$5; Hrs, M-Sat 9am-6pm; Sun, noon-5pm. The ruins are sometimes closed for special functions–phone ahead to ensure they are open ☎ 770-773-7480 or 1-877-773-2447.

To find Barnsley Gardens, take Hall Station Rd from Adairsville, in 5 miles turn right on to Barnsley Garden Rd and drive 2½ miles to the Barnsley Gardens gate; at the gatehouse, they will direct you to the gardens, the ruined manor house and museum.

ter known as *"Pretty Boy" Floyd* when his career of crime started in the mid-1920s.

Wanted for robbing banks and killings armed with a machine gun in the mid '30s, he quickly became the FBI's "Public Enemy No. 1."

Before leaving Adairsville to return to I-75, read the **Insider Tip** about the most romantic place in Georgia. It's not too far from here *(see map on page 58)* and I wouldn't want you to miss it.

Exit 293-Weinman Mineral Museum *(F)*: This museum is undergoing an extensive renovation which will make it a premier attraction in Northwest Georgia, when completed in the Fall of 2008. The original museum galleries are still open during the construction.

If you enjoy rocks and gem stones, there's a treat in store for you at the "Weinman." More than 2,000 exhibits are displayed in three halls. The Georgia room contains many specimens native to the State, as well as a simulated cave and waterfall. Indian artifacts dated back to 8,000 BC and fossils as early as the Paleozoic Era *(see chart on page 94)* are displayed in a second room, while a third contains the international Mayo collections.

To find the museum, take exit 293 and go west for a few yards on route 411–turn left onto Mineral Museum Drive which is just past the motel. [Hrs: M-Sa, 10-5p; Adult/Snr/Child-$3/$2.50/$2; ☎ 770-387-3747].

Exit 288-Cartersville: *(City map on page 58).* A few minutes west lies Cartersville, with many interesting things to see and do. Let's go for a quick tour of the highlights.

Park your car between the railroad tracks and North Wall Street, and walk over to the **Cartersville Visitors Center (G)** housed in the old **Cartersville Train Depot**. Here you'll find all sorts of information about this historic town, in particular, pick up the self-guided walking tour map.

Many visitors incorrectly assume that Cartersville was named after President Carter. Wrong, it was named after Col. Farish Carter (1780-1861), an early landowner.

Before leaving, say *"hi"* to Donna or Susie on the reception desk. Director Ellen, Regina and James, are personal friends of ours so if you see them, please give them our best wishes. All the staff here love to meet and help visitors to this interesting and very historical area. [Hrs, M-F, 8:30-5p; Sa, 11-4p; ☎ 770-387-1357].

Outside and just south of the building, the **Friendship Monument (H)** is worth a visit.

Across Main St on the wall of Young Brothers Pharmacy is the **first outdoor Coca Cola advertisement (J)** in the world, painted by a Coca Cola syrup salesman in 1894.

Cross the road again towards your car and let's stroll along **North Wall St. (K)**. Here you will find the **1929 Grand Theater**, home of the famed Cartersville Opera Co. [☎ 770-386-7343], **Etowah Art Gallery** [11 N. Wall; ☎ 770-382-8277] & the **Bartow History Center** [13 N. Wall; Hrs, Tu-Sa, 10-5p;

INSIDER TIP - the Presidents' Letters

One does not expect to find a world-class museum in the busy Interstate-75 town of Cartersville, but the multi-million dollar, purpose-built building of the **Booth Western Art Museum (L),** with quiet galleries innovatively and dramatically lit to draw the finest detail out of its 200 Western American works of art, would be right at home in Manhattan. Focussed primarily on the art of western life, it also holds a unique and very unusual treasure which makes the two mile trip off I-75, well worth the effort. But more on that later.

Let's go for a tour of the Museum. We start on the ground floor in the *Grand Hall* where a beautifully restored original *1889 stage coach* draws your attention just outside the *Presentation and Orientation theatres*. We'll check the *Museum Gift* shop and perhaps have lunch in the *Café* after spending time in the core of the Museum's permanent collection, the *American West Gallery*. Here finely detailed bronzes and superb paintings by well known artists re-tell the story of the American West.

A glass elevator ride takes us up to the 2nd Floor where two smaller galleries beside the *Cowboy* exhibits introduce us to the wild west of Hollywood through Western movie stars and posters. To our left is the *Special Exhibit Gallery* and just ahead is a large room devoted to contemporary Civil War painting and other artwork–the *War Is Hell Gallery*.

But it's the **President's Gallery** at the end of the hall which I believe is the Museum's real treasure ... for here you will find a letter written and signed by each of the forty-two men who have served as the Nation's Chief Executive.

From George Washington to George W Bush, they are all here with painting or photo, a short bio and an original letter and brief details describing the circumstances behind the letter.

Arguably, this priceless collection of President's Letters is the only one of its kind in the World. In my

Lifesize Bronze of Thomas Jefferson sits pensively in the President's Gallery.

opinion, it's a National treasure . . . and a "must see" for anybody driving I-75 in this area.

The Museum is open Tu,W,Fr,Sa, 10am-5pm; Th, 10am-8pm, Sun, 1-5pm; closed Mon. Adult/Snr/Student/Child under 12, $8/$6/$5/free; ☎ 770-387-1300.

(Both photos courtesy of the Museum; the "shadow" sculpture is *An Honest Day's Work*, by Fred Fellows; the sculpture of *Thomas Jefferson* is by George Lundeen).

Adult/Senior/Child-$3/$2.50/$2; ☎ 770-382-3818]. The latter is well worth a visit to get a glimpse of life in the 1900s.

Continue walking along N Wall St., under the Church St bridge and ahead you will see the beautiful building of the **Booth Western Art Museum** *(L)*. Here you will find a national treasure, arguably the only collection in the world of letters and signatures of the 42 men who became our Nation's Presidents *(see* **Insider Tip***)*.

Return through the Museum's gates and turn left into Church St. *"Under the Bridge."* You'll find some very unusual shops waiting for you in this semi-subterranean street ...

Periwinkle-Patty Richardson's wonderful antique, gift & craft browsing experience. [Hrs, M-Th, 10-6p; F-Sa, 10-8p; ☎ 770-607-7171]. **The Shaving Gallery-**a one-of-a-kind shop, owned and operated by Lauren Cross, a most unusual (in the nicest of senses) New Zealander. [Hrs, M-Sa, 10-7p; ☎ 770-975-9998]. **Appalachian Grill-**great food treats from Jackie. [Hrs, M-Th, 11-9p, F, 11-10p, Sa, noon-10p; ☎ 770-607-5357].

Finally, just 3 miles (4.8km) (11 minutes) southwest of Cartersville is the "not to be missed" **Ancient Indian City** *(M)*–the 1,000 year old Etowah Mounds. It's an easy drive–get directions and a map from the Visitors Center.

Dated from 1000–1500 AD, this entire area was once a huge Indian village. Today, you may explore the remains of three flat topped ceremonial mounds and a moat which encircled the town remain.

Archeological digs have yielded many finds which are on display at the park's Visitor Center. Ranger Steve is very knowledgeable and can answer your questions about this mysterious site. [Hrs, Tu-Sa, 9-5p, Sun 2p-5:30p; Adult/Child, $4/$2:50; ☎ 770-387-3747].

As you leave Cartersville and drive back to I-

75 exit 288, note the dead end just across the interstate bridge. This is very unusual since interstate exits are only built where a substantial route crosses the freeway's path. In the 1980s however, a local judge with influence in all the right places heard that Cartersville was not going to have an exit, so a word in the right quarters... Incidentally, this dead end is a favorite place for police cars to park.

Exit 285-Etowah Bridge and Cooper Iron Works (N): (map on page 58). Follow the map and visit remains of the Etowah Bridge where the locomotive, *Yonah* was commandeered during the Great Locomotive Chase.

Exit 285-Red Top Mountain-Eastern Bluebirds and Deer: A quarter of a mile to the east across the Bethany Bridge, you enter the *Red Top Mountain State Park.* Here wild deer abound. You are almost guaranteed to see them as they graze in the woodlands alongside the road. In more open stretches, the colorful Eastern Bluebirds flit across the meadows to their special "Ranger installed" nesting boxes on old farm fence posts.

At dusk, the deer often come out of the woods and graze on the grass alongside the park's roads and trails. In my mind, there is nothing better than siting on a bench watching the deer in the silvery light of the stars overhead, while listening to the night sounds coming from the nearby woods.

Mile 283-The Georgia Gold Belt: Yep, you heard properly–gold! And there is still lode buried in this area–for it's all part of a band of rock which stretches across North Georgia, called the *Dahlonega Rift.*

Now, perhaps you didn't know the nation's first gold rush did <u>not</u> occur in California, but in Dahlonega, Georgia, 93 miles east along Route 52 from I-75 exit 333. In 1828, the area boomed and more than $6 million in gold coin was minted at the Dahlonega Mint before the Civil War closed it down.

Exit 283-Battle of Allatoona Pass: *(see Special Report, map is on page 60).*

Mile 277-Fast Forward: There are some big plans in the works for improving I-75 between the Cobb County border and Atlanta. In April, 2004, Governor Sonny Perdue announced his *"Fast Forward Transportation Plan"* which provides $15.57 billion to improve transportation statewide. $1.2 billion has been allocated for this area (called the *Northwest Corridor Project)* to expand the number of traffic lanes, commence HOV

The War Between the States–Allatoona Pass

Special Report

A small but significant battle took place about a 1¾ miles east of exit 283 *(see map page 60)*. Known only to the locals, the battlesite is undisturbed with trenches, redoubts and a fort in situ. It has now been opened to the public by the Etowah Valley Historical Society and the Corps of Engineers, and you are invited to wander its wooded trails, but first let me take you back to 1864 and set the scene for you:

By early September, General Sherman had successfully captured Atlanta and the single track Western & Atlantic railroad running through North Georgia had become a vital link for bringing supplies to the occupied city. But Southern President Jeff Davis had announced that he intended to disrupt the route using Confederate raiders. One of the most vulnerable stretches of track was the section at Allatoona where it cuts through a 175ft deep, 360ft long man-made pass; it would be easy work for a small contingent of "Rebs" to block it at this point. For protection, Sherman posted a small detachment of men to fortify Allatoona. Trenches were dug and earthwork defenses built on the high ground either side of the cut–both camps joined by a wooden footbridge 170 feet in the air.

On October 4th, Confederate commander General Hood issued several conflicting orders to General Samuel French, one of which told him to "fill up the deep cut at Allatoona . . ." (an impossible feat of engineering given the 30 hours allowed for the task).

Sherman received early warnings of this as Confederate troop movements were reported in the area. He dispatched reinforcements to Allatoona under the command of General Corse but due to railroad damage inflicted by the "Rebs," only a portion of them arrived. With the scene set for the battle, Corse had a total force of only 2,025 men to defend the Pass against French's force of 3,276.

What developed as the Battle of Allatoona Pass was one of the most vicious and deadliest of the entire war. Its intense hand-to-hand fighting produced many heroes. The Star Fort on the western side of the Pass was the scene of the most intensive action. The defenders under the personal command of Corse, fired their Henry 15 shot repeater rifles so fast that they became too hot to hold. As the fort ran out of ammunition, Pvt. Edwin Fullington crossed the footbridge three times as he was fired upon by enemy snipers, to resupply the defenders. Another defender, Pvt. James Croft, received the Medal of Honor for bravery during this battle. General Corse received a wound to his cheek in the heat of the attack.

At noon, General French received word that Yankee reinforcements were in the area and in view of the heavy casualties his forces had received, he decided to withdraw.

The cost of the day? Out of the 5,301 men engaged in the four hour battle, only 3,698 lived to talk about it–one of the bloodiest days of the entire war.

---

lanes from here, provide HOT lanes (HOV lanes with toll charges) and add dedicated lanes for trucks only. All these possibilities are currently under study and planning, with an implementation program to start in September, 2007. The planned completion date is 2010. We'll keep you informed.

Mile 273-Traffic Sign: We are 14 miles (23km) above the point where we must decide to go around Atlanta on the 25 mile I-285W bypass, or continue through the city for 20 miles on I-75. We have just passed under one of the electronic gantry signs of Atlanta's Advanced Traffic Management System, or ATMS, so check it carefully to see if it is displaying any useful information for us. Also, let's tune in Captain Herb and his traffic team

on 750 AM and get a traffic report.

I do not like the I-285 Bypass. All trucks must use it (unless heading to an Atlanta destination) and it has a high accident rate.

If the Overhead Sign is not reporting I-75 accidents and you have at least 2 people in your car, the decision is easy–continue through Atlanta using the HOV lanes (see Mile 258, below). For the last few years, we have done this regardless of whether it was in rush traffic or not, and have averaged 35 minutes to exit 238, where the Bypass rejoins.

Atlanta's ATMS is billed as the most sophisticated traffic management system in the World. Many technologies such as video cameras and road sensors feed information into a control center where the information is analyzed. Up-to-date traffic information messages are relayed back to travelers via these overhead signs (there are five over I-75 in the Atlanta area)–and to in-car navigational displays, hand-held "Palm" personal communication devices (for people walking), on-line computer services and cable TV. If you have a wireless communication device in your car. visit – http://www.georgia-navigator.com – before you leave home and register on-line. You will then be able to receive the latest traffic information as you drive south through this area.

Exit 273-Southern Museum of Civil War & Locomotive History: *(see* Insider Tip*)*.

Exit 267B (S/Bound), 263 (N/Bound)- Marietta: *(bold letters in this text are referenced on the City map on page 61)*. Many of us zip by Marietta in our haste to get on to the "business" of Atlanta, and yet it has a charming "small town" ambiance–a pleasant grass square, art & craft shops, antiques, small restaurants, bed & breakfast establishments, a fine museum and of course, an excellent Welcome Center. So let's go & take a quick look.

Marietta Square-with angle parking around the perimeter and a round fountain in a parkland setting in the center, it's a great place to just sit and relax under the shady trees, or perhaps go and browse the shops and enjoy the **restaurants** *(E)* surrounding it.

Gardens in Marietta Square

One block along Church Street is an antique browser's idea of heaven for here, and also mingled in with the stores facing the Square, you'll find **antique shops** *(D)* with nooks and crannies to explore for, that special treasure.

Just one block to the west is the old railroad track and an excellent **Visitors' Center** *(A)* inside the c1898 Western & Atlantic Passenger Depot. Say *"hi"* to Mary and the other volunteers–they do a grand job. [Hrs: M-F, 9-5p, Sa, 10-4p, Su. 1-4; ☎ 770-429-1115].

Next to the Center is an historical hotel – called the **Fletcher House** *(B)* during the *"War Between the States,"* and later changed to the *Kennesaw House.* It was here that James Andrews' Raiders (Great Locomotive Chase–see page 117, item 1) stayed–in some cases, four to a bed–before boarding the train

---

INSIDER TIP
Southern Museum of Civil War & Locomotive History

Recently re-opened after a $5.6 million expansion, this museum is now a world class facility, partnered with the Smithsonian in Washington. It houses one of the finest collections of Civil War exhibits outside the Museum of the Confederacy in Richmond, Virginia. For instance, don't miss the extremely rare 1843 Whitworth sniper's rifle, still in its original carrying case.

As you leave the Museum section, you walk through an 19th century engineer's shop and past old railroad wheel patterns, to enter a steam locomotive factory from the 1800s, where you can see an early "iron horse" being assembled.

Finally, you round a corner and pass through a tunnel ... and there she is,the famous locomotive, *General*, which was the subject of the Great Locomotive Chase *(see page 117)*. The locomotive which gave chase, the *Texas* is on display at the Cyclorama in Atlanta (☎ 404-658-7625 for directions).

The primary focus of this museum is to collect, preserve & interpret artifacts relating to the history of Southern steam locomotives, both ante and post bellum. For details and directions, see the map of Kennesaw and the museum on page 59.

MARIETTA - *for Marietta Cobb, believed to have been the wife of Thomas Cobb, after whom Cobb County is named.*

INSIDER TIP – the Marietta Diner never closes

Want fried eggs and chips with a glass of wine at 3 o'clock in the morning? Then the *Marietta Diner* is the place for you. This authentic stainless steel and neon-lit 1950s Diner is a fun place to eat with great food presented on a thirteen page, plastic laminated menu. Breakfast, lunch, dinner, there are meals and prices to satisfy all tastes.

Owner Gus or his mother, Maria, will make you welcome regardless of when you arrive–because they never close. Share a joke with Gus, say *"hi"* to him from me and enjoy

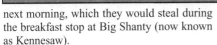

yourself ... for the Marietta Diner is a unique experience not to be missed.

To find the Diner, take exit 263 (S Marietta Pkwy) west; move to the right turn lane well before you reach the lights at US41 (Cobb Pkwy). Turn right and Immediately after, move to the left lane and look for the Diner on your left at 306 Cobb Pkwy. ☎ 770-423-9390

next morning, which they would steal during the breakfast stop at Big Shanty (now known as Kennesaw).

An excellent museum upstairs, the **Marietta Museum of History** *(B)* includes the room used by James Andrews. Curator Dan Cox loves to chat with visitors and tell stories of the past. [Hrs, M-Sa, 10-4p; Adult/Snr/Child-$5/$3/$3; ☎ 770-528-0431].

Next door in the historic Thomas Warehouse building *(B)*, you will find the Shaw-Tumblin **Gone With The Wind** Movie museum. Here you'll see Vivian Leigh's "Oscar," Clark Gable's contract and many other pieces of memorabilia from the famous movie. [Hrs, M-Sa,10-5p; Adult/Snrs/Student/Child-$7/$6/$6/free. ☎ 770-494-5576].

If you have time, drive over to the **Confederate Cemetery** *(C)* which is about half-a-mile south from the Square *(see map)*. When you arrive, drive within the cemetery to the northern end.

More than three thousand Confederate soldiers are buried here on the tranquil slopes of the hill, some from a train crash, others from nearby hospitals but many from the Chickamauga and Atlanta Campaign battlefields. At least 1,000 of these soldiers were never identified; their stones are simply marked, *"Unknown."*

Mile 258-HOV Atlanta Express Lanes: By now, I'm sure you know (and perhaps have used) the restricted HOV, or High Occupancy Vehicle express lanes. They start here and run down to mile 238 (the same for northbound).

Marked with a black diamond symbol, the HOV lanes are dedicated to public and emergency vehicles, and cars with two or more

people on board. Unlike many other cities though, the Atlanta HOV Lanes are *restricted to this traffic 24 hours a day, 7 days a week*. Watch for the black diamond sign and double dashed road markings which identifies these restricted traffic lanes. You may only cross into or from the HOV lane (if you are eligible) at double-dashed line sections; crossing to or from the HOV on a solid line is dangerous, and could earn you a traffic citation

Incidentally, the signage reads *"two person car pools"* but we have checked with the Atlanta authorities and any private car (even with out-of-state license plates) with two or more people in it may use the express lanes.

At present, "AFV," or "Alternate Fuel Vehicles" with special AFV tags, may use the HOV lanes with just one person in the car. However, due to a bureaucratic glitch, hybrid vehicles such as the *Honda Insight* or *Toyota Prius* may <u>not</u> use the HOV lanes unless there are two people in the car.

Atlanta rush hour – note that the cars in the HOV lanes (bounded by the double dashed lines), appear to be moving well.

A word of caution. Since the HOV lanes occupy I-75's left lanes and Atlanta has some left-hand exits, be very careful you don't accidentally leave the interstate on those ramps. All are clearly marked.

However, there are several places where the HOV lanes appear to separate from the rest of I-75 traffic. This happens around mile 252 in the southbound lanes and just past exits 247 and 250 in the northbound lanes. In all cases, the HOV lane ramps are clearly marked *"I-75"* with a directional arrow on the sign. Follow these with confidence since they rejoin I-75 a little further on, usually past all the slow moving traffic in the regular lanes.

On the maps, I've provided separate Atlanta driving instructions for either HOV or regular lanes. The regular lane instructions are in orange boxes and HOV instructions are in white boxes with the black HOV diamond.

The Varsity: at exit 249D lies one of Atlanta's famous landmarks–the Varsity drive-in restaurant.

Now there are several things you need to know about the Varsity before you decide to eat there. It can be crowded, noisy–in fact, sometimes raucous–but it's an Atlanta institution. Anybody who is anybody in Atlanta has eaten there. Presidents Carter, Bush, and most recently, Clinton have graced the Varsity dining rooms where you can choose the room according to the TV channel you would like to watch.

No matter how crowded it is–they serve over 10,000 customers and 17,000 hotdogs each day; they sell more Coke than any other single location in the World–the orders move quickly over the many sales positions along the 150' stainless steel counter.

"Whad'll ya have?? whad'll ya have??" is the constant cry. As founder/owner Frank Gordy says, *"Have your money in your hand and your order in your mind and we will get you to the game on time."*

Alternatively, you can sit in your car and one of the car-hops will come and take your order. Parking isn't always easy to find in the service area, but with a little patience you'll

soon see a happy customer backing out.

You will either love or hate the Varsity, but it <u>will</u> be an unforgettable experience. Frank's daughter, Nancy Sims runs the Varsity along with her staff of very interesting characters –try and get Irvy Walker on the Express Counter to chant the menu for you.

If driving south on I-75, take exit 249D, turn left and the Varsity is immediately on your left just across the bridge. Pull into the first driveway (before the building) for car-hop service or regular parking.

When you leave, drive around the back out onto Spring St, cross the traffic lights at Ponce De Leon and across North Ave., stay left past the I-75 North ramp until you see the I-75 South sign–follow the I-75S ramp back down onto the freeway (also known as the Atlanta Downtown Connector).

If driving north, take exit 249D, cross Spring St and turn left when you reach West

Dixie Highway Motorcade

Oct. 15, 1915–"At 4:30 o'clock this afternoon every auto owner in Atlanta is requested to meet at the Majestic Hotel for the purpose of motoring to Bolton to give the tourists the greatest road reception they have received anywhere along their route." read the Atlanta Constitution's lead. What was it all about?

DH In Georgia, the Dixie Highway project was not moving forward as quickly as some thought it should so in 1915, a group of northern tourists formed a motorcade to drive south and promote the highway's completion. A sign on the baggage truck accompanying the procession said it all, *"600,000 Automobile Owners Are Awaiting the Completion of the Dixie Highway to See the South."*

Can you imagine the sight. I'm sure you sometimes feel as I do that *"every automobile owner in Atlanta"* is on I-75 to greet us when we drive through!

CHATTAHOOCHEE RIVER - *Cherokee name probably, "marked rocks," for painted stones found in the river.*

ATLANTA - *formerly named "Terminus" (in 1837 for the southern end of the Western & Atlantic Railroad), and changed to "Marthasville" in 1843 to honor Gov.. Wilson Lumpkin's daughter. Finally to "Atlanta" in 1845, suggested by the word "Atlantic" in the name of its most important industry, the W&A Railroad.*

Peachtree, turn left again at North Avenue and you will see the Varsity across the road from you.

When you leave, follow the directions above for southbound travelers but take the I-75 North ramp instead.

Exit 249C (S/bound) or 248C (N/bound)- Atlanta Aquarium: The new *Georgia Aquarium* opened in 2006, on the site of the 1996 Olympic Park. Should you wish to visit it, phone 404-581-4000 for information.

Interestingly, I-75 now has more world-class aquariums along its length than any other freeway in the world. At KY exit 192-*Newport Aquarium*, TN exit 2-Chattanooga's *River and Ocean Journey Aquariums*, these exits-new *Atlanta Aquarium*, and at FL exit 261-*Florida Aquarium*. All are absolutely first-class and each is quite different.

Exit 248A (S/bound) or 246A (N/bound)- World of Coca Cola: This major Atlanta attraction is located 3 blocks west of these exits. Phone 404-676-5151 for information.

In mid-2007, a new *World of Coca Cola* will open next to the *Atlanta Aquarium*. We plan to carry more information about these attractions in the next edition of *"Along I-75."*

Turner Field (Olympic Stadium): At mile 246, on your left is Turner Field (named after Atlanta's Ted Turner), site of the 1996 Summer Olympic Opening and Closing ceremonies. The stadium is home for the Atlanta Braves baseball team.

Just to the north of the Stadium is the distinctive open girder statue of the Olympic Torch, honoring the Games.

Mile 239-World's Busiest Airport: At mile 239, you might notice lights on top of stalks in I-75's median. These are the final approach lights of runway 27R, of the world's busiest airport, William B.Hartsfield International.

Built on land originally owned by Asa Chandler, the founder of The Coca Cola Company, as the site of his auto race track, Hartsfield is the world's busiest airport, servicing more than 88.4 million passengers and 980,197 takeoffs and landings last year.

Major construction projects are underway at the airport during the 2000s, each part of an overall expansion plan costing several billion dollars.

At a final cost of $1.28 billion, the new 9,000ft fifth runway bridging I-285W is now open. As reported in the last edition of *"Along I-75,"* some residential neighborhoods and business buildings had to be destroyed to make way for this new facility.

Exit 237-Georgia Farmers Market: Just to the east of I-75 lies the huge *Georgia Farmers' Market*. To reach it, take exit 237 and go east to the second traffic light. Turn left into the double gates & follow the left hand lanes marked *"Shed Area-"Georgia Farmers."*

The whole area is open to the public even though it looks commercial–follow the lanes around the building and there you will find sheds with stands selling–pecans, onions, tomatoes, peanuts–every type of fruit and vegetable you ever wanted. You can drive up and down the rows. When you see something you want, just roll down your window and the stall person will come to you.

Visitors to the Market often miss the huge garden center down in the southwest corner of the property. You will find everything here, from flowers to garden statues, and of course, plants.

Another popular I-75 restaurant has closed. For many years we have recommended *Thomas Marketplace Restaurant* here on the grounds of the Market. But Thomas closed his doors last year and the sign on the door says, *"Gone Fishing."* Hopefully, somebody else will acquire the property soon and start serving Farmers' Market fresh meals again.

Exit 233-The "Road to Tara" Museum: We are now in *"Gone With The Wind"* country. Yes, I know that Margaret Mitchell's great book was a work of fiction ... but don't bother trying to convince anybody in this neighborhood. Wasn't Jonesboro where Scarlett O'Hara used to drive her buggy five miles to catch the train to Atlanta?

While in the mood, let's go and visit the ***Road***

JONESBORO - *originally called "Leakesville," it was renamed after Samuel Jones, an engineer who revived the Macon & Western, a bankrupt railroad.*

FORSYTH - *for John Forsyth (1780-1841) who was Governor of Georgia in 1827 and Secretary of State between 1834-41, under Presidents Jackson and Van Buren.*

To Tara Museum housed in the historic Jonesboro Railroad Depot (incidentally, this same building houses the excellent *Clayton County Information Center)*.

Have your photo taken in front of "Tara."

Here you will find a feast of GWTW photos, artifacts, letters and other memorabilia to satisfy the most ardent "Windie." They even run the movie continuously so you can sit and watch your favorite scene. [Hrs: M-F, 8:30-5:30p; Sa, 10-4p; Adult/Snr/Student/Child-$5/$4/$4/$4; a "package" ticket is also available covering this and four other Atlanta area GWTW attractions; ☎ 770-478-4800; 1-800-662-7829].

Exit 221-Escaping I-75: Once again, I must tell you how helpful those brown "escape" routes are on the colored maps. While driving through here last year, we heard on the radio that I-75 was blocked with a major crash at exit 218. I checked page 36 (yes, I use my book while driving) and found that I could get around the problem by taking exit 221 into McDonough, and then rejoining I-75 at exit 216. It worked beautifully. Not only did we miss a major traffic backup (you should have seen the northbound lanes when we rejoined I-75) but thoroughly enjoyed an impromptu visit to the *"Geranium City"*–McDonough.

Exits 222, 221, 218, 216-McDonough: This lovely historic town (its not really a city) was founded in 1823 and has a charming "Old South" Square where the routes from the above exits, meet in a counter-clockwise one-way road system. This is quite convenient since you can keep circling while you get your bearings and choose a parking space.

The *McDonough Welcome Center* is located in a traditional white & red 1920s Standard Oil Service Station, at 5 Griffin St, on the northwest perimeter of the Square. Enjoy your visit. [☎ 770-898-9311].

Exit 212 - Noah's Ark: If you love children and animals then a visit to this very unusual and special place is for you. Noah's Ark is not an "attraction" but a haven which lovingly brings neglected children and injured or orphaned animals together, providing a place where through animal care therapy, they can help and heal each other.

Set in 40 acres of nature trails and natural habitat, the property includes a center where injured birds and animals are treated and if possible, rehabilitated back to health. More than 1,000 animals–some coming from Georgia's Department of Natural Resources–pass through the hands of the center's professional staff every year. You may visit many of them–domestic, farm, wildlife and exotics of all types–in the fields and pens at Noah's Ark.

At present, a group residence provides a loving foster parent home for about 24 youngsters.

The public is invited to visit the facilities and enjoy the nature trails free of charge (donation appreciated), from Tuesday to Saturday. Phone 770-957-0888 first to make sure the animal habitats are open.

It's 4.3 miles (6.9km) from I-75. Take exit 212 and drive east via Bill Gardner Pkwy towards Locust Grove. Turn right on to US23 /SR42 (south). After .9 mile (1.4km), turn right at the Post Office onto LG Griffin Road. Noah's Ark is 2.8 miles (4.5km) west on the left side of the road.

Exit 198-High Falls State Park: Less than two miles (3.2km) east of I-75 is a pretty place to pause–perhaps for a picnic *(see* **Insider Tip** *on page 88)* beside the 100 foot waterfall–the High Falls State Park. Incidentally, an excellent overnight stop for RVers.

Catfish and seafood dinner service at the *Falls View Restaurant* is as popular as ever and well worth a stop. [Hrs: T-Th, 4-8:30p, F-Sa, 4-9:30p; ☎ 478-994-6050].

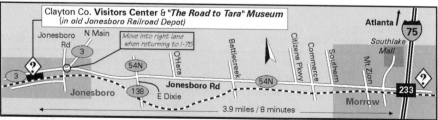

Clayton Co. **Visitors Center** & *"The Road to Tara" Museum*
(in old Jonesboro Railroad Depot)

Jonesboro Rd   N Main   *Move into right lane when returning to I-75*

Atlanta 75

Southlake Mall

Bettiecreek   Citizens Pkwy   Commerce   Southern   Mt Zion

54N   O'Hara

Jonesboro Rd

Jonesboro   138   E Dixie   54N

233

Morrow

◄──────── 3.9 miles / 8 minutes ────────►

INSIDER TIP – Grits Cafe

I've eaten at the Grits Cafe many times and just love it, for here you can dine on exquisitely prepared food in an early 1900s "old brick" setting, with real gas lamps.

Regardless of its humble name, most of the items on the menu–crab, lamb, steak, etc.–are what I would call upscale, casual dining, with dinner entrees in the $12-22 range. Gourmet Chef Wayne Wetendorf and his wife, Terri, will ensure you have a fine meal & enjoyable experience.

Take exit 186 and drive straight ahead for 1 mile. The Grits Cafe will be on your right on the "Square" at 17 W. Johnson St, across from the Forsyth Courthouse.
[Hrs: Lunch, Tu-Sa, 11-2p;   Dinner: Tu-Th, 5:30-9p; F-Sa, 5:30-10p; ☎ 478-994-8325].

As you drive in to High Falls from I-75, you pass several small roadside "villages" of boutique style stores. *Buck Creek Village* (on your right about 1 mile from the interstate) is now the location of "old friends" of ours from Juliette (Whistle Stop Cafe)–*McCrakin Street Sweets*, with hand-made chocolate candies and fabulous fudge. Go in and say "hi" to Larry and Donna for me. [Hrs: W-Sa, 11-5p; ☎ 478-994-4498].

Exit 186-Forsyth Courthouse Square: This lovely "Old South" town is well worth a quick visit and is just one minute off I-75 to the southwest.

Take exit 187 (N Lee St) and drive past the exit services, cross the railroad tracks and you come to Johnson St.–total distance, ½ mile. The old town green is just to your right with its magnificent 1896 Courthouse; you have just entered the Forsyth historical district of *Courthouse Square*. Turn right, stop and park, and enjoy the ambiance of an old southern town.

When ready to leave, go around the Square and turn right onto E Johnston/Tift College Dr and drive east towards I-75 exit 186 (on the other side of the exit, the road leads to Juliette). On the way, you pass the *Mystic Biscuit Coffee House & Sandwich Shop* on your right, a great place to buy freshly made sandwiches and perhaps a Latte, for a picnic lunch [Hrs: M-F, 7-8p. Sa, 9-2p; 211 Tift College Dr; ☎ 478-994-0250].

Exit 186-Juliette & the Whistle Stop Cafe:
(See Town map and other details on page 61).
Do you remember the wonderful movie,

"Fried Green Tomatoes?" If you did, then you might like to visit the tiny village and the actual cafe used as a backdrop for the film.

Whistle Stop Cafe owner Elizabeth Bryant, Betty Clements of *The Gift shop of Southern Grace* and *Habersham Wine Tasting Room*, Penny and Robin of *Juliette Espresso*–and the many other fine people of Juliette are just as friendly and heart-warming as the folk in the movie.

The center of activity is the *Whistle Stop Cafe* (yes–they do serve fried green tomatoes as well as other Southern delicacies).

Across the street is one of my favorite places–the rocking chair in front of Betty's *Southern Grace* antiques. It's wonderful to sit here and chat with Betty, and watch the world go by. Notice the clock behind the counter? Betty keeps *"River Time"* because she doesn't like to change it in the spring or fall ... *"and the nearby Ocmulgee River keeps the same time year round."* In fact, Juliette is timeless, a wonderful place to recharge your soul in today's hectic pace–it's a short trip to another time and age and I heartily recommend it.

Whistle Stop Cafe, Juliette

Jessica Tandy's parting line in the movie mentions the Whistle Stop Cafe ... *"It was never more than a little knockabout place but when I look back on it ... it's funny how a tiny place like this brought so many people together."* Thanks to all the wonderful folk of today's Juliette, it still does.

Mile 180-Macon Welcome Center, "BJ": *(see Macon map on page 196)* The *Macon Welcome Center* is on the interstate just before the road splits between I-75 and the I-475 Bypass. I cannot go by here without stopping to say *"hello"* to that wonderful Southern lady, BJ–her counter partner Bernice, and other staff members at the Center.

BJ and I go back many years (well ... I do;

Macon–the Song & Soul of the South

Without a doubt, Macon is the *"Song & Soul of the South"* and yet so many travelers intent on getting to Florida, pass by on I-475. Why not arrange to spend a night there. Located on the banks of the Ocmulgee River, it is full of history and things to do. Use the map on page 196 to orientate yourself. You'll find reasonably priced motels and inns at exits 171 & 169; many have discount coupons in the free motel books *(see saving tips on pages 67 & 134)*. Or ask the counter staff at the **I-75 Welcome Center** (mile 179; 478-994-8181), they can often get the best lodging rates for you and recommend restaurants. While there, pick up a copy of the free *Macon Visitors' Guide*, it has all the times and admissions you need.

The easiest way to travel downtown is to take I-75, exit 165. At this exit, you join interstate-16 traveling east towards Savannah. Leave I-16 in 2 miles at exit 2 (MLK Blvd). This will take you across the river and into the quiet and spacious downtown area of Macon.

Drive straight across Walnut St–the **Tubman African-American Museum** is on your right–and as you round the curve, my favorite of all museums–the **Georgia Music Hall of Fame**–is on the left. Take care here because MLK Blvd goes off to the right at the intersection of Mulberry St. Stay in the left lane & bear left onto Cherry St Plaza, which becomes 5th Street in a few blocks.

At the intersection of Cherry St and Cherry St plaza, the **Sports Hall of Fame** is on your right. In January, 2007, the downtown Welcome Center relocated from its long tenure at the Terminal Station building, to 450 MLK Blvd, with lots of parking [Hrs: M-Sa, 9a-5p; ☎ 478-743-3401].

I recommend you take the *"Around Town"* self-guided trolley tours. You may enter or leave the trolley as you wish throughout the day. Guides at each attraction will help and answer your questions. This is a great way to see Macon's historic sites such as the **Sidney Lanier Cottage** (Georgia's foremost poet), **Hay House** or **Cannonball House**–or the Macon museums. [Tours, M-Sa. ☎ 478-743-3401 or 800-768-3401 for times; tickets available at the Welcome Center].

If you enjoy ancient history, don't miss the Ocmulgee (pronounced: oak-mul-gee, like the "g" in "geese") **National Monument Indian Village** park (dated back to 9,000BC), visited by Hernando de Soto in 1540 [☎ 478-752-8257].

she's too young!). She has tried to teach me to say *"kudzu"* in the Southern manner–but with my English accent getting in the way, I think she has given up!

Do try and visit Macon. It's an unusual and interesting place; see my *Special Report*, above. [I-75 Welcome Center Hrs, daily, 9a-5:30p; Restrooms 24hrs. ☎ 478-994-8181].

I-475. Exit 15-The Red Tomato: It's so easy to go by the Bolingbroke exit without stopping but once again we have an excuse to head down the ramp and spend some time

Money Saving Tip

If planning to spend the night in Macon, tell the staff at the Macon Welcome Center). Let them make arrangements for you. Tell them what your budget is, they can often arrange much better rates (assuming availability) than you can by yourself.

here–a new restaurant getting rave reviews in the media, *The Red Tomato*. Macon gourmet chef, Michael Falduti, Jr. has taken over the old farmhouse at Alexander Court, and has become the newest hot spot for Continental fare in the Macon area.

Lunch is "cafe/bistro" with prices under $10; dinner (upscale fine dining) has entrees ranging from $16-28. Enjoy!

To find the Red Tomato, at the bottom of the I-75 ramp, turn right towards Bolingbroke. In ½ mile turn right again into *Oak Park Village* (Monroe Bank on the corner). *The Red Tomato* is in the white verandah building set back on your right. [Hrs: Lnch, Tu-Sa, 11-2p; Dnr, Th-Sa, 5:30-9:30p; ☎ 478-994-6336].

I-475. Exit 9-Our favorite Macon stop: This exit seems to grow and grow with new restaurants and shopping facilities. We enjoy stopping at the *Fairfield Inn* here, always a good choice. I call it my *"Macon base"*

MACON- *after Nai Macon (1757-1837), an American Revolutionary patriot and politician.*
ECHECONNEE CREEK - *from Creek Indian, "place where deer are trapped."*

–highly recommended–manager Jonathan & his staff do an excellent job.

A favorite lunch stop of ours is just west of I-475 at 6351 Zebulon Rd–*Polly's Corner Cafe*, a very popular spot for shrimp and catfish [Hrs: Lnch, Tu-Sa, 11-2p; Dnr, Tu-W, 5-9p, F-Sa, 5-10p; ☎ 478-757-9926].

I-475, Exit 3-Big Box Shopping: In the north east quadrant of exit 3, you'll find the 80 acre Eisenhower Crossing Shopping Center Stores already opened are Marshalls, Krogers, Best Buy, Target, Staples, Michaels Crafts, Old Navy and Radio Shack ... and if that's not enough, huge Macon Mall is only another 1.6 miles (2.6km) down the road east from here.

"Legend of the Spanish Moss"

There's an ancient legend
told by Southern folk
About the lacy moss
that garlands the great Live Oak;

A lovely princess and her love
upon their wedding day

Were struck-down by a savage foe
amidst a bitter fray;

Together in death they're buried
so the legends go

'Neath an oak's strong, friendly arms
protected from their foe;

There ... as was the custom
the bride's hair was cut with love

And hung in shining blackness
on the spreading boughs above;

Undisturbed it hung there
for all the world to see

And with the years
the locks turned gray,
and spread from tree to tree.

Mile 155-The Derelict: Wonder what that strange sight is just to the east? Reminiscent of a wrecked ship with torn sails on a lee shore, it was once a golf driving range.

Exit 149-Big Peach Antiques: Another I-75 antique mall mecca. Here you will find hundreds of booths. To reach the building, turn left on to the small road between Pizza Hut and Burger King. [Hrs. M-Sa, 9-7p; Su, noon-6p; ☎ 912-956-6256].

Exit 146-Martin Mace Missile: A CGM-13 Martin Mace guided missile on the south eastern corner of this exit reminds us that to

our east lies Warner Robins, a USAF town.

Mile 140-Forever Georgia: Once we cross *Mossy Creek*, we are in the area I call *"Forever Georgia."* Why? Well, we are now beyond the "hubbub" of the cities and into a much more relaxing part of the South. It's also an area which, apart from conscription, was not touched too badly by *The War.* Of course, you know by now that this refers to the *War Between the States,* or the *Civil War.*

We are also in the land of the Epiphyte. As we travel further south the stands of conifers in the sawmill pinelands and trees draped with Hanging Moss give a much more relaxed, laid back appearance to the roadside. Hanging (or Spanish) Moss (Tillandsia Usneoides) is a peculiar plant, not a moss and not a parasite as many people believe. It's an Epiphyte–a plant that does not grow in soil but clings to another plant or tree for support and lives on the air surrounding it.

Exit 136-Angelina's: If you enjoy fine Italian dining, we have a treat in store for you–*Angelina's Italian Garden Cafe.* This old world cafe restaurant with fountain, brightly colored flower beds and patio umbrellas, is just west of this exit near the Quality Inn. Owner Donald will probably seat you. Buon appetito! [Hrs: Lnch, M-Fr, 11-2:30p; Dnr, M-Th, 5-9:30p, Sa, 5-10p; ☎ 478-987-9494].

Exit 135-Visitor Center: To the east of I-75 is an excellent Visitor Center. It is well stocked with maps and brochures, and friendly advice. Say "hi" to Sheila, Gloria, Evelyn and Lillianne. [Hrs, M-F, 8:30-5p; Sa, 10-4p; in summer also open Sun, 1p-5p; ☎ 478-988-8000].

Mile 130-Hernando de Soto: At Tennessee mile 42, I explained how in 1539, Don Hernando de Soto, the Spanish explorer led his army of 600 men on a journey of exploration of the North American continent. As he moved northward through Georgia, his journal for March, 1540, records how he marched from Montezuma (about 15 miles west of I-

PERRY - *"We have met the enemy and they are ours"* was the naval signal sent by Oliver Hazard Perry (1785-1819) after he beat the British fleet on Lake Erie during the War of 1812. Perry is named in honor of the war hero.

75 mile marker 125), crossed Beaver Creek and arrived at an Indian village at Perry where he observed the women spinning silk from the fibers of mulberry trees. His army would have crossed the terrain of the modern I-75 around mile marker 130. Several days later, the army moved on towards modern Macon and crossed the "Great River"–the Ocmulgee.

Exit 127-Henderson Village: Barely one mile west of this exit is a fascinating 18 acre village of deluxe overnight lodging and fine dining, surrounded by formal gardens and a 3,500 acre hunting preserve (game shooting and wild boar hunting). Definitely not for the budget minded traveler, but perhaps the ultimate stopover for that special occasion–a fine way to celebrate a birthday or anniversary while on the road.

Within the village is the *Langston House Restaurant*–a beautifully renovated 1838 plantation home, decorated throughout with original antiques and divided into small intimate dining rooms. The menu items are freshly prepared by executive chef, Alex Gonzalez, and change regularly to reflect the season. Entrees are in the $15-22 range.

And now to the grounds. Henderson Village is an assembly of historical and heritage buildings from the area–local homes and tenant farmer cottages, all completely renovated and decorated in the finest fashion for a deluxe stay. Winding brick paths meander through the property and old fashioned gas lamps light the way during the evening.

Our favorite tenant farmer's cottage at Henderson Village

I was really taken by the "court" of six inward facing "Tenant" cottages. All the old architectural features that make these buildings so endearing, have been kept. Some have wooden shingle roofs while others are of tin, but all are completely modernized. Modern heating and air-conditioning is hidden away where you cannot see or hear it.

As we enter, we notice the wonderful aromas

of cedar and bayberry. Beautiful old brick hearths (retrofitted with safe but very authentic, glowing ember gas fireplaces) along with functional antique furnishing ensure warm and comfortable interiors.

All buildings have a porch; some with double porch swings, others with rocking chairs or wicker furniture. There is something special about sitting out and quietly rocking the time away while listening to the crickets, on a warm southern night.

In Henderson Village, no expense has been spared to evoke the atmosphere of a peaceful but bygone era.

General Manager Heather Bradham invites *"Along I-75"* readers to take a break from the highway, to come and enjoy the grounds, relax and wander around this unusual community and perhaps, sample some of the delicacies at the Langston House. She has special lower rates for my readers.

[Restaurant hours: Breakfast, 7-10a, Lunch, 11:30-2p; Dinner, 6-9p, closed Sun-Mon; Information/reservations; ☎ toll free 888-615-9722, or 478-988-8696].

Exit 121-Old Time Stuckey: Ah, *Texaco* and *Stuckeys*. Remember the 1960s when a Texaco fill-up (no self service in those days–you weren't allowed to touch the pumps) often came with a box of Pecan Nougat or Peanut Brittle from the adjoining Stuckey Store.

Well, you no longer get the nougat or brittle, and the fill-up is self-service–but at this Texaco, the adjoining Stuckey is about as close as you will come to the "good old days."

Mile 115-Peanuts and Irrigation: Tl elds just to the west (right) of you heiₑ are peanuts. The large wheeled girder units are used for irrigation.

Mile 109.5-Pig BBQ Festival Grounds: As we approach this exit from the north, you will see the grounds of *BBQ City USA* to your right. Home of the annual autumn *Big Pig Jig*, billed as Georgia's oldest (and official) barbeque cooking contest. "Events" include "Whole Hog," "Rib" and "Shoulder." There are also events for "Brunswick Stew" and of course, "Best Sauce." Yeeeee haw!!!

Exit 109-Georgia Cotton Museum: The history of Georgia and cotton have long been closely associated, and now you are in the *"land of cotton"* as you would expect, there is a *Georgia Cotton Museum*. And it tells the story with some very attractive exhibits.

Did you know for instance, that the first Georgia cotton was brought from England in 1733 and planted in the Trustees Garden in Savannah; or that Georgia was the first state to produce cotton commercially?

For more than 250 years, *"King Cotton"* has played a major role in building the economy of Georgia–until it was almost wiped out by the Boll Weevil. But it came back & today is a major Southern crop again.

Cotton Leaf

The museum is more than just a collection of artifacts. Here, you'll learn about the tools used, including Eli Whitney's Cotton Gin (for removing seeds from the white cotton lint) and a weighing beam used to weigh cotton bales. Samples of cotton in various stages of growth are available so you can actually touch & feel Georgia's number one cash crop.

If you've ever wondered about cotton then you're in the right place. Museum custodian Margaret Hegidio knows the plant well, and loves to chat with her visitors. [½ mile west of I-75; Hrs, M-F, 9-4p; ☎ 229-268-2045].

Mile 103-Pecan Orchard: If you didn't have time to stop and visit the Ellis Bros. at exit 109, here's your chance to see a grove of pecan trees beside the interstate. Look for an orchard of trees on the right (west) side as you travel south, between exits 104 and 102.

Exit 101-Cordele: Cordele is known as the *Watermelon Capital of the World.*

If you take this exit west to buy gas, you might be surprised to see a *Titan Rocket.* The Titan was an early space vehicle contained many exotic but corrosive materials–sadly, the rocket is beginning to really show its age and is rapidly deteriorating.

As you continue your drive west, you will see a very attractive wall mural on your right.

The east side of this exit also has several places of interest.

Ramada Antiques-If you love antiques, you must spend a night at this Ramada Inn. Not only are the rates reasonable but the lobby is an antique shop which never closes! So, if you can't sleep at 3 am, just get up and go browsing. If you see something you like, pay for it at the front desk–and then–back to bed. ☎ 229-273-5000.

Charles Seafood-one of our favorites (see exit 62-Tifton) is also now at the Ramada Inn at this exit. [Hrs. daily, Bkfst/Lnch, 6-2p; Dnr, 5-9p; ☎ 229-273-5842].

Vidalia Onions-This exit is also the route to Vidalia, whose onions are well known the world over for their unusual sweetness and flavor. They are also tearless!

INSIDER TIP - A Visit to Ellis Bros.– a family Pecan Farm

"We're Nuts..." is the slogan of *Ellis Bros. Pecans,* and if there's anything you ever wanted to know about these popular nuts, the Ellis family are your experts. The family has been farming the nuts for three generations. In fact, the pecan trees in the grove just to the north of their retail store were planted just after WWI. Pecans are harvested by air blasting them onto strips of clear ground between the trees. Keith Elliot took me for a tour of the shelling plant behind the store and I was surprised at the control he must maintain over the humidity.

Pecan Leaf

In the store, you will find just about every type of coated pecan–coffee, honey, ginger and chocolate, to name a few. The family has an in-house candy kitchen with four marble topped tables to supply this need. The Ellis' also make wonderful *Mayhaw Jelly* as well as sell almonds, cashews, peanuts–and 5 varieties of pecan-Stuart, Desirables, Papershells (Schley/Sumner). Holly at the counter will be happy to help.

To reach Ellis Brothers, take exit 109 east (route 215) and take first left (Tippetville Rd) at the Ellis Bros. sign. Ellis Bros. is well marked, about ¾ mile on left. The store is open 7 days a week, 8am-7pm; ☎ 1-800-635-0616 or 229-268-9041.

CORDELE - *(pronounce, "Cor-deal") after Cordelia Hawkins, daughter of Colonel Samuel Hawkins, president of the Savannah, Americus and Montgomery railroad.*

Why do they taste so different? It's due to the local sandy, low-sulphur soil in the Vidalia area (85 miles/137km to the east). This was discovered by accident in 1931 when local resident Mose Coleman planted some onion seeds from Texas, and could not believe the sweet, juicy results. They're so good that they could be eaten raw.

Today, Vidalia Onions has grown into a multi-million dollar business. Just like fine wines, only onions from a certain areas are allowed to bear the Vidalia logo. The best time to buy is in the spring. Genuine Vidalia onions may be found at many outlets along I-75 in Georgia; we like to buy ours at the Georgia State Farmers Market (exit 237) if driving north.

Mile 100: Just south of this exit on the right is a cotton field which might be of interest if you don't live in the South. If you missed the Cotton Museum at exit 109, here's your chance to see a cotton field from your car.

Keep an eye on this field–green for most of the summer, it bursts into a field of thigh high cotton balls–*Southern Snow*–in mid-August.

Mile 82-The Peanut Monument: How many

of you have zipped by the tall peanut just south of this exit and wondered what it is. We did a little "off-roading" and found out that it's a memorial; here's the plaque:

"This monument to the Peanut, Turner County's most important agricultural prod- uct is dedicated to the memo- ry of Nora Lawrence Smith, December 25, 1886–July 17, 1971, member, Georgia Jour- nalism Hall of Fame, Editor and Co-Publisher of the Wire- grass Farmer, Turner Coun- ty's award winning newspa- per, & an untiring supporter of Turner Co. and its agricultural economy."

Exit 82-Ashburn: Hang around at the *Crime & Punishment Museum*; enjoy lunch at the *Last Meal Cafe*–see **Insider Tip**.

Exit 78-Jefferson Davis Capture Site: If you were a few miles east of here in May, 1865, you were probably hunting (or helping) Jefferson Davis, ex-President of the Southern Confederacy. He had been on the run from his capital, Richmond, Virginia, since early April and had a $100,000 reward of gold on his head. With his wife, an escort of 20 men and $300,000 in gold and silver from the Confed- erate Treasury, the party decided to camp in a pine grove beside a stream.

Imagine their feelings when they were woken up in the early morning by two Federal caval- ries shooting at each other and everything

---

INSIDER TIP - Crime & Punishment Museum, Last Meal Cafe

This is probably the most unusual museum on I-75, for it was here that criminals were held and in some cases, exe- cuted for heinous crimes.

The iron-barred cages (sepa- rate cells for male, female, black & white), hanging noose and trap, and even an empty coffin are all here for you to see, along with many other prison exhibits.

And now to food. There's an eatery on the premises–the *Last Meal Cafe*–which serves lunch on reproduction prison dinnerware. Of course, the food is much better than prison fare (I think)–regular soup and sandwiches.

It's also much more wholesome than actual last meals ordered by the condemned; their menus are framed on the wall. For instance, mass-murderer Michael Durocher ordered *5lbs fried jumbo shrimp with catsup & melt- ed butter, a pint of chocolate ice cream and 2 liters of Coca Cola*, before heading to the noose. [Hrs: Tu-Sa, 10-4:30p; Adult/Snr/ Child-$6/$4/$2; 241 E College Ave (see map 42); ☎ 800-471-9696].

INSIDER TIP - The French Market

We visited this interesting shop in Ashburn, and found 50-60 well organized booths and sections of collectibles,small antique jewel- ry, interesting & unusual decorator pieces. So interesting in fact, that I purchased all the gifts for our "house & pet sitter" here.

Better still, The French Market includes a nice cafe where you can get an excellent sandwich lunch.

Owner Barbara Coley opened this market of eclectic collectibles in April, 2003, and wel- comes your visit.

Drive west from exit 82 on Route 112 (Washington St) for .8 mile (1.3km). The shop is on the right side of the road just past traffic lights at Johnson St and between Ace Hardware and Movie Gallery (look for "Freds" on left). [Hrs: M-F, 10-6p; Sa, 10-5p; ☎ 229-567-0131].

Tin Can Tourists

Among the early users of the *Dixie Highway* were the *"Tin Can Tourists,"* the fore-runners of today's RVers.

Formed at Tampa, Florida's DeSoto Park in 1919, the organization got its name from the popularity of the members canned "on-the-go" meals and that many members converted the Ford Model T (the *Tin Lizzy),* into their mobile home–this was long before the availability of manufactured RVs.

TCTs had an official black & tan diamond shaped badge on their license plate, but were much easier to recognize from the tin can each soldered onto their car's radiator cap. They also had a secret handshake (sawing motion) and had an unfairly earned reputation of being vagabonds. As one member wrote, *"most people would have nothing to do with us ... many sheriffs met us at the county line."*

Since the *Dixie Highway* ran through many towns between Michigan and Florida, the annual procession of TCTs was seen by some as a nuisance. Just like today, others capitalized on this mobile market.

else in sight. A soldier aimed at Jefferson but his wife offered herself as a target instead; Jefferson surrendered quickly to save her life.

Exit 75-Daylilies: I'm a keen gardener and have known about the *Bells Daylily Garden* for some years now ... but every time I've gone in to visit, I've had the feeling that they do not like writers or publicity. However, with more than 876 varieties of daylily in their catalog, I can't ignore this valuable gardening resource any more.

INSIDER TIP - Pit Stop Bar-B-Que

By now you know that my two loves when I travel are history & eating. Some people have even subtitled this book, "Dave eats his way to Florida!" But I don't want you to miss this excellent BBQ restaurant just west of I-75 at exit 63B. After your meal, go and visit the smoke house at the back, say "hi" to owner Don Davis for me.

[Hrs: Su-Th, 11a-9p; F-Sa, 11a-10p; ☎ 229-387-0888].

You will find the farm east of I-75. Drive ½ mile east on Inaha Rd, turn left and drive ½ mile north, turn right and drive ½ to the Gardens. Incidentally, according to a sign at the entrance, it costs $1 to enter, unless buying. Good luck. [Hrs: W-Sa, 8-4p; ☎ 229-256-1234].

Mile 74.5-Concrete: The road surfaces on the northbound lanes have been rehabilitated and are now new concrete, one of the most enduring (and expensive) methods of surfacing a freeway. How enduring? Well, did you know that concrete was used extensively by the ancient Romans and many of their buildings are still around?

In 20CE, the Roman architect, Vitruvius. described the process in detail. Equal parts of powdered burnt limestone, pozzolan volcanic ash and small stones were mixed with a little water, and the resulting stiff grey mixture was tamped heavily into the cracks and spaces between rocks laid in wooden forms, layer by layer. A chemical reaction took place in this ancient mortar which resulted in a long lasting concrete, as strong as any modern roller compacted material.

Many ancient Roman aqueducts, cisterns and buildings-such as the famous Pantheon in Rome–were built in this manner and are still standing today. I wonder if this road surface will still be here 2,000 years from now?

Mile 63-Tifton: *(Town map on page 53).*

Exit 63B-Georgia Agrirama: Two minutes west at exit 63 (Eighth St.), country life in the late 19th century is the focus of this living outdoor museum. The town's guides wear costumes from the period and practice the trades and skills which would have been required to live in this rural community.

As you wander around the town, visit the steam-powered sawmill, water wheel grist mill, smokehouse, sugar cane mill and turpentine still, among other rural industries. All in all, a pleasant way to spend an hour or so, off the road.

Peanut leaflets

I have heard that there are plans to move the *National Peanut Museum* into Agrirama, but at time of writing, have no details. [Open year round: Tu-Sa, 9a-5p; Adult/Senior/Child-$10/$8/$6 ☎ 229-386-3344].

TIFTON *-founded in 1841 by Capt. Henry Tift, a Yankee from Mystic, Connecticut, who sought wood for shipbuilding and built a sawmill in the area.*

Tifton–the Birthplace of Interstate-75

Special Report

Have you ever wondered exactly when and where the construction of I-75 started? Well, it was here at milepost 63 in Tifton, Georgia. This is the birthplace of not only Interstate-75, but also the entire Interstate system since it was the first interstate construction project to receive Federal approval and funding! And it all came about because Tifton wanted to get rid of the heavy "snowbird" traffic flowing through town.

Like many other communities located between the northern states and Florida, the *Dixie Highway* (in this area, old US 41) went right through the center of town causing heavy congestion, especially in winter months. Cadillacs, Packards and Roadmasters from Illinois, Ohio and Michigan gave rush hour a new meaning. So Tifton decided to build a US41 bypass around town. Years of study and careful planning went into this project and in May, 1956, bids were requested & contracts awarded.

Ironically a month later in Washington, President Eisenhower signed a Bill which officially launched the Interstate system *(see page 69)*. Federal transportation officials needed to get the process "off the ground" quickly and the Tifton Bypass project was a perfect place to start since legal "rights-of-way" on all the necessary land had been acquired and all the planning completed.

So, the 4 mile *Tifton US41 Bypass* became the first 4 miles of *I-75*–the first stretch of interstate constructed and completed anywhere in the USA; it ran from a point near Tifton Junior HS (north of exit 63) in the north, to Southwell Blvd (exit 59) in the south and was completed in 1960.

Interestingly, when enacted the federal interstate planning regulations allowed only one exit every eight miles. But Tifton had designed eight for the bypass–and construction had already begun. That's why Tifton has more exits than most I-75 communities.

The Eisenhower Interstate Monument, Tifton, Georgia

Some Interesting Facts about the first four miles:
- four lanes of concrete roadway
- eight planned exits
- 4.953 miles of grading and paving
- 2,138,500 cubic yds of excavation
- 129 property owners affected
- 286 acres of land cleared
- construction started in 1957
- construction completed in 1960

Just to the west of I-75 at exit 63B stands the *Eisenhower Monument*, dedicated to the former President, Georgian politicians and Tifton highway engineer, Earl Olson–all who made it all happen.

Exit 62: *Adcock Pecans*-Just to the east of exit 62 is the giant retail outlet of the Sunbelt Plantation company–*Adcock Pecans*. I'm always impressed with the huge array of jellies, jams, relish, salsa, sauces and spreads on display. At the last count, there were 88 different varieties in stock, from pumpkin butter to guava jelly to chow chow–you never know what you'll find. [Hrs: daily, 7:30-9p; ☎ 229-382-5566].

A short distance east of Adcock's is a fascinating showroom for those who enjoy antique cars–*Auto Quest*. Here owner Bob Kennon keeps a splendid inventory of antiques and classics, and invites you to have a look.

The oldest is a very rare dark green 1917 Haynes; the most expensive, a yellow 1931 Cadillac sedan. Both remarkable vehicles.

And so spouses don't get bored while significant others are drooling over these mechanical wonders, Bob's wife, Ann, has opened an upscale clothing store–*The Cabin Shop*–at the rear of the auto showroom. Now that is very thoughtful! [Hrs: M-F, 9-5p, Sa, 10-3p; ☎ 229-382-4750].

Charles Seafood Restaurant, is everything I expected–fresh seafood at reasonable prices.

The menu ranges from the usual range of seafood such as grouper–to the unusual such as 'gator tail. If you're not sure about the latter, try it as an appetizer.

Incidentally, there is plenty of non-seafood choice for the landlubber. All fried foods are prepared with cholesterol-free oil.

Money Saving Tip
Before you leave Georgia, fill up with gas–even if you only need a 1/4 of a tank. Florida gas is much more expensive than Georgia's.

Just 1/3rd mile east of exit 22 lies *Charlie Tripper's*, an "epicurean jewel" specializing in gourmet American fare. As you step through the canopied front door, you know this is going to be a very special experience. White linen tables with glistening silverware are set about the oak paneled rooms. Everywhere, eclectic artwork enhances the intimacy of this fine restaurant.

The menu is seasonal and entrees beautifully prepared by the hands of *CT's* master chef who obviously enjoys his work. *Filet of Beef, Rack of Lamb* and many other entrees tempt us. Surprisingly, prices are very reasonable ranging from $14 to $20.

Kathy and I very much enjoy *CT's* and hope you do as well. Say *"hello"* to owner Tripp or manager Mark for us. [Hrs: M-Sa, 6p-10p, Lounge opens at 5p. ☎ 229-247-0366].

The restaurant is closed on Sunday, but open the rest of the week. Lunch hours are 11-2pm; diner is served from 5-10pm. [☎ 229-382-9696].

Exit 55-Magnolia Plantation: I can never seem to get my car (or my wife, Kathy) past the *Magnolia Plantation* without a mandatory stop to check out the large stock of local relishes, honey, jellies, jams or marmalades. We always come away with at least a few jars of Vidalia Onion relish.

Mile32-Motorsports: The track you can see off to the east is the *South Georgia Motorsports Park*, the local venue for stock car "C" and dragster racing.

Mile 31-Lowdnes County: For a number of years, this stretch of I-75 from here to the Florida border has been very rigidly patrolled by the Valdosta police with radar. In fact, several years ago, the AAA were very close to adding it to the infamous Waldo and Lawtey radar traps in Florida.

Times have changed, thanks to the recently constructed concrete median barrier wall with sliding gates. Police can no longer sit in the median monitoring oncoming traffic, make fast "U" turns on the grassy strip and give chase. Now they must drive to a sliding barrier gate (notice the gates at mile 25.2 & 21), get out of their car & unlock it, drive through and re-lock it, and then chase the offender.

However, life goes on and as you will probably see at exit 13, the police have switched to a "wolf pack" technique.

Exit 22-Charlie Tripper's: –see **Insider Tip**.

Exit 18-Valdosta Beach Party: When you pull into the parking area of this unusual restaurant, you might be forgiven for thinking that you have landed at a beach party. Flaming torches light a sandy shoreline complete with volleyball.

Inside the building–an ex-service station innovatively converted to provide food service–you might be surprised to find tables with holes in the center, paper towel on a stalk and beach furniture hanging upside-down from the ceiling.

This is a transplanted eat-in-the-rough Florida "food-factory," serving seafood goodies wrapped in tinfoil. Unwrap, enjoy, throw the foil and leftover bits down the hole, wipe your hand on the paper towel; you've just enjoyed a beachside meal at the *Steamhouse Seafood & Beachside Bar*. [West of the exit, turn left at first road. Hrs: Tu-Sa, 4-10p; 3008 James Rd; ☎ 229-245-9008].

Exit 16-LuLu's: –see **Insider Tip**.

Mile 13-Radar Trap: Whether traveling north or south, be very careful near exit 13. The police sit on the overpass with radar and have a squad of cars on the ramp ready to pull offenders over (see inset map on page 44). For safety, it's probably best to drive in L2

Several miles east of exit 16 is an excellent restaurant which received rave reviews in *"Southern Living"* magazine. With linen table service, a long narrow room and French posters, *LuLu's* has a definite European ambience. A large collection of wines are available by the glass and chefs work "in front" in full display of the patrons. At the door, you'll meet owner Mary Anna, who loves greeting her guests and making them feel welcome.

For dinner, Kathy and I enjoyed a very tasty Wild Mushroom soup, followed by Grilled Tuna. I selected a caramelized Creme Brule for dessert. The meal was memorable.

Lunches are $6-9; Dinner entrees range from $14-$23. Hrs: Lunch, Tu-Sa, 11-2p; Dinner, Th-Sa, 5:30-10p; Su Brunch, 11-2p

To find LuLu's, from exit 16 drive east on Rt84 (Hill Ave) for 2.4 miles (3.9km); turn left onto Ashley St; drive 1 block & turn left onto Central Ave; drive 1 block & turn left onto N.Patterson. LuLu's is on your right at 132 N. Patterson ☎ 229-242-4000

Well not quite the Hamptons of Long Island but if you are planning a stay in the Valdosta (exit 16) or Lake Park (exit 5), I know you will enjoy either of these Hampton Inns. Operated by the same owner, these properties are well furnished, clean and reasonably prices.

We enjoy the smaller *Lake Park Hampton* at exit 5, (☎ 229-559-5565) with many rooms opening onto its interesting atrium. I know manager Mike will make you feel very welcome.

The *Valdosta Hampton* (exit 16, ☎ 229-241-1234) is a larger "conference-style" facility and has more amenities. We highly recommend them both.

through here to allow the fast moving ramp cars clear access to I-75.

Of course, if you see a patrol car on the soft shoulder, it is the law that you must move to the lane on your left as soon as safe to do so.

Exit 5-The "FarmHouse": For home cooked style southern food, don't overlook the very popular family-owned *FarmHouse Restaurant* east at this exit–you can see it from I-75.

The food is excellent with lots of choices (the house specialty is quail) and very reasonable prices (entrees, $10-17). They also serve an all-day breakfast.

Danny or Greg will make sure that you have a great visit. [Hrs: daily, 7a-9p; ☎ 229-559-5445].

Georgia Mile 2-N/bound Welcome Center: If you are traveling north from Florida, stop in and say *"hello"* for me to my friends at the

Georgia Welcome Center. Hilda, Cathy, Cheryl, Eric, Patty and Teresa will help make your journey northward through Georgia, as interesting as possible. If you plan any stops, they can often make reservations for you at very favorable rates.

FLORIDA: Mile 472-the Florida Border: Florida's Department of Transport is now in its final phase of exit number changes–removing the "old exit" numbers. If you still need an old number, you'll find old and new in my new book, *"Along Florida's Expressways."*

FL Mile 471-Florida Welcome Center: Since Florida's major industry is tourism, the State has a wonderful counter staff to greet and help you. Say *"hi"* from me to manager Patrick and Barbara, Doreen, Dot, Glenda, Helen, Patricia, and Rosetta. Oh, and don't forget to pick up your free orange or grapefruit juice.

The Center's information section is very well stocked, and open daily from 8-5p, daily. Restrooms are open 24 hours; the area is patrolled at night. [☎ 386-938-2981].

Incidentally, if you arrive here after hours, go over to the newspaper boxes outside the vending machine area–you will find a good supply of the free Florida motel and restaurant guides, and coupon books here.

Well–we are now in Florida and if you have a copy of my other book, *"Along Florida's Expressways"* in your car, turn to map 27 (stories on page 125) to continue our drive together. The book covers all the *Florida expressways and toll routes, so I'll be with you no matter where your final destination.

If you don't have a copy, you can buy it at any bookstore, or by phoning **1-800-431-1579**.

But for now, I've enjoyed riding along with you to the Georgia border, sharing adventures and stories along the way. Drive safely and enjoy your time in the sun.

*Psst! As a bonus, I've included several sample Florida's I-75 maps on the next two pages – just to tempt you!

FLORIDA - *named by explorer Ponce de Leon, who discovered the land on Easter Sunday (Pascua Florida), in 1512. Florida means "flowering" in Spanish. Ponce de Leon's original Florida claim encompassed all the land up to and including Newfoundland in Canada.*

Northbound to Georgia

Weigh Station

Weigh Station

Camp Branch

Florida Phone Numbers
Emergency: 911 or
Cell: *FHP (*347) or *FTP (*387)
Police Information: 850-488-6676

Florida has statewide 511 traffic
information system (see page 85)

G-Texco
L-DQ Subwy

old 85

129

451

US129
Live Oak
Jasper

H

G-BP
F-CowbyBBQ

41

25

SAMPLE MAP

JASPER

FL Sheriff's Boys
Camp
Spirit of Suwannee
Music Park

Hamilton Co.

Highway Advisory
1640 AM
when lights are
flashing

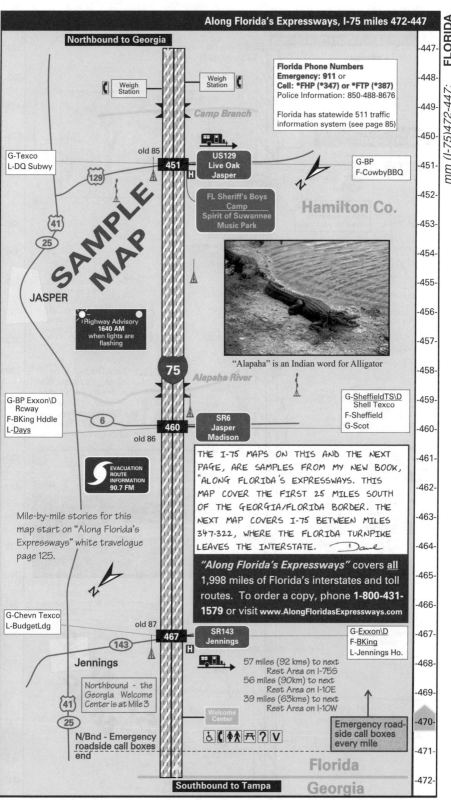

"Alapaha" is an Indian word for Alligator

75

Alapaha River

G-BP Exxon\D
Rcway
F-BKing Hddle
L-Days

6

460

old 86

SR6
Jasper
Madison

G-SheffieldTS\D
Shell Texco
F-Sheffield
G-Scot

EVACUATION
ROUTE
INFORMATION
90.7 FM

Mile-by-mile stories for this
map start on "Along Florida's
Expressways" white travelogue
page 125.

THE I-75 MAPS ON THIS AND THE NEXT
PAGE, ARE SAMPLES FROM MY NEW BOOK,
"ALONG FLORIDA'S EXPRESSWAYS. THIS
MAP COVER THE FIRST 25 MILES SOUTH
OF THE GEORGIA/FLORIDA BORDER. THE
NEXT MAP COVERS I-75 BETWEEN MILES
347-322, WHERE THE FLORIDA TURNPIKE
LEAVES THE INTERSTATE. _Dave_

"Along Florida's Expressways" covers **all**
1,998 miles of Florida's interstates and toll
routes. To order a copy, phone **1-800-431-
1579** or visit www.AlongFloridasExpressways.com

G-Chevn Texco
L-BudgetLdg

old 87

143

467

H

SR143
Jennings

G-Exxon\D
F-BKing
L-Jennings Ho.

Jennings

Northbound - the
Georgia Welcome
Center is at Mile 3

41

25

N/Bnd - Emergency
roadside call boxes
end

Welcome
Center

♿ 🚻 👪 🎪 ? V

57 miles (92 kms) to next
Rest Area on I-75S
56 miles (90km) to next
Rest Area on I-10E
39 miles (63kms) to next
Rest Area on I-10W

Emergency road-
side call boxes
every mile

Florida
Georgia

Southbound to Tampa

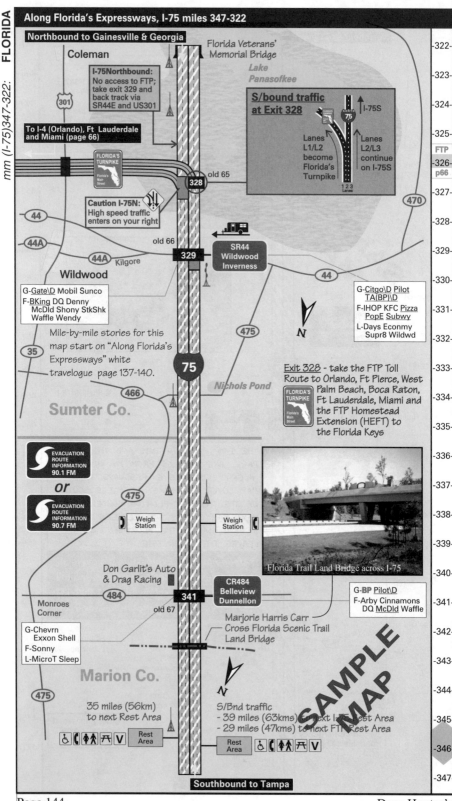

Northbound to Gainesville & Georgia

Coleman

Florida Veterans' Memorial Bridge

Lake Panasofkee

I-75Northbound:
No access to FTP;
take exit 329 and
back track via
SR44E and US301

301

S/bound traffic at Exit 328

I-75S

Lanes
L1/L2
become
Florida's
Turnpike

Lanes
L2/L3
continue
on I-75S

1 2 3
Lanes

To I-4 (Orlando), Ft Lauderdale
and Miami (page 66)

FLORIDA'S
TURNPIKE
Florida's
Main
Street

old 65

328

470

FTP
p66

Caution I-75N:
High speed traffic
enters on your right

44

old 66

329

SR44
Wildwood
Inverness

44A

44A Kilgore

Wildwood

44

G-Gate\D Mobil Sunco
F-BKing DQ Denny
McDld Shony StkShk
Waffle Wendy

G-Citgo\D Pilot
TA(BP)\D
F-IHOP KFC Pizza
PopE Subwy
L-Days Econmy
Supr8 Wildwd

Mile-by-mile stories for this
map start on "Along Florida's
Expressways" white
travelogue page 137-140.

35

475

75

Nichols Pond

466

<u>Exit 328</u> - take the FTP Toll
Route to Orlando, Ft Pierce, West
Palm Beach, Boca Raton,
Ft Lauderdale, Miami and
the FTP Homestead
Extension (HEFT) to
the Florida Keys

FLORIDA'S
TURNPIKE
Florida's
Main
Street

Sumter Co.

EVACUATION
ROUTE
INFORMATION
90.1 FM

or

EVACUATION
ROUTE
INFORMATION
90.7 FM

475

Weigh
Station

Weigh
Station

Don Garlit's Auto
& Drag Racing

Florida Trail Land Bridge across I-75

484

341

old 67

CR484
Belleview
Dunnellon

G-BP Pilot\D
F-Arby Cinnamons
DQ McDld Waffle

Monroes
Corner

Marjorie Harris Carr
Cross Florida Scenic Trail
Land Bridge

G-Chevrn
Exxon Shell
F-Sonny
L-MicroT Sleep

Marion Co.

SAMPLE MAP

475

35 miles (56km)
to next Rest Area

Rest
Area

S/Bnd traffic
- 39 miles (63kms) to next I-75 Rest Area
- 29 miles (47kms) to next FTP Rest Area

Rest
Area

Southbound to Tampa

Things You Need to Know

Local Knowledge ... think about it, it's the one category of information which helps you feel comfortable and in control when you travel far away from home. All the information in this book is based on local knowledge acquired over more than 40 years of I-75 travel and from the many friends we've made along the way. In this section, I've gathered information for you which is better presented in table form, rather than on the maps or in the text sections of the book.

For instance, with the wider availability of portable "severe weather" radio alert units at electronic stores (see page 147), I've included the FIPS/SAME codes for all I-75 counties-very difficult to obtain once traveling. These codes allow you to program an alert unit so it is specific to your I-75 route and location.

Not only does the FIPS/SAME system provide timely alerts and information about dangerous and pending weather conditions, but also "Amber" alerts and other serious police warnings–all delivered in "text" directly to your car. For $50 this is important information for a road traveler many miles from home. Some safety experts say that an FIPS/SAME capable alert unit in your car is the equivalent of a smoke detector in the home.

If you can think of other questions which need answers, let me know (see page 203), and I will try and oblige in a future edition:

© 2007 Mile Oak Publishing Inc.

Radio on the Road

AM radio signals travel much farther in the dark. To avoid interference, the FCC requires that many stations reduce their night "distance" coverage by performing an antenna "pattern" change at dusk. By agreement, some powerful (50,000 watt) AM stations provide nighttime extended coverage and their signals can cover as much as 750 miles after dark. This is useful to know if you are on a night drive since you can stay with the same station for many miles. Here are the powerful AM stations covering your I-75 drive:

MI: Detroit, WJR-760; OH: Cincinnati, WLW-700; KY: Louisville, WHAS-840;

TN: Nashville, WLAC-1510; GA: Atlanta, WSB-750; FL: non assigned

In Ontario, Canada, I recommend the 50,000 watt station, CHWO-740

If you enjoy radio, consider one of the two satellite radio services XM or Sirius. These provide hundreds of channels of music, sports, talk, all distortion free & superb sound... and you can stay tuned to the same program for the entire trip. Receivers are available at most electronic stores (monthly service fee required) Not available in Canada

The Triple "A" for Help

One of the best investments you can make for a long distance drive is to join the AAA (or CAA in Canada). It doesn't cost a lot of money–annual membership fees vary by location but are usually in the $50-70 range–and yet the peace of mind provided when traveling long distances is well worth the money. Should you experience a breakdown or other car emergency, help is only a national toll free 1-800 phone call away:

USA - **1-800-AAA-HELP**   Canada - **1-800-CAA-HELP**
(1-800-222-4357)   (1-800-222-4357)

I-75 HOTEL TOLL FREE RESERVATION PHONE NUMBERS

Baymont Inns	877-229-6668	Hampton Inn	800-426-7866
Best Inns, America's	800-432-7992	Howard Johnson	800-446-4656
Best Value Inns	888-315-2378	Jameson Inns	800-526-3766
Best Western	800-937-8376	Knights Inn	800-843-5644
Budget Host	800-283-4678	La Quinta Inns	800-531-5900
Budget Inn	800-780-5733	Microtel	888-771-7171
Comfort Inn	800-424-6423	Motel6	800-466-8356
Country Inns/Suites	800-456-4000	Quality Inn	800-424-6423
Courtyard Marriott	800-321-2211	Ramada Inn	800-272-6232
Days Inn	800-329-7466	Red Roof Inns	800-733-7663
EconoLodge	800-424-6423	Rodeway Inn	800-424-6423
Extended Stay	800-398-7829	Scottish Inn	800-251-1962
Fairfield Inn	800-228-2800	Sleep Inn	800-424-6423
Garden Inn	877-782-9444	Super 8 Motels	800-800-8000
Guesthouse	800-214-8378	TraveLodge	800-578-7878
Holiday Inn	800-465-4329	Wingate Inns	800-228-1000

STATE	Gas Tax (¢)	Sales Tax (%)			Notes:
		State	Avg Local	Combined	
Michigan	.268	6%	---	6%	**State Gas Tax** - this is presented to give an approximation of which states will have the lower gas prices
Ohio	.28	6%	1.25%	7.25%	
Kentucky	.187	6%	---	6%	**Sales Tax** - these three columns show the state percentages, average local/city tax, combined percentage.
Tennessee	.17	7%	2.4%	9.4%	
Georgia	.1277	4%	2.9%	6.9%	**Lodging Tax and Surcharges** - these have become to varied to report. Always ask about miscellaneous surcharges at <u>check-in</u> time.
Florida	.2937	6%	.7%	6.7%	

TORNADO WATCH

Special note: this section is not intended to alarm you - but to make sure that you are well informed and prepared should a Tornado emergency occur in your area, while traveling the I-75.

 It was six o'clock in the evening. Kathy and I had checked into a m o t e l i n M i a m i s b u r g, Ohio, and were beginning to relax after a long day on the interstate . . . when we were interrupted by a loud banging on the door -

> *"Everybody to the basement - three tornados have been spotted in Preble County!"*

Where was Preble County? We had no idea.

What should we do to minimize our risk? We didn't know.

After the emergency was over, I decided to find the answers to these very important questions & share them with you.

Over the last few years we have certainly gained a heightened awareness of tornados

Tornado Safety Tips

If in a sturdy building:

- go to the lowest level, interior room in the building.
- take a flashlight and battery radio.
- stay away from large rooms, such as auditoriums, ballrooms, etc.
- avoid rooms with windows & outside walls.
- hide under something that is sturdy.
- cover yourself with blankets, pillows, coats (to protect from flying debris).
- protect your neck and head areas. Put on a crash or safety helmet, if you have one.

If in a weak structure or RV home:

- get out and seek a sturdy shelter.

If caught in the open:

- if in a car, get right away from it.
- lay flat in a ditch face down (1st choice) or behind a sturdy hedge. Cover head with arms.

SPECIAL NOTE: studies indicate that it is unsafe to take shelter in the "V" created by the concrete banks of an overpass. Tornado winds can create killer suctions in this area.

INSIDER TIP
Your Personal Severe Weather Alert System

Again this summer, we had a tornado warning while staying overnight in Ohio. We were in Montgomery Co. at the time and by using the maps on the following pages, we were able to determine the activity was to our southeast in Warren County . . . so we were probably safe since tornados do not normally (but sometimes can) double back or swing northwest.

My regular readers know that I do not travel without a severe weather warning system. Normally, I recommend several models (portable and for the home) but Radio Shack now has a powerful hand-held unit covering *National Weather Service's 7 NWS frequencies*, and with built-in *NWS "Alert" signal* and *SAME* (see below) capability. The **Model T581** (catalog 12-259) runs on 3 "AA" batteries, costs $49.95 and is well worth every penny.

That evening, we dined at a nearby Red Lobster and with the small unit clipped to my belt, were able to keep the restaurant's manager informed of the situation.

A 110volt adapter is also available so at home, it's easy to plug in (the batteries serve as back-up) and leave it on standby permanently, ready to warn of any changing or dangerous weather conditions in your area. A great safety feature.

As mentioned, the unit receives the special *Specific Area Message Encoding* (**SAME**) signals. Using 6 digit *Federal Information Processing System* (or **FIPS**) codes, you can program your T581 to provide specific alerts for your area, rather than on a broad county basis. The local 6 digit FIPS codes are obtained from the NWS internet site but for convenience, I have included all the ones you will need on I-75, on the following maps.

Incidentally, messages are sent to the T581 for many types of dangerous conditions - severe thunder, flooding, tornados, hurricane, etc., - and you can choose which ones you would like to receive, or those to be ignored. *(Canadians, FIPS codes are only available for U.S. locations; the T581 cannot be purchased outside the USA although it will receive Canada's regular weather broadcasts).*

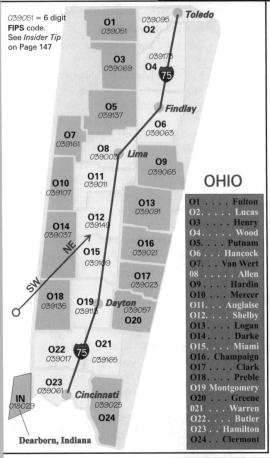

039051 = 6 digit **FIPS** code. See *Insider Tip* on Page 147

OHIO

O1 . . . . . Fulton	
O2 . . . . . Lucas	
O3 . . . . Henry	
O4 . . . . . Wood	
O5 . . . . Putnam	
O6 . . . Hancock	
O7 . . . Van Wert	
08 . . . . . Allen	
O9 . . . . Hardin	
O10 . . . Mercer	
O11. . . Auglaise	
O12. . . . Shelby	
O13. . . . Logan	
O14. . . . Darke	
O15. . . . Miami	
O16. Champaign	
O17. . . . Clark	
O18. . . . Preble	
O19 Montgomery	
O20 . . . . Greene	
021 . . . . Warren	
O22. . . . Butler	
O23. . Hamilton	
O24. . Clermont	

(or twisters, as they are often known), as we travel. In April, 1996, a section of the small town of Berea was devastated by a tornado which swept across the I-75 and slammed into the "old town" area. And of course, we are all aware of the terrible damage done by a tornado which touched down just east of Kissimmee, Florida during the 1997/8 winter. Here are some tornado facts:

Tornados tend to travel from the south-west quadrant of a storm system to the north east. Never try to outrun a tornado in your

County Maps

Tornado warnings are issued by county name. I have shown all the counties through which **I-75** runs (in yellow), along with at least one other county either side (in green). The 6 digit FIPS code is also shown.

The **southwest-northeast axis** is also shown since this tends to be the general path of tornado spawning storms.

KENTUCKY

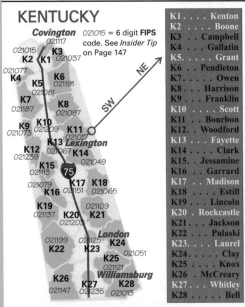

021015 = 6 digit **FIPS** code. See *Insider Tip* on Page 147

K1 . . . . Kenton	
K2 . . . . Boone	
K3 . . Campbell	
K4 . . . Gallatin	
K5 . . . . . Grant	
K6 . . Pendleton	
K7 . . . . . Owen	
K8 . . Harrison	
K9 . . . Franklin	
K10 . . . . Scott	
K11 . . Bourbon	
K12. . Woodford	
K13 . . . Fayette	
K14 . . . . Clark	
K15 . Jessamine	
K16 . . Garrard	
K17 . . Madison	
K18 . . . . Estill	
K19 . . . Lincoln	
K20 . Rockcastle	
K21 . . . Jackson	
K22 . . . Pulaski	
K23. . . . Laurel	
K24 . . . . . Clay	
K25 . . . . Knox	
K26 . McCreary	
K27 . . . Whitley	
K28 . . . . . Bell	

TENNESSEE

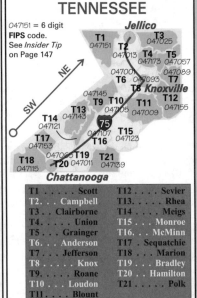

047151 = 6 digit **FIPS** code. See *Insider Tip* on Page 147

T1 . . . . . Scott		T12 . . . . Sevier	
T2. . . . Campbell		T13. . . . . Rhea	
T3 . . Clairborne		T14 . . . . Meigs	
T4. . . . . Union		T15 . . . Monroe	
T5 . . . Grainger		T16. . . McMinn	
T6. . . Anderson		T17 . Sequatchie	
T7. . . Jefferson		T18 . . . Marion	
T8 . . . . . Knox		T19 . . Bradley	
T9. . . . Roane		T20 . . Hamilton	
T10 . . . Loudon		T21 . . . . . Polk	
T11 . . . Blount			

car, but if there is clear sky to your south-east, that is the direction to go.

A storm that can spawn tornados is often preceded with lightning, hail and heavy rain. They tend to happen in late afternoon, early evenings during the late-spring/early summer.

Most injuries are caused by flying debris. A tornado can come in many strengths, from one which damages light trees, branches or billboards (known as an F0) to a very rare F5 which can hurtle a wooden plank projectile at speeds up to 200 mph.

Pressure differential in tornados does not play a big role in terms of damage. Forget the dated advice about opening a window on the opposite side to the storm; experts say it makes no difference.

In terms of risk, here are annual average tornado frequencies by state, compiled by the *National Severe Storm Center* in Kansas City: Texas-189, Kansas-92, Oklahoma-64, Michigan-21, Ohio-61, Kentucky-11, Tennessee-8 and Georgia-19.

Interstate-75 is no more vulnerable to tornados than any of the other major corridor routes between the mid-west and Florida.

In fact, the tips in this story can be equally as well applied to your home area. I consider my home weather alert system as important as my smoke detectors or security system, and keep it running at all times.

I hope you never encounter a tornado, but if you do—you are well prepared.

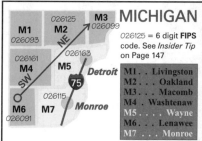

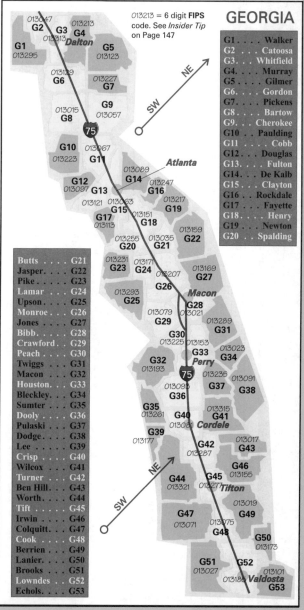

Butts	G21
Jasper. . . .	G22
Pike	G23
Lamar . . .	G24
Upson. . . .	G25
Monroe . . .	G26
Jones	G27
Bibb.	G28
Crawford. .	G29
Peach	G30
Twiggs . .	G31
Macon . .	G32
Houston. . .	G33
Bleckley. . .	G34
Sumter . . .	G35
Dooly	G36
Pulaski . . .	G37
Dodge. . . .	G38
Lee	G39
Crisp	G40
Wilcox . . .	G41
Turner . . .	G42
Ben Hill. . .	G43
Worth. . . .	G44
Tift	G45
Irwin	G46
Colquitt. . .	G47
Cook	G48
Berrien . . .	G49
Lanier. . . .	G50
Brooks . . .	G51
Lowndes . .	G52
Echols. . . .	G53

INTERSTATE-75 RV PARK & CAMPGROUND SITES

State I-75 Exit	Direction	Campground	Phone	# of Sites	Open	Rates	Distance in Miles	Driving Directions
MI 11	W	Harbortown RV Resort	734-384-4700	250	all year	$28-35/family	1/2	1/2 mile West on Laplaisance Rd; Entrance on left
OH 179	W	Fire Lake	888-879-2267	100	4/15-10/15	$23-26/2people	2½	1½ miles W on 6; ½ m S on 25; ½ m W on Kramer Rd; on right
OH 164	E	Pleasant View	419-299-3897	300	all year	$19-23/fam.	1	¾ m E on 613; ¼ m SE on 218; Entrance on right
OH 161	E	Shady Lake	419-423-3490	139	all year	$22/fam.	2½	½ m E on 99; 1½ m N on CR 220; ½ m W on 101; Ent on right
OH 145	E	Twin Lake Park	888-436-3610	85	4/1-11/1	$26-40/fam.	.6	.1 m S on 235; ½ m E on 34; Entrance on left
OH 110	E	KOA Wapakonata	419-738-6016	73	2/4-12/4	$27-35/2p	1½	.2 m E to first intersection; ¾ m N on Cemetery Rd; Ent on left
OH 82	E	Poor Farmer's	937-368-2449	540	4/15-11/30	$17/fam.	6¾	6 m E on US36; ¾ m S on Lost Creek-Shelby Rd; Ent on left
OH 14	W	Quality Inn RV Park	513-771-5252	11	all year	$25/RV	1/4	¼ mile west on Glendale-Milford Rd; Entrance on left
OH 10	W	Woodland Trailer	513-931-8845	20	all year	$25/2p	4¼	4 m W on Galbraith; ¼ m S on Daly; Entrance on right
KY 171	W	Oak Creek Campground	859-485-9131	105	all year	$18.50-24/2p	1	1m SW on Hwy 16; Entrance on right.
KY 166	E	KOA Cincinnati - South	859-428-2000	101	all year	$22-32/2p	2¼	¼ m E on 491; 2.6 m S on US25; Entrance on right
KY 159	W	Dry Ridge Camper's Village	859-824-5836	70	all year	$20/RV	1.2	50 yds W on 22; 1 m N on Service Rd; Entrance at end of road
KY 120	E	Kentucky Horse Park SP	800-370-6416	260	all year	phone for rates	1/2	½ m E on 1973; Entrance on left
KY 95	E	Fort Boonesborough SP	606-527-3131	167	all year	phone for rates	5.9	4.9 m E on 627; ½m S on 338
KY 76	W	Oh Kentucky Campground	859-986-1150	152	all year	$10-14/RV	1/4	¼ m W on Hwy 21; Entrance on right
KY 76	W	Walnut Meadow Campground	859-986-6180	123	all year	$10-20/2p	1/2	½m W on Hwy 21; Entrance on left
KY 62	E	KOA Renfro Valley	606-256-2474	133	all year	$19-31/2p	1½	1½ m E on Hwy 25; Entrance on right
KY 62	E	Renfro Valley RV Park	800-765-7464	199	3/1-12/31	$21.20-25.44/RV	1/4	¼ mile east on Highway 25; Entrance on right
KY 38	E	Levi Jackson Wilderness Rd S/P	606-878-8000	146	all year	phone for rates	4.3	2 m E on 192; 2 3/10 m S on 25; Entrance on left
KY 29	W	KOA Corbin	606-528-1534	90	all year	$17-27/2p	1/2	¼ m W on 770; ¼ m S (follow signs); Entrance on right
KY 11	W	Williamsburg Travel Trailer Park	800-426-3267	56	all year	$12/RV	---	50 yds W on Hwy 92; Entrance on right
TN 134	W	Cove Lake SP	423-566-9701	100	all year	phone for rates	1/2	½ m NE on Hwy 25; park entrance on left
TN 141	E	Royal Blue RV Park	423-566-4847	45	all year	$19.75/RV	1/2	½ m S on Luther Seibers Rd (at the giant cross)
TN 128	E	Norris Dam State Park	865-426-7461	85	all year	phone for rates	7	see map on page 55; 7 miles east on US441; Entrance on left
TN 122	E	Big Ridge SP	865-992-5523	52	all year	phone for rates	12	12 E on Hwy 61; Entrance on left
TN 122	E	Fox Inn Campground	865-494-9386	93	all year	$16-26/2p	1/5	1/5 m E on Hwy 61; Entrance on left
TN 62	W	KOA Sweetwater Valley	865-213-3900	53	all year	$24-29/fam.	1	¾ m W on Oakland; follow signs S ¼ m; Entrance on left
TN 1	W	Holiday Trav-L-Park	800-693-2877	178	all year	$23/2p	3/4	¼ m W on Hwy 41; ½ m S on Mack Smith Rd; Ent on right

INTERSTATE-75 RV PARK & CAMPGROUND SITES

State I-75 Exit Direction	Campground	Phone	# of Sites	Open	Rates	Distance in Miles	Driving Directions
TN 49 E	Athens I-75 Campground	423-745-9199	60	5/15 - 9/15	$19-20/2p	1/5	1/5 m E on Hwy 30; Entrance on right
TN 20 W	KOA Cleveland	423-472-8928	92	all year	$22-28/2p	1	½ m W on county Rd; follow signs ½ m; Entrance on right
GA 350 W	KOA Chattanooga S KOA	706-937-4166	145	all year	$23-29/2p	1/4	¼m W on Hwy 2, Entrance on right (New Owner)
GA 315 E	KOA Calhoun	706-629-7511	89	all year	$21-27/2people	1½	1½ m E on Hwy 156; Entrance on right
GA 296 W	KOA Cartersville	770-382-7330	117	all year	$21-23/2p	1/4	¼ m W on Cassville Rd; Entrance on left
GA 285 E	Red Top Mountain SP	770-975-0055	92	all year	phone for rates	1¼	1 ¼ m E on Red Top Mountain Rd; follow signs in park
GA 283 E	Allatoona Landing	800-346-7305	140	all year	$19.75-28.35/4p	2	2 miles E on Allatoona Rd; Entrance on left
GA 269 W	KOA Atlanta N (Kennesaw)	770-427-2406	230	all year	$28-30/2people	2 1/10	1½ m W on Barrett; ½ m N on Hwy 41; 1/10 m Battlefield Pkwy
GA 198 W	High Falls Campground	800-428-0132	124	all year	$18/family	1/10	1/10 m W on High Falls Rd; Entrance on right
GA 186 E	KOA Forsyth	478-994-2019	141	all year	$22-24/2people	3/5	100 ft E on Juliette Rd; ½ m N on Frontage Rd; Ent on right
GA 5 W	Lake Tobesofkee Park	478-474-8770	110	all year	phone for rates	5.9	3.5 m W on Rt 74; turn left on Lower Thomaston; 2.4 m on left
GA 136 E	Boland's RV Park	478-987-3371	65	all year	$18-20/2people	1/3	¼ m E on Hwy 341; 1/10 m N on Perimeter Rd; Ent on left
GA 136 W	Crossroads Travel Park	478-987-3141	64	all year	$21/2people	1/10	1/10 m W on Hwy 341; Entrance on left
GA 135 W	Fair Harbor RV Park	877-988-8844	153	all year	$22/RV	1/4	¼ m W of exit 42; Entrance on right
GA 97 W	KOA Cordele	229-273-5454	73	all year	$24-26/2p	1/4	¼ m W on Rockhouse Rd; Entrance on right
GA 92 W	Southern Gates RV	229-273-6464	46	all year	$18/family	1/4	¼m W on Deep Creek Rd; Entrance on right
GA 84 W	Ashburn RV Park	229-567-3334	77	all year	$8.95/2people	1/10	1/10m W on Amboy Rd; Entrance on right
GA 60 W	Amy's South GA RV Park	229-386-8441	86	all year	$18/2people	1	1m W on South Central Ave; Entrance on right.
GA 39 W	Reed Bingham SP	229-896-3551	44	all year	phone for rates	6	6m W on Hwy 37; watch for sign
GA 18 W	River Park	229-244-8397	62	all year	$18-19/2people	1/10	1/10 m W on Hwy 133; Entrance on right
GA 5 E	Eagles Roost Campground	229-559-5192	140	all year	$22/2people	3/5	100 ft E; ½ m S on Frontage Rd; Entrance on left

We recommend that you purchase a current copy of *Woodall's Campground Directory* (available from most bookstores, or phone 1-800-323-9076). This comprehensive directory covers all the key parks and campgrounds state by state, across North America.

In addition, if you are not already a member, consider joining the *Good Sam Club.* The benefits are numerous, and include discounts at various campgrounds and on propane purchases, special RV insurance, etc. Good Sam publishes the *Trailer Life Campground and RV Park & Services Directory,* another excellent source of parks and campgrounds. Phone 1-800-234-3450 for membership information and services.

Both of these directories include information about RV services and suppliers (parts) -- and tourist attractions along the way.

INTERSTATE-75 PUBLIC GOLF COURSES

State Exit	Location	Golfcourse	Address	Phone #	Semi Prvt/ Public	Total Yds/ # Tees	Par	Fees $ Week/ Wkend	Directions	Notes (see below)
OH187	Perrysburg	Tanglewood GC	9802 Dowling Road	419-833-1725	S	5822/3	72	13/15	.6m E on 582; 1.4m N on Dunbridge; .9m on 17 to Dowling	1
OH161	Findlay	Hillcrest GC	800 West Bigelow	419-423-7211	S	6981/3	72	19/22	.5m E on Twp99; 1m S on N Main; .6 W on W Bigelow	2
OH130	Lima	Springbrook	4200 Ottawa Rd	419-225-8037	P	6045/3	71	17/19	3.5m W on Bluelick; .6 N on 65; bear right @ fork for .1m	2
OH 63	Vandalia	Castle Hills	125 Clubhouse Rd	937-890-1300	P	6617/4	71	22/26	.5m E to Brownschool; .2m N to GC	3
OH 44	Miamisburg	Mound GC	757 Mound Rd	937-866-2211	P	5605/2	72	13/14	2.7m W on 725; .4m S on S 6th to Mound Road	2
OH 29	Middletown	Pleasant Hill	6487 Hankins Rd	513-539-7221	P	6586/2	71	21/21	3.5m W on 63; 1m S on Salzman; .3m E on Hankins	2
KY181	Florence	World of Sport	7400 Woodspoint Dr	859-371-8255	P	2997/2	58	18/18	.1m NW on Burlington Pk; .3m NE on Woodspoint	2
KY104	Lexington	Lakeside Munic.	3725 Richmond Rd	859-263-5315	P	6844/3	72	18/18	2.5m NW on SR418; join Richmond Rd (US25) NW for .6m	2
KY 77	Berea	Berea CC	128 Lorriane Ct	859-986-7141	S	6134/3	72	14/18	2.1m E of exit - see Berea map on page 52	2
KY 38	London	Crooked Creek	781 Crooked Creek Dr	606-877-1993	S	7007/5	72	35/35	.2m E on 192; 1.7m S on 229; turn L onto Conley; .3m to GC	2
KY ---	Williamsburg	The Golf Course	690 Airport Rd	606-549-4215	S	3300/3	36	12/12	S/Bnd-exit 25 W 6.6m; N/Bnd-exit 15 W 6.8m	2
TN 76	Loudon	Riverview GC	101 Club Dr	865-986-6972	P	6072/3	72	11/16	E of exit; turn right on Hotchkiss Valley Rd 1.7m	2
TN 2	Chattanoga	Brainerd GC	5203 Old Mission Rd	423-855-2692	P	6468/4	72	13/17	1.2m on I-24W to exit 184; .3m S Moore; .9m N to GC	2
GA317	Calhoun	Calhoun Elks	143 Craigtown Rd NE	706-629-4091	S	5985/3	71	9/14	.1m E on SR225	2
GA306	Adairsville	Indian Ridge GC	4333 Adairsville Rd NE	706-291-9049	P	5720/2	72	12/22	8.6m west on Adairsville Rd (SR140)	2
GA277	Acworth	Centennial	5225 Woodstock Rd	770-975-1000	P	6849/4	72	42/52	.1m S to Baker (SR92); 1.1m E to Woodstock; 8m NW to GC	2
GA ---	Marietta	City Club	510 Powder Springs	770-528-4653	P	5738/3	71	39/49	see map on page 61 for I-75 exits and golf course location	2
GA187	Forsyth	Forsyth GC	400 Country Club Dr	478-994-5328	P	6053/3	72	10/12	.6 S on SR83; .8m W on Johnson; .7m on CountryClub to GC	2
GA ---	Macon	Barrington Hall	7100 Zebulon Rd	478-757-8358	S	7062/5	72	29/39	I-475 exit 9 - 1.9m W on Zebulon (do not turn at Lamar)	2
GA101	Cordele	Georgia Vets	2315 Hwy 280 W	229-276-2377	P	6869/4	72	17-21	6.8m W on SR280	4
GA 66	Tifton	Forest Lakes	260 Sutton Rd	229-382-7626	P	6806/4	72	22-22	3.5m E on Brighton Rd; .4m NE on Clements Simmons to GC	2
GA 22	Valdosta	Northlake G&CC	4025 Northlake Dr	229-247-8613	P	5193/2	68	9/12	E on Valdosta Rd (US41N); first turn on your left	2
GA 22	Valdosta	Stone Creek	4300 N Coleman Rd	229-247-2527	S	6705/4	72	35-45	.3 E on N Valdosta; .4 S on Coleman to GC	2
GA 5	Lake Park	Francis Lake	5366 Golf Dr	229-559-7961	S	6458/4	72	26-35	.3m E on SR376 to GC	2

I hope you enjoy this selection of Public (P) and Semi-Private (S) golf courses on your Interstate-75 drive. The fees quoted are peak season fees, so may be lower when you pass by. There are many more - the best place to find them is on the internet at www.golfcourse.com. Please refer to the codes in the last column (key below) to determine the course's season.

NOTES: 1 = Open Apr 1-Oct 31,   2 = Open all year,   3 = Open Feb 1-Dec 15,   4 = Open all year, except Mondays.

Northbound Route

First time readers: please read the *"Quick Start Hints"* on the inside of the front cover - this will quickly explain how the book is laid out in sections to help you on your journey.   The Key to the road speed colors and map symbols is located on the front cover flap.

When I designed the first edition of this book in 1992, I had to make a difficult decision. Should the book be laid out so it presents information in a logical sequence for southbound travelers, or for those driving north?

Since our primary market is the *"snowbird couple"* driving to Florida for the winter, setting the book out in southbound sequence was the natural choice.

If you are **Northbound** and joining the book for the first time, I don't want you to miss important tips or helpful information, so here's a table of useful page references you should check before setting off.

Insider Tip for Northbound Travelers
Northbound Photographs

Driving north with the sun over your shoulder makes the roadside scenery much more interesting and acceptable for in-car photography. In particular, look closely at the rock cuts in north Tennessee and south Kentucky. Early morning sun angled across cuts on the west side of the interstate and late afternoon sun lighting rock cuts on the east will reveal all sorts of interesting things such as the vertical drill holes used for the dynamite charges when the road was being built.

If using an automatic camera from inside the car, don't forget to turn off the auto focusing feature (otherwise it will tend to focus on your car window glass) and set for as high a shutter speed as possible. If you don't have a high shutter speed, then try and "lock" your camera on the subject by panning as the car moves forward.

Something I sometimes forget is to make sure my windshield is clean, both inside and out...it's amazing the improvement in your photos if shooting through clean glass.

Never pull on to the soft shoulder for your photograph - an interstate shoulder is a very dangerous place to be and should only be used for emergency stops.

(onst both pages (none 2010)

-25-
-24-
-23-
-22-
-21-
-20-
-19-
-18-
-17-
-16-
-15-
-14-
-13-
-12-
-11-
-10-
-9-
-8-
-7-
-6-
-5-
-4-
43 m
69 k
-2-
-1-
-0-

DH

EVACUATION ROUTE INFORMATION 90.1 FM

Tillman

Church Street

Weigh Station

Mineola

Swamp

GEORGIA Phone Numbers
Emergency: 911, 404-624-6077,
Cell: *GSP (*477)
Police Information: 404-657-9300
Road Construction
   and Conditions: 404-635-8000

22
Rts S41 N75
N Valdosta Rd
Moody AFB

H

41

Exit 22
G-BP Shell\D
F-BaskR CharlieTripr
   KspyKrm Subwy

EXIT 22, INSIDER TIP
CHARLIE TRIPPER'S
FINE DINING

Exit 22
G-Citgo\D
F-BKing-I DQ
   Stucky
L-Days

Exit 18
G-BP\DL Rcway Shell
F-StmrsSeafd
L-BestW Econo Sleep

Withlacoochee River

Valdosta
Colonial Mall

Exit 18
G-BP BigFt Texco\D
F-Applb Arby **BKing**
   Brustrs **ChickF-I** CrkBrl
   Denny ElPetro Fazoli
   Hooter **Hrdee** KFC
   Krystal LongH **McDld**
   OldTmBft OldTmStk
   OutBk RedLb Sonny
   Starbcks Subwy Taco
   VineYd Waffle Wendy
L-CmfrtSte CrtYrd
   CtryInnSte Fairfld
   H/Inn Hmptn HoJo
   Jamson Jolly LaQnt
   QltyInn Scot

18
Rt 94 Valdosta
Moultrie

94

Super
Wal-Mart

Gornto

Normann St Augustin M Patterson Ashley

?
S

EXIT 16, INSIDER TIP
- LULU'S FINE DINING RESTAURANT
- THE HAMPTONS

Exit 16
G-Shell\D
F-AustnStk Hddle BriarWd
L-Comfrt Knght

16
Rts 84 221
Valdosta
Quitman

84

Valdosta
Pop: 46,900

Exit 16
G-BP\D BigFt Chevn
   Citgo\D Danfair
   Phil66 Shell\D
F-BKing BaskR Blimp
   IHOP **McDld**
   OldSouth Pizza
   Shony Sonic
   Stucky Subwy
   Waffle Wendy
L-Days GuestHs
   H/Inn Hmptn
   Motel6 NewVldsta
   QltyInn Ramda
   Supr8

Patrol car on bridge, beaming radar on northbound traffic . . .

. . . radios "chase" car with speeder's description

Exit 13

"chase" cars on ramp, ready to roll

Radar

Trees hide radar car

Traffic from Florida

Mud Creek

41

13
Old Clyattville Rd
Valdosta

Madison

31

DH

11
Rt 31
Valdosta
Clyattville

Grand Oaks Plaza

S

P

Exit 11
G-HessTS\D PilotTS\D
F-CircStar RedMtn
   Stucky Subwy Waffle
L-TravInn

Patterson

41

Northbound - to get the most from these maps, please read the notes on the previous page. See the *"Key to the Map Symbols"* on the front cover flap for road speed colors and other map information.

EXIT 5,
INSIDER TIP
THE HAMPTONS

WinnDixie

Post Office

G

5
Rt 376
Twin Lakes

R

Lake Park Mill Outlet Stores

Lake Park

Exit 5
G-BP Chevn Phil66
   Rcway Shell
F-ChickF-I FarmHse
   Hrdee Shony
   Sonic Sonny
   Subwy Waffle
L-GuestHs H/InnX
   Shony

Peterson Bellville

Exit 5
G-Citgo\D Shell\D
F-CrkBrl IceCrm
   McDld Pizza Subwy
   Taco Wendy
L-Days Hmptn Supr8
   TravL

Welcome Center

? V

Information: 8:30-5:30 daily
Restrooms: 24 hours

RADAR

Lowndes Co.

Exit 2
G-FlyJ(Conco)\LD
F-CtryMkt MgDrgn
   Pepproni
L-LkPkInn

2
Bellville Rd
Lake Park

DH

Exit 2
G-Mobil Shell TA(BP)\D
F-Arby DQ HubCafe

THE OLD "DIXIE HIGHWAY"
- SEE PAGES 68 AND 114

9:00 /10

FLORIDA-GEORGIA BORDER

956

mm 25-50

Lenox

Exit 49
G-BP\D Phil66

49
Kinard Br Rd
Lenox

Exit 49
G-Dixie\D
F-LenorDnr
Pizza
L-Knght

-49-

-48-

41

-47-

SOUTHERN GEORGIA IS
FAMOUS FOR ITS DAYLILLIES

No Information - Restrooms: 24 hours

Rest Area ♿ ☕ ♟♀♂ ⛺ ☂ V

39 m
63 k

▲

45
Barneyville
Road

Barneyville

Exit 45
L-RedC

-45-

-44-

41

-43-

↗ N

Sparks

-42-

41
Roundtree Rd
Sparks

Exit 41
G-Citgo

-41-

-40-

Exit 39
G-BP CitgoTS\D
F-BKing CaptD
Hddle IHOP
KFrog MamaTbl
PopE Stucky
Taco WSizz
L-Days Hmptn

W
39 Rt 37
H Adel
R Moultrie

Adel

🏭 *Weyhauser Paper*

Exit 39
G-Shell\D Texco\D
F-Hrdee **McDld-I**
Waffle
L-BdgLdg **Scot Supr8**

-39-

-38-

i

Georgia Forestry
watch tower

37 Adel

9 39 am

gas

-37-

-36-

DH

Tune your radio to 92.1
FM for shopping
information at exit 39

-35-

-34-

*South Georgia
Motorsports Park*

Cecil

-33-

Exit 32
G-Chevn

32 Old Coffee Rd
Cecil

🏕️ ←

Cook Co.

✕

-32-

41

-31-

Lowndes Co.

🚓

-30-

Exit 29
G-BP\D BigFt
Citgo
SavATon\D
F-AppleVl
Blimp TCBY
L-Supr8

W
29 Rts 122 N41
Hahira/Barney
Lakeland

Hahira

-29-

9:20 '10

-28-

🚓

9:21 am
'07

-27-

41

window chip

-26-

🚸 →

-25-

Tillman

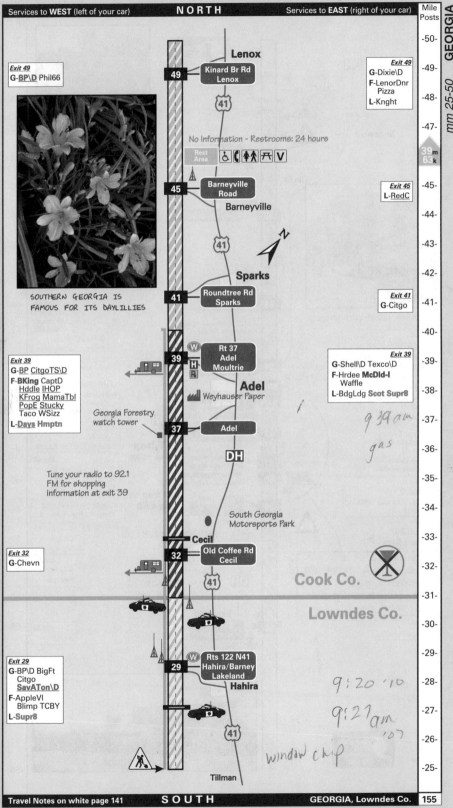

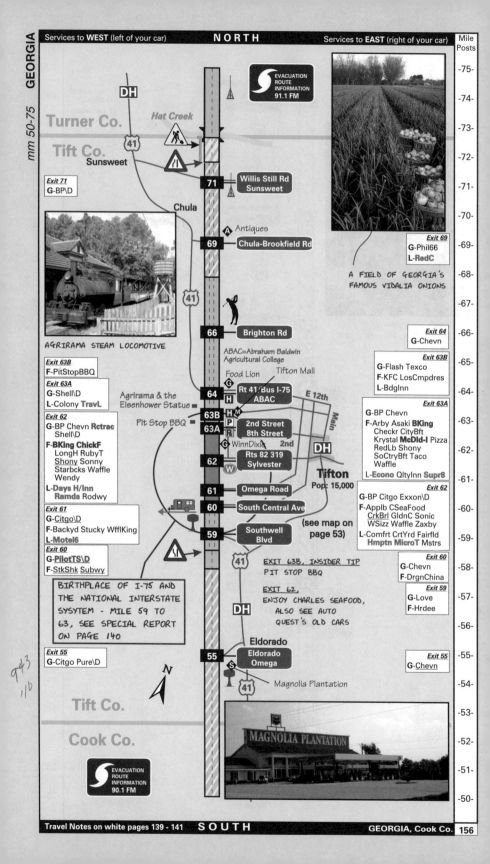

EVACUATION ROUTE INFORMATION 91.1 FM

-75-

DH

-74-

Hat Creek

Turner Co.

-73-

Tift Co.

(41)

-72-

Sunsweet

71 | Willis Still Rd Sunsweet

-71-

Exit 71
G-BP\D

Chula

-70-

A Antiques

69 | Chula-Brookfield Rd

-69-

Exit 69
G-Phil66
L-RedC

-68-

A FIELD OF GEORGIA'S FAMOUS VIDALIA ONIONS

(41)

-67-

AGRIRAMA STEAM LOCOMOTIVE

66 | Brighton Rd

-66-

Exit 64
G-Chevn

ABAC=Abraham Baldwin Agricultural College

-65-

Exit 63B
F-PitStopBBQ

Food Lion　　Tifton Mall

Exit 63B
G-Flash Texco
F-KFC LosCmpdres
L-BdgInn

Exit 63A
G-Shell\D
L-Colony TravL

64 | Rt 41/Bus I-75 ABAC

H M

E 12th

-64-

Agrirama & the Eisenhower Statue ■

63B
63A

2nd Street 8th Street

H P R T

Main

Exit 63A
G-BP Chevn
F-Arby Asaki **BKing**
　Checkr CityBft
　Krystal **McDld-I** Pizza
　RedLb Shony
　SoCtryBft Taco
　Waffle
L-**Econo** QltyInn **Supr8**

-63-

Exit 62
G-BP Chevn **Rctrac**
　Shell\D
F-**BKing ChickF**
　LongH RubyT
　Shony Sonny
　Starbcks Waffle
　Wendy
L-Days H/Inn
　Ramda Rodwy

Pit Stop BBQ ■

A WinnDixie

2nd

62 | Rts 82 319 Sylvester

W

DH

-62-

Tifton
Pop: 15,000

-61-

61 | Omega Road

Exit 61
G-Citgo\D
F-Backyd Stucky WfflKing
L-Motel6

60 | South Central Ave

(see map on page 53)

Exit 62
G-BP Citgo Exxon\D
F-Applb CSeaFood
　CrkBrl GldnC Sonic
　WSizz Waffle Zaxby
L-Comfrt CrtYrd Fairfld
　Hmptn MicroT Mstrs

-60-

Exit 60
G-PilotTS\D
F-StkShk Subwy

59 | Southwell Blvd

-59-

BIRTHPLACE OF I-75 AND THE NATIONAL INTERSTATE SYSYSTEM - MILE 59 TO 63, SEE SPECIAL REPORT ON PAGE 140

(41)

EXIT 63B, INSIDER TIP
PIT STOP BBQ

Exit 60
G-Chevn
F-DrgnChina

-58-

EXIT 62,
ENJOY CHARLES SEAFOOD,
ALSO SEE AUTO
QUEST'S OLD CARS

Exit 59
G-Love
F-Hrdee

-57-

DH

-56-

Eldorado

Exit 55
G-Citgo Pure\D

55 | Eldorado Omega

-55-

N

S

Exit 55
G-Chevn

Tift Co.

(41)　Magnolia Plantation

-54-

-53-

Cook Co.

MAGNOLIA PLANTATION

-52-

EVACUATION ROUTE INFORMATION 90.1 FM

-51-

-50-

1037

Services to **WEST** (left of your car)   **N O R T H**   Services to **EAST** (right of your car) | Mile Posts | **GEORGIA**

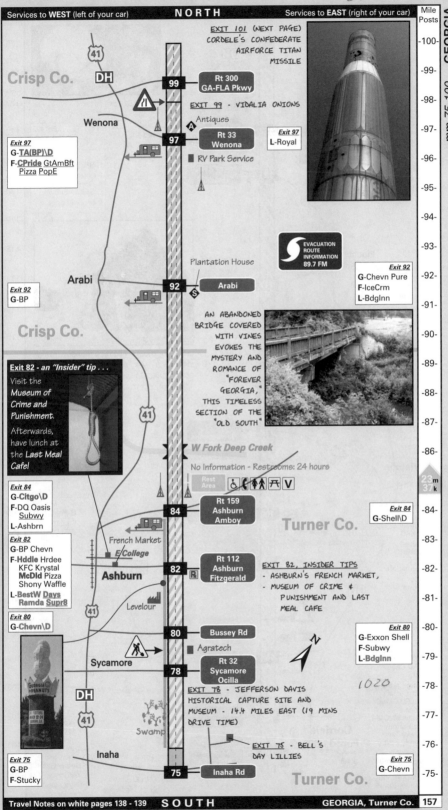

EXIT 101 (NEXT PAGE)
CORDELE'S CONFEDERATE
AIRFORCE TITAN
MISSILE

mm 75-100

Crisp Co.

DH

99   Rt 300 GA-FLA Pkwy

EXIT 99 - VIDALIA ONIONS

Wenona

Antiques
A

97   Rt 33 Wenona

Exit 97
L-Royal

RV Park Service

Exit 97
G-TA(BP)\D
F-CPride GtAmBft
Pizza PopE

Plantation House

Arabi

92   Arabi   S

Exit 92
G-BP

Exit 92
G-Chevn Pure
F-IceCrm
L-BdgInn

Crisp Co.

EVACUATION
ROUTE
INFORMATION
89.7 FM

AN ABANDONED
BRIDGE COVERED
WITH VINES
EVOKES THE
MYSTERY AND
ROMANCE OF
"FOREVER
GEORGIA,"
THIS TIMELESS
SECTION OF THE
"OLD SOUTH"

Exit 82 - an "Insider" tip . . .
Visit the
Museum of
Crime and
Punishment.

Afterwards,
have lunch at
the Last Meal
Cafe!

W Fork Deep Creek

No Information - Restrooms: 24 hours

Rest Area

23 m
37 k

Exit 84
G-Citgo\D
F-DQ Oasis
Subwy
L-Ashbrn

84   Rt 159 Ashburn Amboy

Exit 84
G-Shell\D

Turner Co.

Exit 82
G-BP Chevn
F-**Hddle** Hrdee
KFC Krystal
McDld Pizza
Shony Waffle
L-BestW **Days**
Ramda **Supr8**

French Market
E/College

Ashburn

82   Rt 112 Ashburn Fitzgerald

EXIT 82, INSIDER TIPS
- ASHBURN'S FRENCH MARKET,
- MUSEUM OF CRIME &
  PUNISHMENT AND LAST
  MEAL CAFE

Levelour

Exit 80
G-Chevn\D

80   Bussey Rd

Exit 80
G-Exxon Shell
F-Subwy
L-BdgInn

Agratech

DH

Sycamore

78   Rt 32 Sycamore Ocilla

N

1020

EXIT 78 - JEFFERSON DAVIS
HISTORICAL CAPTURE SITE AND
MUSEUM - 14.4 MILES EAST (19 MINS
DRIVE TIME)

GEORGIA
PEANUTS

Swamp

Inaha

EXIT 75 - BELL'S
DAY LILLIES

Exit 75
G-BP
F-Stucky

75   Inaha Rd

Exit 75
G-Chevn

Turner Co.

GEORGIA

mm 100-125

-125-

DH

-124-

Houston Co.

-123-

Dooly Co.

GEORGIA COTTON

Exit 122
G-Pure
L-RedC

122 RT 230
Unadilla
Byromville
Clothing Carnival

Unadilla

-122-

EVACUATION ROUTE INFORMATION 89.7 FM

Exit 122
G-Colonial

Exit 121
G-Pure
L-RedC

Exit 121
G-CitgoTS\D
L-Regncy

121 Rt 41
Unadilla

P

-121-

Exit 121
G-BP Shell Texco
F-CPtch DQ
DonPMex GldnC
Stucky Subwy
L-Econmy Scot

-120-

41

-119-

Pinehurst

-118-

Exit 117
G-BP\D
Danfair

117 Pinehurst

-117-

-116-

-115-

WHY DID GREAT BRITAIN ALMOST ENTER THE CIVIL WAR ON THE SIDE OF THE CONFEDERACY? ASK AT THE EXCELLENT GEORGIA COTTON MUSEUM (EXIT 109).

N

irrigation system in peanut fields

-114-

Sandy Mount Creek

-113-

Exit 112
G-Mrthn

112 Rt 27
Hawkinsville

Exit 112
G-Pure

-112-

27

EXIT 109, INSIDER TIP
ELLIS BROS. PECANS

-111-

Vienna

Pig BBQ Festival Grounds

-110-

Exit 109
G-Citgo\D
ElCheapo
Shell\D
F-Hddle
JackBBQ
PopE
ViennaCafe
L-Exec

W A H

109 Rt 215
Vienna/Pitts

Exit 109
G-PilotTS\D
F-McDld

-109-

EXIT 109 - GEORGIA
COTTON MUSEUM

No Information - Restrooms: 24 hours

Rest Area ♿ 🚻 👫 🍽 V

56 m
90 k

Pennahatchee Creek

-107-

DH

Dooly Co.

-106-

-105-

257

Crisp Co.

Exit 101
G-BP\D Chevn
Libty
F-BKing CrkBrl
CuttrStk DQ
GinaFD GldnC
Hrdee KFC
Krystal McDld-I
Pizza Shony
Subwy Taco
Wendy Zaxby
L-Ashbrn Athens
BestW Comfrt
Deluxe Econo
H/InnX Hmptn
Premier Supr8

104 Farmers Market Rd

-104-

41

Pecan Orchards

-103-

Exit 102
G-Citgo

257

H

102 Rt 257/Cordele
Hawkinsville

-102-

Cordele
Pop: 11,600

G
S

101 Rts 280 90
Cordele
Abbeville

280

-101-

Exit 101
G-Exxon\D
PilotTS\D
Shell Texco
F-Arby
CSeaFood
Denny GldnC
Waffle
L-Days Ramda

280

R V

EXIT 101
- SLEEP IN AN ANTIQUE SHOP
- CHARLES SEAFOOD

-100-

Super Wal-Mart
WinnDixie

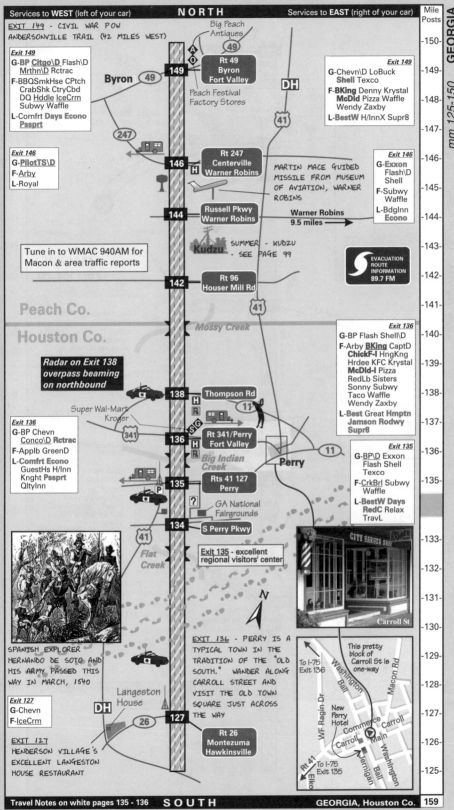

Services to **WEST** (left of your car) **N O R T H** Services to **EAST** (right of your car) | Mile Posts | GEORGIA

mm 125-150

EXIT 149 - CIVIL WAR POW
ANDERSONVILLE TRAIL (42 MILES WEST)

Exit 149
G-BP <u>Citgo\D</u> Flash\D
<u>Mrthn</u>\D Rctrac
F-BBQSmkHse CPtch
CrabShk CtryCbd
DQ <u>Hddle</u> <u>IceCrm</u>
Subwy Waffle
L-Comfrt Days Econo
<u>Pssprt</u>

Big Peach
Antiques

Rt 49
Byron
Fort Valley

149

DH

Byron (49)

Peach Festival
Factory Stores

(41)

Exit 149
G-<u>Chevn</u>\D LoBuck
Shell Texco
F-**BKing** Denny Krystal
McDld Pizza Waffle
Wendy Zaxby
L-**BestW** H/InnX Supr8

Exit 146
G-<u>PilotTS</u>\D
F-<u>Arby</u>
L-Royal

(247)

146 H

Rt 247
Centerville
Warner Robins

MARTIN MACE GUIDED
MISSILE FROM MUSEUM
OF AVIATION, WARNER
ROBINS

Exit 146
G-<u>Exxon</u>
Flash\D
Shell
F-Subwy
Waffle
L-Bdglnn
Econo

144

Russell Pkwy
Warner Robins

Warner Robins
9.5 miles →

Tune in to WMAC 940AM for
Macon & area traffic reports

142

Rt 96
Houser Mill Rd

Kudzu

SUMMER - KUDZU
- SEE PAGE 99

EVACUATION
ROUTE
INFORMATION
89.7 FM

Peach Co.

Houston Co.

Mossy Creek

(41)

Exit 136
G-BP Flash Shell\D
F-Arby **BKing** CaptD
ChickF-I HngKng
Hrdee KFC Krystal
McDld-I Pizza
RedLb Sisters
Sonny Subwy
Taco Waffle
Wendy Zaxby
L-Best Great Hmptn
Jamson Rodwy
Supr8

**Radar on Exit 138
overpass beaming
on northbound**

138 H R

Thompson Rd

(11)

Super Wal-Mart
Kroger

Exit 136
G-BP Chevn
<u>Conco</u>\D Rctrac
F-Applb GreenD
L-Comfrt Econo
GuestHs H/Inn
Knght <u>Pssprt</u>
Qltylnn

(341)

136 H R

Rt 341/Perry
Fort Valley

(11)

Perry

Big Indian
Creek

135

Rts 41 127
Perry

Exit 135
G-<u>BP</u>\D Exxon
Flash Shell
Texco
F-<u>CrkBrl</u> Subwy
Waffle
L-BestW Days
RedC Relax
TravL

(41)

?

134

S Perry Pkwy

GA National
Fairgrounds

Exit 135 - excellent
regional visitors' center

CITY BARBER SHOP

Flat
Creek

N

Carroll St

SPANISH EXPLORER
HERNANDO DE SOTO AND
HIS ARMY PASSED THIS
WAY IN MARCH, 1540

EXIT 136 - PERRY IS A
TYPICAL TOWN IN THE
TRADITION OF THE "OLD
SOUTH." WANDER ALONG
CARROLL STREET AND
VISIT THE OLD TOWN
SQUARE JUST ACROSS
THE WAY

This pretty
block of
Carroll St is
one-way

To I-75
Exit 136

WF Ragin Dr

Washington

Ball

Macon Rd

New
Perry
Hotel

Commerce

Carroll

Main

Washington

Carroll

Langeston
House

DH

(26)

127

Rt 26
Montezuma
Hawkinsville

Exit 127
G-Chevn
F-<u>IceCrm</u>

EXIT 127 -
HENDERSON VILLAGE'S
EXCELLENT LANGESTON
HOUSE RESTAURANT

Rt 41
To I-75
Exit 135

Elko

Jernigan

Ball

Washington

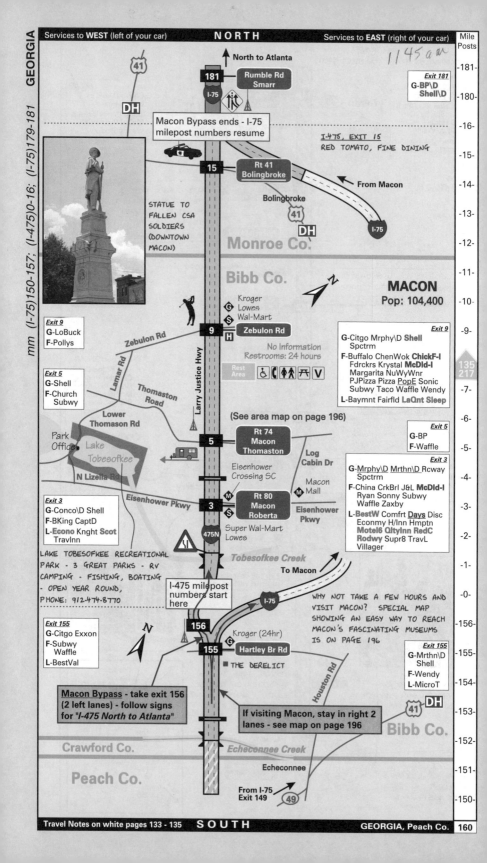

North to Atlanta

181 I-75
Rumble Rd
Smarr

Macon Bypass ends - I-75 milepost numbers resume

Exit 181
G-BP\D
Shell\D

-181
-180
-16

I-475, EXIT 15
RED TOMATO, FINE DINING

-15

15
Rt 41
Bolingbroke

From Macon

Bolingbroke
41
DH

-14
-13
-12

STATUE TO FALLEN CSA SOLDIERS (DOWNTOWN MACON)

Monroe Co.

Bibb Co.

MACON
Pop: 104,400

-11
-10

Exit 9
G-LoBuck
F-Pollys

Zebulon Rd

Kroger
Lowes
Wal-Mart

9 Zebulon Rd

No Information
Restrooms: 24 hours

Rest Area ♿ ⛽ 🚻 ⛲ V

Exit 9
G-Citgo Mrphy\D **Shell** Spctrm
F-Buffalo ChenWok **ChickF-I** Fdrckrs Krystal **McDld-I** Margarita NuWyWnr PJPizza Pizza PopE Sonic Subwy Taco Waffle Wendy
L-Baymnt Fairfld **LaQnt Sleep**

-9
-8

135
217
-7

Exit 5
G-Shell
F-Church Subwy

Lamar Rd

Thomaston Road

Lower Thomason Rd

Park Office

Lake Tobesofkee

N Lizella Rd

Larry Justice Hwy

(See area map on page 196)

5
Rt 74
Macon Thomaston

Eisenhower Crossing SC

Log Cabin Dr

Macon Mall

Eisenhower Pkwy

Exit 5
G-BP
F-Waffle

Exit 3
G-Mrphy\D Mrthn\D Rcway Spctrm
F-China CrkBrl J&L **McDld-I** Ryan Sonny Subwy Waffle Zaxby
L-**BestW** Comfrt **Days** Disc Econmy H/Inn Hmptn **Motel6 QltyInn RedC Rodwy** Supr8 TravL Villager

-6
-5
-4

Exit 3
G-Conco\D Shell
F-BKing CaptD
L-**Econo** Knght **Scot** TravInn

Eisenhower Pkwy

3
Rt 80
Macon Roberta

M
S

Super Wal-Mart
Lowes

-3
-2

LAKE TOBESOFKEE RECREATIONAL PARK - 3 GREAT PARKS - RV CAMPING - FISHING, BOATING - OPEN YEAR ROUND, PHONE: 912-474-8770

475N

Tobesofkee Creek

To Macon

I-75

WHY NOT TAKE A FEW HOURS AND VISIT MACON? SPECIAL MAP SHOWING AN EASY WAY TO REACH MACON'S FASCINATING MUSEUMS IS ON PAGE 196

-1
-0

I-475 milepost numbers start here

156

-156

Exit 155
G-Citgo Exxon
F-Subwy Waffle
L-BestVal

Kroger (24hr)

155 Hartley Br Rd

■ THE DERELICT

Exit 155
G-Mrthn\D Shell
F-Wendy
L-MicroT

Houston Rd

-155
-154

Macon Bypass - take exit 156 (2 left lanes) - follow signs for "I-475 North to Atlanta"

If visiting Macon, stay in right 2 lanes - see map on page 196

41 **DH**

Bibb Co.

-153

Crawford Co.

Echeconnee Creek

-152
-151

Peach Co.

Echeconnee

From I-75
Exit 149
49

-150

1145 am

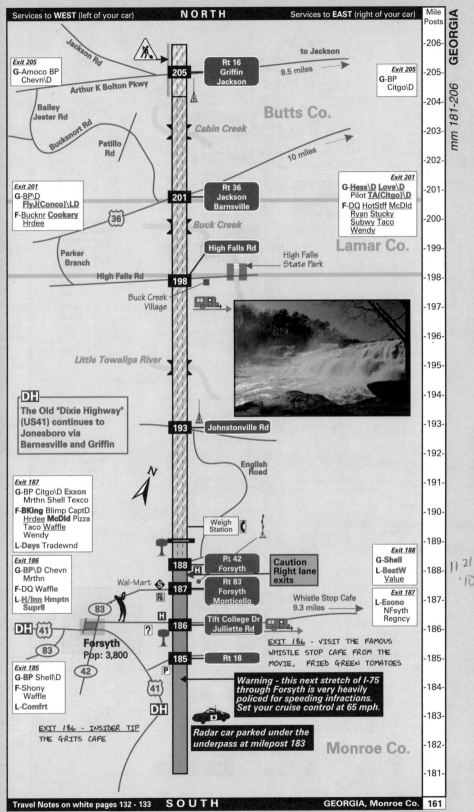

mm 181-206

Jackson Rd

Exit 205
G-Amoco BP Chevn\D

Arthur K Bolton Pkwy

Rt 16
Griffin
Jackson

to Jackson
8.5 miles

Exit 205
G-BP Citgo\D

-206-
-205-
-204-

Bailey Jester Rd

Bucksnort Rd

Patillo Rd

Butts Co.

Cabin Creek

10 miles

-203-
-202-

Exit 201
G-BP\D
FlyJ(Conco)\LD
F-Bucknr Cookery
Hrdee

36

Rt 36
Jackson
Barnsville

Buck Creek

Exit 201
G-Hess\D Love\D
Pilot TA(Citgo)\D
F-DQ HotStff McDld
Ryan Stucky
Subwy Taco
Wendy

-201-
-200-

Lamar Co.

Parker Branch

High Falls Rd

High Falls Rd

High Falls
State Park

High Falls Rd

-199-
-198-

Buck Creek
Village

-197-
-196-

Little Towaliga River

-195-
-194-

DH
The Old "Dixie Highway"
(US41) continues to
Jonesboro via
Barnesville and Griffin

193

Johnstonville Rd

-193-
-192-

English Road

-191-
-190-

Exit 187
G-BP Citgo\D Exxon
Mrthn Shell Texco
F-BKing Blimp CaptD
Hrdee McDld Pizza
Taco Waffle
Wendy
L-Days Tradewnd

N

Weigh
Station

188

Rt 42
Forsyth

**Caution
Right lane
exits**

Exit 188
G-Shell
L-BestW
Value

-189-
-188-

Exit 186
G-BP\D Chevn
Mrthn
F-DQ Waffle
L-H/Inn Hmptn
Supr8

83

Wal-Mart

187

Rt 83
Forsyth
Monticello

Whistle Stop Cafe
9.3 miles

Exit 187
L-Econo
NFsyth
Regncy

-187-

DH 41
83

Forsyth
Pop: 3,800

186

Tift College Dr
Julliette Rd

EXIT 186 - VISIT THE FAMOUS
WHISTLE STOP CAFE FROM THE
MOVIE, FRIED GREEN TOMATOES

-186-

Exit 185
G-BP Shell\D
F-Shony
Waffle
L-Comfrt

42

185

Rt 18

41

DH

Warning - this next stretch of I-75
through Forsyth is very heavily
policed for speeding infractions.
Set your cruise control at 65 mph.

-185-
-184-
-183-

EXIT 186 - INSIDER TIP
THE GRITS CAFE

**Radar car parked under the
underpass at milepost 183**

Monroe Co.

-182-
-181-

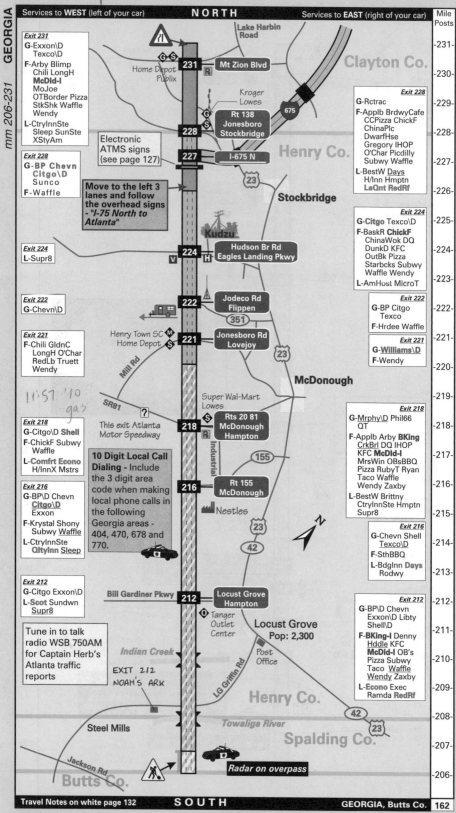

Handwritten: '07 1225pm

Lake Harbin Road

Exit 231
G-Exxon\D Texco\D
F-Arby Blimp Chili LongH **McDld-I** MoJoe OTBorder Pizza StkShk Waffle Wendy
L-CtryInnSte Sleep SunSte XStyAm

⚠ **231** Mt Zion Blvd ®
Home Depot Publix Ⓖ Ⓢ

Clayton Co.

Kroger Lowes
675

Exit 228
G-BP Chevn Citgo\D Sunco
F-Waffle

Ⓖ **228** Rt 138 Ⓢ Jonesboro Stockbridge

Electronic ATMS signs (see page 127)

227 I-675 N
23

Exit 228
G-Rctrac
F-Applb BrdwyCafe CCPizza ChickF ChinaPlc DwarfHse Gregory IHOP O'Char Picdilly Subwy Waffle
L-BestW Days H/Inn Hmptn LaQnt RedRf

Henry Co.

Move to the left 3 lanes and follow the overhead signs - "*I-75 North to Atlanta*"

Stockbridge

Exit 224
L-Supr8

Kudzu

V **224** H Hudson Br Rd Eagles Landing Pkwy

Exit 224
G-Citgo Texco\D
F-BaskR **ChickF** ChinaWok DQ DunkD KFC OutBk Pizza Starbcks Subwy Waffle Wendy
L-AmHost MicroT

Exit 222
G-Chevn\D

222 Jodeco Rd Flippen
351

Exit 222
G-BP Citgo Texco
F-Hrdee Waffle

Exit 221
F-Chili GldnC LongH O'Char RedLb Truett Wendy

Henry Town SC Ⓜ Home Depot Ⓢ **221** Jonesboro Rd Lovejoy
23

McDonough

Handwritten: 11:57 '10 gas

Mill Rd

SR81

?

This exit Atlanta Motor Speedway

Super Wal-Mart Lowes

Exit 221
G-Williams\D
F-Wendy

Ⓢ **218** Rts 20 81 Ⓡ McDonough Hampton

Exit 218
G-Citgo\D Shell
F-ChickF Subwy Waffle
L-Comfrt Econo H/InnX Mstrs

10 Digit Local Call Dialing - Include the 3 digit area code when making local phone calls in the following Georgia areas - 404, 470, 678 and 770.

155

Exit 218
G-Mrphy\D Phil66 QT
F-Applb Arby **BKing** CrkBrl DQ IHOP KFC **McDld-I** MrsWin OBsBBQ Pizza RubyT Ryan Taco Waffle Wendy Zaxby
L-BestW Brittny CtryInnSte Hmptn Supr8

Exit 216
G-BP\D Chevn Citgo\D Exxon
F-Krystal Shony Subwy Waffle
L-CtryInnSte QltyInn Sleep

Industrial

216 Rt 155 McDonough

Nestles

23
42

Exit 216
G-Chevn Shell Texco\D
F-SthBBQ
L-BdgInn Days Rodwy

Tune in to talk radio WSB 750AM for Captain Herb's Atlanta traffic reports

Exit 212
G-Citgo Exxon\D
L-Scot Sundwn Supr8

Bill Gardiner Pkwy **212** Locust Grove Hampton

Tanger Outlet Center

Indian Creek

Handwritten: EXIT 212 NOAH'S ARK

Locust Grove Pop: 2,300

Post Office

LG Griffin Rd

Exit 212
G-BP\D Chevn Exxon\D Libty Shell\D
F-BKing-I Denny Hddle KFC **McDld-I** OB's Pizza Subwy Taco Waffle Wendy Zaxby
L-Econo Exec Ramda RedRf

Henry Co.

Steel Mills

Towaliga River

Spalding Co.

42
23

Jackson Rd

Butts Co.

⚠ Radar on overpass

Handwritten: 12:05 pm '07

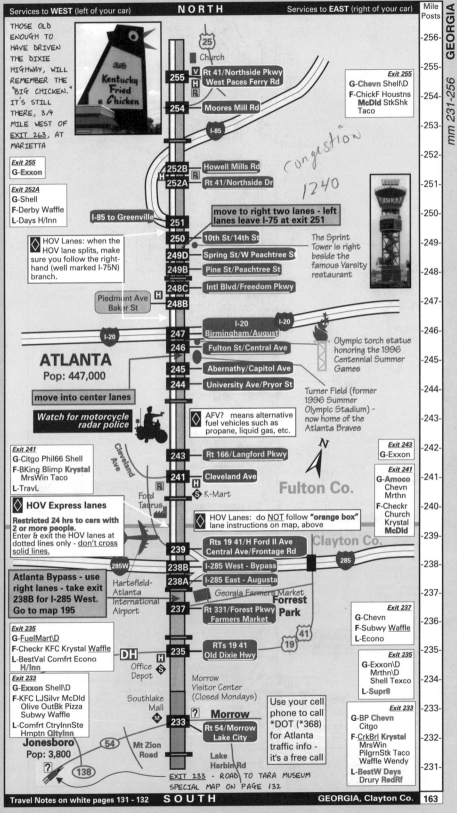

1248

THOSE OLD ENOUGH TO HAVE DRIVEN THE DIXIE HIGHWAY, WILL REMEMBER THE "BIG CHICKEN." IT'S STILL THERE, 3/4 MILE WEST OF EXIT 263, AT MARIETTA

Kentucky Fried Chicken

-256-
-255-
-254-
-253-
-252-
-251-
-250-
-249-
-248-
-247-
-246-
-245-
-244-
-243-
-242-
-241-
-240-
-239-
-238-
-237-
-236-
-235-
-234-
-233-
-232-
-231-

25
Church

255 — Rt 41/Northside Pkwy West Paces Ferry Rd

254 — Moores Mill Rd

I-85

Exit 255
G-Exxon

Exit 252A
G-Shell
F-Derby Waffle
L-Days H/Inn

252B — Howell Mills Rd
252A — Rt 41/Northside Dr

I-85 to Greenville

251 — **move to right two lanes - left lanes leave I-75 at exit 251**

250 — 10th St/14th St

◇ HOV Lanes: when the HOV lane splits, make sure you follow the right-hand (well marked I-75N) branch.

The Sprint Tower is right beside the famous Varsity restaurant

249D — Spring St/W Peachtree St
249B — Pine St/Peachtree St
248C — Intl Blvd/Freedom Pkwy

Piedmont Ave Baker St
248B

I-20 — 247 — I-20 Birmingham/August

246 — Fulton St/Central Ave

I-20

Olympic torch statue honoring the 1996 Centennial Summer Games

ATLANTA
Pop: 447,000

245 — Abernathy/Capitol Ave
244 — University Ave/Pryor St

move into center lanes

Watch for motorcycle radar police

◇ AFV? means alternative fuel vehicles such as propane, liquid gas, etc.

Turner Field (former 1996 Summer Olympic Stadium) - now home of the Atlanta Braves

Cleveland Ave

243 — Rt 166/Langford Pkwy

Exit 243
G-Exxon

Exit 241
G-Citgo Phil66 Shell
F-BKing Blimp **Krystal** MrsWin Taco
L-TravL

241 — Cleveland Ave

Ford Taurus

K-Mart

Fulton Co.

Exit 241
G-Amoco Chevn Mrthn
F-Checkr Church Krystal **McDld**

◇ **HOV Express lanes**
Restricted 24 hrs to cars with 2 or more people.
Enter & exit the HOV lanes at dotted lines only - don't cross solid lines.

◇ HOV Lanes: do NOT follow "orange box" lane instructions on map, above

Clayton Co.

285

239 — Rts 19 41/H Ford II Ave Central Ave/Frontage Rd

285W — 238B — I-285 West - Bypass
238A — I-285 East - Augusta

Atlanta Bypass - use right lanes - take exit 238B for I-285 West. Go to map 195

Hartsfield-Atlanta International Airport

Georgia Farmers Market

Forrest Park

237 — Rt 331/Forest Pkwy Farmers Market

Exit 237
G-Chevn
F-Subwy Waffle
L-Econo

Exit 235
G-FuelMart\D
F-Checkr KFC Krystal Waffle
L-BestVal Comfrt Econo H/Inn

DH
Office Depot

235 — RTs 19 41 Old Dixie Hwy

41
19

Exit 235
G-Exxon\D Mrthn\D Shell Texco
L-Supr8

Exit 233
G-Exxon Shell\D
F-KFC LJSilvr McDld Olive OutBk Pizza Subwy Waffle
L-Comfrt CtryInnSte Hmptn QltyInn

Morrow Visitor Center (Closed Mondays)

Southlake Mall

M

Morrow

233 — Rt 54/Morrow Lake City

Use your cell phone to call *DOT (*368) for Atlanta traffic info - it's a free call

Exit 233
G-BP Chevn Citgo
F-CrkBrl Krystal MrsWin PilgrnStk Taco Waffle Wendy
L-BestW Days Drury RedRf

Jonesboro
Pop: 3,800

54
Mt Zion Road

138

Lake Harbin Rd

EXIT 233 - ROAD TO TARA MUSEUM SPECIAL MAP ON PAGE 132

congestion 1240

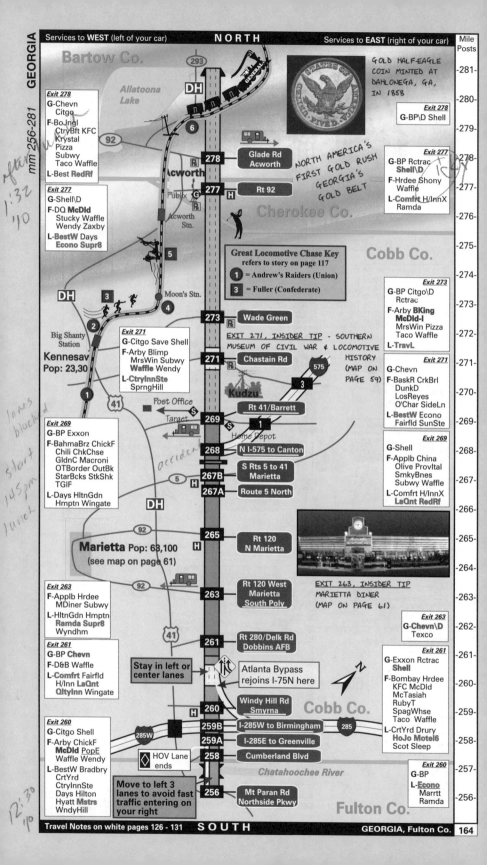

mm 256-281

after 1:32 '10

Bartow Co.

Allatoona Lake

GOLD HALF-EAGLE COIN MINTED AT DAHLONEGA, GA, IN 1858

-281-
-280-

DH

Exit 278
G-Chevn Citgo
F-BoJngl CtryBft KFC Krystal Pizza Subwy Taco Waffle
L-Best RedRf

Exit 278
G-BP\D Shell

-279-

293

92

6

278 Glade Rd Acworth

NORTH AMERICA'S FIRST GOLD RUSH GEORGIA'S GOLD BELT

Acworth

277 Rt 92 **H**

Publix

Exit 277
G-Shell\D
F-DQ McDld Stucky Waffle Wendy Zaxby
L-BestW Days Econo Supr8

Acworth Stn.

Cherokee Co.

Exit 277
G-BP Rctrac Shell\D
F-Hrdee Shony Waffle
L-Comfrt H/InnX Ramda

-278-
-277-
-276-

5

Cobb Co.

Great Locomotive Chase Key
refers to story on page 117
1 = Andrew's Raiders (Union)
3 = Fuller (Confederate)

Exit 273
G-BP Citgo\D Rctrac
F-Arby BKing McDld-I MrsWin Pizza Taco Waffle
L-TravL

-275-
-274-
-273-

DH

3

Moon's Stn.

273 Wade Green

EXIT 271, INSIDER TIP - SOUTHERN MUSEUM OF CIVIL WAR & LOCOMOTIVE HISTORY (MAP ON PAGE 59)

-272-

2

4

Big Shanty Station

Kennesav
Pop: 23,30

1

Exit 271
G-Citgo Save Shell
F-Arby Blimp MrsWin Subwy Waffle Wendy
L-CtryInnSte SprngHill

41

271 Chastain Rd

575

3

Exit 271
G-Chevn
F-BaskR CrkBrl DunkD LosReyes O'Char SideLn
L-BestW Econo Fairfld SunSte

-271-
-270-

lanes blocked

start

145 pm

lunch

Post Office

Target

Kudzu

269 Rt 41/Barrett

S

Home Depot

Exit 269
G-BP Exxon
F-BahmaBrz ChickF Chili ChkChse GldnC Macroni OTBorder OutBk StarBcks StkShk TGIF
L-Days HltnGdn Hmptn Wingate

Exit 269
G-Shell
F-Applb China Olive ProvItal SmkyBnes Subwy Waffle
L-Comfrt H/InnX LaQnt RedRf

-269-
-268-

5

accident

268 N I-575 to Canton

267B S Rts 5 to 41 Marietta **H**
267A Route 5 North

-267-
-266-

DH

92

Marietta Pop: 68,100
(see map on page 61)

92

265 Rt 120 N Marietta **H**

-265-
-264-

Exit 263
F-Applb Hrdee MDiner Subwy
L-HltnGdn Hmptn Ramda Supr8 Wyndhm

41

263 Rt 120 West Marietta South Poly

EXIT 263, INSIDER TIP MARIETTA DINER (MAP ON PAGE 61)

-263-

Exit 263
G-Chevn\D Texco

-262-

Exit 261
G-BP Chevn
F-D&B Waffle
L-Comfrt Fairfld H/Inn LaQnt QltyInn Wingate

41

261 Rt 280/Delk Rd Dobbins AFB

Exit 261
G-Exxon Rctrac Shell
F-Bombay Hrdee KFC McDld McTasiah RubyT SpagWhse Taco Waffle
L-CrtYrd Drury HoJo Motel6 Scot Sleep

-261-
-260-

Stay in left or center lanes

Atlanta Bypass rejoins I-75N here

Windy Hill Rd Smyrna

260 **H**

Cobb Co.

-259-

Exit 260
G-Citgo Shell
F-Arby ChickF McDld PopE Waffle Wendy
L-BestW Bradbry CrtYrd CtryInnSte Days Hilton Hyatt Mstrs WndyHill

285W

259B I-285W to Birmingham
259A I-285E to Greenville

285

HOV Lane ends

258 Cumberland Blvd

Chatahoochee River

Exit 260
G-BP
L-Econo Marrtt Ramda

-258-
-257-

Move to left 3 lanes to avoid fast traffic entering on your right

256 Mt Paran Rd Northside Pkwy

-256-

12:30 '10

Fulton Co.

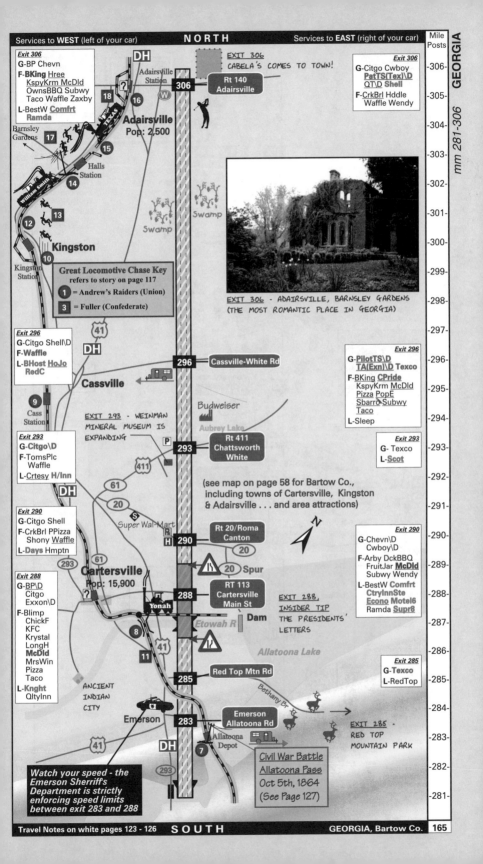

Exit 306
G-BP Chevn
F-BKing Hree
 KspyKrm McDld
 OwnsBBQ Subwy
 Taco Waffle Zaxby
L-BestW Comfrt
 Ramda

DH

Adairsville
Station

306 | Rt 140
Adairsville

EXIT 306
CABELA'S COMES TO TOWN!

Exit 306
G-Citgo Cwboy
 PatTS(Tex)\D
 QT\D Shell
F-CrkBrl Hddle
 Waffle Wendy

-306-

-305-

18   16

Adairsville
Pop: 2,500

Barnsley
Gardens

17

15

-304-

-303-

Swamp

Halls
Station

14

Swamp

-302-

-301-

12   13

-300-

Kingston

-299-

Kingston
Station

10

Great Locomotive Chase Key
refers to story on page 117
1 = Andrew's Raiders (Union)
3 = Fuller (Confederate)

EXIT 306 - ADAIRSVILLE, BARNSLEY GARDENS
(THE MOST ROMANTIC PLACE IN GEORGIA)

-298-

41

DH

296 | Cassville-White Rd

-297-

-296-

Exit 296
G-Citgo Shell\D
F-Waffle
L-BHost HoJo
 RedC

Cassville

Exit 296
G-PilotTS\D
 TA(Exn)\D Texco
F-BKing CPride
 KspyKrm McDld
 Pizza PopE
 Sbarro Subwy
 Taco
L-Sleep

-295-

9

Cass
Station

Budweiser

Aubrey Lake

**EXIT 293 - WEINMAN
MINERAL MUSEUM IS
EXPANDING**

-294-

P

411

293 | Rt 411
Chattsworth
White

Exit 293
G- Texco
L-Scot

-293-

Exit 293
G-Citgo\D
F-TomsPlc
 Waffle
L-Crtesy H/Inn

DH

61

20

(see map on page 58 for Bartow Co.,
including towns of Cartersville, Kingston
& Adairsville . . . and area attractions)

-292-

-291-

Exit 290
G-Citgo Shell
F-CrkBrl PPizza
 Shony Waffle
L-Days Hmptn

Super Wal-Mart

S

H

290 | Rt 20/Roma
Canton

20

N

Exit 290
G-Chevn\D
 Cwboy\D
F-Arby DckBBQ
 FruitJar McDld
 Subwy Wendy
L-BestW Comfrt
 CtrylnnSte
 Econo Motel6
 Ramda Supr8

-290-

61

293

Cartersville
Pop: 15,900

Yonah

20 Spur

-289-

-288-

Exit 288
G-BP\D
 Citgo
 Exxon\D
F-Blimp
 ChickF
 KFC
 Krystal
 LongH
 McDld
 MrsWin
 Pizza
 Taco
L-Knght
 QltyInn

?

288 | RT 113
Cartersville
Main St

**EXIT 288,
INSIDER TIP
THE PRESIDENTS'
LETTERS**

8

Etowah R.   Dam

-287-

11   41

Allatoona Lake

-286-

285 | Red Top Mtn Rd

Bethany Br

Exit 285
G-Texco
L-RedTop

-285-

ANCIENT
INDIAN
CITY

Emerson

283 | Emerson
Allatoona Rd

-284-

-283-

41

DH

Allatoona
Depot

7

293

**EXIT 285 -
RED TOP
MOUNTAIN PARK**

Civil War Battle
Allatoona Pass
Oct 5th, 1864
(See Page 127)

-282-

*Watch your speed - the
Emerson Sherriff's
Department is strictly
enforcing speed limits
between exit 283 and 288*

-281-

ISSUED IN 1995 THIS STAMP HONORS CSA GEN. JOHNSTON - THE MAN WHO ALMOST STOPPED GEN. SHERMAN'S MARCH ON ATLANTA

Joseph E. Johnston

-331-

-330-

-329-

30

Exit 328
G-FlCity\D
Phil66

328 Rt 3 to US 41

41

DH

Green's Station (Tilton)

29

28

-328-

-327-

Exit 328
G-BP\D
PilotTS\D
F-Arby Blimp
KspyKrm
Waffle Wendy
L-Supr8

Exit 326
G-BP Exxon
GldnGln
Phil66\D
F-KspyKrm

326 Carbondale Rd

-326-

-325-

Exit 326
G-Chevn\D
PilotTS\D
F-McDld Subwy

-324-

26 **27**

General Sherman
Union Army
104,000 men
(Casulaties - 2,747)

General Johnston
Confederate Army
43,000 men
(Casualties - 2,800)

Resaca
Resaca Station

-323-

-322-

Civil War Battle
of Resaca
13-15th May, 1864
(see page 120, Map
Page 57)

Gordon Co.

-321-

320 Rt 136, Resaca La Fayette

25

-320-

Exit 320
G-Conco
FlyJ\DL
F-**Cookery**
Pepproni

Exit 318
G-RghtStff Shell
F-Chuckwgn
L-Bdglnn Best
Duffy Smith
Supr8

Oostanaula
River

Confederate retreat to Cassville

-319-

318 Rt 41/Resaca

24

Trail of Tears Hwy

-318-

Exit 318
G-Hess\D
Wilco\D
F-DQ Hrdee
Stucky
Wendy
L-Knight

317 Rt 225 Chatsworth

-317-

23
22

Trail of Tears Hwy
EXIT 315,
INSIDER TIP
NEW ECHOTA
SMOKEHOUSE

EXIT 317 - NEW ECHOTA, THE CHEROKEE NATION CAPIAL

-316-

41

H

315 Rt 156 Red Bud Rd Calhoun

-315-

Exit 315
G-Citgo\D
Kgroo
F-GldnC
Waffle
L-Scot

Calhoun Station

20 **21**

Calhoun

Exit 315
G-Chevn Libty
Texco\DL
F-Arby Shony
L-Days Ramda

A
Redbud Antiques

Great Locomotive Chase Key
refers to story on page 117
1 = Andrew's Raiders (Union)
3 = Fuller (Confederate)

-314-

-313-

WinnDixie

G

312 Rt 53 Calhoun

P

-312-

Exit 312
G-BP Chevn\D
Citgo Exxon
Fina Kgroo
F-A&W Arby
CaptD Checkr
ChickF-I
China DQ
GldnC Hddle
HickH IHOP
KFC **Krystal**
KspyKrm
LJSilvr
McDld-I Pizza
Subwy Taco
Wendy Zaxby
L-Comfrt Guest
H/InnX Hmptn
Jamson Royal

19

41

DH

Prime Outlet Shopping

N

VINTAGE AIRCRAFT (MERCER FIELD)

No Information - Restrooms: 24 hours

Rest Area

Gordon Co.

Exit 312
G-Kgroo
Shell\D
F-CrkBrl
L-BHost
QltyInn

-311-

-310-

-309-

-308-

47 m
76 k

-307-

Bert Lance Highway

Bartow Co.

-306-

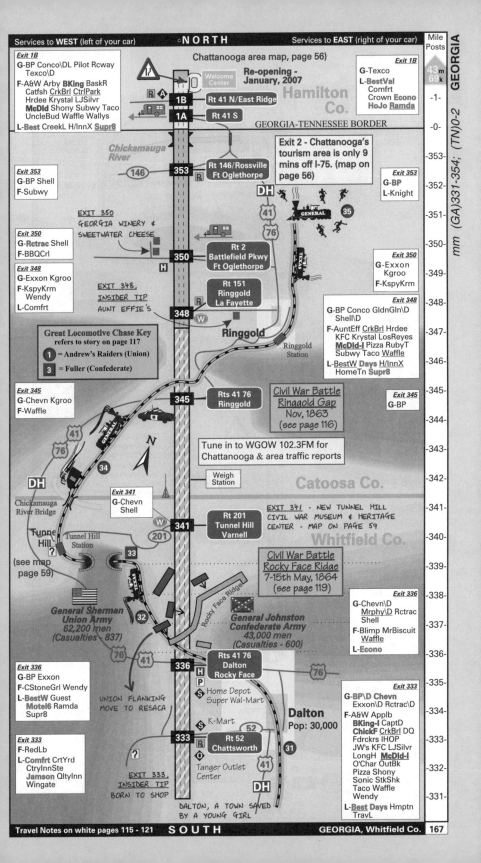

Services to **WEST** (left of your car)

Services to **EAST** (right of your car)

mm (GA)331-354; (TN)0-2

Exit 1B
G-BP Conco\DL Pilot Rcway Texco\D
F-A&W Arby **BKing** BaskR Catfsh CrkBrl CtrlPark Hrdee Krystal LJSilvr **McDld** Shony Subwy Taco UncleBud Waffle Wallys
L-**Best** CreekL H/InnX **Supr8**

Exit 1B
G-Texco
L-BestVal Comfrt Crown Econo HoJo Ramda

43 m
69 k
-1-
-0-

Re-opening - January, 2007

Welcome Center

Rt 41 N/East Ridge

Rt 41 S

Hamilton Co.

GEORGIA-TENNESSEE BORDER

Chickamauga River

146 | 353 | Rt 146/Rossville Ft Oglethorpe

Exit 2 - Chattanooga's tourism area is only 9 mins off I-75. (map on page 56)

-353-
-352-

Exit 353
G-BP Shell
F-Subwy

DH

41
76

GENERAL

35

Exit 353
G-BP
L-Knight

EXIT 350
GEORGIA WINERY & SWEETWATER CHEESE

-351-

350 | Rt 2 Battlefield Pkwy Ft Oglethorpe

-350-

Exit 350
G-Rctrac Shell
F-BBQCrl

H

Exit 350
G-Exxon Kgroo
F-KspyKrm

Exit 348
G-Exxon Kgroo
F-KspyKrm Wendy
L-Comfrt

EXIT 348, INSIDER TIP AUNT EFFIE'S

348 | Rt 151 Ringgold La Fayette

-349-
-348-

R
W

Ringgold

Exit 348
G-BP Conco GldnGln\D Shell\D
F-AuntEff CrkBrl Hrdee KFC Krystal LosReyes **McDld-I** Pizza RubyT Subwy Taco Waffle
L-BestW Days H/InnX HomeTn Supr8

-347-

Great Locomotive Chase Key
refers to story on page 117
1 = Andrew's Raiders (Union)
3 = Fuller (Confederate)

Ringgold Station

-346-

Exit 345
G-Chevn Kgroo
F-Waffle

345 | Rts 41 76 Ringgold

Civil War Battle Ringgold Gap Nov, 1863 (see page 116)

-345-
-344-

Exit 345
G-BP

41
76

GENERAL

34

N

Tune in to WGOW 102.3FM for Chattanooga & area traffic reports

-343-

Weigh Station

Catoosa Co.

-342-

Chickamauga River Bridge

Exit 341
G-Chevn Shell

W

341 | Rt 201 Tunnel Hill Varnell

EXIT 341 - NEW TUNNEL HILL CIVIL WAR MUSEUM & HERITAGE CENTER - MAP ON PAGE 59

-341-

DH

Tunnel Hill

Tunnel Hill Station

201

Whitfield Co.

-340-

(see map page 59)

33

Civil War Battle Rocky Face Ridge 7-15th May, 1864 (see page 119)

-339-

Exit 336
G-Chevn\D Mrphy\D Rctrac Shell
F-Blimp MrBiscuit Waffle
L-Econo

-338-

General Sherman Union Army 62,200 men (Casualties - 837)

32

General Johnston Confederate Army 43,000 men (Casualties - 600)

-337-

-336-

Exit 336
G-BP Exxon
F-CStoneGrl Wendy
L-BestW Guest Motel6 Ramda Supr8

76

41

336 | Rts 41 76 Dalton Rocky Face

76

-335-

H
P
S | Home Depot Super Wal-Mart

Dalton
Pop: 30,000

Exit 333
G-BP\D Chevn Exxon\D Rctrac\D
F-A&W Applb BKing-I CaptD **ChickF** CrkBrl DQ Fdrckrs IHOP JW's KFC LJSilvr LongH **McDld-I** O'Char OutBk Pizza Shony Sonic StkShk Taco Waffle Wendy
L-**Best** Days Hmptn TravL

-334-

UNION FLANKING MOVE TO RESACA

S | K-Mart

52

Exit 333
F-RedLb
L-**Comfrt** CrtYrd CtryInnSte **Jamson** Qltylnn Wingate

333 | Rt 52 Chattsworth

31

-333-

R

-332-

Tanger Outlet Center

DH

41

EXIT 333, INSIDER TIP BORN TO SHOP

-331-

DALTON, A TOWN SAVED BY A YOUNG GIRL

ON ALMOST EVERY I-75 DRIVE, WE HAVE SEEN DEER FEEDING IN THE ROADSIDE TREE FRINGE OR IN THE WIDE MEDIAN AREAS - PLEASE BE CAREFUL SINCE THEY SCARE EASILY AND MAY BOLT ACROSS THE ROAD IN FRONT OF YOU.

Important - Watch for Deer crossing the road during the next 40 miles

DH

60 11

25

W

Rt 60 Cleveland/Dayton

H R V

-27-
-26-
-25-
-24-

Exit 25
G-BP Chevn\D
Rctrac
Shell\D

F-BKing
CancunMex
CrkBrl Hrdee
McDld
Roblyn
Schltzky
Sharky
Waffle Zaxby

L-**Colnial Days**
Douglas
Econmy
Econo
Qltyinn
Travinn

Exit 25
G-Shell
L-**Baymnt** H/Inn
Wingate

Candies Creek Ridge

Truck Inspection
(no facilities)

74 64

Cleveland
Pop: 38,200

-23-
-22-
-21-

64
11

60

20 H

Rt 64 Bypass East to Cleveland

-20-
-19-

Exit 20
G-Exxon\DL

TENNESSEE HAS A VERY ACTIVE WILDFLOWER PLANTING PROGRAM ALONG ITS FREEWAYS

-18-

Watch for radar in the gaps in the trees in the median

Whiteoak Mountain

-17-
-16-
-15-

Bradley Co.

Hamilton Co.

N

Stay right except to pass

DH

64
11

TENNESSEE Phone Numbers
Emergency: 911
Cell: *THP (*847)
Police Information: 615-251-5175
Road Weather Info: 800-342-3258
Road Construction: 800-858-6349

-14-
-13-
-12-

Exit 11
G-BP ExnTS)\D
Kgroo
F-Krystal Waffle
L-Supr8

11 Rts N11 E64 Ooltewah

Exit 11
G-Chevn Rctrac
Shell
F-Arby BKing-I
Hrdee McDld-I
Taco

-11-
-10-

Exit 7B
G-Texco
L-Best BestW Comfrt
Econo Motel6
ParkInn Wellsly

45 mph

9 Enterprise S Industrial Pk

45 mph

EXIT 4A, INSIDER TIPS
- STICKY FINGERS
- FAMOUS DAVE'S

-9-
-8-

Exit 5
G-BP Citgo Exxon
F-Applb CrkBrl Fazoli GlenGene McDld MexGrl O'Aces O'Char RBravo Shony Subwy TexRdHse Waffle Wendy
L-CtryInnSte Days Fairfld GuestHs H/Inn H/InnX HltnGdn Hmptn HomeWd Knght LaQnt MicroT Ramda RedRf Sleep

7B Rt 317W/Bonny Oaks Dr/Lee Hwy

7A Rt 317/Summit Collegedale

Shallowford

5 S

Gunbarrel

Exit 5
F-Acropolis
Alexndr
Arby
CntryPlace
ElMeson
FmDave
Krystal Olive
OutBk
RedLb
StkShk
StkyFngr
Taco
L-Comfrt
CrtYrd
Wingate

-7-
-6-

EXIT 4 - TENNESSEE VALLEY RAILROAD

11

Hamilton Place Mall

5 Shallowford Rd

4A M

-5-

CHATTANOOGA
Pop: 159,700

Eastgate Mall M

Missionary Ridge

4A M Hamilton Place Blvd

4 Rt N153/Chickamauga Dam

Sticky Fingers

Famous Daves

Exit 3A
G-Exxon
F-Subwy

-4-
-3-

I-24 **I-24 West to Chattanooga**

2

3B Rt 320W/E Brainerd Rd

3A Rt 320E/E Brainerd Rd

EXIT 2, INSIDER TIP
A PRIVATE PARLOR CAR FOR THE NIGHT

-2-

Use 2 right lanes

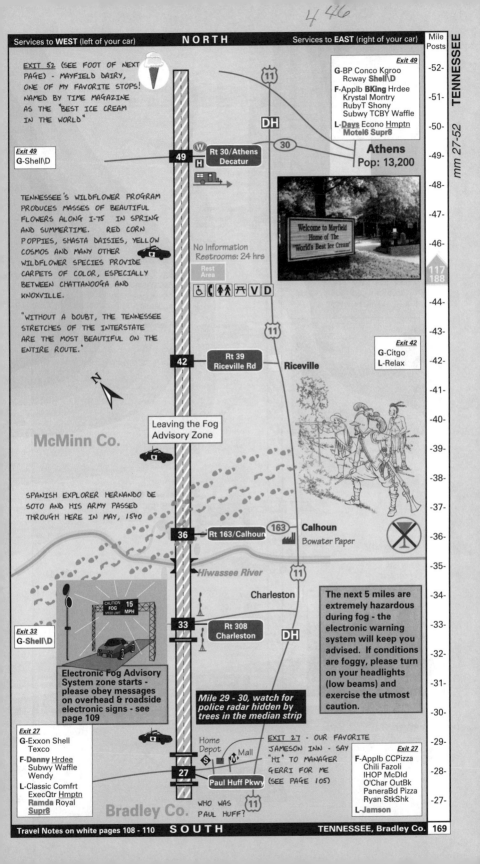

4 46

mm 27-52

EXIT 52 (SEE FOOT OF NEXT PAGE) - MAYFIELD DAIRY, ONE OF MY FAVORITE STOPS! NAMED BY TIME MAGAZINE AS THE "BEST ICE CREAM IN THE WORLD"

Exit 49
G-BP Conco Kgroo
  Rcway **Shell\D**
F-Applb **BKing** Hrdee
  Krystal Montry
  RubyT Shony
  Subwy TCBY Waffle
L-**Days** Econo **Hmptn**
  Motel6 Supr8

Athens
Pop: 13,200

Exit 49
G-Shell\D

49 — Rt 30/Athens Decatur

W H

TENNESSEE'S WILDFLOWER PROGRAM PRODUCES MASSES OF BEAUTIFUL FLOWERS ALONG I-75 IN SPRING AND SUMMERTIME. RED CORN POPPIES, SHASTA DAISIES, YELLOW COSMOS AND MANY OTHER WILDFLOWER SPECIES PROVIDE CARPETS OF COLOR, ESPECIALLY BETWEEN CHATTANOOGA AND KNOXVILLE.

"WITHOUT A DOUBT, THE TENNESSEE STRETCHES OF THE INTERSTATE ARE THE MOST BEAUTIFUL ON THE ENTIRE ROUTE."

Welcome to Mayfield
Home of The
"World's Best Ice Cream"

No Information
Restrooms: 24 hrs

Rest Area

117 188

42 — Rt 39 Riceville Rd — Riceville

Exit 42
G-Citgo
L-Relax

Leaving the Fog Advisory Zone

McMinn Co.

SPANISH EXPLORER HERNANDO DE SOTO AND HIS ARMY PASSED THROUGH HERE IN MAY, 1540

36 — Rt 163/Calhoun — 163 **Calhoun** Bowater Paper

Hiwassee River

11

Charleston

33 — Rt 308 Charleston

DH

The next 5 miles are extremely hazardous during fog - the electronic warning system will keep you advised. If conditions are foggy, please turn on your headlights (low beams) and exercise the utmost caution.

Exit 33
G-Shell\D

CAUTION FOG SPEED LIMIT **15** MPH

Electronic Fog Advisory System zone starts - please obey messages on overhead & roadside electronic signs - see page 109

Mile 29 - 30, watch for police radar hidden by trees in the median strip

Exit 27
G-Exxon Shell
  Texco
F-**Denny** Hrdee
  Subwy Waffle
  Wendy
L-Classic Comfrt
  ExecQtr **Hmptn**
  Ramda Royal
  Supr8

Home Depot

Mall

27 — Paul Huff Pkwy

EXIT 27 - OUR FAVORITE JAMESON INN - SAY "HI" TO MANAGER GERRI FOR ME (SEE PAGE 105)

Exit 27
F-Applb CCPizza
  Chili Fazoli
  IHOP McDld
  O'Char OutBk
  PaneraBd Pizza
  Ryan StkShk
L-Jamson

WHO WAS PAUL HUFF?

11

Bradley Co.

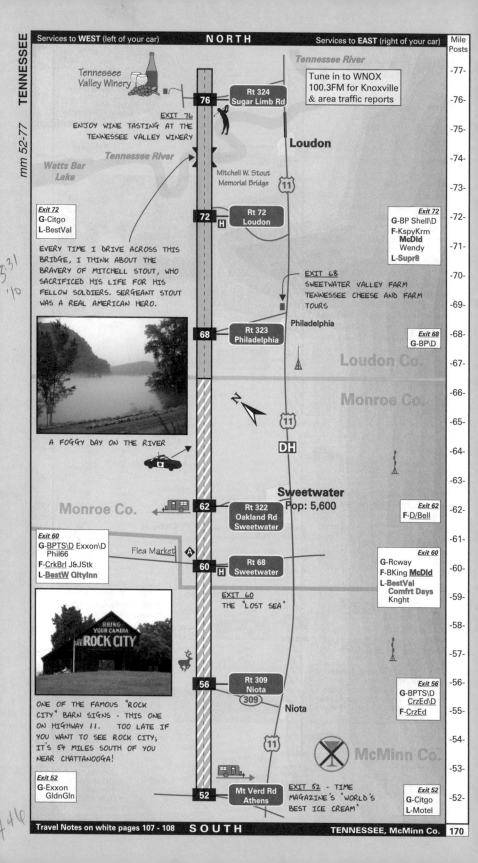

TENNESSEE

mm 52-77

Tennessee River

-77-

Tennessee Valley Winery

76 Rt 324 Sugar Limb Rd

Tune in to WNOX 100.3FM for Knoxville & area traffic reports

-76-

EXIT 76
ENJOY WINE TASTING AT THE TENNESSEE VALLEY WINERY

-75-

Loudon

Tennessee River

-74-

Watts Bar Lake

Mitchell W. Stout Memorial Bridge

11

-73-

Exit 72
G-Citgo
L-BestVal

72 H Rt 72 Loudon

Exit 72
G-BP Shell\D

F-KspyKrm
McDld
Wendy

L-Supr8

-72-

-71-

EVERY TIME I DRIVE ACROSS THIS BRIDGE, I THINK ABOUT THE BRAVERY OF MITCHELL STOUT, WHO SACRIFICED HIS LIFE FOR HIS FELLOW SOLDIERS. SERGEANT STOUT WAS A REAL AMERICAN HERO.

EXIT 68
SWEETWATER VALLEY FARM TENNESSEE CHEESE AND FARM TOURS

-70-

-69-

68 Rt 323 Philadelphia

Philadelphia

-68-

Exit 68
G-BP\D

A FOGGY DAY ON THE RIVER

Loudon Co.

-67-

Monroe Co.

-66-

N

11

-65-

DH

-64-

-63-

Sweetwater
Pop: 5,600

Monroe Co.

62 Rt 322 Oakland Rd Sweetwater

Exit 62
F-D/Bell

-62-

Exit 60
G-BPTS\D Exxon\D
Phil66
F-CrkBrl J&JStk
L-BestW QltyInn

Flea Market A

60 H Rt 68 Sweetwater

Exit 60
G-Rcway
F-BKing **McDld**
L-BestVal
Comfrt Days
Knght

-61-

-60-

-59-

EXIT 60
THE "LOST SEA"

-58-

BRING YOUR CAMERA SEE ROCK CITY

-57-

56 Rt 309 Niota

309   Niota

-56-

Exit 56
G-BPTS\D
CrzEd\D
F-CrzEd

-55-

ONE OF THE FAMOUS "ROCK CITY" BARN SIGNS - THIS ONE ON HIGHWAY 11.   TOO LATE IF YOU WANT TO SEE ROCK CITY; IT'S 54 MILES SOUTH OF YOU NEAR CHATTANOOGA!

11

-54-

McMinn Co.

-53-

Exit 52
G-Exxon
GldnGln

52 Mt Verd Rd Athens

EXIT 52 - TIME MAGAZINE'S "WORLD'S BEST ICE CREAM"

Exit 52
G-Citgo
L-Motel

-52-

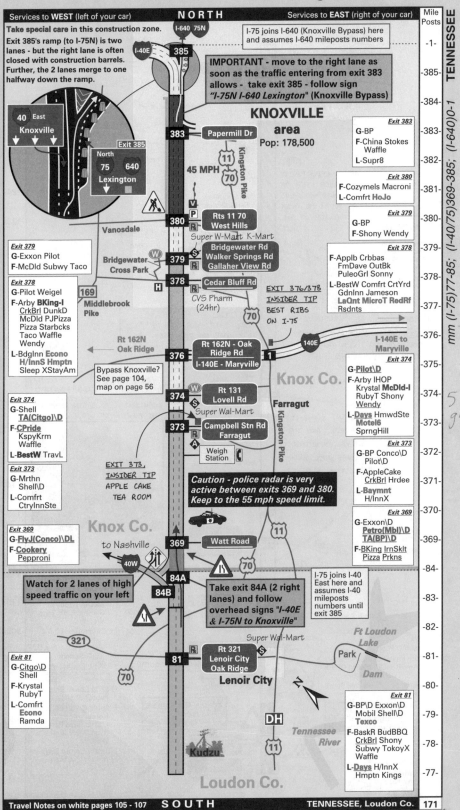

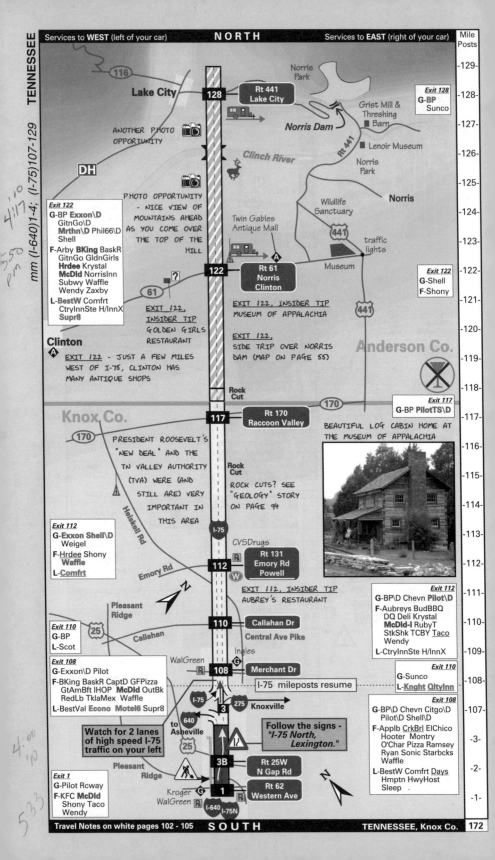

TENNESSEE

mm (I-640)1-4; (I-75)107-129

116

Lake City

128 — Rt 441 Lake City

-129-
-128-

Norris Park

Exit 128
G-BP Sunco

Grist Mill & Threshing Barn

Norris Dam

-127-

ANOTHER PHOTO OPPORTUNITY

Rt 441

Lenoir Museum

-126-

DH

Clinch River

Norris Park

-125-

PHOTO OPPORTUNITY - NICE VIEW OF MOUNTAINS AHEAD AS YOU COME OVER THE TOP OF THE HILL

Twin Gables Antique Mall

Wildlife Sanctuary

441

Norris

traffic lights

-124-
-123-

Exit 122
G-Shell
F-Shony

Exit 122
G-BP Exxon\D
GitnGo\D
Mrthn\D Phil66\D
Shell
F-Arby BKing BaskR
GitnGo GldnGirls
Hrdee Krystal
McDld Norrisinn
Subwy Waffle
Wendy Zaxby
L-BestW Comfrt
CtryInnSte H/InnX
Supr8

61

122 — Rt 61 Norris Clinton

EXIT 122, INSIDER TIP
MUSEUM OF APPALACHIA

EXIT 122, SIDE TRIP OVER NORRIS DAM (MAP ON PAGE 55)

Museum

441

Anderson Co.

-122-
-121-
-120-
-119-

EXIT 122, INSIDER TIP
GOLDEN GIRLS RESTAURANT

Clinton

EXIT 122 - JUST A FEW MILES WEST OF I-75, CLINTON HAS MANY ANTIQUE SHOPS

Rock Cut

117 — Rt 170 Raccoon Valley

170

-118-
-117-

Exit 117
G-BP PilotTS\D

Knox Co.

170

PRESIDENT ROOSEVELT'S "NEW DEAL" AND THE TN VALLEY AUTHORITY (TVA) WERE (AND STILL ARE) VERY IMPORTANT IN THIS AREA

BEAUTIFUL LOG CABIN HOME AT THE MUSEUM OF APPALACHIA

-116-
-115-

Rock Cut

ROCK CUTS? SEE "GEOLOGY" STORY ON PAGE 94

I-75

-114-
-113-

Exit 112
G-Exxon Shell\D
Weigel
F-Hrdee Shony
Waffle
L-Comfrt

Heiskell Rd

CVSDrugs

R
W

112 — Rt 131 Emory Rd Powell

-112-

Emory Rd

EXIT 112, INSIDER TIP
AUBREY'S RESTAURANT

-111-

Exit 112
G-BP\D Chevn Pilot\D
F-Aubreys BudBBQ
DQ Deli Krystal
McDld-I RubyT
StkShk TCBY Taco
Wendy
L-CtryInnSte H/InnX

Pleasant Ridge

25

Callahan

110 — Callahan Dr

Central Ave Pike

-110-
-109-

Exit 110
G-BP
L-Scot

Exit 110
G-Sunco
L-Knght QltyInn

Exit 108
G-Exxon\D Pilot
F-BKing BaskR CaptD GFPizza
GtAmBft IHOP McDld OutBk
RedLb TklaMex Waffle
L-BestVal Econo Motel6 Supr8

WalGreen

R
Ingles
G

108 — Merchant Dr

I-75 mileposts resume

-108-

Exit 108
G-BP\D Chevn Citgo\D
Pilot\D Shell\D
F-Applb CrkBrl ElChico
Hooter Montry
O'Char Pizza Ramsey
Ryan Sonic Starbcks
Waffle
L-BestW Comfrt Days
Hmptn HwyHost
Sleep

I-75

3
275

Knoxville

to Asheville

640

25

-107-

Watch for 2 lanes of high speed I-75 traffic on your left

Follow the signs - "I-75 North, Lexington."

Pleasant Ridge

3B — Rt 25W N Gap Rd

-3-
-2-

Exit 1
G-Pilot Rcway
F-KFC McDld
Shony Taco
Wendy

Kroger
WalGreen
G

1 — Rt 62 Western Ave

R

I-640 I-75N

N

-1-

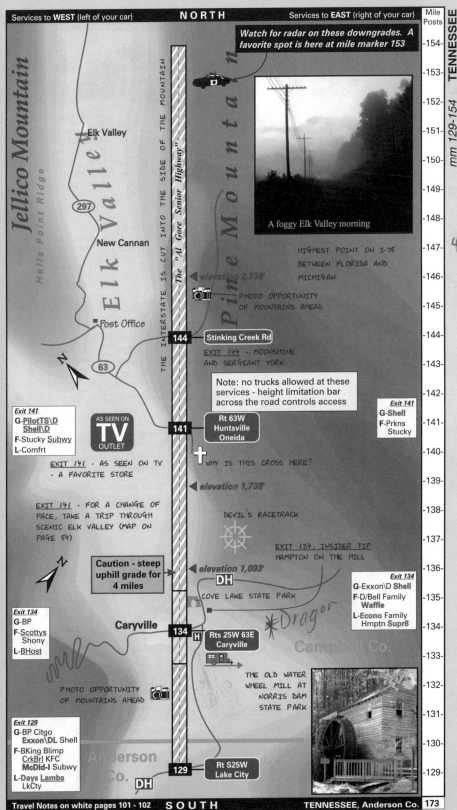

4:41 :10   615

TENNESSEE

mm 129-154

Watch for radar on these downgrades. A favorite spot is here at mile marker 153

-154-
-153-
-152-
-151-
-150-
-149-
-148-

A foggy Elk Valley morning

4:35 :10

HIGHEST POINT ON I-75
BETWEEN FLORIDA AND
MICHIGAN

Jellico Mountain

Hells Point Ridge

Elk Valley

Pine Mountain

297

New Cannan

THE INTERSTATE IS CUT INTO THE SIDE OF THE MOUNTAIN

The "Al Gore Senior Highway"

◄ *elevation 2,238'*

📷 PHOTO OPPORTUNITY
OF MOUNTAINS AHEAD

Post Office

63

-147-
-146-
-145-
-144-

144 ⬛ Stinking Creek Rd

EXIT 144 - MOONSHINE
AND SERGEANT YORK

-143-

Note: no trucks allowed at these
services - height limitation bar
across the road controls access

-142-

AS SEEN ON
TV
OUTLET

141 ⬛ Rt 63W
Huntsville
Oneida

-141-
-140-

EXIT 141 - AS SEEN ON TV
- A FAVORITE STORE

✝ WHY IS THIS CROSS HERE?

◄ *elevation 1,738'*

-139-
-138-

EXIT 141 - FOR A CHANGE OF
PACE, TAKE A TRIP THROUGH
SCENIC ELK VALLEY (MAP ON
PAGE 54)

DEVIL'S RACETRACK

-137-

EXIT 134, INSIDER TIP
HAMPTON ON THE HILL

-136-

Caution - steep
uphill grade for
4 miles

◄ *elevation 1,093'*

DH

COVE LAKE STATE PARK

Dragon

-135-

Caryville

134 ⬛ H ⬛ Rts 25W 63E
Caryville

Campbell Co.

-134-
-133-

PHOTO OPPORTUNITY
OF MOUNTAINS AHEAD 📷

THE OLD WATER
WHEEL MILL AT
NORRIS DAM
STATE PARK

-132-
-131-

*Anderson
Co.*

-130-

129 ⬛ Rt S25W
Lake City

DH

-129-

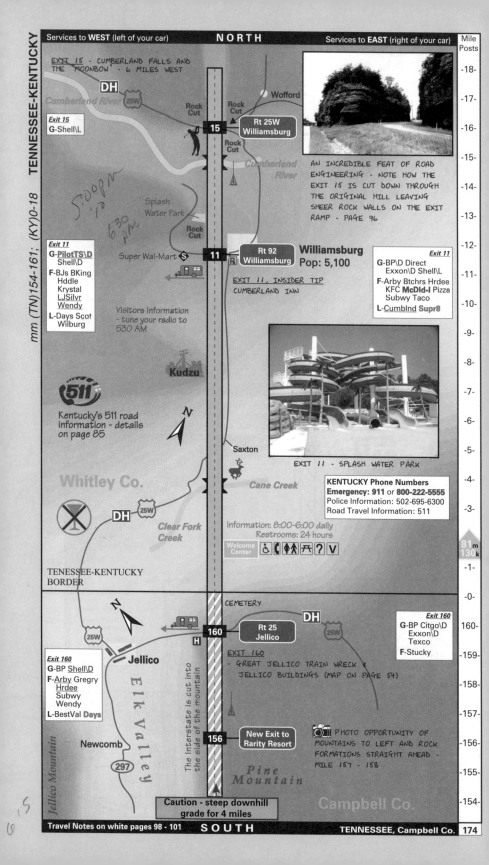

EXIT 15 - CUMBERLAND FALLS AND
THE MOONBOW - 6 MILES WEST

DH

-18-

Cumberland River

25W

Wofford

-17-

Rock Cut

Rock Cut

Rt 25W
Williamsburg

15

-16-

Exit 15
G-Shell\L

Rock Cut

-15-

Cumberland River

AN INCREDIBLE FEAT OF ROAD
ENGINEERING - NOTE HOW THE
EXIT 15 IS CUT DOWN THROUGH
THE ORIGINAL HILL LEAVING
SHEER ROCK WALLS ON THE EXIT
RAMP - PAGE 96

-14-

5:00pm

-13-

6:30 pm

Splash
Water Park

Rock Cut

Exit 11
G-PilotTS\D
Shell\D
F-BJs BKing
Hddle
Krystal
LJSilvr
Wendy
L-Days Scot
Wilburg

Super Wal-Mart

11

Rt 92
Williamsburg

Williamsburg
Pop: 5,100

-12-

R

EXIT 11, INSIDER TIP
CUMBERLAND INN

Exit 11
G-BP\D Direct
Exxon\D Shell\L
F-Arby Btchrs Hrdee
KFC **McDld-I** Pizza
Subwy Taco
L-CumbInd **Supr8**

-11-

Visitors Information
- tune your radio to
530 AM

-10-

-9-

Kudzu

-8-

-7-

511

Kentucky's 511 road
information - details
on page 85

-6-

N

-5-

Saxton

EXIT 11 - SPLASH WATER PARK

Whitley Co.

-4-

Cane Creek

**KENTUCKY Phone Numbers
Emergency: 911** or **800-222-5555**
Police Information: 502-695-3300
Road Travel Information: 511

DH

25W

-3-

Clear Fork
Creek

Information: 8:00-6:00 daily
Restrooms: 24 hours

Welcome Center ♿ 🚻 🚹🚺 🪑 ? V

81 m
130 k

TENESSEE-KENTUCKY
BORDER

-1-

-0-

CEMETERY

25W

DH

25W

160-

N

160

Rt 25
Jellico

Exit 160
G-BP Citgo\D
Exxon\D
Texco
F-Stucky

H

Jellico

EXIT 160
- GREAT JELLICO TRAIN WRECK &
JELLICO BUILDINGS (MAP ON PAGE 54)

-159-

Exit 160
G-BP Shell\D
F-Arby Gregry
Hrdee
Subwy
Wendy
L-BestVal Days

E l k   V a l l e y

-158-

-157-

The Interstate is cut into
the side of the mountain

Newcomb

156

New Exit to
Rarity Resort

📷 PHOTO OPPORTUNITY OF
MOUNTAINS TO LEFT AND ROCK
FORMATIONS STRAIGHT AHEAD -
MILE 157 - 158

-156-

297

Pine
Mountain

-155-

Jellico Mountain

Caution - steep downhill
grade for 4 miles

Campbell Co.

-154-

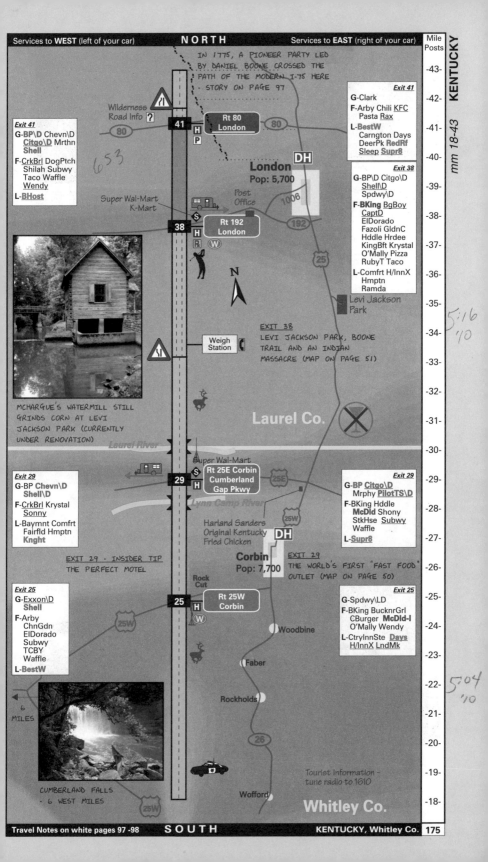

IN 1775, A PIONEER PARTY LED BY DANIEL BOONE CROSSED THE PATH OF THE MODERN I-75 HERE - STORY ON PAGE 97

Wilderness Road Info ?

Rt 80 London — 80

Exit 41
G-BP\D Chevn\D Citgo\D Mrthn Shell
F-CrkBrl DogPtch Shilah Subwy Taco Waffle Wendy
L-BHost

Super Wal-Mart K-Mart

Rt 192 London

Post Office

London Pop: 5,700 DH

Exit 41
G-Clark
F-Arby Chili KFC Pasta Rax
L-BestW Carngton Days DeerPk RedRf Sleep Supr8

Exit 38
G-BP\D Citgo\D Shell\D Spdwy\D
F-BKing BgBoy CaptD ElDorado Fazoli GldnC Hddle Hrdee KingBft Krystal O'Mally Pizza RubyT Taco
L-Comfrt H/InnX Hmptn Ramda

Levi Jackson Park

EXIT 38
LEVI JACKSON PARK, BOONE TRAIL AND AN INDIAN MASSACRE (MAP ON PAGE 51)

Weigh Station

Laurel Co.

MCHARGUE'S WATERMILL STILL GRINDS CORN AT LEVI JACKSON PARK (CURRENTLY UNDER RENOVATION)

Laurel River

Super Wal-Mart

Rt 25E Corbin Cumberland Gap Pkwy — 25E

Lynn Camp River

Exit 29
G-BP Chevn\D Shell\D
F-CrkBrl Krystal Sonny
L-Baymnt Comfrt Fairfld Hmptn Knght

Exit 29
G-BP Citgo\D Mrphy PilotTS\D
F-BKing Hddle McDld Shony StkHse Subwy Waffle
L-Supr8

Harland Sanders Original Kentucky Fried Chicken DH

Corbin Pop: 7,700

EXIT 29 - INSIDER TIP THE PERFECT MOTEL

EXIT 29
THE WORLD'S FIRST "FAST FOOD" OUTLET (MAP ON PAGE 50)

Rock Cut

Rt 25W Corbin

Exit 25
G-Exxon\D Shell
F-Arby ChnGdn ElDorado Subwy TCBY Waffle
L-BestW

Exit 25
G-Spdwy\LD
F-BKing BucknrGrl CBurger McDld-I O'Mally Wendy
L-CtryInnSte Days H/InnX LndMk

Woodbine

Faber

Rockholds

6 MILES

CUMBERLAND FALLS - 6 WEST MILES

Wofford

Tourist Information - tune radio to 1610

Whitley Co.

Services to **WEST** (left of your car) **N O R T H** Services to **EAST** (right of your car) Mile Posts

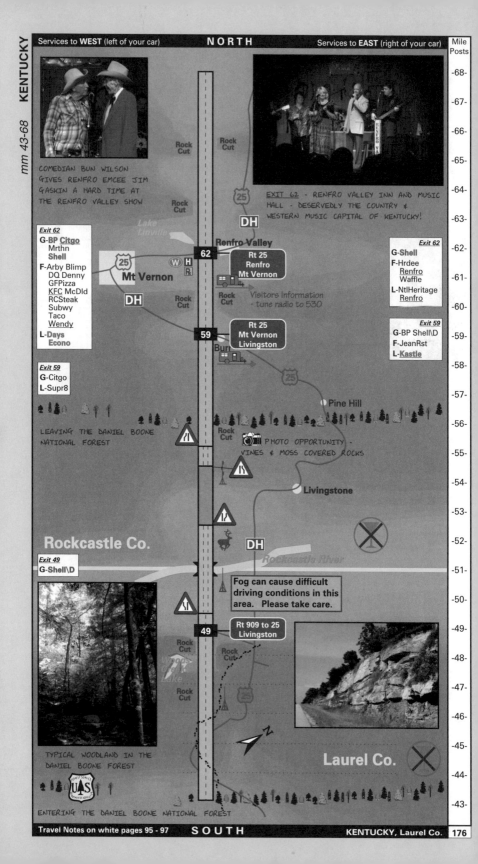

COMEDIAN BUN WILSON GIVES RENFRO EMCEE JIM GASKIN A HARD TIME AT THE RENFRO VALLEY SHOW

EXIT 62 - RENFRO VALLEY INN AND MUSIC HALL - DESERVEDLY THE COUNTRY & WESTERN MUSIC CAPITAL OF KENTUCKY!

Rock Cut

Rock Cut

Rock Cut

Rock Cut

Lake Linville

Exit 62
G-BP <u>Citgo</u>
Mrthn
Shell
F-Arby Blimp
DQ Denny
GFPizza
<u>KFC</u> McDld
RCSteak
Subwy
Taco
<u>Wendy</u>
L-Days
Econo

Renfro Valley

Rt 25
Renfro
Mt Vernon

Mt Vernon

Visitors Information
- tune radio to 530

Exit 62
G-Shell
F-Hrdee
<u>Renfro</u>
Waffle
L-NtlHeritage
<u>Renfro</u>

Rt 25
Mt Vernon
Livingston

Exit 59
G-BP Shell\D
F-JeanRst
L-<u>Kastle</u>

Exit 59
G-Citgo
L-Supr8

Burr

Pine Hill

LEAVING THE DANIEL BOONE NATIONAL FOREST

PHOTO OPPORTUNITY - VINES & MOSS COVERED ROCKS

Livingstone

Rockcastle Co.

Rockcastle River

Exit 49
G-Shell\D

Fog can cause difficult driving conditions in this area. Please take care.

Rt 909 to 25
Livingston

Rock Cut

Rock Cut

Rock Cut

Woods of Lake

TYPICAL WOODLAND IN THE DANIEL BOONE FOREST

Laurel Co.

ENTERING THE DANIEL BOONE NATIONAL FOREST

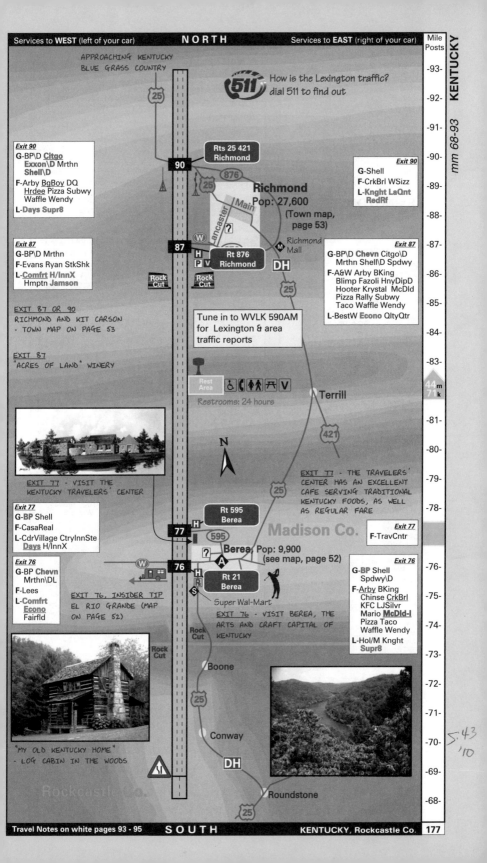

APPROACHING KENTUCKY
BLUE GRASS COUNTRY

25

-93-
-92-
-91-
-90-

511 How is the Lexington traffic?
dial 511 to find out

Rts 25 421
Richmond

876

Richmond
Pop: 27,600
(Town map,
page 53)

25

Main
Lancaster

90

Exit 90
G-BP\D Citgo
Exxon\D Mrthn
Shell\D
F-Arby BgBoy DQ
Hrdee Pizza Subwy
Waffle Wendy
L-Days Supr8

Exit 90
G-Shell
F-CrkBrl WSizz
L-Knght LaQnt
RedRf

-89-
-88-
-87-

Richmond
Mall

87

W
H
P V

Rt 876
Richmond

DH

25

M

Exit 87
G-BP\D Mrthn
F-Evans Ryan StkShk
L-Comfrt H/InnX
Hmptn Jamson

Rock
Cut

Rock
Cut

Exit 87
G-BP\D Chevn Citgo\D
Mrthn Shell\D Spdwy
F-A&W Arby BKing
Blimp Fazoli HnyDipD
Hooter Krystal McDld
Pizza Rally Subwy
Taco Waffle Wendy
L-BestW Econo QltyQtr

-86-
-85-
-84-

EXIT 87 OR 90
RICHMOND AND KIT CARSON
- TOWN MAP ON PAGE 53

Tune in to WVLK 590AM
for Lexington & area
traffic reports

EXIT 87
"ACRES OF LAND" WINERY

-83-

Rest
Area

♿ 🍴 🚻 ⛽ V

Restrooms: 24 hours

Terrill

44 m
71 k

-82-
-81-

421

N

-80-

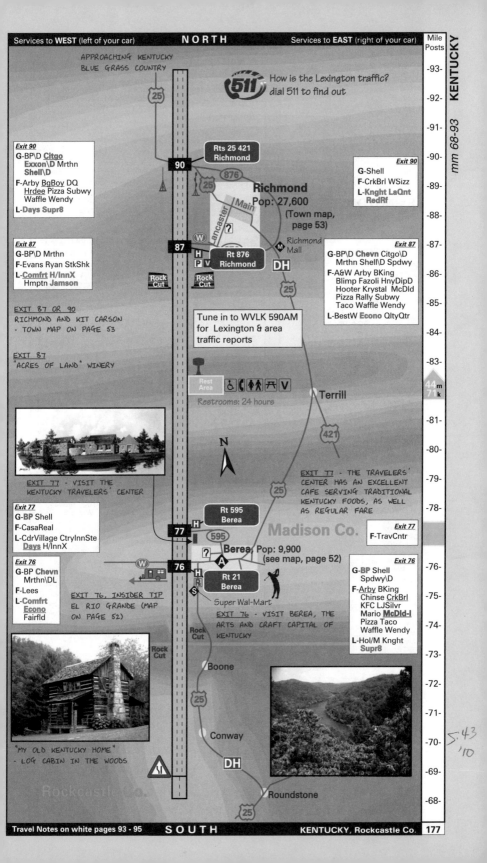

EXIT 77 - VISIT THE
KENTUCKY TRAVELERS' CENTER

25

EXIT 77 - THE TRAVELERS'
CENTER HAS AN EXCELLENT
CAFE SERVING TRADITIONAL
KENTUCKY FOODS, AS WELL
AS REGULAR FARE

-79-
-78-

Exit 77
G-BP Shell
F-CasaReal
L-CdrVillage CtryInnSte
Days H/InnX

77

H

Rt 595
Berea

595

Madison Co.

Exit 77
F-TravCntr

Berea, Pop: 9,900
(see map, page 52)

?
A

-77-

Exit 76
G-BP Chevn
Mrthn\DL
F-Lees
L-Comfrt
Econo
Fairfld

76

W

EXIT 76, INSIDER TIP
EL RIO GRANDE (MAP
ON PAGE 52)

H
R
S

Rt 21
Berea

Super Wal-Mart

EXIT 76 - VISIT BEREA, THE
ARTS AND CRAFT CAPITAL OF
KENTUCKY

Exit 76
G-BP Shell
Spdwy\D
F-Arby BKing
Chinse CrkBrl
KFC LJSilvr
Mario McDld-I
Pizza Taco
Waffle Wendy
L-Hol/M Knght
Supr8

-76-
-75-
-74-
-73-

Rock
Cut

Rock
Cut

Boone

25

-72-
-71-

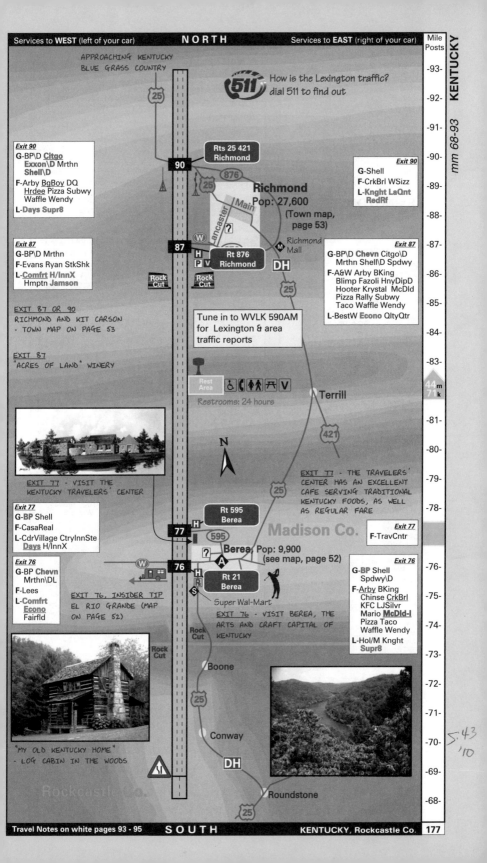

"MY OLD KENTUCKY HOME"
- LOG CABIN IN THE WOODS

Conway

DH

-70-

S:43
'10

Rockcastle Co.

-69-

Roundstone

25

-68-

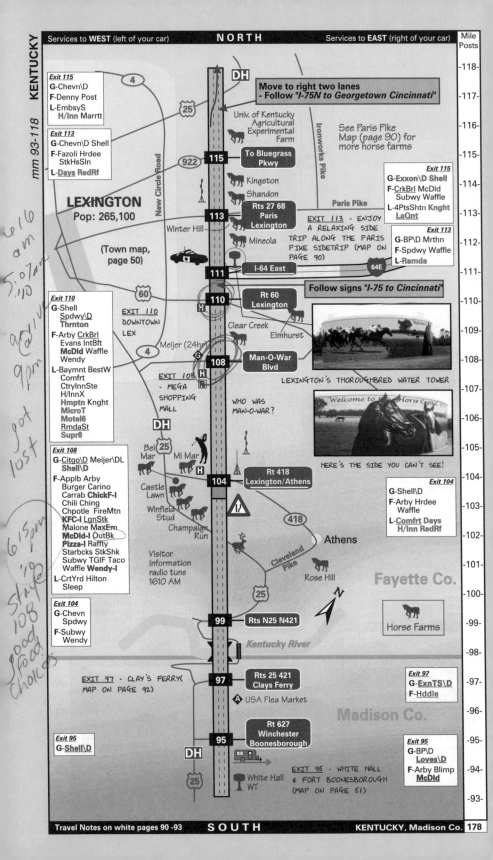

Handwritten margin notes (left side):
616 am
5:07 am
5:10
a drive
9pm
got lost
615pm stayed 108 good food choices

-118-
-117-

DH

Move to right two lanes
- Follow "I-75N to Georgetown Cincinnati"

Exit 115
G-Chevn\D
F-Denny Post
L-EmbsyS
H/Inn Marrtt

4
25

Univ. of Kentucky
Agricultural
Experimental
Farm

Ironworks Pike

See Paris Pike
Map (page 90) for
more horse farms

-116-

Exit 113
G-Chevn\D Shell
F-Fazoli Hrdee
StkHsSln
L-Days RedRf

922

115

To Bluegrass
Pkwy

Kingston

Exit 115
G-Exxon\D Shell
F-CrkBrl McDld
Subwy Waffle
L-4PtsShtn Knght
LaQnt

-115-
-114-

Shandon

LEXINGTON
Pop: 265,100

New Circle Road

113

Rts 27 68
Paris
Lexington

Paris Pike

Exit 113
G-BP\D Mrthn
F-Spdwy Waffle
L-Ramda

-113-

Winter Hill

Mineola

EXIT 113 - ENJOY
A RELAXING SIDE
TRIP ALONG THE PARIS
PIKE SIDETRIP (MAP ON
PAGE 90)

-112-

(Town map,
page 50)

111

I-64 East

64E

-111-

60

110

Rt 60
Lexington

Follow signs "I-75 to Cincinnati"

-110-

EXIT 110
DOWNTOWN
LEX

Clear Creek

Elmhurst

-109-

Exit 110
G-Shell
Spdwy\D
Thrnton
F-Arby CrkBrl
Evans IntBft
McDld Waffle
Wendy
L-Baymnt BestW
Comfrt
CtrylnnSte
H/InnX
Hmptn Knght
MicroT
Motel6
RmdaSt
Supr8

4

Meijer (24hr)
G

108

Man-O-War
Blvd

LEXINGTON'S THOROUGHBRED WATER TOWER

-108-

EXIT 108
- MEGA
SHOPPING
MALL

WHO WAS
MAN-O-WAR?

Welcome to the Horse Capital

-107-

-106-

DH
25

Bel
Mar

Mi Mar

HERE'S THE SIDE YOU CAN'T SEE!

-105-

Exit 108
G-Citgo\D Meijer\DL
Shell\D
F-Applb Arby
Burger Carino
Carrab ChickF-I
Chili Ching
Chpotle FireMtn
KFC-I LgnStk
Malone MaxEm
McDld-I OutBk
Pizza-I Raffty
Starbcks StkShk
Subwy TGIF Taco
Waffle Wendy-I
L-CrtYrd Hilton
Sleep

Castle
Lawn

Winfield
Stud

104

Rt 418
Lexington/Athens

418

Exit 104
G-Shell\D
F-Arby Hrdee
Waffle
L-Comfrt Days
H/Inn RedRf

-104-

-103-

Champaign
Run

Athens

-102-

Exit 104
G-Chevn
Spdwy
F-Subwy
Wendy

Visitor
Information
radio tune
1610 AM

Cleveland Pike

Rose Hill

Fayette Co.

-101-

25

-100-

99

Rts N25 N421

Horse Farms

-99-

Kentucky River

-98-

EXIT 97 - CLAY'S FERRY
(MAP ON PAGE 92)

97

Rts 25 421
Clays Ferry

USA Flea Market

Madison Co.

Exit 97
G-ExnTS\D
F-Hddle

-97-

-96-

Exit 95
G-Shell\D

95

Rt 627
Winchester
Boonesborough

White Hall
WT

EXIT 95 - WHITE HALL
& FORT BOONESBOROUGH
(MAP ON PAGE 51)

Exit 95
G-BP\D
Loves\D
F-Arby Blimp
McDld

-95-

DH
25

-94-

-93-

mm 118-143

Scott Co.

Stonewall

(25)

WHITE (AND SOMETIMES, BLACK) FENCES MEAN WE ARE STILL IN KENTUCKY'S FAMOUS HORSE FARM COUNTRY
WHY BLACK? SEE PAGE 91

North Rays River

Sadieville

Exit 136
G-Mrthn

136 Rt 32 Sadieville

DH

N

WELDING A CAR BODY AT THE TOYOTA PLANT

(25)

620

Weigh Station

Exit 129
G-PilotTS\D Shell
F-McDld

129 Rt 620 Delaplain Rd

Delaplain
Railroad yards
No Information
Restrooms: 24 hours

1387

TOYOTA PLANT TOURS

Exit 129
G-PilotTS\D
F-Grdma GtAmBft Subwy Waffle Wendy
L-Days Motel6

49 m
79 k

Factory Stores of America

Rest Area ♿ 🚻 🏕 ⛽ V

62

Super Wal-Mart WinnDixie

see map page 52

Georgetown
Pop: 18,000

460

H
?
O

126 Rt 62-Georgetown Cynthiana

125 Rt 460-Georgetown Paris

Exit 126
G-BP Mrphy\D Shell
F-Arby BgBoy McDld PlumTree
L-Econo

K-Mart

EXIT 125 - VICTORIAN GEORGETOWN, (TOWN MAP ON PAGE 52)

If you exit at 125, re-enter I-75N by following the Service Road on the east side of the freeway, northwards to exit 126

Exit 125/126
G-BP\L Citgo Mrthn Shell Spdwy\D Swfty
F-Applb CrkBrl DQ Fazoli KFC LJSilvr RubyT Subwy Taco Waffle Wendy
L-BestW Comfrt CtryInnSte Fairfld Hmptn IvyLdg MicroT Supr8 WCirc

DH
(25)

NEED WINE OR BEER?

Scott Co.

Exit 120
G-Citgo\D

120 Rt 1973 Ironworks Pike

Fayette Co.

Flying I Ranch

Kentucky Horse Park

EXIT 120
KENTUCKY HORSE PARK
(1/4 MILE TO EAST)

118

I-64 West Frankfort Louisville
64W

Ironworks Pike

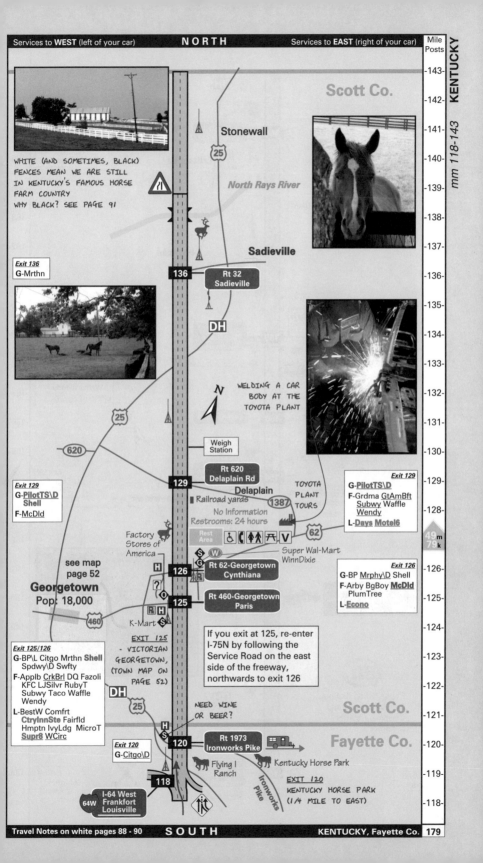

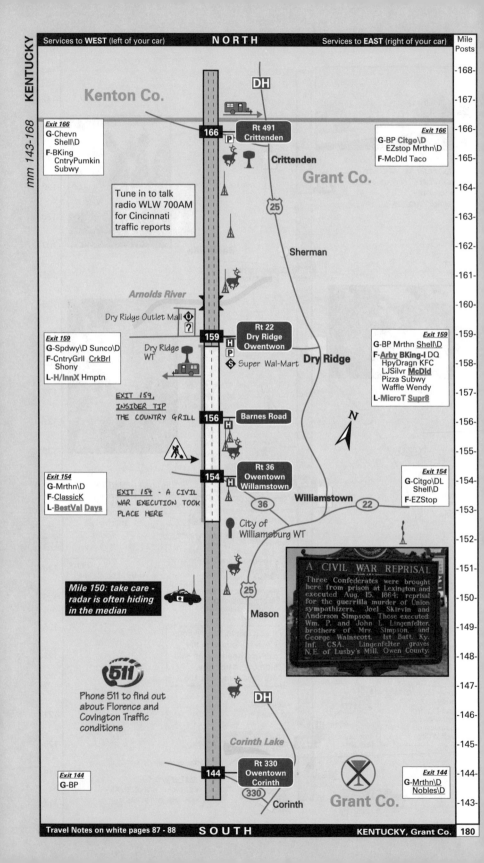

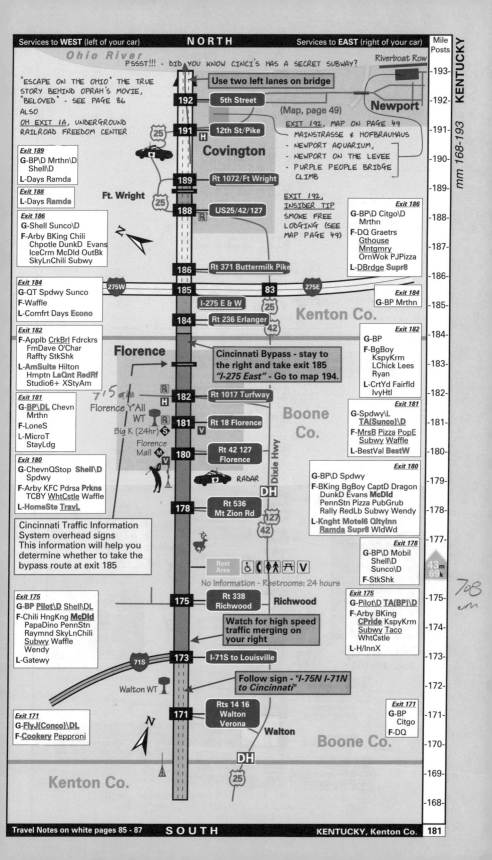

Ohio River

PSSST!!! - DID YOU KNOW CINCI'S HAS A SECRET SUBWAY?

Riverboat Row

-193-

Use two left lanes on bridge

"ESCAPE ON THE OHIO" THE TRUE
STORY BEHIND OPRAH'S MOVIE,
"BELOVED" - SEE PAGE 86
ALSO

OH EXIT 1A, UNDERGROUND
RAILROAD FREEDOM CENTER

192 | 5th Street

(Map, page 49)

Newport

-192-

191 | 12th St/Pike

US 25

H

EXIT 192, MAP ON PAGE 49
- MAINSTRASSE & HOFBRAUHAUS
- NEWPORT AQUARIUM,
- NEWPORT ON THE LEVEE
- PURPLE PEOPLE BRIDGE
  CLIMB

Covington

-191-

-190-

mm 168-193

Exit 189
G-BP\D Mrthn\D
Shell\D
L-Days Ramda

189 | Rt 1072/Ft Wright

US 25

Ft. Wright

EXIT 192,
INSIDER TIP
SMOKE FREE
LODGING (SEE
MAP PAGE 49)

-189-

188 | US25/42/127

R

Exit 186
G-BP\D Citgo\D
Mrthn
F-DQ Graetrs
Gthouse
Mntgmry
OrnWok PJPizza
L-DBrdge Supr8

-188-

Exit 188
L-Days Ramda

Exit 186
G-Shell Sunco\D
F-Arby BKing Chili
Chpotle DunkD Evans
IceCrm McDld OutBk
SkyLnChili Subwy

186 | Rt 371 Buttermilk Pike

-187-

-186-

Exit 184
G-BP Mrthn

Exit 184
G-QT Spdwy Sunco
F-Waffle
L-Comfrt Days Econo

275W | **185** | **83** | **275E**

I-275 E & W | US 25

184 | Rt 236 Erlanger

Kenton Co.

-185-

US 42

-184-

Florence

**Cincinnati Bypass - stay to
the right and take exit 185
"I-275 East" - Go to map 194.**

Exit 182
G-BP
F-BgBoy
KspyKrm
LChick Lees
Ryan
L-CrtYd Fairfld
IvyHtl

Exit 182
F-Applb CrkBrl Fdrckrs
FmDave O'Char
Raffty StkShk
L-AmSuite Hilton
Hmptn LaQnt RedRf
Studio6+ XStyAm

-183-

**Boone
Co.**

7:15 am

R
H

182 | Rt 1017 Turfway

-182-

Exit 181
G-BP\DL Chevn
Mrthn
F-LoneS
L-MicroT
StayLdg

Florence Y'All
WT
Big K (24hr)

R
V
S

181 | Rt 18 Florence

Exit 181
G-Spdwy\L
TA(Sunco)\D
F-MrsB Pizza PopE
Subwy Waffle
L-BestVal BestW

-181-

Florence
Mall

M
V

180 | Rt 42 127
Florence

Exit 180
G-ChevnQStop Shell\D
Spdwy
F-Arby KFC Pdrsa Prkns
TCBY WhtCstle Waffle
L-HomeSte TravL

RADAR

DH

Exit 180
G-BP\D Spdwy
F-BKing BgBoy CaptD Dragon
DunkD Evans McDld
PennStn Pizza PubGrub
Rally RedLb Subwy Wendy
L-Knght Motel6 QltyInn
Ramda Supr8 WldWd

-179-

178 | Rt 536
Mt Zion Rd

US 127
US 42

-178-

Cincinnati Traffic Information
System overhead signs
This information will help you
determine whether to take the
bypass route at exit 185

-177-

Rest
Area | ♿ 🚻 👨‍👩‍👧 🏕 V

Exit 178
G-BP\D Mobil
Shell\D
Sunco\D
F-StkShk

43 m
69 k

No Information - Restrooms: 24 hours

-176-

Exit 175
G-BP Pilot\D Shell\DL
F-Chili HngKng McDld
PapaDino PennStn
Raymnd SkyLnChili
Subwy Waffle
Wendy
L-Gatewy

175 | Rt 338
Richwood | **Richwood**

Exit 175
G-Pilot\D TA(BP)\D
F-Arby BKing
CPride KspyKrm McDld
Subwy Taco
WhtCstle
L-H/InnX

-175-

-174-

**Watch for high speed
traffic merging on
your right**

71S | **173** | I-71S to Louisville

-173-

Walton WT

**Follow sign - "I-75N I-71N
to Cincinnati"**

-172-

N

Exit 171
G-FlyJ(Conco)\DL
F-Cookery Pepproni

171 | Rts 14 16
Walton
Verona | **Walton**

Exit 171
G-BP
Citgo
F-DQ

-171-

Boone Co.

-170-

DH

US 25

Kenton Co.

-169-

-168-

leave 830 am
stop 745 am

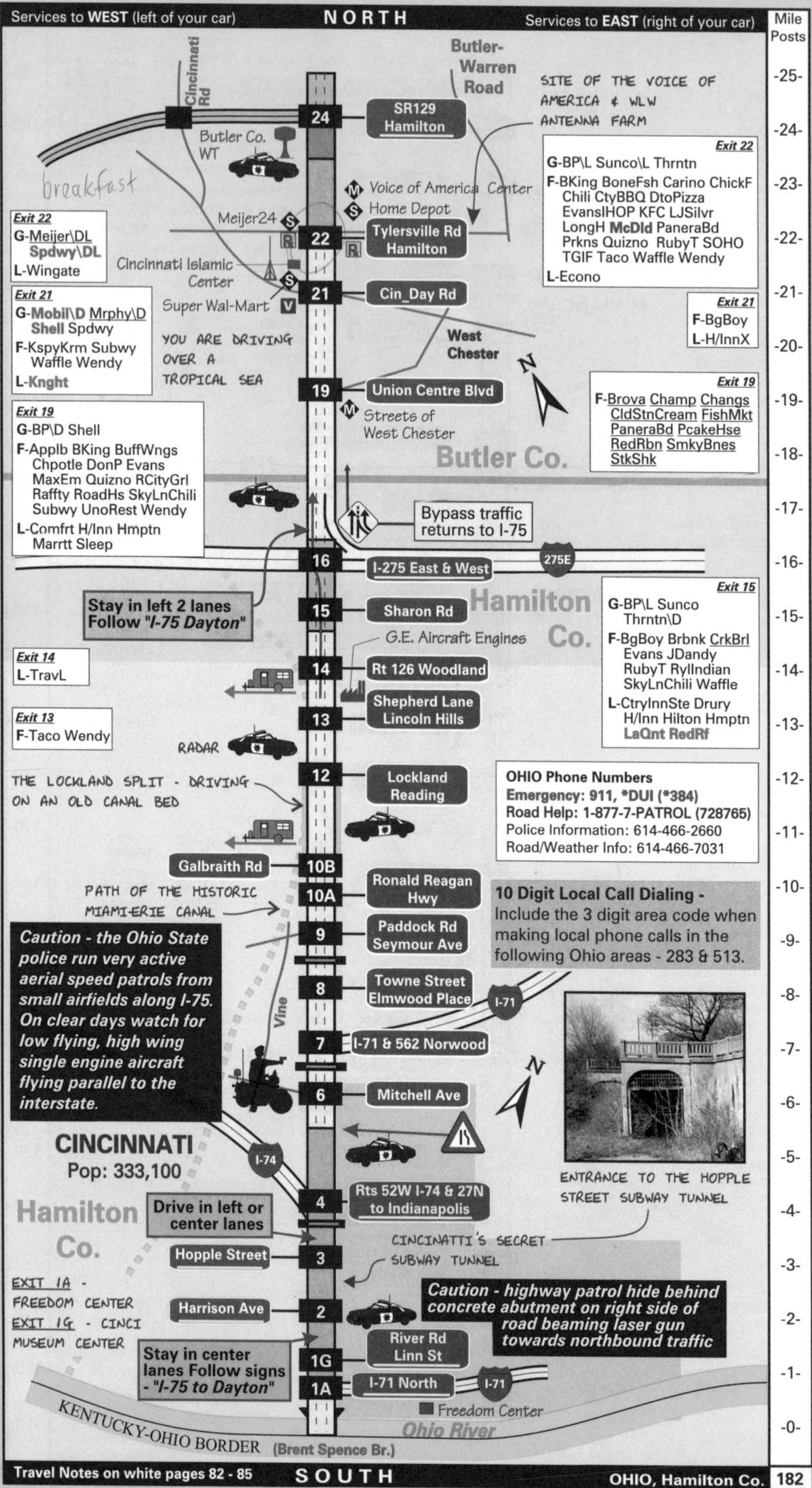
Services to WEST (left of your car)
NORTH
Services to EAST (right of your car)
Mile Posts
Butler-Warren Road
Cincinnati Rd
SITE OF THE VOICE OF AMERICA & WLW ANTENNA FARM
24
SR129 Hamilton
Butler Co. WT
breakfast
Exit 22
G-BP\L Sunco\L Thrntn
F-BKing BoneFsh Carino ChickF Chili CtyBBQ DtoPizza EvansIHOP KFC LJSilvr LongH McDld PaneraBd Prkns Quizno RubyT SOHO TGIF Taco Waffle Wendy
L-Econo
Voice of America Center
Home Depot
Meijer24
Exit 22
G-Meijer\DL Spdwy\DL
L-Wingate
22
Tylersville Rd Hamilton
Cincinnati Islamic Center
21
Cin_Day Rd
Super Wal-Mart
Exit 21
G-Mobil\D Mrphy\D Shell Spdwy
F-KspyKrm Subwy Waffle Wendy
L-Knght
Exit 21
F-BgBoy
L-H/InnX
West Chester
YOU ARE DRIVING OVER A TROPICAL SEA
19
Union Centre Blvd
Exit 19
F-Brova Champ Changs CldStnCream FishMkt PaneraBd PcakeHse RedRbn SmkyBnes StkShk
Streets of West Chester
Exit 19
G-BP\D Shell
F-Applb BKing BuffWngs Chpotle DonP Evans MaxEm Quizno RCityGrl Raffty RoadHs SkyLnChili Subwy UnoRest Wendy
L-Comfrt H/Inn Hmptn Marrtt Sleep
Butler Co.
Bypass traffic returns to I-75
16
I-275 East & West
275E
Stay in left 2 lanes Follow "I-75 Dayton"
15
Sharon Rd
Hamilton Co.
Exit 15
G-BP\L Sunco Thrntn\D
F-BgBoy Brbnk CrkBrl Evans JDandy RubyT RylIndian SkyLnChili Waffle
L-CtryInnSte Drury H/Inn Hilton Hmptn LaQnt RedRf
G.E. Aircraft Engines
Exit 14
L-TravL
14
Rt 126 Woodland
Shepherd Lane Lincoln Hills
13
Exit 13
F-Taco Wendy
RADAR
12
Lockland Reading
THE LOCKLAND SPLIT - DRIVING ON AN OLD CANAL BED
OHIO Phone Numbers
Emergency: 911, *DUI (*384)
Road Help: 1-877-7-PATROL (728765)
Police Information: 614-466-2660
Road/Weather Info: 614-466-7031
Galbraith Rd
10B
10A
Ronald Reagan Hwy
PATH OF THE HISTORIC MIAMI-ERIE CANAL
10 Digit Local Call Dialing - Include the 3 digit area code when making local phone calls in the following Ohio areas - 283 & 513.
Caution - the Ohio State police run very active aerial speed patrols from small airfields along I-75. On clear days watch for low flying, high wing single engine aircraft flying parallel to the interstate.
9
Paddock Rd Seymour Ave
8
Towne Street Elmwood Place
I-71
Vine
7
I-71 & 562 Norwood
6
Mitchell Ave
CINCINNATI
Pop: 333,100
I-74
4
Rts 52W I-74 & 27N to Indianapolis
ENTRANCE TO THE HOPPLE STREET SUBWAY TUNNEL
Hamilton Co.
Drive in left or center lanes
Hopple Street
3
CINCINATTI'S SECRET SUBWAY TUNNEL
EXIT 1A - FREEDOM CENTER
EXIT 1G - CINCI MUSEUM CENTER
Harrison Ave
2
Caution - highway patrol hide behind concrete abutment on right side of road beaming laser gun towards northbound traffic
Stay in center lanes Follow signs - "I-75 to Dayton"
1G
River Rd Linn St
1A
I-71 North
I-71
Freedom Center
Ohio River
KENTUCKY-OHIO BORDER (Brent Spence Br.)
-25- -24- -23- -22- -21- -20- -19- -18- -17- -16- -15- -14- -13- -12- -11- -10- -9- -8- -7- -6- -5- -4- -3- -2- -1- -0-

723

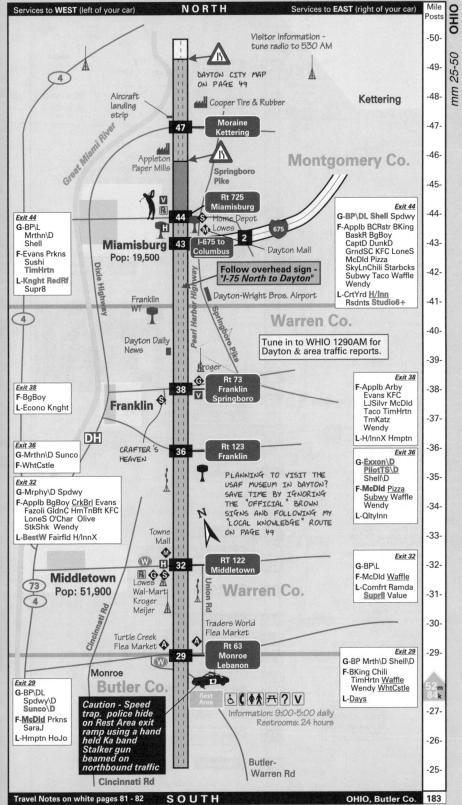

851

Visitor Information - tune radio to 530 AM

DAYTON CITY MAP ON PAGE 49

Cooper Tire & Rubber

Kettering

Aircraft landing strip

47 Moraine Kettering

-50-
-49-
-48-
-47-
-46-

Appleton Paper Mills

Springboro Pike

Montgomery Co.

-45-

44 Rt 725 Miamisburg
Home Depot
Lowes
675
2

Exit 44
G-BP\DL Shell Spdwy
F-Applb BCRstr BKing
BaskR BgBoy
CaptD DunkD
GrndSC KFC LoneS
McDld Pizza
SkyLnChili Starbcks
Subwy Taco Waffle
Wendy
L-CrtYrd H/Inn
Rsdnts Studio6+

-44-
-43-
-42-

43 I-675 to Columbus

Exit 44
G-BP\L
Mrthn\D
Shell
F-Evans Prkns
Sushi
TimHrtn
L-Knght RedRf
Supr8

Miamisburg
Pop: 19,500

Dayton Mall

Follow overhead sign - "I-75 North to Dayton"

Dayton-Wright Bros. Airport

Dixie Highway

Franklin WT

Warren Co.

-41-
-40-

Dayton Daily News

Tune in to WHIO 1290AM for Dayton & area traffic reports.

Kroger

Pearl Harbor Highway

Springboro Pike

-39-

Exit 38
F-BgBoy
L-Econo Knght

38 Rt 73 Franklin Springboro

Franklin

Exit 38
F-Applb Arby
Evans KFC
LJSilvr McDld
Taco TimHrtn
TmKatz
Wendy
L-H/InnX Hmptn

-38-
-37-

DH

CRAFTER'S HEAVEN

36 Rt 123 Franklin

-36-

Exit 36
G-Mrthn\D Sunco
F-WhtCstle

Exit 36
G-Exxon\D
PilotTS\D
Shell\D
F-McDld Pizza
Subwy Waffle
Wendy
L-QltyInn

-35-
-34-

Exit 32
G-Mrphy\D Spdwy
F-Applb BgBoy CrkBrl Evans
Fazoli GldnC HmTnBft KFC
LoneS O'Char Olive
StkShk Wendy
L-BestW Fairfld H/InnX

PLANNING TO VISIT THE USAF MUSEUM IN DAYTON? SAVE TIME BY IGNORING THE "OFFICIAL" BROWN SIGNS AND FOLLOWING MY "LOCAL KNOWLEDGE" ROUTE ON PAGE 49

N

-33-

Towne Mall

32 RT 122 Middletown

Exit 32
G-BP\L
F-McDld Waffle
L-Comfrt Ramda
Supr8 Value

-32-
-31-

Middletown
Pop: 51,900

73
4

Lowes
Wal-Mart
Kroger
Meijer

Union Rd

Warren Co.

-30-

Traders World Flea Market

Rt 63 Monroe Lebanon

Exit 29
G-BP Mrth\D Shell\D
F-BKing Chili
TimHrtn Waffle
Wendy WhtCstle
L-Days

-29-

Cincinnati Rd

Turtle Creek Flea Market

29

Monroe

Butler Co.

52 m
84 k

-28-

Exit 29
G-BP\DL
Spdwy\D
Sunco\D
F-McDld Prkns
SaraJ
L-Hmptn HoJo

Caution - Speed trap. police hide on Rest Area exit ramp using a hand held Ka band Stalker gun beamed on northbound traffic

Rest Area

♿ ☕ 🚶 ♿ ? V

Information: 9:00-5:00 daily
Restrooms: 24 hours

Butler-Warren Rd

-27-
-26-
-25-

Cincinnati Rd

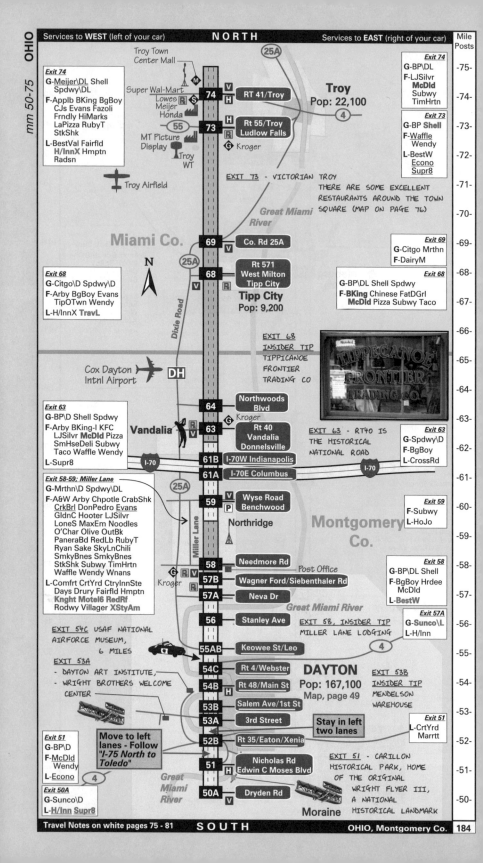

Exit 74
G-Meijer\DL Shell
Spdwy\DL
F-Applb BKing BgBoy
CJs Evans Fazoli
Frndly HiMarks
LaPizza RubyT
StkShk
L-BestVal Fairfld
H/InnX Hmptn
Radsn

25A

Troy Town Center Mall

Super Wal-Mart
Lowes
Meijer
Honda

74 — RT 41/Troy

Troy
Pop: 22,100

Exit 74
G-BP\DL
F-LJSilvr
McDld
Subwy
TimHrtn

-75-

-74-

73 — Rt 55/Troy
Ludlow Falls

MT Picture Display

Troy WT

Kroger

Exit 73
G-BP Shell
F-**Waffle**
Wendy
L-BestW
Econo
Supr8

-73-

-72-

Troy Airfield

EXIT 73 - VICTORIAN TROY
THERE ARE SOME EXCELLENT
RESTAURANTS AROUND THE TOWN
SQUARE (MAP ON PAGE 76)

Great Miami River

-71-

-70-

Miami Co.

N

69 — Co. Rd 25A

Exit 69
G-Citgo Mrthn
F-DairyM

-69-

25A

Exit 68
G-Citgo\D Spdwy\D
F-Arby BgBoy Evans
TipOTwn Wendy
L-H/InnX TravL

68 — Rt 571
West Milton
Tipp City

Tipp City
Pop: 9,200

Exit 68
G-BP\DL Shell Spdwy
F-BKing Chinese FatDGrl
McDld Pizza Subwy Taco

-68-

-67-

EXIT 68
INSIDER TIP
TIPPICANOE
FRONTIER
TRADING CO

-66-

-65-

Cox Dayton Intnl Airport

DH

-64-

Exit 63
G-BP\D Shell Spdwy
F-Arby BKing-I KFC
LJSilvr **McDld** Pizza
SmHseDeli Subwy
Taco Waffle Wendy
L-Supr8

64 — Northwoods Blvd

Kroger

Vandalia

63 — Rt 40
Vandalia
Donnelsville

EXIT 63 - RT40 IS
THE HISTORICAL
NATIONAL ROAD

Exit 63
G-Spdwy\D
F-BgBoy
L-CrossRd

-63-

-62-

I-70

61B — I-70W Indianapolis

61A — I-70E Columbus

I-70

-61-

25A

Exit 58-59; Miller Lane
G-Mrthn\D Spdwy\DL
F-A&W Arby Chpotle CrabShk
CrkBrl DonPedro Evans
GldnC Hooter LJSilvr
LoneS MaxEm Noodles
O'Char Olive OutBk
PaneraBd RedLb RubyT
Ryan Sake SkyLnChili
SmkyBnes SmkyBnes
StkShk Subwy TimHrtn
Waffle Wendy Wnans
L-Comfrt CrtYrd CtryInnSte
Days Drury Fairfld Hmptn
Knght Motel6 RedRf
Rodwy Villager XStyAm

59 — Wyse Road
Benchwood

Northridge

Montgomery Co.

Exit 59
F-Subwy
L-HoJo

-60-

-59-

58 — Needmore Rd

Post Office

57B — Wagner Ford/Siebenthaler Rd

Kroger

57A — Neva Dr

Exit 58
G-BP\DL Shell
F-BgBoy Hrdee
McDld
L-BestW

-58-

-57-

Great Miami River

56 — Stanley Ave

EXIT 58, INSIDER TIP
MILLER LANE LODGING

Exit 57A
G-Sunco\L
L-H/Inn

-56-

EXIT 54C USAF NATIONAL
AIRFORCE MUSEUM,
6 MILES

EXIT 53A
- DAYTON ART INSTITUTE,
- WRIGHT BROTHERS WELCOME
CENTER

55AB — Keowee St/Leo

4

54C — Rt 4/Webster

54B — Rt 48/Main St

53B — Salem Ave/1st St

DAYTON
Pop: 167,100
Map, page 49

EXIT 53B
INSIDER TIP
MENDELSON
WAREHOUSE

Exit 51
L-CrtYrd
Marrtt

-55-

-54-

-53-

53A — 3rd Street

Exit 51
G-BP\D
F-McDld
Wendy
L-Econo

Move to left
lanes - Follow
*"I-75 North to
Toledo"*

52B — Rt 35/Eaton/Xenia

Stay in left
two lanes

-52-

51 — Nicholas Rd
Edwin C Moses Blvd

EXIT 51 - CARILLON
HISTORICAL PARK, HOME
OF THE ORIGINAL
WRIGHT FLYER III,
A NATIONAL
HISTORICAL LANDMARK

-51-

Exit 50A
G-Sunco\D
L-H/Inn Supr8

4

Great Miami River

50A — Dryden Rd

Moraine

-50-

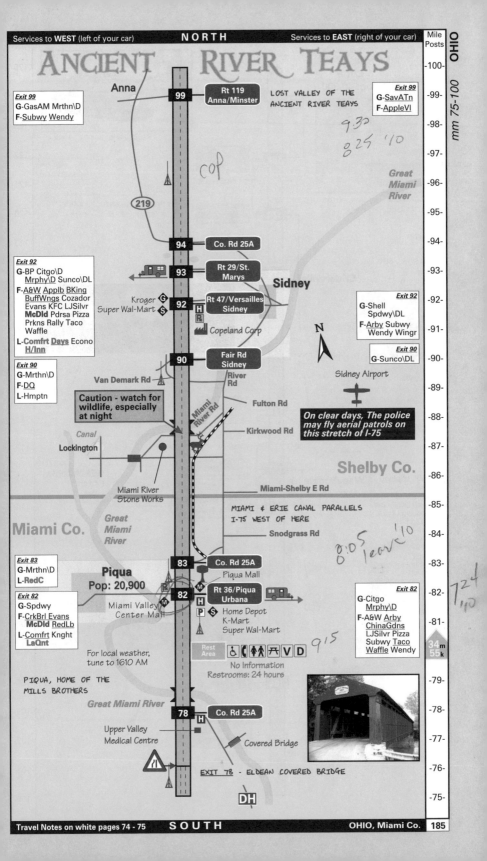

ANCIENT RIVER TEAYS

-100-
mm 75-100

Anna

99 | Rt 119 Anna/Minster

LOST VALLEY OF THE ANCIENT RIVER TEAYS

-99-

Exit 99
G-GasAM Mrthn\D
F-Subwy Wendy

Exit 99
G-SavATn
F-AppleVl

9.30
8 25 '10

-98-

-97-

COP

-96-

Great Miami River

(219)

-95-

94 | Co. Rd 25A

-94-

Exit 92
G-BP Citgo\D
   Mrphy\D Sunco\DL
F-A&W Applb BKing
   BuffWngs Cozador
   Evans KFC LJSilvr
   McDld Pdrsa Pizza
   Prkns Rally Taco
   Waffle
L-Comfrt Days Econo
   H/Inn

93 | Rt 29/St. Marys

Sidney

-93-

Kroger **G**
Super Wal-Mart **S**

92 | Rt 47/Versailles Sidney

H R

Copeland Corp

-92-

Exit 92
G-Shell
   Spdwy\DL
F-Arby Subwy
   Wendy Wingr

-91-

90 | Fair Rd Sidney

Exit 90
G-Sunco\DL

-90-

Exit 90
G-Mrthn\D
F-DQ
L-Hmptn

Van Demark Rd

River Rd

Sidney Airport

-89-

Miami River Rd

Caution - watch for wildlife, especially at night

Fulton Rd

Kirkwood Rd

On clear days, The police may fly aerial patrols on this stretch of I-75

-88-

Canal
Lockington

-87-

Shelby Co.

-86-

Miami River Stone Works

Miami-Shelby E Rd

-85-

Miami Co.

Great Miami River

MIAMI & ERIE CANAL PARALLELS I-75 WEST OF HERE

Snodgrass Rd

-84-

8:05 1eor '10

83 | Co. Rd 25A

-83-

Exit 83
G-Mrthn\D
L-RedC

Piqua
Pop: 20,900

Piqua Mall

M

-82-

7 24 '10

Exit 82
G-Spdwy
F-CrkBrl Evans
   McDld RedLb
L-Comfrt Knght
   LaQnt

82 | Rt 36/Piqua Urbana

Miami Valley Center Mall

H P S

Home Depot
K-Mart
Super Wal-Mart

Exit 82
G-Citgo
   Mrphy\D
F-A&W Arby
   ChinaGdns
   LJSilvr Pizza
   Subwy Taco
   Waffle Wendy

-81-

For local weather, tune to 1610 AM

Rest Area ♿ 🚻 👫 ⛺ V D

915

34 m
55 k

PIQUA, HOME OF THE MILLS BROTHERS

No Information
Restrooms: 24 hours

-79-

Great Miami River

78 | Co. Rd 25A

-78-

H

-77-

Upper Valley Medical Centre

Covered Bridge

-76-

⚠️

EXIT 78 - ELDEAN COVERED BRIDGE

-75-

DH

HOME OF THE SECRET "KRYPTONITE" ROOM
Lima
Pop: 40,300

-125-
-124-

124 P   4th Street

-123-

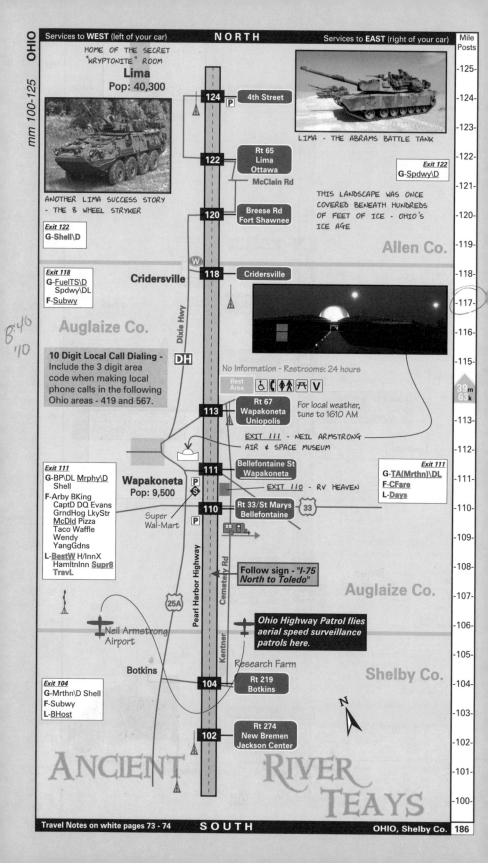

LIMA - THE ABRAMS BATTLE TANK

-122-

122 Rt 65
Lima
Ottawa
McClain Rd

Exit 122
G-Spdwy\D

-121-

ANOTHER LIMA SUCCESS STORY
- THE 8 WHEEL STRYKER

THIS LANDSCAPE WAS ONCE
COVERED BENEATH HUNDREDS
OF FEET OF ICE - OHIO'S
ICE AGE

-120-

120 Breese Rd
Fort Shawnee

Exit 122
G-Shell\D

-119- Allen Co.

Exit 118
G-FuelTS\D
  Spdwy\DL
F-Subwy

Cridersville

118 Cridersville

-118-
-117-

Auglaize Co.

Dixie Hwy

DH

-116-
-115-

10 Digit Local Call Dialing -
Include the 3 digit area
code when making local
phone calls in the following
Ohio areas - 419 and 567.

No Information - Restrooms: 24 hours

Rest Area   ♿ 🚹🚺 🎎 V

39 m
63 k

-114-

113 Rt 67
Wapakoneta
Uniopolis

For local weather,
tune to 1610 AM

-113-

EXIT 111 - NEIL ARMSTRONG
AIR & SPACE MUSEUM

-112-

Exit 111
G-BP\DL Mrphy\D
  Shell
F-Arby BKing
  CaptD DQ Evans
  GrndHog LkyStr
  McDld Pizza
  Taco Waffle
  Wendy
  YangGdns
L-BestW H/InnX
  HamltnInn Supr8
  TravL

111 Bellefontaine St
Wapakoneta

Exit 111
G-TA(Mrthn)\DL
F-CFare
L-Days

-111-

Wapakoneta
Pop: 9,500

P
$

EXIT 110 - RV HEAVEN

110 Rt 33/St Marys
Bellefontaine   33

-110-

Super
Wal-Mart

P

-109-

Pearl Harbor Highway

Cemetery Rd

**Follow sign - "I-75
North to Toledo"**

-108-

Auglaize Co.

-107-

25A

✈ Neil Armstrong
  Airport

Kentner

**Ohio Highway Patrol flies
aerial speed surveillance
patrols here.**

-106-
-105-

Botkins

Research Farm

Shelby Co.

-104-

Exit 104
G-Mrthn\D Shell
F-Subwy
L-BHost

104 Rt 219
Botkins

N

-103-
-102-

102 Rt 274
New Bremen
Jackson Center

-101-

ANCIENT RIVER TEAYS

-100-

B:46
'10

VORTAC FDY

••• • || •• || •• • — —• — ——

THE FOXTROT DELTA YANKEE MORSE SIGNAL OF THE FINDLAY "VORTAC ON J47"

IN 1784, IN THIS AREA YOU WOULD BE LEAVING VIRGINIA AND ENTERING CONNECTICUT

BLUFFTON'S NORTH MAIN STREET IS A PRETTY DIVERSION FROM THE INTERSTATE. WATCH FOR THE TEDDY BEAR SHOP ON THE CORNER

CR313

145 Rt 235/Ada Mt Cory

Hancock Co.

H **142** Rt 103/Arlington Bluffton

Bluffton
W

Exit 142
G-BP\D Mrthn
F-BKing KFC **McDld** Subwy Taco
L-Comfrt

Exit 142
G-BP Sunco
L-Knght

Riley Creek

Bluffton Airport

H **140** Bentley Rd Bluffton

Norfolk & Western Railway

BRONZE BUST OF IKE HONORING HIS ROLE IN CREATING THE INTERSTATE SYSTEM OF HIGHWAYS, LOCATED IN TIFTON, GEORGIA - SITE OF THE FIRST I-75 MILES (PAGE 140)

Phillips Rd

Exit 135
G-**FlyJ\DL** PilotTS\DL
F-Cookery McDld Pepproni Subwy

Napoleon

Beaverdam

LINCOLN HIGHWAY **L**

San Francisco

Old Route 30 Lincoln Hwy

30

IKE'S CONVOY PASSED HERE IN 1919

Washington

Exit 135
G-Spdwy\DL

135 to Rt 30/Delphos Upper Sandusky

134 Rt 696 Beaverdam Napoleon Rd

EXIT 135 - TO THE "OLD LINCOLN HIGHWAY"

N

I-75 WAS BUILT ON TOP OF THE OLD DIXIE HIGHWAY FOR MOST OF THE DISTANCE BETWEEN LIMA AND FINDLAY

Power Grid Substation

DH

Note - no n/bound return at exit 134

Allen Co.

130 Blue Lick Rd

Dixie Hwy

Exit 130
G-Mrthn\D
L-BestVal

U.S. Plastics Retail Outlet (1/2 mile N on Neubrecht Rd)

DH

S

Exit 127B
G-Mrthn\D
F-Waffle
L-Comfrt Days Econo

Strip Mining Operations

127B Rt 81/Lima

127A Rt 81/Ada

Ottawa River

Exit 125
G-Shell
F-IgnaGrl Kwpee PJPizza
L-Econmy Supr8

Lima

H **125** Rt 309 117 Kenton/Lima
W
R

S Super Wal-Mart/K-Mart

Exit 125
G-BP\D Mrphy\D Spdwy\LD
F-Arby BKing CaptD CrkBrl Evans Hunan McDld Olive Pdrsa Pizza Rally Ralph RedLb Ryan SkylnStk Taco TexStk Wendy
L-H/Inn Hmptn Knght Motel6

900
110

9:26 10
10 30

Portage River

-175-
-174-
-173-
-172-

DH
US 25

LOOK TO THE
EAST (RIGHT) AS
I-75 RISES OVER
THE SMALL HILL
- ALL THIS LAND
WAS ONCE THE
"BLACK SWAMP"

EXIT 179 (NEXT PAGE)
SNOOK'S DREAM CARS

171
Rt 25
Cygnet

-171-

Cygnet

-170-

Insley Road
CR603 Grant Rd

SNOOK'S GARAGE   Oil Center Rd

-169-

Needles Rd

OHIO'S ROAD WEATHER
INFORMATION SYSTEM
(RWIS) MONITOR STATION
IN THE MEDIAN

168
Quarry Road
Eagleville Rd

Wood Co.

-168-

Exit 168
G-FuelTS\DL

North
Baltimore

S
Petro Shopping Center

Exit 167
L-Crown

167
Rt 18
N Baltimore/Fostoria

-167-

W

Exit 167
G-Mobil\DL PetroTS\D
F-IrnSklt McDld Pizza

Rocky Ford

ROUTE 18 IS A
"RIDGE" HIGHWAY

-166-

Hancock Co.

-165-

Exit 164
G-PilotTS\D
F-Subwy Taco

Priebe
Airport

164
Rt 613
Fostoria
McComb

Van Buren

-164-

Whirlpool

-163-

ENTERING THE "BLACK SWAMP"

-162-

A

161
Twp Rd 99

220

EXIT 161 - JEFFREY'S
ANTIQUES

-161-

P

-160-

"DAVID COPPERFIELD" HOUSE

159
Rts 15 & 224
Ottawa/Tiffin

-159-

Super
Wal-Mart   S R

Exit 159
G-Mrphy\D Shell\D
F-ChinaGdns CrkBrl
DennyDnr Evans
JacPizza OutBk
Waffle
L-CtyInnSte H/InnX
Hmptn QltyInn

Blanchard River

Main St

Exit 159
G-BP\DL Spdwy\D
Swfty\D
F-BKing DktaGrl KFC
LJSilvr McDld
Mings Pdrsa Pizza
Ralph StkShk
Subwy Wendy
L-RedRf Rodwy Supr8
TravInn

-158-

"FLAG CITY"

157
Rt 12/Findlay

12

-157-

V

EXIT 157, INSIDER TIP
"BISTRO ON MAIN" FINE DINING

156
Rts S68 E15
Carey

Findlay
Pop: 39,200

-156-

H
15

Exit 157
G-TrvlCntr\D
F-Frckers
L-Econo

Pioneer
Sugar

Lima Ave

Exit 157
G-GasAm\D
Mrthn\D
F-Blimp
L-BestVal

-155-

Findlay Municipal
Airport

-154-

N

Rest Area

Visitor information -
tune radio to 530 AM

25 m
40 k

Dayton
100 MILES
161 KILOMETERS

No Information - Restrooms: 24 hours

-152-

EXIT 159
- "DAVID COPPERFIELD" HOUSE

313

-151-

SOUTHBOUND SIGN - 161
KILOMETERS TO DAYTON
(PAGE 71)

-150-

9 06
1 10

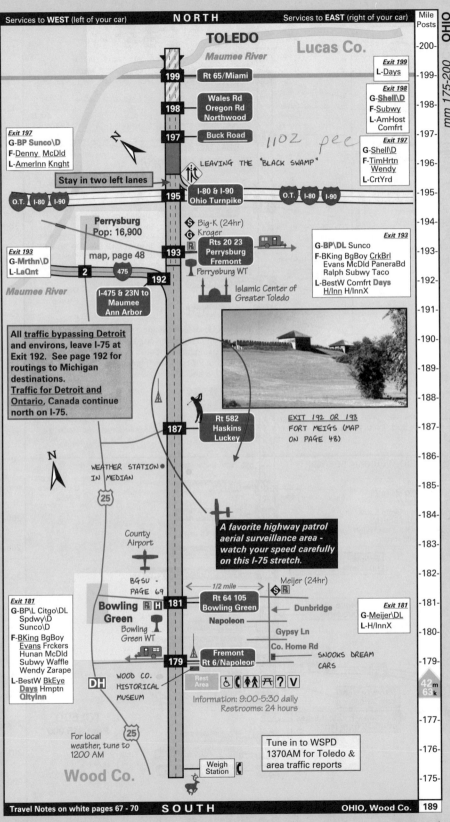

TOLEDO

Maumee River

Lucas Co.

-200-

199 | Rt 65/Miami

-199-

Exit 199
L-Days

198 | Wales Rd / Oregon Rd / Northwood

-198-

Exit 198
G-Shell\D
F-Subwy
L-AmHost Comfrt

197 | Buck Road

1102 pee

-197-

Exit 197
G-Shell\D
F-TimHrtn Wendy
L-CrtYrd

-196-

Exit 197
G-BP Sunco\D
F-Denny McDld
L-AmerInn Knght

LEAVING THE "BLACK SWAMP"

Stay in two left lanes

195 | I-80 & I-90 / Ohio Turnpike

O.T. | I-80 | I-90   O.T. | I-80 | I-90

-195-

-194-

Perrysburg
Pop: 16,900

Big-K (24hr)
Kroger

193 | Rts 20 23 / Perrysburg / Fremont

Perrysburg WT

-193-

Exit 193
G-Mrthn\D
L-LaQnt

map, page 48

2 | 475 | 192

I-475 & 23N to Maumee Ann Arbor

Maumee River

Islamic Center of Greater Toledo

Exit 193
G-BP\DL Sunco
F-BKing BgBoy CrkBrl
Evans McDld PaneraBd
Ralph Subwy Taco
L-BestW Comfrt Days
H/Inn H/InnX

-192-

-191-

-190-

All <u>traffic bypassing Detroit</u> and environs, leave I-75 at Exit 192. See page 192 for routings to Michigan destinations.
<u>Traffic for Detroit and Ontario</u>, Canada continue north on I-75.

187 | Rt 582 / Haskins / Luckey

EXIT 192 OR 193
FORT MEIGS (MAP ON PAGE 48)

-189-

-188-

-187-

WEATHER STATION IN MEDIAN

-186-

N

25

-185-

County Airport

A favorite highway patrol aerial surveillance area - watch your speed carefully on this I-75 stretch.

-184-

-183-

BGSU - PAGE 69

-182-

Meijer (24hr)

1/2 mile

Exit 181
G-BP\L Citgo\DL
Spdwy\D
Sunco\D
F-BKing BgBoy
Evans Frckers
Hunan McDld
Subwy Waffle
Wendy Zarape
L-BestW BkEye
Days Hmptn
QltyInn

Bowling Green

181 | Rt 64 105 / Bowling Green

Dunbridge

-181-

Exit 181
G-Meijer\DL
L-H/InnX

Napoleon

Gypsy Ln

-180-

Bowling Green WT

Co. Home Rd

SNOOKS DREAM CARS

-179-

DH

179 | Fremont / Rt 6/Napoleon

WOOD CO. HISTORICAL MUSEUM

Rest Area

♿ 🚻 🚶 ⛽ ? V

42 m
63 k

Information: 9:00-5:30 daily
Restrooms: 24 hours

-178-

-177-

25

For local weather, tune to 1200 AM

Tune in to WSPD 1370AM for Toledo & area traffic reports

-176-

Weigh Station

-175-

Wood Co.

9:26 /10

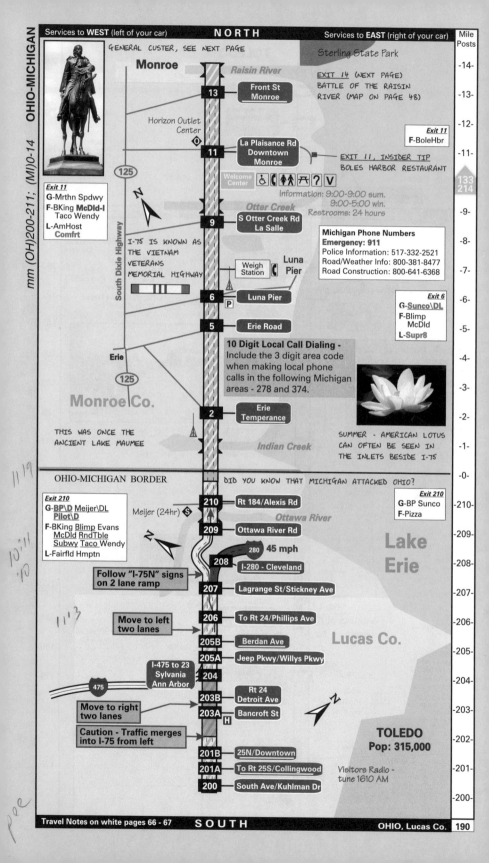

GENERAL CUSTER, SEE NEXT PAGE

Sterling State Park

Monroe   *Raisin River*

-14-

EXIT 14 (NEXT PAGE)
BATTLE OF THE RAISIN
RIVER (MAP ON PAGE 48)

13   Front St
Monroe

-13-

Horizon Outlet
Center

Exit 11
F-BoleHbr

-12-

11   La Plaisance Rd
Downtown
Monroe

EXIT 11, INSIDER TIP
BOLES HARBOR RESTAURANT

-11-

(125)

Welcome
Center 🚻♿🚶🏕️?V

133
214

Exit 11
G-Mrthn Spdwy
F-BKing McDld-I
Taco Wendy
L-AmHost Comfrt

Information: 9:00-9:00 sum.
9:00-5:00 win.
Restrooms: 24 hours

Otter Creek

-9-

9   S Otter Creek Rd
La Salle

I-75 IS KNOWN AS
THE VIETNAM
VETERANS
MEMORIAL HIGHWAY

Michigan Phone Numbers
Emergency: 911
Police Information: 517-332-2521
Road/Weather Info: 800-381-8477
Road Construction: 800-641-6368

-8-

Weigh
Station 🅲   **Luna Pier**

-7-

6   Luna Pier

🅿

Exit 6
G-Sunco\DL
F-Blimp
McDld
L-Supr8

-6-

5   Erie Road

-5-

Erie

10 Digit Local Call Dialing -
Include the 3 digit area code
when making local phone
calls in the following Michigan
areas - 278 and 374.

-4-

(125)

-3-

Monroe Co.

2   Erie
Temperance

-2-

THIS WAS ONCE THE
ANCIENT LAKE MAUMEE

SUMMER - AMERICAN LOTUS
CAN OFTEN BE SEEN IN
THE INLETS BESIDE I-75

-1-

Indian Creek

-0-

OHIO-MICHIGAN BORDER   DID YOU KNOW THAT MICHIGAN ATTACKED OHIO?

Exit 210
G-BP\D Meijer\DL
Pilot\D
F-BKing Blimp Evans
McDld RndTble
Subwy Taco Wendy
L-Fairfld Hmptn

Meijer (24hr) 🆂

210   Rt 184/Alexis Rd

Exit 210
G-BP Sunco
F-Pizza

-210-

Ottawa River

209   Ottawa River Rd

-209-

280 **45 mph**

208   I-280 - Cleveland

**Lake
Erie**

-208-

Follow "I-75N" signs
on 2 lane ramp

207   Lagrange St/Stickney Ave

-207-

Move to left
two lanes

206   To Rt 24/Phillips Ave

-206-

205B   Berdan Ave

Lucas Co.

205A   Jeep Pkwy/Willys Pkwy

-205-

I-475 to 23
Sylvania
Ann Arbor

475

204

-204-

203B   Rt 24
Detroit Ave

Move to right
two lanes

203A   Bancroft St

H

Caution - Traffic merges
into I-75 from left

201B   25N/Downtown

TOLEDO
Pop: 315,000

-202-

201A   To Rt 25S/Collingwood

Visitors Radio -
tune 1610 AM

-201-

200   South Ave/Kuhlman Dr

-200-

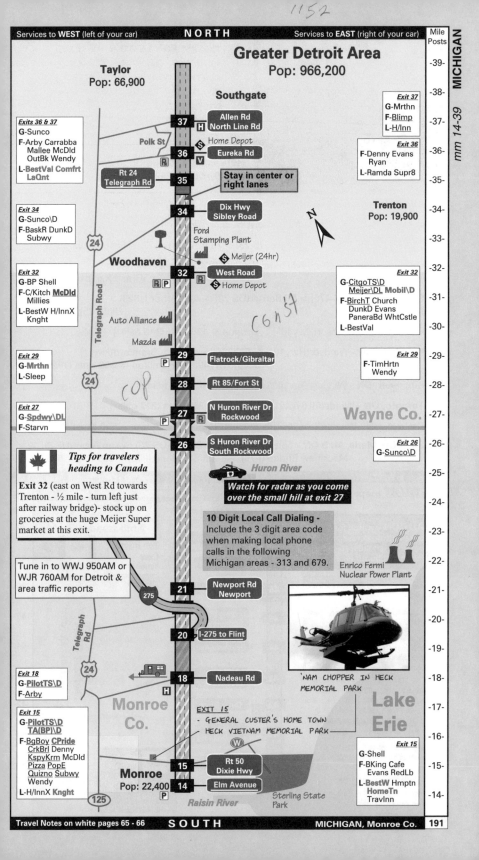

1152

Services to **WEST** (left of your car) **N O R T H** Services to **EAST** (right of your car) | Mile Posts | **MICHIGAN**

mm 14-39

Greater Detroit Area
Pop: 966,200

Taylor
Pop: 66,900

Southgate

-39-
-38-

Exit 37
G-Mrthn
F-Blimp
L-H/Inn

-37-

| 37 | H |
| **Allen Rd** **North Line Rd** |

Polk St

-36-

Home Depot

| 36 | S V |
| **Eureka Rd** |
R

Exit 36
F-Denny Evans
Ryan
L-Ramda Supr8

Exits 36 & 37
G-Sunco
F-Arby Carrabba
Mallee McDld
OutBk Wendy
L-BestVal Comfrt
LaQnt

Rt 24
Telegraph Rd | 35 |

-35-

**Stay in center or
right lanes**

| 34 | **Dix Hwy** **Sibley Road** |

-34-

Trenton
Pop: 19,900

Exit 34
G-Sunco\D
F-BaskR DunkD
Subwy

Ford
Stamping Plant

-33-

N

Woodhaven

S Meijer (24hr)

-32-

| 32 | R P | **West Road** |
S Home Depot

Exit 32
G-CitgoTS\D
Meijer\DL Mobil\D
F-BirchT Church
DunkD Evans
PaneraBd WhtCstle
L-BestVal

Exit 32
G-BP Shell
F-C/Kitch McDld
Millies
L-BestW H/InnX
Knght

Telegraph Road

Auto Alliance

-31-

-30-

Mazda

| 29 | P | **Flatrock/Gibraltar** |

-29-

Exit 29
G-Mrthn
L-Sleep

24

COP

Exit 29
F-TimHrtn
Wendy

| 28 | **Rt 85/Fort St** |

-28-

| 27 | R | **N Huron River Dr** **Rockwood** |
P

Exit 27
G-Spdwy\DL
F-Starvn

Wayne Co.

-27-

| 26 | **S Huron River Dr** **South Rockwood** |

-26-

Exit 26
G-Sunco\D

Huron River

-25-

C6n57

**Tips for travelers
heading to Canada**

Exit 32 (east on West Rd towards
Trenton - ½ mile - turn left just
after railway bridge)- stock up on
groceries at the huge Meijer Super
market at this exit.

**Watch for radar as you come
over the small hill at exit 27**

-24-

10 Digit Local Call Dialing -
Include the 3 digit area code
when making local phone
calls in the following
Michigan areas - 313 and 679.

Enrico Fermi
Nuclear Power Plant

-23-

-22-

Tune in to WWJ 950AM or
WJR 760AM for Detroit &
area traffic reports

275

| 21 | **Newport Rd** **Newport** |

-21-

-20-

| 20 | **I-275 to Flint** |

-19-

'NAM CHOPPER IN HECK
MEMORIAL PARK

Telegraph
Rd

24

| 18 | H | **Nadeau Rd** |

-18-

Monroe Co.

Exit 18
G-PilotTS\D
F-Arby

Lake Erie

-17-

Exit 15
G-PilotTS\D
TA(BP)\D
F-BgBoy CPride
CrkBrl Denny
KspyKrm McDld
Pizza PopE
Quizno Subwy
Wendy
L-H/InnX Knght

EXIT 15
- GENERAL CUSTER'S HOME TOWN
HECK VIETNAM MEMORIAL PARK

W

-16-

Exit 15
G-Shell
F-BKing Cafe
Evans RedLb
L-BestW Hmptn
HomeTn
TravInn

Monroe
Pop: 22,400

| 15 | **Rt 50** **Dixie Hwy** |
| 14 | **Elm Avenue** |
P

-15-

Sterling State
Park

-14-

125

Raisin River

View from the Grand Hotel, Mackinac Island, Michigan

THANKS FOR LETTING ME RIDE
WITH YOU ON YOUR JOURNEY
NORTH. HAVE A SAFE TRIP,
NO MATTER WHERE YOUR FINAL
DESTINATION LIES.

Dave

Here is a handy guide to some *Michigan* and *Ontario* (Canada) Destinations . . .

Ann Arbor - Toledo(I-475) > MI Border(US23) > Ann Arbor = **52** miles

Lansing - Toledo(I-475) > MI Border(US23) > Brighton(I-96) > Lansing = **115** miles

Flint - Toledo(I-475) > MI Border(US 23) > Ann Arbor(US23) > Flint = **106** miles

Grand Rapids - Toledo(I-475) > MI Border(US23) > Brighton(I-96) >
Grand Rapids = **179** miles

Saginaw - Toledo(I-475) > MI Border(US 23) > Ann Arbor(US23) >
Flint(I-75) = **138** miles

London, ON - Windsor(Hwy401) > London = **190** Kms (118 miles)

Hamilton, ON - Windsor(Hwy401) > Exit235(Hwy403) > Brantford(Hwy2)
> Jnctn(Hwy403) > Hamilton = **309** Kms (192 miles)

Kitchener, ON - Windsor(Hwy401) > = **286** Kms (178 miles)

Toronto, ON - Windsor(Hwy401) > Toronto = **350** Kms (217 miles)

Ottawa, ON - Windsor(Hwy401) > Prescott(Hwy16) > Ottawa = **800** Kms (497 miles)

Sault Ste Marie, MI & ON - Toledo(I-475) > MI Border(US 23) > Ann Arbor(US23) >
Mackinaw Bridge (I-75) > Sault Ste Marie (I-75) = **395** miles (636 kms)

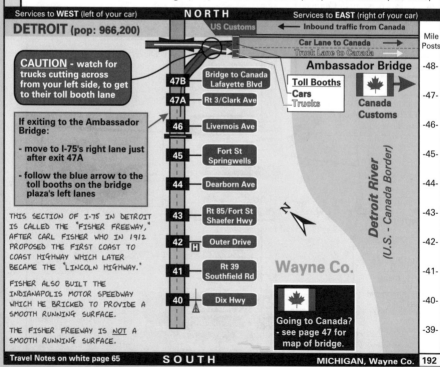

Services to **WEST** (left of your car)   **NORTH**   Services to **EAST** (right of your car)

DETROIT (pop: 966,200)

US Customs   ← **Inbound traffic from Canada**

Car Lane to Canada →
Truck Lane to Canada →

Ambassador Bridge

	Mile Posts

CAUTION - watch for trucks cutting across from your left side, to get to their toll booth lane

Toll Booths
Cars
Trucks

Canada Customs

-48-

47B — Bridge to Canada Lafayette Blvd

47A — Rt 3/Clark Ave

-47-

If exiting to the Ambassador Bridge:

46 — Livernois Ave

-46-

- move to I-75's right lane just after exit 47A

45 — Fort St Springwells

-45-

- follow the blue arrow to the toll booths on the bridge plaza's left lanes

44 — Dearborn Ave

-44-

THIS SECTION OF I-75 IN DETROIT IS CALLED THE "FISHER FREEWAY," AFTER CARL FISHER WHO IN 1912 PROPOSED THE FIRST COAST TO COAST HIGHWAY WHICH LATER BECAME THE "LINCOLN HIGHWAY."

43 — Rt 85/Fort St Shaefer Hwy

-43-

42 H — Outer Drive

-42-

Detroit River (U.S. - Canada Border)

Wayne Co.

FISHER ALSO BUILT THE INDIANAPOLIS MOTOR SPEEDWAY WHICH HE BRICKED TO PROVIDE A SMOOTH RUNNING SURFACE.

41 — Rt 39 Southfield Rd

-41-

40 — Dix Hwy

-40-

Going to Canada?
- see page 47 for map of bridge.

THE FISHER FREEWAY IS <u>NOT</u> A SMOOTH RUNNING SURFACE.

-39-

Beating the Rush Hour Blues

Nobody likes rush hour traffic and each year it seems to get worse no matter where you are. Fortunately, I-75 cities have some of the best traffic reporters in the Nation–on the ground and in the air–to speed you through the interstate cities. To help you on your drive through their areas, I've assembled the **best-of-the-best**, as my **I-75 Traffic Reporter Team**. You'll also find bypass maps for Cincinnati and Atlanta on the following pages, as well as a special map of the Macon area.

Detroit - morning rush hours are 7:00-9:00; afternoon, 4:00-6:30. *"On the 8's"* (every 8 minutes), tune in the team of *John Bailey* (on the ground) and *Mike Howard* (in the air), supported by *Chris Morgan*, on **WWJ-950AM**. Road construction reports at 18 and 48 minutes past each hour.

Toledo - **WSPD-1370AM's** *Lynn Cassidy* will keep you moving through the 6-9 am rush hour with reports *"on the 10's"* (every 10 mins); *Kristyn Marie* will look after your afternoon drive reports, from 3 to 4pm.

Dayton - morning rush hours are 7-9; afternoons, 4-6. Who knows traffic better than the police? **WHIO-1290AM's** *Sgt. Mark Bowron,* supported by *Harley D.* and *Capt. Cooper* will keep you rolling.

Cincinnati - morning rush hours are 5:30-9:00; afternoon, 3:30-6:30. Traffic reports from **WLW 700AM's** *John Phillips*, *Dave Armbruster* and *Chuck Ingram* on the 10s in rush time & *"top-of-the-hour"* at other times.

Lexington - morning rush hours are 6:30-8:30; afternoons, 4:30-6:00. **WVLK-590AM's** traffic reporter, *Leslie* reports on the bluegrass rush traffic from 6 to 8:40am and from 4 to 6pm. Leslie certainly doesn't horse around!

Knoxville - morning rush hours are 7:00-9:00; afternoon, 4:30-6:00. Check out *Jay Kersting* on **WNOX-100.3FM** - he'll keep you moving on I-75 and I-40.

Chattanooga - morning rush hours are 6:00-9:00; afternoon, 3:30-6:30 ... but they shouldn't bother you unless morning I-24 traffic backs up onto I-75. Stay tuned to **WGOW-102.3FM's** *Sean Paul* and *Christie Clark* during rush hours.

Atlanta - morning rush hours are 6:30-9:30; afternoon, 4:00 (2:00 on Fri.)-6:30. My friend who taught me that the *"Brookwood Split"* isn't a soda fountain dessert, **WSB-750AM's** *Captain Herb Emory* is in the air in the WSB chopper –on the job *every 6 minutes*–all over the city and bypass routes, supported by his team of *Mark Arum, Calandra Corder, Denise Maunder, Kim McCarthy* and *Nancy Plum.*.

Macon - You're on the I-475 Macon Bypass so you should be OK ... but keep and ear open for **WMAC-940AM's** traffic reports ... and if the traffic's OK, then just relax and enjoy the *"Jami G. and Kenny B"* morning show.

After that, it's all "downhill" to Florida, folks!

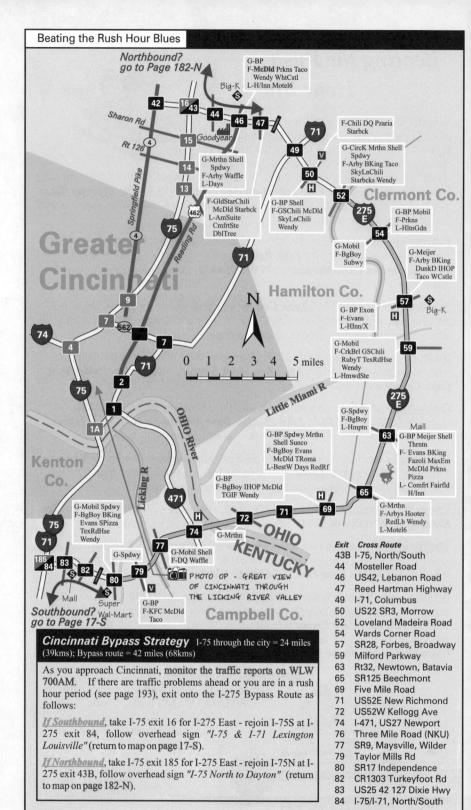

Northbound?
go to Page 182-N

G-BP
F-**McDld** Prkns Taco
Wendy WhtCstl
L-H/Inn Motel6

Big-K

Sharon Rd

Rt 126

Goodyear

F-Chili DQ Pzaria
Starbck

G-CircK Mrthn Shell
Spdwy
F-Arby BKing Taco
SkyLnChili
Starbcks Wendy

Clermont Co.

G-Mrthn Shell
Spdwy
F-Arby Waffle
L-Days

F-GldStarChili
McDld Starbck
L-AmSuite
CmfrtSte
DblTree

G-BP Shell
F-GSChili McDld
SkyLnChili
Wendy

G-BP Mobil
F-Prkns
L-HltnGdn

G-Meijer
F-Arby BKing
DunkD IHOP
Taco WCstle

G-Mobil
F-BgBoy
Subwy

Greater Cincinnati

Hamilton Co.

G- BP Exon
F-Evans
L-HInn/X

Big-K

G-Mobil
F-CrkBrl GSChili
RubyT TexRdHse
Wendy
L-HmwdSte

N

0 1 2 3 4 5 miles

Little Miami R

G-Spdwy
F-BgBoy
L-Hmptn

Mall

G-BP Meijer Shell
Thrntn
F- Evans BKing
Fazoli MaxEm
McDld Prkns
Pizza
L- Comfrt Fairfld
H/Inn

G-BP Spdwy Mrthn
Shell Sunco
F-BgBoy Evans
McDld TRoma
L-BestW Days RedRf

OHIO RIVER

Kenton Co.

G-BP
F-BgBoy IHOP McDld
TGIF Wendy

G-Mrthn
F-Arbys Hooter
RedLb Wendy
L-Motel6

Licking R

G-Mobil Spdwy
F-BgBoy BKing
Evans SPizza
TexRdHse
Wendy

OHIO

G-Spdwy

G-Mobil Shell
F-DQ Waffle

KENTUCKY

G-Mrthn

Mall

Super
Wal-Mart

G-BP
F-KFC McDld
Taco

PHOTO OP - GREAT VIEW
OF CINCINNATI THROUGH
THE LICKING RIVER VALLEY

Campbell Co.

Southbound?
go to Page 17-S

Exit	Cross Route
43B	I-75, North/South
44	Mosteller Road
46	US42, Lebanon Road
47	Reed Hartman Highway
49	I-71, Columbus
50	US22 SR3, Morrow
52	Loveland Madeira Road
54	Wards Corner Road
57	SR28, Forbes, Broadway
59	Milford Parkway
63	Rt32, Newtown, Batavia
65	SR125 Beechmont
69	Five Mile Road
71	US52E New Richmond
72	US52W Kellogg Ave
74	I-471, US27 Newport
76	Three Mile Road (NKU)
77	SR9, Maysville, Wilder
79	Taylor Mills Rd
80	SR17 Independence
82	CR1303 Turkeyfoot Rd
83	US25 42 127 Dixie Hwy
84	I-75/I-71, North/South

Cincinnati Bypass Strategy I-75 through the city = 24 miles
(39kms); Bypass route = 42 miles (68kms)

As you approach Cincinnati, monitor the traffic reports on WLW
700AM.   If there are traffic problems ahead or you are in a rush
hour period (see page 193), exit onto the I-275 Bypass Route as
follows:

If Southbound, take I-75 exit 16 for I-275 East - rejoin I-75S at I-
275 exit 84, follow overhead sign *"I-75 & I-71 Lexington
Louisville"* (return to map on page 17-S).

If Northbound, take I-75 exit 185 for I-275 East - rejoin I-75N at I-
275 exit 43B, follow overhead sign *"I-75 North to Dayton"* (return
to map on page 182-N).

Dave Hunter's

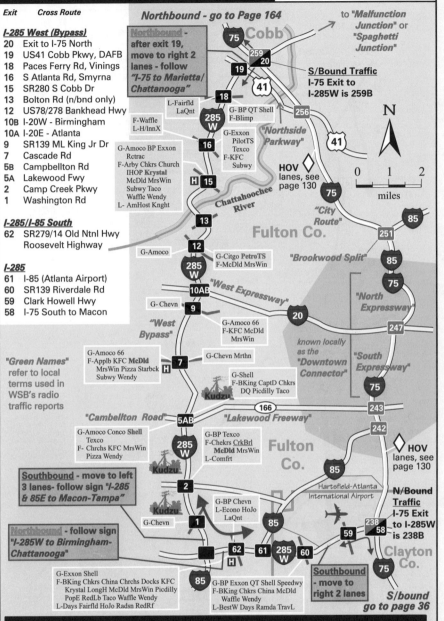

Atlanta Bypass Strategy   I-75 through the city = 20 miles (32kms); Bypass route = 25 miles (40kms)

As you approach Atlanta, **monitor the traffic reports on WSB 750AM.**   If there are traffic problems ahead exit onto the I-285 Bypass Route as follows:

Southbound - leave I-75 at exit 259, stay in *two left lanes* on ramp and follow *"I-285W."* On I-285W, just after exit 60, move to *two right lanes* - leave I-285W at exit 58 & follow overhead sign *"I-75 Macon Tampa"* - on ramp, stay right & follow *"I-75 South"* - after ramp splits, move to *left quickly* because ramp becomes single lane. Rejoin I-75 South at mile 238 (return to map on page 36).

Northbound - leave I-75N at exit 238B, for I-285W. Just past exit 19, move to *two right lanes* - take exit 20 and follow overhead sign *"I-75 to Marietta/Chattanooga"* - on ramp, move to the *two left lanes* and - *slow down*, very tight left corner coming up. Rejoin I-75N (return to map on page 164).

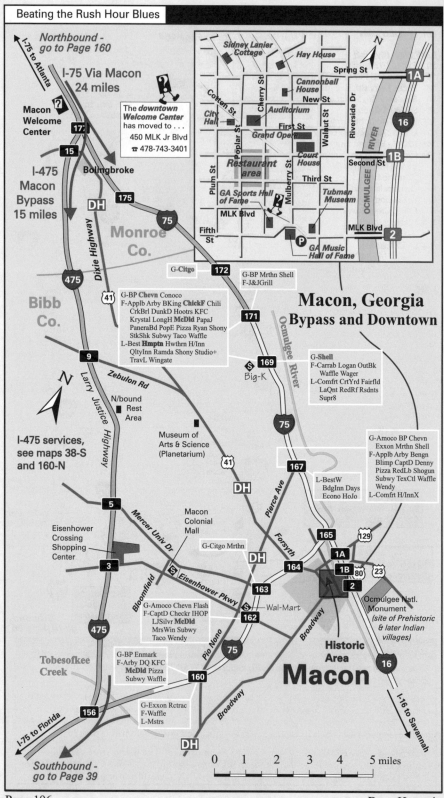

Beating the Rush Hour Blues

Northbound -
go to Page 160

I-75 to Atlanta

I-75 Via Macon
24 miles

Macon Welcome Center

The *downtown* Welcome Center has moved to . . .
450 MLK Jr Blvd
☎ 478-743-3401

172

15

I-475 Macon Bypass 15 miles

Bolingbroke

DH

175

75

Monroe Co.

G-Citgo 172

G-BP Mrthn Shell
F-J&JGrill

41

Bibb Co.

9

G-BP **Chevn** Conoco
F-Applb Arby BKing **ChickF** Chili
CrkBrl DunkD Hootrs KFC
Krystal LongH **McDld** PapaJ
PaneraBd PopE Pizza Ryan Shony
StkShk Subwy Taco Waffle
L-Best **Hmptn** Hwthrn H/Inn
QltyInn Ramda Shony Studio+
TravL Wingate

171

Ocmulgee River

Macon, Georgia
Bypass and Downtown

169

Big-K

G-**Shell**
F-Carrab Logan OutBk
Waffle Wager
L-Comfrt CrtYrd Fairfld
LaQnt RedRf Rsdnts
Supr8

Zebulon Rd

N/bound Rest Area

I-475 services, see maps 38-S and 160-N

5

Museum of Arts & Science (Planetarium)

41

DH

75

167

L-BestW
BdgInn Days
Econo HoJo

G-Amoco BP Chevn
Exxon Mrthn Shell
F-Applb Arby Bengn
Blimp CaptD Denny
Pizza RedLb Shogun
Subwy TexCtl Waffle
Wendy
L-Comfrt H/InnX

Eisenhower Crossing Shopping Center

3

Mercer Univ Dr

Macon Colonial Mall

G-Citgo Mrthn

DH

165

129

164

1A

1B 80 23

2

163

Bloomfield

Eisenhower Pkwy

162 Wal-Mart

G-Amoco Chevn Flash
F-CaptD Checkr IHOP
LJSilvr **McDld**
MrsWin Subwy
Taco Wendy

Pio Nono

75

Broadway

Ocmulgee Natl. Monument
(site of Prehistoric & later Indian villages)

Tobesofkee Creek

G-BP Enmark
F-Arby DQ KFC
McDld Pizza
Subwy Waffle

160

Historic Area
Macon

16

I-16 to Savannah

475

156

G-Exxon Rctrac
F-Waffle
L-Mstrs

Broadway

I-75 to Florida

DH

Southbound -
go to Page 39

0 1 2 3 4 5 miles

Macon Downtown inset

Sidney Lanier Cottage

Hay House

Spring St

1A

Cherry St

Cannonball House

New St

Cotten St

City Hall

Auditorium

Walnut St

Riverside Dr

16

First St

Grand Opera

Plum St

Poplar St

Mulberry St

Court House

Third St

1B

Second St

Restaurant area

Fifth St

GA Sports Hall of Fame

MLK Blvd

Tubman Museum

MLK Blvd

2

P

GA Music Hall of Fame

OCMULGEE RIVER

Dixie Highway

Larry Justice Highway

Pierce Ave

Forsyth

Page 196

Dave Hunter's

A word about these listings

The Internet's World Wide Web has become such an information resource that wherever possible, I've included the appropriate website address.

American Association of Retired Persons (AARP) - [www.aarp.org] - 601 E Street NW, Washington DC 20049. Everybody 50 or older should join this organization; the annual membership is so low and the benefits broad; ☎ 1-800-687-2277.

American Automobile Association (AAA) - [www.aaa.com] - Check your phone book for number of your local club. Emergency road number: **1-800-AAA-HELP** I wouldn't consider traveling by car without my membership. I have had to use AAA emergency services on several occasion and always found them to be responsive and my problems solved easily. Great peace of mind!

Canadian Association of Retired Persons (CARP) - [**www.fifty-plus.net**] - 27 Queen Street East, Suite 1304, Toronto ON M5C 2M6; ☎ 416-363-8748.

Canadian Automobile Association (CAA) - [**www.caa.ca**] - See my comments under "AAA." Emergency road number: **1-800-CAA-HELP**. Check your phone book for your local club.

Canadian Snowbird Association - [**www.snowbirds.org**] - 180 Lesmill Road, Toronto ON M3B 2T5; ☎ 1-800-265-3200. If you are Canadian, and spend your winters in the South, you should consider becoming a member of this organization. Low annual membership fees, many discounts and benefits, this 100,000+ members organization is the "voice" of the Canadian "snowbird."

MA - Market America Motel Discount Coupon Books - Box 7069, Gadsden AL 35906; ☎ 256-547-4321. The familiar red covered motel discount coupon books available at I-75 welcome centers. MA also has a website where you can print and clip your discount coupons before you travel. Visit **www.travelcoupons.com**.

Microsoft Street & Trips - (available at most electronic stores) - by far the best street mapping software for the traveler. While driving, I use this product in my laptop, connected to a Garmin Street Pilot GPS. It gives me instant information about where I am and the streets around me. The software can also be purchased with its own GPS receiver, in the box.

State Travel Information - how to get official travel information for each I-75 state.

Michigan:	1-888-78-GREAT (784-7328);	www.Michigan.org/Travel
Ohio:	1-800-BUCKEYE (282-5393);	www.discoverOhio.com
Kentucky:	1-800-225-TRIP (225-8747);	www.KentuckyTourism.com
Tennessee:	1-800-GO2-TENN (462-8366);	www.TNvacation.com
Georgia:	1-800-VISIT-GA (847-4842);	www.Georgia.org
Florida:	1-888-7FLA USA (735-2872);	www.visitFlorida.com

"Trailer Life RV Park & Services Directory" (*Amzn*) - Box 11097, Des Moines IA 50336; ☎ 1-800-234-3450. One of the two essential campground and RV services guides to have aboard your RV [**www.goodsamclub.com**]. (see also, *"Woodall's,"* below).

Traveler Discount Guide Hotel Coupons - 4205 NW 6th Street, Gainesville FL 32609; ☎ 1-800-332-3948. The familiar green covered motel discount coupon books available at I-75 welcome centers and rest areas. The company also has an excellent website where you can print your discount coupons before you travel. Visit **www.roomsaver.com**.

Valentine Research - [**www.valentine1.com**]. - 10280 Alliance Road, Cincinnati OH 45242; ☎ 1-800-331-3030. Annual tests conducted by major car magazines, consistently rate the Valentine One radar detector with laser warning as the best detection equipment available, by far. This is the *"Rolls Royce"* of detectors.

"Woodall's Campground Directory" (*Amzn*) - [**www.woodalls.com**] - 2575 Vista Del Mar Drive, Ventura CA 93001; ☎ 1-877-680-6155. Available at RV dealers, most large bookstores or at Woodall's website, this is one of the two essential campground and RV services guides to have aboard your RV (the other is *"Trailer Life"* - see above).

RECOMMENDED BOOKS - I-75 travelers might enjoy or find useful some of the following books, many of which I use for reference. A tip for searching on Amazon.com. Click on *"Books"* in the *"Browse"* sub-menu on the left of your screen; click on *"Advanced Search"* in the top bar; enter the 10 digit ISBN number (shown below) with no dashes - you will be taken directly to the book you are looking for, if it's available through Amazon.

Title	Author	ISBN
Brief Description [Purchasing Information]		

Allatoona Pass (Civil War) — William Scaife — none
Well researched book detailing this horrendous Civil War battle [Etowah Valley Historical Society, GA, ☎ 770-606-8862, online books at www.evhsonline.org].

Barnsley Gardens at Woodlands — Clent Coker — 0-9701936-1-0
The definitive history of the tragic Barnsley family, their house and beautiful garden estate. [The Julia Company, ☎ 770-698-9299; or same as *"Allatoona Pass"* (above)].

Battlefield Atlas of the Civil War — Craig Symonds — 0-933852-40-1
[NAPAC, Baltimore MD, ☎ 301-659-0220, also available at amazon.com].

Battle of Resaca, The (Civil War) — Philip Secrist — 0-86554-601-0
An excellent book which not only explains the entire battle in great detail, but also deals with the archaeological situation (and subsequent reports) resulting from the I-75 construction in the battlefield area. [Mercer University Press, Macon GA, ☎ 478-301-2880; also available online at amazon.com].

City Behind A Fence, Oak Ridge TN, 1942-46 — Johnson & Jackson — 0-87049-309-4
Indispensable source for anyone interested in the development of the atomic bomb, and the role played by Oak Ridge during the war years. [Univ of TN Press, Knoxville TN, ☎ 865-974-3321, also available online at amazon.com].

Civil War Battlefield Guide — Frances Kennedy — 0-395-740-12-6
Excellent maps. [through your bookstore or available at amazon.com].

DeLorme Gazateers for I-75 states — various
We wouldn't travel to Florida without our DeLorme large scale guide (Atlas and Gazetteer) in our car. [DeLorme Mapping Co., Yarmouth MN, ☎ 800-561-5105].

Drive I-95 — Sandra & Stan Posner — 1-894979-99-0
Written by my journalist friends, Sandra Phillips and Stan Posner, especially for those who drive the I-95 "Atlantic" route to Florida. An award winner; I highly recommend it. [TravelSmart, PO Box3, Roxboro QC Canada H8Y 3E8, ☎ 888-484-3395].

PassPorter Walt Disney World 2007 — J Watson & D Marx — 0-58771-033-1
Highly recommend for those planning a visit to WDW. It's a WDW travel guide, planner, organizer . . . and unusual journal and keepsake, providing a wonderful memento of your visit. [Passporter Travel Press, ☎ 877-929-3273, or online at www.passporter.com].

Traveling with your Pet — 1-5625-1406-7
The definitive book for people traveling with pets [Any AAA or CAA travel centers].

Unofficial Guide to Walt Disney World — Bob Sehlinger — 0-764-58341-7
Far superior to any of the other guides ("official" and "unofficial") because of its objective point of view. Many money and time saving tips. [all bookstores or at amazon.com].

War of 1812, The Invasion of Canada — Pierre Berton — 0-385-65838-7
War of 1812, Flames Across the Border — Pierre Berton — 0-385-65838-9
Excellent, very readable books about the War of 1812. Well researched; great detail. [Out of print but copies can usually be found through a search at www.abebooks.com].

Wilderness Road, The (Daniel Boone) — Robert Kincaid — none
The definitive book about the Wilderness Road which was used by many pioneers in the 1700s for their journeys across the mountains and into Kentucky and Tennessee. [Out of print but copies can usually be found through a search at www.abebooks.com].

Abbreviations used in our maps

Space limitations necessitate the use of abbreviations for many of the fuel stations, restaurants and motels listed. For your convenience, the less familiar abbreviations are listed on the next two pages.

GAS, DIESEL & LPG

BP . . . . BP Oil	
BigFt . . . . Big Foot	
Chevn . . . Chevron USA	
Conco . . . . Conoco	
Exxn . . . . Exxon	
Fina. . . . . Fina Oil	
FlyJ . . . . FlyingJ	
GldnGln . Golden Gallon	
Hess . . . . Hess Oil	
Kgroo . . . . Kangaroo	
Libty . . . . Liberty	
Mrthn . . . . Marathon Oil	
Mrphy . . . . Murphy USA	
(Wal-Mart)	

Phil66 . . . . Philips66	
Pilot . . . . Pilot Gas	
QT . . . . Quick Time Gas	
Racewy. . . . . . Raceway	
Rctrac. . . . . . . Racetrac	
RghtStff . . . . . RightStuff	
SavATn . . . . Save A Ton	
Shell. . . . . Shell Oil	
Spdwy. . . . . . Speedway	
Sunco . . . . Sunoco	
Swfty . . . . Swifty	
TA(brand) . . . . . . Travel-	
. . . . Centers of America	
Texco . . . . Texaco	
Thrntn . . . . . . Thorntons	

NOTE:

1. Gas Stations offering <u>Diesel</u> or <u>LPG</u> (propane) are listed on the maps with "\D" or "\L" appended to their name. Eg., "BP\DL" indicates a gas station with diesel pump(s) and stocking propane.

2. Truck Stops are listed with the gas brand, followed by "TS."

3. Truck Stops often have a separate pump area for automobiles, and gas is often a few cents cheaper. Try Pilot or FlyingJ gas bars.

4. See the **Key to the Map Symbols** (on cover flap) for the color codes indicating *"open 24 hour"* or *"mechanic on duty."*

FOOD

A&W. . . A&W Fast Food	
Alexndr . . . . . Alexander	
Applb . . . . Applebee's	
AppleVl . . . Apple Valley	
Arby . . . . Arbys	
AuntEff . . . . Aunt Effie's	
BKing . . . . . Burger King	
BaskR . Baskin-Robbins	
Ice Cream	
BgBoy . . . . Big Boy	
Family Restaurant	
Blimp . . . . Blimpies	
Brbnk. . . Burbanks BBQ	
BudBBQ. . . . Bud's BBQ	
BuffWngs Buffalo Wings	
C/Kitch. Country Kitchen	
CCPizza . . . . CiCi's	
CPride. . . Country Pride	
CPtch . . . . Cotton Patch	
Restaurant	
CaptD . . . . . Captain D's	
Carino . . Carion's Italian	
CharlSeaFd . . . Charles	
Sea Food	
Checkr . . . . . . Checkers	
ChickF . . . . . Chick-Fil-A	
Chili. . . . . . GoldStar Chili	
China. . . . . China Buffet	
ChinaGdns. . . . . . China	
Gardens	
Chpotle. . . Chipotle Mex	
Church . . . . Chicken	
Cookery	
CityBft. . . . . . City Buffet	
Cookery . . . . . . Flying J	
CrabShk . . . CrabShack	
CrkBrl. . . Cracker Barrel	
CrzEd. . Crazy Eds Rest	
CtrlPark. . . Central Park	
CtryBft . . Country Buffet	
CtryGrill. . . Country Grill	
CuttrsStk . . . . . Cutters	
Steakhouse	
D/Bell. . . . . . Dinner Bell	

DQ . . . . . . Dairy Queen	
Denny. . . . . Denny's	
DennyDnr . . . . Denny's	
Diner	
DktaGrl. . . . Dakota Grill	
Dudly . . . . Dudley's	
DunkD . . . . Dunkin	
Doughnut	
ElDorado . . . . El Dorado	
Mexican	
Evans. . . . . . Bob Evans	
FmDave . . . . . . Famous	
Dave's	
Family. . . . . Family Rest	
Fazoli . . . . Fazzoli's	
Fdrckrs . . . Fuddruckers	
Frckers. . . Fricker's Rest	
FruitJr . . . Fruit Jar Rest	
GFPizza . . . . Godfather	
Pizza	
GinaFD . . . . Gina's Fine	
Dining	
GitnGo . . . . . . Git 'n Go	
GldnC . . . Golden Corral	
GldnGirls. . Golden Girls	
Grdma . . . . . Grandma's	
Kitchen	
GrndSC . . . Grindestone	
Charlies	
GtAmBft . . . . Great	
American Buffet	
Gthouse. . . . Gatehouse	
Hddle . . . Huddle House	
HickH . . . Hickory House	
HngKng. . . . Hong Kong	
HnyDipD. . . . Honey Dip	
Donuts	
Hooter. . . . . Hooters	
Hrdee . . . Hardee's Rest	
Hunan. . Hunan Chinese	
IHOP . . . . . International	
House of Pancakes	
IceCrm . . . . . Ice Cream	
Churn	

IntBft . . . . . International	
Buffet	
IrnSklt. . . . . . Iron Skillet	
J&L . . . . . . J&L Famous	
Pit BBQ	
KFC . . . . Kentucky Fried	
Chicken	
Krystal . . . . Krystal Rest	
KspyKrm. . KrispyKreme	
Doughnuts	
LChick. . . Lee's Country	
Chicken	
LJSilvr . . . . . Long John	
Silver	
Lees . . Lees Restaurant	
LgnStk. . . . Logan Steak	
LkyStr. . . . . Lucky Steer	
Restaurant	
LoneS . . . . . . Lone Star	
Steaks	
LongH . . . . . . Longhorn	
Steaks	
Macroni. . . . . Macaronis	
MamaTbl . Mama's Table	
MaxEm . . Max&Emma's	
McDld . . . . . McDonalds	
MexGrl . . . Mexican Grill	
Mntgmry . . Montgomery	
Montry. . . . . . Monterrey	
MrsWin . . . Mrs Winners	
Chicken	
NuWyWnr . . . . NewWay	
Weiner	
O'Char . . . . . O'Charlies	
OTBorder. . . . . . On The	
Border	
Olive. . . . . Olive Garden	
OrnWok . . Oriental Wok	
OutBk. . . . . Outback	
Steakhouse	
PJPizza . . . Papa Jones	
Pizza	
PaneraBd. . . . . . Panera	
Bread	

PapaDino . . PaPaDino's	
Pizza	
Pdrsa . . . . . Ponderosa	
Steaks	
Pepproni . . . . . . Flying J	
Picdilly . . . . Picadilly	
PitStop . . . PitStop BBQ	
Pizza . . . . . . Pizza Hut	
PopE. . . . . Popeye's	
Prkns. . . Perkin's Family	
Restaurant	
Quizno . . . Quizno's Sub	
RCSteak . . . Rockcastle	
Steak	
Raffty . . . . Rafferty's	
Rally . . . . Rally Drive-In	
Ralph. . . . . . . Ralphies	
Rax. . . Rax Restaurants	
RedLb . . . . Red Lobster	
RoadHs. . . Road House	
RubyT. . . Ruby Tuesday	
Ryan . . . . Ryan's Family	
Steakhouse	
SaraJ . . . . . . Sara Jane	
Sbarro . . . . Sbarro's	

Continued on next page

Fast Food restaurants with <u>outdoor play areas</u> for children are shown on our maps in Red.

Example - **BKing**.

Restaurants with <u>indoor play areas</u> are shown in red, and appended with the letter "I."

Example - **McDld-I**.

Please note that all <u>Chick-Fil-A</u> restaurants close on Sundays.

FOOD, continued

Schltzky.... Schlotzky's Deli
Shony....... Shoney's
SkyLnChili..... Skyline Chili
SmkyBnes..... Smoky Bones BBQ
Sonic..... 50's Drive In
Sonny.... Sonny's BBQ
SpagWhse... Spaghetti Warehouse
Starbcks.... Starbuck's
Starvn.. Starvin' Marvin
StkHsSln.. Steak House Saloon
StkShk.. Steak & Shake Burgers
StkyFngr. Sticky Fingers
Stucky...... Stuckey's
Subwy........ Subway
TCBY... The Country's Best Yogurt
TGIF....... TGI Friday
Taco....... Taco Bell
TexRdHse...... Texas Roadhouse
TexStk..... West Texas Steakhouse
TimHrtn... Tim Hortons
TipOTwn... Tip O' Town
WSizz. Western Sizzlin'
Waffle.... Waffle House
Wendy....... Wendy's
WfflKing... Waffle King
WhtCstl... White Castle Hamburgers
Wingr........ Wingers
Zaxby. Zaxby's Chicken

LODGING

4PtsShtn... Four Points Sheraton
AmerInn.. American Inn
AmHost. AmeriHost Inns
Ashbrn.... Ashburn Inn
BHost.... Budget Host
Baymnt...... Baymont Inns & Suites
BdgInn... Budget Inn of America
Best.... America's Best Inns
BestVal..... BestValue Motel
BestW... Best Western
BkEye...... Buckeye
Bradbry...... Bradbury
Brittny... Brittany Motor Inn
Colnial.... Colonial Inn
Comfrt.... Comfort Inn
Crown..... Crown Inn
CrtYrd...... Courtyard by Marriot
Crtesy....... Courtesy
CtryInnSte.... Country Inns & Suites
Cumberlnd.......... Cumberland Inn
DBrdge... Drawbridge
Days........ Days Inn
Drury..... Drury Motel
Duffy..... Duffy's Motel
Econmy..... Economy Motel
EconoL... Econo Lodge
EmbsyS..... Embassy Suites
Exec..... Executive Inn

Fairfld..... Fairfield Inn
Family..... Family Inns of America
Guest....... Guest Inn
GuestHs.. Guest House Inn
H/Inn...... Holiday Inn
H/InnS.... Holiday Inn Select
H/InnX..... Holiday Inn Express
Hilton.... Hilton Hotels
HltnGdn........ Hilton Garden
Hmptn.... Hampton Inn
HoJo.. Howard Johnson
Hol/M... Holiday Motel
HomeTn.... Hometown Motel
HomeWd... Homewood Motel
Hrtge... Heritage Motel
Hyatt..... Hyatt Hotels
Jamson... Jameson Inn
Jolly......... Jolly Inn
Kings....... Kings Inn
Knght..... Knights Inn
LaQnt.... La Quinta Inn
LkCty....... Lake City
LndMk...... Landmark
Marrtt.... Marriot Hotels
MicroT.. Microtel Inns
Motel.. any independent unknown motel
Motel6......... Motel6
Mstrs..... Masters Inn
NFsyth.... New Forsyth Inn
Pssprt.... Passport Inn
QltyInn..... Quality Inn

QltyQtr........ Quality Quarter Inn
Radsn.... Radisson Inn
Ramda... Ramada Inn
RedC..... Red Carpet Inns
RedRf.... Red Roof Inn
Regncy... Regency Inn
Relax....... Relax Inn
Renfro... Renfro Valley Motel
RmdaSt...... Ramada Suites
Rodwy... Rodeway Inn
Royal...... Royal Inns
Rsdnts... Residents Inn
Scot...... Scottish Inn
Shony...... Shoney's Inn
Sleep....... Sleep Inn
SprngHill..... Springhill Suites (Marriott)
Studio6+.. Studio6 Plus
Supr8.. Super 8 Motels
TradeWd.. Trade Winds Motel
TravInn...... Travel Inn
TravL...... Travelodge
Value...... Value Inns
Villager.... Villager Inn
Wilburg... Williamsburg Motel
Wingate... Wingate Inn
WldWd... Wildwood Inn
Wyndm..... Wyndham
XstayAm..... Extended Stay America

A Word to our Readers . . .

Please note: we have not listed gas, food or lodgings in the downtown areas of Detroit, Toledo, Dayton, Cincinnati and Atlanta. We feel that access to such facilities (and easy return to the Interstate) is often difficult for those not familiar with streets in the area.

Also, downtown facilities tend to be higher priced, catering more to the business traveler than vacationer - travel bargains will generally be found elsewhere. This Guide has been written with the long distance interstate traveler in mind, and accordingly we recommend staying or eating at facilities outside these areas.

Nobody has paid to be listed or recommended in this guide; furthermore, we do NOT accept advertising. "Along I-75" contains no commercial content.

Unless a facility or service is specifically mentioned in an **Insider Tip**, inclusion in this book does not constitute a recommendation on the part of the publisher or author. We are however, interested in receiving your comments about facilities

Finally - every effort is made to ensure the accuracy of the guide's listings. Prior to publishing each edition, we drive a minimum of three personal I-75 car trips, cross-checking information and ensuring that the exit services shown on our maps are correct and where they are supposed to be. The most recent survey is always completed just a month prior to publication. We also include all major road construction projects encountered on this trip, although some of these may be completed before you head south.

DATE (M/D)	DAY	MILEAGE			FUEL	DAILY EXPENSE RECORD						OVERNIGHT STOP			
		START	STOP	DIFF	(Gals)	B/FAST	LUNCH	DINNER	GAS	MISC	TOTAL	STATE	EXIT#	LOCATION	MOTEL
A	B	C	D	E	F	G	H	I	J	K	L	M	N	O	P

- Enter the **Date** (month/day), and the **Day** of the week (e.g.. Mon, Tues, etc.) in columns A & B.

- At the beginning of the first day, record your car's odometer reading in **Mileage Start** (column C). After finishing with the car each evening, record the odometer reading in **Mileage Stop** (column D). Post the same number in column C for the next day.

- To calculate the number of miles driven during the day, deduct column C from column D, and enter the result in **Difference** (column E).

- To calculate your daily **Miles per Gallon**, make sure you fill up your tank before you start your journey (do not enter these gallons on the chart).

Keep a note of the number of fuel gallons purchased during each day. Each morning before you start, fill up your car and add these gallons to the fuel purchased during the previous day's run. Record this total for the previous day in column F.

Divide the total number of miles driven during the previous day (column E) by the total number of gallons used (column F). The result will be your Miles per Gallon for the previous day.

- **Daily expenses** can be recorded in columns G to K, and totaled for the day in column L. Post your motel costs and sundry expenses in column L.

- Record details of your **Overnight Stops** in columns M to P.

DATE (M/D)	DAY	MILEAGE			FUEL	DAILY EXPENSE RECORD						OVERNIGHT STOP			
		START	STOP	DIFF	(Gals)	B/FAST	LUNCH	DINNER	GAS	MISC	TOTAL	STATE	EXIT#	LOCATION	MOTEL
A	B	C	D	E	F	G	H	I	J	K	L	M	N	O	P

- Enter the **Date** (month/day), and the **Day** of the week (e.g.. Mon, Tues, etc.) in columns A & B.

- At the beginning of the first day, record your car's odometer reading in **Mileage Start** (column C). After finishing with the car each evening, record the odometer reading in **Mileage Stop** (column D). Post the same number in column C for the next day.

  To calculate the number of miles driven during the day, deduct column C from column D, and enter the result in **Difference** (column E).

- To calculate your daily **Miles per Gallon**, make sure you fill up your tank before you start your journey (do not enter these gallons on the chart).

  Keep a note of the number of fuel gallons purchased during each day. Each morning before you start, fill up your car and add these gallons to the fuel purchased during the previous day's run. Record this total for the previous day in column F.

  Divide the total number of miles driven during the previous day (column E) by the total number of gallons used (column F). The result will be your Miles per Gallon for the previous day.

- **Daily expenses** can be recorded in columns G to K, and totaled for the day in column L. Post your motel costs and sundry expenses in column L.

- Record details of your **Overnight Stops** in columns M to P.

Help me write the next edition of "Along Interstate-75"

Please help me continue to make this *your* book. Each year, I receive many interesting letters from my readers. Before going to press, Kathy and I *review every suggestion* and put them on our list to check during our next I-75 trip. If they meet our standards, we try and incorporate as many of them as possible into the next edition ... that way, we can make sure the book *continues to meet your needs*.

Please use the space below to record your recommendations or changes to the book's information. Use the other side for your comments and other suggestions. Tell me what you like about the guide, or what you don't like — we are constantly trying to improve it for you. To be considered for the next edition we must have your request by April 30th each year, to ensure it's included on our next I-75 "review" trip.

As a thank-you for your suggestion/comments, in September, I will send you a *15% discount coupon* for any of our books.

To: *Dave Hunter, c/o Mile Oak Publishing Inc.,*
Suite 81, 20 Mineola Road East,
Mississauga ON Canada L5G 4N9

From:

Name: _____ Phone: _____

Address: _____

City: _____ State/Prov: _____ Zip/PC: _____

e.mail address: _____

My recommendation or change in information:

(if recommending a facility, please include as much information as possible - thanks).

Facility Name: _____

Owner or Manager's Name: _____ Phone: _____

Where is it? - State: _____ Exit#: _____ East/West?: _____

Recommendation or Information to be changed:

_____
_____
_____
_____
_____
_____
_____

Please use the other side for your comments or suggestions

My comments and suggestions for the next edition:

Free Offer

Offer expires July 31, 2008

Dave Hunter's Florida Newsletter
with news for Florida's winter visitors

☐ Check (✔) box to left; fill in your name & address in the space below and mail or fax this form to Mile Oak Publishing (see address and fax number below), we will send you a free copy of Dave Hunter's *Florida Newsletter*.

In addition, in September we will send you a *15% discount coupon* for either of our books ... as a thank-you for being a regular customer.

Please note, your name, address and other personal information is completely safe with us. We treat it as confidential information and do NOT share it with anybody else.

Name:

Address:

City: _____ State/Prov.:

ZIP/Postal Code: _____ Phone:

E.Mail Address:

How to contact us:

By mail: **Mile Oak Publishing Inc.,**
Suite 81, 20 Mineola Road East,
Mississauga, ON Canada L5G 4N9

Phone: **905-274-4356**; Fax: **905-274-8656**; Email: **mile_oak@compuserve.com**

To order additional copies, either visit our website at **www.i75online.com,** or phone **1-800-431-1579**. We mail your book within 24 hours of receiving your order.

If you've enjoyed my book, why not buy a gift copy for a traveling friend? I'll even personalize and autograph it for you ... free!

Now, what could be a better gift?

Visit our website at www.i75online.com *to learn more about my personalized gift service.*

NOTES